Mini Indonesian Dictionary

Indonesian-English
English-Indonesian

Compiled by Katherine Davidsen

TUTTLE Publishing

Tokyo | Rutland, Vermont | Singapore

Published by Tuttle Publishing, an imprint of Periplus Editions (HK) Ltd.

www.tuttlepublishing.com

© 2018 by Periplus Editions (HK) Ltd

All rights reserved.

ISBN 978-0-8048-5081-0

Distributed by:

Indonesia
PT Java Books Indonesia
Jl. Rawa Gelam IV No. 9, Kawasan Industri Pulogadung
Jakarta 13930
Tel: (62) 21 4682-1088 | Fax: (62) 21 461-0206
crm@periplus.co.id; www.periplus.com

North America, Latin America and Europe
Tuttle Publishing
364 Innovation Drive, North Clarendon, VT 05759-9436 USA
Tel: 1(802) 773-8930 | Fax: 1(802) 773-6993
info@tuttlepublishing.com; www.tuttlepublishing.com

Asia Pacific
Berkeley Books Pte. Ltd.
61 Tai Seng Avenue #02-12, Singapore 534167
Tel: (65) 6280-1330 | Fax: (65) 6280-6290
inquiries@periplus.com.sg; www.periplus.com

22 21 20 19 18   5 4 3 2 1   1804RR
Printed in China

TUTTLE PUBLISHING® is a registered trademark of
Tuttle Publishing, a division of Periplus Editions (HK) Ltd.

Contents

Introduction

A brief introduction to Indonesian

Indonesian is the national language of the world's fourth-largest nation, spoken by at least 70% of the nation's 250 million people. It is a mother tongue to over 27%, connecting speakers of 750 regional languages. As a variety of Malay, it is also understood in Singapore and Malaysia, making it a major language of Southeast Asia. An Austronesian language, modern Indonesian developed from Riau Malay into the official language of post-war independent Indonesia. It has borrowed widely from other languages and absorbed myriad influences, making it dynamic and always in flux.

Indonesian is considered relatively easy to learn, having very regular grammar. Adjectives follow the noun, as in French, and there is a wide range of verbs. Word order generally follows a subject-verb-object pattern. Words may be left out if the context is clear. Pronunciation is similar to Spanish or Italian, although accents vary.

Vowels:	**a**	as in *father*
	e	mostly as in *loosen* (swallowed "shwa" sound); sometimes as in *egg*. In older texts this is written as **é**
	i	as in *marine*

o	as in *open*
u	as in *blue*

Diphthongs:

ai	as in *aisle*
au	as in *sauerkraut*

Consonants: as in English, except for:

c	like **ch** in *child*
g	always hard, as in *gum*, never soft as in *gem*
kh	throaty sound as in *loch*
ng	as in *thing*
ngg	as in *finger* (ng+g)
r	rolled, as in Spanish
sy	**sh** as in *show*

The *Tuttle Mini Indonesian Dictionary* aims to represent the modern, standard usage of Indonesian, through common entries, new terminology and authentic terms, as well as identify parts of speech. A helpful, unusual feature is that this volume does not presume knowledge of word structure, which is vital when using most quality Indonesian dictionaries. For example, the word **mengalahkan** is listed under **mengalahkan** as well as its base, **kalah** in this dictionary. In most dictionaries, only the latter would appear.

Introduction

Selection of entries

By definition, a mini dictionary is a selection of useful words and phrases, rather than a complete compendium. This dictionary attempts to reflect general, everyday usage throughout Indonesia and the English-speaking world, including words that are important to students, language learners and tourists. American spelling is used. Entries cover survival language for tourists, common everyday words, national culture and language heard on the street.

Guide to using this dictionary

The dictionary is divided into two sections, Indonesian–English and English–Indonesian.

menghadap	entry (in bold type)
halang: halangan	first word is not found (or commonly used) alone. Sub-entries follow after semi-colon, in bold black type
v	word type (ie part of speech). Not always given if more than one word type exists. eg. **cas** charge (could be **N, v**)
child N children	irregular plurals follow the noun symbol **N**
put v put put	irregular past tense forms (simple past and past perfect) follow the verb symbol **v**

[nait]	irregularly-spelt words are given in Indonesian phonetic pronunciation
malam	meaning (in plain type)
session, meeting; hearing	Similar meanings are divided by commas; other meanings are divided by a semi-colon
~ *tiri* stepmother; *bahasa* ~ mother tongue	Entries or sub-entries are indicated by ~ (in italics). On the left, ~ represents *ibu*.
ouch! ow! (expressions of pain) to (be able to) speak or use a language	Round brackets contain additional information; or perhaps an extra meaning.
baik ... maupun ... both ... and ...	... represents any word, in a set phrase
bersih, membersihkan, pembersih **handwriting ← hand**	Where possible, all entries and sub-entries are grouped alphabetically. A left-pointing arrow indicates the base word.
abis → habis **became → become**	A right-pointing arrow shows an entry for further information or reference; or the base of an irregular past tense verb form.

Introduction

Acknowledgments

I would like to thank everyone involved in this dictionary project. In particular, thanks to Eric M. Oey, Associate Professor Stuart O. Robson of Monash University, Nancy Goh, Tony Mansanulu, Judo Suwidji, and of course Johansjah Sugianto. I must also thank countless patient and helpful friends, the Sumirat family, the family of Moch. Yunus, the household of Fauzi Bowo, my own family in Melbourne, the Zeed family, and my students over the years.

Terima kasih banyak.

List of Abbreviations

ABBREV	abbreviation	**ISL**	Islamic
ADJ	adjective	**M**	masculine
ADV	adverb	**N**	noun
ARCH	archaic	**PL**	plural
CATH	Catholic	**POL**	polite
CHILD	child(ren)	**PREF**	prefix
CHR	Christian	**PREP**	preposition
COLL	colloquial	**PRON**	pronoun
CONJ	conjunction	**S**	singular
DEROG	derogatory	**SL**	slang
EJAC	ejaculation	**SUF**	suffix
F	feminine	**V**	verb
GR	greeting	**V, AUX**	auxiliary verb
HIND	Hindu	**V, PF**	past perfect form of verb

Indonesian–English

A

abad N century; age, era; ~ *keemasan* golden age

abadi eternal, everlasting; *cinta* ~ endless love

abang N, PRON elder brother; ~ *None* Mr and Miss Jakarta → **bang**

abis COLL → **habis**

abjad N alphabet

abon N shredded dry meat, eaten as a side-dish

ABRI ABBREV *Angkatan Bersenjata Republik* Indonesia Indonesian Armed Forces

abu N ash; ~ *rokok* cigarette ash

abu-abu ADJ gray

AC ABBREV air-conditioner, airconditioning

acar N finely-cut pickles, eaten with fried rice, satay etc

acara agenda, program, event; **pengacara** N lawyer, solicitor

acung: acungan N ~ *jempol* thumbs-up

AD ABBREV *Angkatan Darat* Army

ada V to be (present); to have, exist; ~ *Firman?* Is Firman here?; ~ *apa?* What's up? What's wrong?; *tidak* ~ there isn't, there aren't; not here; **adalah** V is, are (followed by a noun); **adanya** N the existence of; *apa* ~ as it is, without any pretensions; **berada** V to be somewhere; ADJ well-to-do, well-off; **keadaan** N situation, condition; ~ *darurat* emergency situation; **mengadakan** V to create, organize, make available; **seadanya** ADJ what's there; *makan* ~ eat what's there

adalah V is, are (followed by a noun) → **ada**

adanya *apa* ~ as it is, without any pretensions ← **ada**

adat N tradition, custom, customary law, esp. of an ethnic group; ~ *istiadat* customs and traditions; ~ *Sunda* Sundanese traditions

adegan N scene

adik N younger brother or sister; ~ *ipar* (younger) brother- or sister-in-law; ~ *laki-laki* (younger) brother; *kakak-ber~* siblings; ~ *kandung* (younger) blood brother or sister; ~ *sepupu* cousin (of lower status)

adil ADJ just, righteous; **keadilan** N justice; **pengadilan** N court of justice or law, trial

administrasi N administration, management

adon: adonan N batter, dough, mixture

adu: mengadu V to complain, report; ~ *domba* to play two parties against each other; **pengaduan** N complaint; *surat* ~ letter of complaint

aduh EJAC ouch! ow! (expression of pain); EXCL oh! (expression of sorrow); wow!

aduk *campur* ~ mixed up; **mengaduk** V to stir, mix

adzan → **azan**

Afrika N Africa; *orang* ~ African; ~ *Selatan (Afsel)* South Africa

agak ADV rather, somewhat; ~ *gemuk* rather fat

agama N religion; ~ *Budha* Buddhism; **beragama** V to have a religion; ADJ religious

agar CONJ in order that/to

agar, agar-agar N a kind of jelly made from seaweed

agén N agent, agency, distributor

agénda N agenda; appointment diary

agrowisata N agricultural tourism

agung ADJ high, supreme

Agustus *bulan* ~ August

ah EXCL oh (showing mild annoyance)

Ahad → **Minggu**

ahli N expert, specialist; member; ~ *bedah* surgeon; ~ *waris* heir

air N water; juice; ~ *jeruk* orange juice; ~ *ledeng* reticulated water; ~ *mata* tears; ~ *minum*, ~ *putih* drinking water; ~ *pasang* incoming tide; ~ *terjun* waterfall; *buang* ~ to go to the toilet

ajaib ADJ miraculous, strange

ajak: mengajak V to invite,

ask out; to urge; ~ *jalan-jalan* to ask out

ajar: ajaran N teaching; **belajar** v to learn, study; **mempelajari** v to study something in depth; **mengajar** v to teach; **pelajar** N pupil, student; **pelajaran** N lesson; **terpelajar** ADJ educated; **pengajar** N teacher

akad N contract, agreement; ~ *nikah* Muslim marriage contract

akal N mind, intellect; *mencari* ~ to find a way

akan v will, going to (marks future time); *minggu yang ~ datang* next week; PREP about, concerning, regarding; ~ *tetapi* however

akar N root

akhir N end; ~*nya* finally; **berakhir** v to end; **mengakhiri** v to end, finish something; **terakhir** ADJ last, final, latest

aki N vehicle battery

akibat N result, consequence; CONJ due to, consequently; ~*nya* as a result

akrab ADJ close, intimate, friendly

aksén N accent

aksi N action, demonstration; **beraksi** v to take action, do something

akta, akte N official document, certificate; ~ *lahir,* ~ *kelahiran* birth certificate; ~ *nikah,* ~ *pernikahan* marriage certificate

aktif ADJ activated, active, on, working; **aktivitas** N activity

aktual ADJ latest, up-to-date; *berita* ~ current affairs

aku PRON I, me; **mengaku** v to admit, confess, acknowledge; to claim; ~ *salah* to admit guilt

akuntan N accountant; **akuntansi** N accounting

AL ABBREV *Angkatan Laut* Navy

ala ADJ in the style of, à la

alam N nature, world; ~ *(ter-) buka* open-air

alam: mengalami v to experience; **pengalaman** N experience

alamat N address; sign, omen

alangkah ADV how ...! what a ...!

3

alas N foundation, basis, base; ~ *kaki* footwear; **alasan** N cause, reason, motive

alat N tool, instrument, means; ~ *kontrasepsi*, ~ *KB* form of contraception; ~ *tulis* stationery; **peralatan** N equipment

album N album; ~ *foto* photo album

alérgi allergy, allergic; ~ *terhadap mangga* allergic to mangoes

alhamdulillah EJAC, ISL thanks be to God; bless you! (when sneezing)

alih v to shift, change position

alir flow aliran N stream, current; ideology, school, sect; **mengalir** v to flow

alis N eyebrow; *mengangkat* ~ to raise your eyebrows

aljabar N algebra

Alkitab N the Bible

alkohol N alcohol; **beralkohol** v containing alcohol

Allah N God, Allah

almarhum ADJ, M, ISL the late; **almarhumah** ADJ, F, ISL the late

alpukat, apokat, avokat N

avocado; *jus* ~ avocado drink

Alqur'an, Al-quran, Alquran N the Koran

AL(RI) ABBREV *Angkatan Laut (Republik Indonesia)* (Indonesian) Navy

alu N pestle; ~ *lumpang* mortar and pestle

alun-alun N town square

amal N charity

aman ADJ safe, in peace; **keamanan** N safety, security; **mengamankan** v to make safe, restore order; place in custody

amat ADV very, extremely

amat: mengamati v to watch closely, keep an eye on; **pengamat** N observer; **pengamatan** N observation, monitoring

ambeien N hemorrhoids, piles

ambil v to take; to subtract; to bring; ~ *saja* help yourself; **mengambil** v to take, get, fetch

ambisi N ambition

ambruk v to collapse, break, crash

ambulans N ambulance

amén: (me)ngamén v to

4

sing in the street for money, busk; **pengamén** N street singer, busker

Amérika N America; ~ *Serikat* United States of America

amin EJAC amen

amis ADJ putrid, smelling fishy

amplop N envelope; COLL bribe

ampuh ADJ powerful, potent

ampun N mercy, forgiveness, pardon; EJAC Mercy! (expression of astonishment or disapproval); *minta* ~ beg for mercy

amuk: mengamuk V to run amok, go berserk

anak N child; young (of an animal); member of a group; small part of a whole; ~ *angkat* adopted child; ~ *buah* assistants, staff; ~ *bungsu* youngest child; ~ *cucu* descendants; ~ *emas* favorite; ~ *haram* illegitimate child; ~ *jalanan* street kid; ~ *kunci* key; ~ *perempuan* daughter; ~ *sulung* eldest child; ~ *tiri* stepchild; ~ *tunggal* only child; ~ *yatim* orphan; **anak-anak** N, PL children; **beranak**

V (of animals) to give birth to, have offspring; **peranakan** N of mixed Chinese and Indonesian blood, Straits Chinese

analisa, analisis N analysis

ancam V to threaten; **ancaman** N threat; **mengancam** V to threaten, intimidate; **terancam** ADJ threatened

anda, Anda PRON you (neutral, without status)

andai, andaikan, andainya, seandainya CONJ if, supposing that

andal ADJ reliable; **mengandalkan** V to rely on, trust

andong N four-wheeled horse-drawn carriage in Jogja and Solo

anéh ADJ strange, peculiar; ~*nya* the strange thing is...

anéka ADJ all kinds of, various; ~ *jenis* all sorts; ~ *macam*, ~ *ragam* varied

anggap V to consider; **menganggap** V to consider, regard

anggaran N budget, estimate

anggota N member; ~ *badan* limb; ~ *DPR* Member of Parliament; ~ *keluarga* family member; **keanggota-an** N membership; *kartu ~* membership card

anggrék N orchid

angguk, mengangguk V to nod

anggun ADJ elegant, stylish, graceful

anggur N wine, grapes; *~ putih* white wine; *buah ~* grapes

anggur: pengangguran N unemployment, unemployed person

angin N wind, breeze

angka N figure, numeral, digit; score, mark; *~ Romawi* Roman numeral

angkasa N space, sky

angkat V to lift; *~ besi* weight-lifting; *~ tangan* give up; raise your hand; *~ telepon* to pick up, answer the phone; **angkatan** N generation, year level (at school or university); force; *~ darat (AD)* army; **berangkat** V to depart, leave; **keberangkatan** N departure; *pintu ~* departure gate; **mengangkat** V to lift or pick up, raise; appoint; to remove, amputate

angkét N survey (form)

angklung N bamboo instrument, played in an orchestra

angkot N, COLL public minibus ← **angkutan kota**

angkut V to carry, lift, transport; **angkutan** N transport, transportation; *~ kota (angkot)* city transportation; *~ umum* public transport

angpao, angpau N a red envelope containing money, given at Chinese New Year

angsa N goose

anjing N dog (also insult)

anjlok V to derail; *kereta api ~* derailed train

anjung: anjungan N gallery, upper level, ship's bridge

anjur: menganjurkan V to suggest, propose

anoa N dwarf buffalo of Sulawesi

antar take, escort; *~ jemput* pick up and take home, door-to-door; **mengantar** V to take, escort, accompany; **mengantarkan** V to take someone or something

antara CONJ between; among them; **perantara** N broker,

6

intermediary, go-between

antarpropinsi ADJ inter-provincial

antem: berantem V, COLL to fight, scuffle → **hantam**

anti- PREF, ADJ against, resistant to; ~ *perang*, anti-war

anting N earring

antré, antri queue; **antréan** N queue; **mengantri** V to queue

anut, menganut V to follow; **penganut** N follower, believer

anyam, menganyam V to weave, plait, braid; **anyaman** N plait, braid

apa INTERROG, N what; ~ *lagi* what else?; ~ *saja* anything; ~ *kabar?* how are you?; **apa-apa** N something; ~ *tidak* ~ it doesn't matter; **apabila** CONJ if, when; **berapa** INTERROG how many? what number?; ~ *harganya?* how much is it?; *umur* ~ how old; **beberapa** ADJ several, a number of; *jauh* ~ as far as; **mengapa** INTERROG why; *tak* ~ it doesn't matter; **ngapain** SL why, do what; **siapa** INTERROG, N who;

~ *saja* whoever; **siapa-siapa** N anybody

apakah, apa (question marker) ← **apa**

apalagi ADV, CONJ especially, moreover

apartemén N apartment, flat

apel N apple

api N fire, flame; **berapi** V to produce fire; **perapian** N fireplace, oven

apik ADJ neat, tidy

apoték N pharmacy, chemist (shop), dispensary; **apotéker** N pharmacist

April *bulan* ~ April

apung, mengapung V to float, be suspended

Arab *bahasa* ~ Arabic; *orang* ~ an Arab

arah N direction; *satu* ~ one way; same direction

arak N alcoholic drink

arang N charcoal

arca N statue

arén N areca palm

argo, argométér N taxi meter

arit N sickle

arogan ADJ arrogant

arsip N archive, file

arti N meaning; ~ *nya* it

7

means, that is to say; **berarti v** to mean; ADJ meaningful

artikel N article (in print media)

artis N celebrity; actor, actress or singer

arung ~ *jeram* white water rafting

arus N stream, current, flow; ~ *listrik* electric current

AS ABBREV *Amerika Serikat* the United States

asal N origin; ~*usul* origins; **berasal v** to come from

asal, asalkan CONJ as long as, providing that

asam, asem sour, tamarind; acid; ~ *manis* sweet and sour

asap N smoke, exhaust, pollution; vapor; **berasap** ADJ smoky

asar N, ISL the afternoon prayer

asas, azas: asasi, azazi ADJ basic

asbak N ashtray

ASI ABBREV *air susu ibu* breast milk

Asia N Asia; ~ *Tenggara* Southeast Asia

asin ADJ salty, salted; **asinan** N sour vegetable and fruit dish

asing ADJ strange, alien, foreign; *orang* ~ stranger; foreigner

asli ADJ original, indigenous; *orang* ~, *penduduk* ~ indigenous person, native

asma N asthma

asong: asongan N street vendor; goods sold on the street (cigarettes, magazines, drinking water etc)

aspal N asphalt

asrama N boarding house, dormitory; MIL barracks

asri ADJ beautiful, scenic (of a view)

assalamualaikum, assalamu alaikum salam alaikum GR, ISL peace be upon you

asuh care; *orang tua* ~ foster parents; **pengasuh** N carer; ~ *anak* nursemaid, babysitter

asuransi N insurance

asyik ADJ fun; ADV absorbed, engrossed; eager

atap N roof; **beratap v** to have a roof

atas PREP up; N upper part; *di* ~ on (top of), upon, above, over; upstairs; **atasan** N

superior, boss; **mengatasi** v
to overcome

atau conj or

ati ampela n liver and
gizzards

atlét, atlit n athlete

atur arrange; **aturan** n rule,
regulation; **mengatur** v to
arrange, organize, regulate;
peraturan n rule, regulation;
teratur adj organized,
regular

aula n hall (at school),
auditorium

AU(RI) abbrev *Angkatan
Udara (Republik Indonesia)*
(Indonesian) Air Force

Australia n Australia; *orang ~*
Australian

awak n person; *~ pesawat*
cabin crew

awal beginning, early;
awalan n prefix; **berawal** v
to begin with

awan n cloud; **berawan** adj
cloudy, overcast

awas ejac be careful, beware;
mengawasi v to supervise

awét adj durable, long-lasting

ayah, Ayah n, pron father; *~
bunda* parents

ayam n chicken, hen; *~
kampung* free-range chicken;
~ negeri battery hen

ayat n verse (of a religious
text)

ayo come on, let's go

ayu adj beautiful

ayun: ayunan n swings

azan, adzan n call to prayer

B

bab n chapter

babi n pig, boar (also as an
insult); *~ hutan* wild boar;
daging ~ pork

baca v to read; **bacaan** n
reading material; **membaca** v
to read; **pembaca** n reader

badai n hurricane, storm; *~
topan* typhoon

badak n rhino, rhinoceros

badan n body; board,
committee

badut n clown

bagai conj like, as; **berbagai**
adj various, several; **sebagai**
conj like, as

bagaimana interrog, conj
how, in what way

9

bagasi N baggage; boot (of vehicle); hold (of ship or aircraft)

bagi V divide; **bagian** N part, share, section; **berbagi** V to share; **membagi** V to divide, distribute; **sebagian** N some, a section of

bagi PREP for

bagus ADJ good, fine, excellent (external qualities of concrete objects)

bahagia ADJ happy, joyous; **berbahagia** V to be happy

bahan N materials, ingredients; cloth, fabric; ~ *bakar* fuel

bahas V to discuss; **membahas** V to discuss, debate

bahasa N language; ~ *Indonesia* Indonesian; **berbahasa** V to (be able to) speak or use a language

bahaya N danger; **berbahaya** V to be dangerous

bahkan CONJ moreover; on the contrary; indeed, even

bahu N shoulder

bahwa CONJ that

baik ADJ good, fine, well, OK (i.e. internal qualities of abstract objects); **baik-baik**
ADJ fine; respectable; ~ *hati* kind; **membaik** V to improve; **memperbaiki** V to repair, fix; **perbaikan** N repair, improvement; **sebaiknya** ADV preferably, it's best if; **terbaik** ADJ the best

baja N steel

bajaj N three-wheeled motorized form of transport in Jakarta

bajak N plow; **membajak** V to plow

bajak, membajak V to hijack; to copy illegally; **bajakan** ADJ pirated; *CD* ~ pirated CD

baju N, INF clothes; clothing for the upper body; ~ *dalam* singlet; underwear

bak N tub; ~ *mandi* large tank in the bathroom from which water is taken

bakal ADJ future, potential

bakar V to burn; **kebakaran** N fire; **membakar** V to burn; **terbakar** ADJ burnt

bakat N talent, gift; **berbakat** ADJ talented, gifted

bakau N mangrove

bakmi, bami N Chinese noodles

bakpao N steamed white bread with filling of nuts or chicken

bakpia N sweet cake from Jogja with nutty filling

bakso, baso N meatball; meatball soup; ~ *tahu* meatballs and tofu (specialty of Bandung)

bakul N basket hung on a pole for selling goods

bakwan N dish of various sweetmeats, a specialty of Malang

balai ~ *kota* town hall

balap race; **balapan** N race; **membalap** v to race

balas reply; **balasan** reply, answer; **membalas** v to reply, respond

balét N ballet

Bali N *pulau* ~ Bali; *bahasa* ~, *orang* ~ Balinese

balik v to return, reverse, retreat; N back, flipside; return; **membalik** v to return, reverse, turn over; **membalikkan** v to turn something over; **sebaliknya** CONJ on the contrary; **terbalik** ADJ overturned, upside-down, opposite

balon N balloon

balut: pembalut N sanitary pad

bambu N bamboo

ban N tire; ~ *serep* spare tire

bandara N airport ← **bandar udara**

bandel ADJ naughty, disobedient

banding: membandingkan v to compare something; **perbandingan** N comparison, ratio

bandrék N ginger drink

bang PRON older brother (in Jakarta or Malay areas) → **abang**

banget ADJ, SL fast, quick

bangga ADJ proud

bangkai N corpse (usually of animals); *bunga* ~ the Rafflesia flower

bangkit v to rise, get up

bangkrut ADJ bankrupt

bangku N bench (for sitting); stool; desk

bangsa N people, nation, race

bangun v get up, wake up; **membangunkan** v to wake someone up

bangun: bangunan N build-

11

ing; **membangun v** to build or create; **pembangunan n** development

banjir n flood

bank n bank; ~ *negara* state-owned bank; **perbankan adj** banking; **bankir n** banker

bantal cushion; pillow

banteng n (Javan) ox

banting: membanting v to throw down (with a bang)

bantu v to help; **bantuan n** assistance, help, aid; **membantu v** to help (someone); **pembantu n** servant, maid; assistant

banyak adj many, much; **kebanyakan n, adj** too much; most

Bapa pron Father (title for own father or respected older man), also **Bapak**; **chr** God, Father, Lord

Bapak pron Father (title for own father or respected older man)

bapak n father

baptis adj Baptist

barang n goods, things

barangkali conj perhaps, maybe

Barat n the West

barat adj west; ~ *daya* southwest; ~ *laut* northwest

Barelang *Batam, Rempang, Galang* group of islands in Riau Archipelago province

bareng conj, sl with; **v** to go together

baris n line, row, rank; **barisan n** line; forces; **berbaris v** to line up

barongsai n Chinese dragon for dance performances

baru adj new, recent; just; ~~ *ini* just the other day; **terbaru adj** latest, newest; **barusan adv, sl** just now

basa-basi n good manners, politeness; platitudes

basah adj wet, moist, soaked

basi adj off, rotten, inedible (of food)

batagor n fried tofu and meatballs, a specialty of Bandung ← **bakso tahu goreng**

Batak adj ethnic group of North Sumatra

batal adj cancelled; broken (a fast); **membatalkan v** to cancel, repeal

batang N trunk, stem, stick (of a tree); shaft; handle; penis; counter for long cylindrical objects

batas N limit, border; **berbatasan** V to be adjacent to; **perbatasan** N border, frontier; **terbatas** ADJ limited

baterai N battery

batik N application of wax onto fabric to create a pattern after dyeing; fabric or clothes with designs produced in this manner; ~ *cap* stamped batik; ~ *tulis* handmade batik; **membatik** V to apply wax onto fabric

batu N stone; **berbatu** ADJ rocky, stony

batuk V cough

bau N, V, ADJ smell, smelly; **berbau** V to smell, have connotations of

baut N bolt

bawa V to take, bring, carry; to conduct; **membawa** V to take, bring, carry; to conduct; **terbawa** ADJ (accidentally) taken away

bawah PREP below; *di ~* below, under; *di ~ umur* underage

bawang N onion; ~ *putih* garlic

baya N age; *setengah ~* middle-aged

bayam, bayem N spinach

bayang N shadow, image; **bayangan** N shadow; **terbayang** ADJ imagined, conceivable

bayar V to pay; **membayar** V to pay; **pembayaran** N payment

bayi N baby

béa N tax, duty, excise; ~ *cukai* customs

béasiswa N scholarship, bursary

beban N burden, load; responsibility

bébas ADJ free

bébék N duck

beberapa ADJ several, a number of ← *apa, berapa*

becak N pedicab, rickshaw tricycle; *tukang ~ bécak* driver

bécék ADJ muddy, wet

béda ADJ different; ~*nya ...* the difference is, ...; **berbéda** ADJ different; **membédakan** V to discriminate, differentiate

13

between, consider different; **perbédaan** N difference

bedah N surgery

bedak N powder

begadang v to stay up all night; to sleep late

begini ADV like this, in this manner ← **ini**

begitu ADV like that, in that manner ← **itu**

béha N bra

bekal N provisions

bekas ADJ used, old, former (for objects)

bekerja v to work; ~ *sama* to co-operate, work together ← **kerja**

beku ADJ frozen; **membeku** v to freeze

bél N bell

béla v defend; ~ *diri* self-defense; **membéla** v to defend

belah N crack, fissure, divide, splinter; **belahan** N half, side; **membelah** v to split in two; **sebelah** PREP next to; N half, side; (*din kanan*) on the right (side)

belajar v to learn, study ← **ajar**

belakang PREP, N behind; back, rear; **belakangan** ADV recently; after others; ~ *ini* recently

belalang N grasshopper, locust

Belanda N the Netherlands, Holland; *bahasa* ~; *orang* ~ Dutch

belanja v to go shopping; **belanjaan** N shopping; **ber-belanja** v to go shopping; **perbelanjaan** *pusat* ~ shopping center, mall

belas N number between 10–20; *lima* ~ fifteen; **belasan** N dozens; **sebelas** N, ADJ eleven

belérang N sulfur

Bélgia N Belgium

beli v to buy; **membeli** v to buy, purchase; **pembelian** N purchase

beliau PRON he, she; him, her (respectful form of **dia**)

belimbing N starfruit

bélok turn; **bélokan** N bend, turn in the road; **berbélok, membélok** v to bend, turn

belum ADV not yet; ~ *pernah* until now, never (but pos-

14

sibly in the future); **sebelum** ADJ before; **sebelumnya** ADV previously, before

belut N eel

benang N thread

benar, bener ADJ true, correct, right; **benar-benar** ADV truly, really; **kebenaran** N truth; **membenarkan** V to confirm, verify; to justify; **sebenarnya** ADV in fact, actually

bencana N disaster, catastrophe

benci V to hate; **membenci** V to hate

bendéra N flag

béndi N two-wheeled horse-carriage

bendung: bendungan N dam

bener → **benar**

bengkak ADJ swollen

béngkél N garage; workshop

béngkok ADJ bent, crooked

bening ADJ clear, transparent, clean (of glass, water etc)

bénjol, bénjolan N mole, lump, tumor

bénsin N petrol, gasoline

bénténg N fort, fortress

bentrok V to clash head-on; **bentrokan** N clash, conflict

bentuk N shape, form; **berbentuk** ADJ shaped, with the shape of; **membentuk** V to form, set up something (eg. committee); **terbentuk** ADJ formed, shaped, created

benua N continent

bepergian V to travel, be away ← **pergi**

beracun ADJ poisonous, containing poison ← **racun**

berada V to be somewhere; ADJ well-to-do, well-off ← **ada**

beragam ADJ various ← **ragam**

beragama ADJ religious; V to have a religion

bérak V poo, defecate; N poo, feces

berakhir V to end ← **akhir**

beralkohol V containing alcohol; *minuman* ~ alcoholic drink ← **alkohol**

berambut ADJ hairy; V to have hair

beranak V (of animals) to give birth to, have offspring ← **anak**

beranda N veranda, balcony; home (on webpage)

berang ADJ furious, enraged

15

berangkat v to depart, leave; **keberangkatan** N departure ← **angkat**

berani ADJ brave, courageous; **keberanian** N bravery, courage

berantakan ADJ messy, in a mess ← **antak**

berantas, memberantas v to wipe out, fight against

berantem v, COLL to fight, scuffle ← **antem, hantam**

berapa INTERROG how many? what number?; ~ *harganya?* how much is it?; *umur* ~ how old; **beberapa** ADJ several, a number of ← **apa**

berapi ADJ burning, fire-producing (of volcanoes) ← **api**

berarti v to mean; ADJ meaningful ← **arti**

beras N rice (husked and uncooked, as sold in shops)

berasal v to come from ← **asal**

berasap ADJ smoky ← **asap**

berat heavy, severe, difficult; weight; **keberatan** N objection; v to object

beratap v to have a roof ← **atap**

berawal v to begin with ← **awal**

berawan ADJ cloudy, overcast ← **awan**

berbagai ADJ various, several ← **bagai**

berbagi v to share ← **bagi**

berbahagia v to be happy ← **bahagia**

berbahasa v to (be able to) speak or use a language ← **bahasa**

berbahaya v to be dangerous ← **bahaya**

berbakat ADJ talented, gifted ← **bakat**

berbaris v to line up ← **baris**

berbatasan v to be adjacent to ← **batas**

berbatu ADJ rocky, stony ← **batu**

berbau v to smell, have connotations of ← **bau**

berbéda ADJ different ← **béda**

berbelanja v to go shopping ← **belanja**

berbentuk ADJ shaped, with the shape of ← **bentuk**

berbicara v to speak; ~ *dalam bahasa Sunda* to speak in Sundanese ← **bicara**

berbincang, berbincang-bincang v to chat, discuss ← **bincang**

berbintang v to have a star ← **bintang**

berbisa ADJ poisonous; *ular* ~ poisonous snake ← **bisa**

berbisnis v to do business ← **bisnis**

berbohong v to lie ← **bohong**

berbuah v to bear fruit, produce ← **buah**

berbuat v to do ← **buat**

berbuka ~ *puasa* to break the fast ← **buka**

berbukit ADJ hilly ← **bukit**

berbunyi v to sound, make a noise ← **bunyi**

bercampur ADJ mixed with ← **campur**

bercanda v to joke ← **canda**

bercelana v to wear trousers, trousered ← **celana**

bercerita v to tell (a story) ← **cerita**

bercinta v to make love; to be in love ← **cinta**

berciuman v to kiss each other ← **cium**

berdagang v to trade, do business ← **dagang**

berdamai v to make peace ← **damai**

berdampak v to have a (negative) effect ← **dampak**

berdandan v to dress, put on make-up ← **dandan**

berdansa v to dance (Western-style) ← **dansa**

berdarah v to bleed ← **darah**

berdebar v to beat quickly ← **debar**

berdebat v to have a debate ← **debat**

berdebu ADJ dusty ← **debu**

berdekatan ADJ close (of two or more things) ← **dekat**

berdémo v to hold a protest ← **démo**

berdering v to ring, tinkle ← **dering**

berdesakan v to push each other ← **desak**

berdoa v to pray, say a prayer ← **doa**

berdosa v to sin, commit a sin ← **dosa**

berdua ADJ together, in pairs ← **dua**

berduka ~ *(cita)* to grieve, be in mourning ← **duka**

berduri ADJ thorny ← **duri**

17

berebut v to fight for; **berebutan** v to fight each other for ← **rebut**

berékor v to have a tail ← **ékor**

berempat ADJ in a group of four ← **empat**

berenang v to swim ← **renang**

berencana v to plan ← **rencana**

béres finished, ready; **membéréskan** v to clear up, make ready

berfungsi v to work, go; to act as ← **fungsi**

bergabung v to join together ← **gabung**

bergambar ADJ illustrated ← **gambar**

berganti v to change; ~*ganti*, ~*an* in turns ← **ganti**

bergaris ADJ lined ← **garis**

bergaul v to mix or associate with ← **gaul**

bergaya ADJ stylish, with style ← **gaya**

bergegas-gegas v to hurry ← **gegas**

bergelar v titled ← **gelar**

bergelombang ADJ wavy ← **gelombang**

bergembira v to be happy, joyous ← **gembira**

bergéngsi ADJ prestigious ← **géngsi**

bergerak v to move ← **gerak**

bergilir, bergiliran ADJ in turns ← **gilir**

bergizi ADJ nutritious ← **gizi**

bergosip v to gossip ← **gosip**

bergoyang v to shake, sway; to dance ← **goyang**

bergulat v to wrestle, fight ← **gulat**

berguna ADJ useful, worthwhile ← **guna**

berhadapan v (~ *muka*) face to face ← **hadap**

berhadiah ADJ with prizes ← **hadiah**

berhak v to have a right to, be entitled to ← **hak**

berhalangan v to be prevented from, unable ← **halang**

berharap v to hope ← **harap**

berharga ADJ precious, valuable ← **harga**

berhari-hari ADV for days ← **hari**

berhasil v to succeed ← **hasil**

berhenti v to stop, cease ← **henti**

18

berhubung conj in connection to, related with; **berhubungan** v, pl to have a link or connection ← **hubung**

beri v give; ~ *tahu* inform, let know → **beritahu; memberi** v to give; **memberikan** v to give someone (as an act of kindness); to give something (for someone)

beribu, beribu-ribu adj thousands of ← **ribu**

berikut adj following ← **ikut**

berimbang adj balanced, proportional ← **imbang**

beringin n banyan (tree)

berisi v to contain; adj full, filled out ← **isi**

berisik adj noisy, loud; to rustle ← **risik**

berisiko v to be risky ← **risiko**

beristeri, beristri adj, m married ← **isteri, istri**

beristirahat v to rest, take a break ← **istirahat**

berita n news, information; **memberitakan** v to report

beritahu, beri tahu v to inform, let know; **memberitahu** v to advise, inform, tell; **pemberitahuan** n

berjabat, berjabatan ~ *tangan* to shake hands ← **jabat**

berjalan v to walk, move ← **jalan**

berjam-jam adj for hours and hours ← **jam**

berjamur adj moldy ← **jamur**

berjanji v to promise ← **janji**

berjemur v to sunbathe, sun yourself ← **jemur**

berjénggot adj bearded ← **jénggot**

berjilbab v to wear the veil ← **jilbab**

berjogét v to dance ← **jogét**

berjuang v to fight, struggle ← **juang**

berjudi v to gamble ← **judi**

berjudul v to have a title; adj titled ← **judul**

berjumlah v to number ← **jumlah**

berjumpa v to meet ← **jumpa**

berjuta v to have millions of ← **juta**

berkali-kali adv repeatedly, again and again ← **kali**

berkapasitas v with a capacity of ← **kapasitas**

19

berkarat ADJ rusty ← **karat**

berkas N bundle; file, dossier, brief

berkata v to say, speak ← **kata**

berkawan v to have or be friends with ← **kawan**

berkedip v to blink (two eyes) or wink (one eye); **berkedip-kedip** ADJ blinking ← **kedip**

berkelahi v to quarrel, fight, fall out ← **kelahi**

berkelas ADJ classy ← **kelas**

berkeliling v to go around ← **keliling**

berkeluarga v to have a family, be married ← **keluarga**

berkémah v to camp, go camping ← **kémah**

berkembang v to develop, expand; *negara* ~ developing country ← **kembang**

berkencan v to go on a date ← **kencan**

berkeringat v to sweat ← **keringat**

berkesan ADJ impressive ← **kesan**

berkibar v to wave, flutter ← **kibar**

berkilau ADJ glittering, spar-

kling ← **kilau**

berkisah v to tell a story ← **kisah**

berkisar v to revolve, rotate, turn ← **kisar**

berkoméntar v to (make a) comment ← **koméntar**

berkorban v to make sacrifices, do without ← **korban**

berkualitas ADJ quality ← **kualitas**

berkuasa ADJ powerful, mighty ← **kuasa**

berkuda v to ride a horse, go (horse-)riding ← **kuda**

berkuku ADJ having nails or claws; clawed ← **kuku**

berkulit to have skin, skinned ← **kulit**

berkumpul v to assemble, meet ← **kumpul**

berkumur(-kumur) v to gargle ← **kumur**

berkunjung v to visit, pay a visit to ← **kunjung**

berkurang v to decrease, diminish, subside ← **kurang**

berlaku ADJ effective, valid; v to behave ← **laku**

berlambang v to have a

symbol ← **lambang**

berlangganan v to subscribe to ← **langgan**

berlangsung v to take place ← **langsung**

berlari v to run ← **lari**

berlayar v to sail ← **layar**

berlebihan ADJ excessive ← **lebih**

berlian N diamond

berlibur v to go or be on holiday ← **libur**

berlindung v to (take) shelter ← **lindung**

berlomba v to compete, race ← **lomba**

berlumuran ADJ smeared, stained ← **lumur**

berlutut to kneel (down) ← **lutut**

bermacam-macam ADJ various ← **macam**

bermain v to play ← **main**

bermaksud v to intend ← **maksud**

bermalam v to spend or stay the night ← **malam**

bermalas-malas(an) v to lie or laze around, be lazy ← **malas**

bermanfaat ADJ useful, of

benefit ← **manfaat**

bermasalah ADJ problematic, troublesome ← **masalah**

bermérek ADJ branded ← **mérek**

bermimpi v to dream ← **mimpi**

berminggu-minggu ADV for weeks ← **minggu**

berminyak ADJ oily, greasy ← **minyak**

bermotif v to have a design ← **motif**

bermuka v to have a face; ~ *dua* two-faced ← **muka**

bermula v to start, begin ← **mula**

bermutu ADJ quality ← **mutu**

bernafaskan, bernapaskan v with a breath of ← **nafas**

bernafsu ADJ passionate, lusty ← **nafsu**

bernama ADJ named ← **nama**

berniat v to intend ← **niat**

bernyanyi v to sing ← **nyanyi**

berobat v to go to the doctor, seek medical advice ← **obat**

beroda ADJ wheeled ← **roda**

berolahraga v to do or play sport ← **olahraga**

berombak ADJ wavy ← **ombak**

21

berontak, memberontak
v to rebel, revolt; **pemberontakan** N rebellion, revolt,
mutiny

berotot ADJ muscular ← **otot**

berpakaian ADJ dressed in
← **pakai**

berpangkat v to have the rank
of ← **pangkat**

berpegang v to hold onto ←
pegang

berpendapat v to have an
opinion, believe ← **dapat**

berpendidikan ADJ educated; v
to have an education

berpengaruh ADJ influential
← **pengaruh**

berperan v to play the role or
part ← **peran**

berperang v to wage war, go
to war ← **perang**

berpésta v to (have a) party
← **pésta**

berpidato v to make a speech,
give an address ← **pidato**

berpihak v to take sides ←
pihak

berpikir v to think ← **pikir**

berpindah v to move ← **pindah**

berpisah v to part, separate
← **pisah**

berpose v to pose for a
photograph ← **pose**

berpréstasi ADJ prestigious;
successful ← **préstasi**

berpuasa v to fast ← **puasa**

berpusar N to revolve, whirl
← **pusar**

berpusat ~ *pada* to focus or
center on ← **pusat**

berputar v to rotate, turn ←
putar

bersabar v to be patient ←
sabar

bersahabat ADJ to be friends
← **sahabat**

bersaing v to compete; *harga*
~ competitive price ← **saing**

bersalah ADJ guilty ← **salah**

bersalin v to give birth ←
salin

bersalju ADJ snowy, snow-
covered ← **salju**

bersama ADV together; jointly
← **sama**

bersambung ADJ in parts; to
be continued ← **sambung**

bersampingan ADJ next to
each other ← **samping**

bersandar v to lean ← **sandar**

bersangka v to suspect or
think ← **sangka**

bersangkutan ADJ concerned, involved ← **sangkut**

bersatu v to unite ← **satu**

bersaudara v to be related; to have brothers and sisters; ~ *enam* to be one of six (children) ← **saudara**

bersayap ADJ winged ← **sayap**

bersedia v to be prepared or willing ← **sedia**

bersedih v to be or feel sad ← **sedih**

bersejarah ADJ historic, historical ← **sejarah**

bersekolah v to go to school ← **sekolah**

berselancar v to surf, go surfing ← **lancar**

berselingkuh v to have an affair ← **selingkuh**

bersemangat ADJ spirited, enthusiastic ← **semangat**

bersembahyang v to pray, perform a prayer ← **sembahyang**

bersembunyi v to hide (yourself) ← **sembunyi**

bersenang-senang v to enjoy yourself, have fun ← **senang**

bersenda ~ *gurau* to joke around ← **senda**

bersendawa v to burp, belch ← **sendawa**

bersenjata ADJ armed ← **senjata**

bersepatu ADJ in shoes ← **sepatu**

bersepéda v to ride a bicycle ← **sepéda**

bersiap v to get ready; **bersiap-siap** v to make preparations ← **siap**

bersifat v to have the quality of ← **sifat**

bersih ADJ clean, neat; **kebersihan** N cleanliness, hygiene; **membersihkan** v to clean; wipe out (eg. disease); **pembersih** N cleaning agent

bersikap v to display an attitude ← **sikap**

bersikeras v to maintain, stick to, be obstinate ← **keras**

bersilaturahmi v to maintain good relations, visit or meet friends ← **silaturahmi**

bersin v to sneeze

bersinar v to shine, gleam ← **sinar**

bersiul v to whistle ← **siul**

berskala v to be on a scale; ~ *besar* large-scale ← **skala**

23

bersoda ADJ carbonated; *minuman* ~ carbonated drink ← **soda**

bersolék v to put on make-up, dress up ← **solék**

bersorak v to cheer, shout ← **sorak**

bersuami ADJ, F married

bersuara v to sound, have a voice ← **suara**

bersulang v to toast, drink to ← **sulang**

bersumpah v to swear ← **sumpah**

bersyarat ADJ conditional ← **syarat**

bersyukur ADJ grateful ← **syukur**

bertaburan ADJ scattered over ← **tabur**

bertahap ADJ in stages ← **tahap**

bertahun-tahun ADV for years and years ← **tahun**

bertambah v to increase ← **tambah**

bertanda ADJ marked ← **tanda**

bertanding v to compete, play ← **tanding**

bertanggung jawab ADJ responsible ← **tanggung jawab**

bertanya v to ask; **bertanya-tanya** v to wonder, ask yourself ← **tanya**

bertaruh v to bet ← **taruh**

berteduh v to take shelter ← **teduh**

berteman v to be friends ← **teman**

bertempat v to take place or happen ← **tempat**

bertemu v to meet; *sampai ~ lagi* see you later, so long ← **temu**

bertengkar v to quarrel ← **tengkar**

bertentangan ADJ contradictory, contrary, opposing ← **tentang**

bertepuk tangan v to clap, applaud ← **tepuk tangan**

berteriak v to scream or shout ← **teriak**

berterima kasih v to be grateful or thankful ← **terima kasih**

bertiga ADJ in a three ← **tiga**

bertingkat ADJ having different levels ← **tingkat**

bertinju v to box ← **tinju**

bertumpuk v to be in piles ← **tumpuk**

berturut-turut ADJ consecutive, successive ← **turut**

beruang N bear; ~ *putih* polar bear

berubah V to change ← **ubah**

berulang V to happen again, recur; **berulang-ulang** ADV again and again, repeatedly ← **ulang**

berumur ADJ aged ← **umur**

beruntung ADJ lucky, fortunate ← **untung**

berupa ADJ in the shape or form of ← **rupa**

berurusan V to have dealings with, deal with ← **urus**

berusaha V to try, make an effort ← **usaha**

berusia V to be (aged) ← **usia**

berutang V to owe; ~ *budi* to have a debt of gratitude ← **utang**

berwarna ADJ colored ← **warna**

berziarah V to make a pilgrimage, visit a holy place ← **ziarah**

bésan N relationship between two couples whose children have married

besar ADJ big, large, great; ~ *kepala* big-headed, arrogant;

besar-besaran ADJ large-scale; **kebesaran** ADJ too big; **membesarkan** V to bring up, raise (children); **memperbesar** V to enlarge something; **terbesar** ADJ largest, biggest

beserta CONJ along with, and ← **serta**

besi N iron

bésok ADV tomorrow; COLL in the future ← **ésok**

besuk V to visit someone in hospital

betah V settle in, feel at home

betapa ADV how (very); ~ *cantiknya!* How pretty she is! → **alangkah**

Betawi original inhabitants of Jakarta (since 1527)

betina ADJ female (of animals); *anjing* ~ bitch

betis N calf, lower part of leg

beton N concrete

betul ADJ true, correct, right; **betul-betul** ADV truly, completely; **kebetulan** ADV by chance, accidentally; N coincidence; **membetulkan** V to correct, repair; **sebetulnya** ADV in fact, actually

25

bi PRON Aunt; term of address for older housemaid ← **bibi**

biar let, no matter if; ~*lah!* Never mind!; **membiarkan** V to let, allow, permit

biasa ADJ normal, usual, common, ordinary; ~*nya* usually; **kebiasaan** N habit, custom; **terbiasa** ADJ used to, accustomed

biaya N cost, expense (for a service)

bibi N, PRON aunt, sister of parent; mother's female cousin ← **bi**

bibir N lips

bibit N seedling

bicara V speak; **berbicara** V to speak; **membicarakan** V to discuss; **pembicaraan** N discussion

bidan N midwife

bidang ADJ spacious, wide; N area, field

bihun N vermicelli noodles

bijak ADJ wise; **kebijakan** N policy

biji N seed, grain; counter for very small objects; SL counter

bikin V, COLL to make; ~ *marah* make angry; **bikinan** N product; **dibikin** V to be made → **buat**

biksu N Buddhist monk

bila CONJ if

bilang V, SL say; **dibilang** V to be said

bilas, membilas V rinse

biliar, bilyar N billiards

biliun, bilyun N billion (1 000 000 000)

bimbing V to lead, guide; **membimbing** V to lead, guide, coach

bina V build up; **membina** V to build up, found

binatang N animal

binatu N (commercial) laundry

bincang: berbincang(-bincang) V to chat, discuss

bingkai N frame(s)

bingkis: bingkisan N wrapped or free gift

bingung ADJ confused; **membingungkan** ADJ confusing

bintang N star; **berbintang** V to have a star; **membintangi** V to star (in)

bintik N spot, stain, freckle

biodata N personal profile

26

(name, address, date of birth, hobbies etc)

biola N violin, fiddle

bioskop N cinema, movie theater

bir N beer

biro N office, center; ~ *perjalanan* travel agent

biru ADJ blue; ~ *tua* dark blue

bis ~ *surat* letter box, mailbox (for posting)

bis, bus N bus

bisa V, AUX can, be able; **sebisanya, sebisa-bisanya** ADV as well as you can, to the best of your ability

bisa N poison (of animals), venom; **berbisa** ADJ poisonous; *ular* ~ poisonous snake

bisbol N baseball

bisik whisper; V to whisper; **membisik** V to whisper something

bisnis N business, trade; **berbisnis** V to do business

bistik N steak

bisu ADJ mute, dumb; ~ *tuli* deaf-mute

bius N drug; *obat* ~ anesthetic; **membius** V to drug, anesthetize

blangko N form

blasteran ADJ mixed, hybrid; *Sari* ~ *Sunda-Jerman* Sari is half-Sundanese, half-German

bléwah N kind of melon

blits N flash (of camera)

blok N block (in addresses)

blokir, memblokir V to block

blong ADJ loose, not taut

blus N blouse

bobo, bobok V, SL to sleep (children's language)

bocor V to leak; **kebocoran** N leak; **membocorkan** V to leak something

bodoh ADJ stupid

bohlam N light bulb

bohong lie; **berbohong** to lie; **membohong** V to lie; **pembohong** N liar

boikot N boycott; **memboikot** V to boycott something

boks N playpen, bassinet

bola N ball; football, soccer; ~ *basket* basketball; *main* ~ play football

bolak-balik ADV back and forth, to and fro, there and back

boléh may, can; allowed, permitted; okay; ~~~ *saja*

27

sure you can; **memperbo-léhkan v** to allow, permit

boling N ten-pin bowling

bolong ADJ holey, perforated

bolos, membolos v to skip, be absent, play truant, wag, skive

bolpoin N ballpoint pen, biro

bom N bomb; **mengebom v** to bomb something

bon N bill, check, receipt

bonéka N doll (like a person); soft toy (animal); puppet

bongkar, membongkar v to pull apart, dismantle; unpack; to unearth

bor N drill; *mata ~* drill bit

bordir, bordiran N embroidery, lace edging; **membordir v** to embroider

borgol N handcuffs

boro-boro CONJ what's the point of ...? It's not even worth ...

borong, memborong v to buy up, buy in bulk; **borongan N** goods bought in bulk; *taksi ~* un-metered taxi; **pemborong N** developer, contractor

boros ADJ wasteful

bos PRON, SL boss, sir; **N** boss

bosan ADJ bored, fed up with, tired of; **membosankan ADJ** boring, tiresome

botak ADJ bald

botok, bothok N Javanese side-dish of shredded coconut and fresh vegetables

botol N bottle; *teh ~* bottled tea

brahmana, brahmin, brahma N highest Hindu caste in Bali

brankas, brangkas N safe

bréngsék EXCL blast! damn!; **N** bastard!; **ADJ** damn, bloody

brem N a soft white biscuit made from fermented rice

bréwok, beréwok N beard, whiskers, sideburns; **bréwokan ADJ** whiskered, bearded

brokoli N broccoli

bros N brooch

brosur N brochure

bu PRON Mother (to respected older women); Mum(my), Mom(my)

buah N fruit; piece, general counter for objects; *~ nangka* jackfruit; **buah-buahan N** fruit(s); **sebuah ADJ** a, one

(generic counter)

buang v to throw (away); ~ *air* to urinate; **membuang** v to throw out; waste; exile; **terbuang** ADJ thrown out, wasted

buas ADJ fierce, wild

buat PREP for; v to do, make; **buatan** N made in, product of; **berbuat** v to do; **membuat** v to make; **pembuat** N producer; **pembuatan** N production, manufacture; **perbuatan** N act, deed

buaya N crocodile, alligator

bubar v to disperse, break up, spread out; **membubarkan** v to break something up

bubuk N powder, dust

bubur N porridge; ~ *ayam* chicken porridge

budak N slave

budaya N culture; **kebudayaan** N culture, civilization

Budha *agama* ~ Buddhism; *orang* ~ Buddhist

bufét N buffet meal

bugar ADJ fit; **kebugaran** *pusat* ~ gym, fitness center

Bugis ethnic group from South Sulawesi

bujang ADJ single, unmarried (man); **bujangan** N bachelor

bujuk, membujuk v to coax

bujur N longitude; vertical line down a sphere; ~ *timur* east longitude

buka open; ~ *baju* take off clothes; **berbuka** ~ *puasa* to break the fast; **membuka** v to open; **terbuka** ADJ open

bukan no, not (of things, nouns); *Ini* ~ ? This one, isn't it?

bukit N hill; **berbukit** ADJ hilly

bukti N proof, evidence; **membuktikan** v to prove; **terbukti** ADJ proven

buku N book; ~ *pelajaran* textbook; ~ *panduan* guide(book)

bulak-balik → **bolak-balik**

bulan N moon; month; ~ *Februari* February; ~ *madu* honeymoon; ~ *puasa* fasting month, Ramadan; ~ *purnama* full moon

bulat ADJ round; fat; **bulatan** N circle

bulé N, DEROG white person, whitey, paleface; albino

bulu N feather; fur; body hair; ~ *mata* eyelashes; ~ *tangkis* badminton

bumbu N spice

bumerang N boomerang

bumi N earth, ground

buncis N string bean

buncit ADJ pot-bellied, fat

bundar, bunder ADJ round; **bundaran** N roundabout

Bung PRON brother; ~ *Karno* President Soekarno; *ayo* ~! Come on, mate!

bunga N flower, blossom; interest; ~ *mawar*, ~ *ros* rose

bungalo N bungalow, cottage, one-story house

bungkus N takeaway, pack; *nasi* ~ a takeaway rice meal; **membungkus** V to wrap; ~ *kado* to wrap a gift

bungsu N youngest child in a family; *anak* ~, *si* ~ youngest child

buntu ADJ one-way, useless; *jalan* ~ dead-end; cul-de-sac, court

buntut N tail; *sop* ~ oxtail soup

bunuh, membunuh V to kill; **pembunuh** N murderer,

killer; **pembunuhan** N murder, killing; **terbunuh** ADJ killed

bunyi N sound, noise; **berbunyi** V to sound, make a noise; **membunyikan** V to sound, ring something

bupati N regent; **kabupatén** N regency

buram ADJ cloudy, frosted, dull

bursa N exchange; ~ *efek* stock exchange

buru, memburu V to hunt, chase; **buruan, buron** N the hunted; **keburu** SL in time; too early; **pemburu** N hunter; **terburu-buru** ADJ in a hurry

buruh N laborer

buruk ADJ bad (of a situation, weather); ugly

burung N bird; ~ *béo* parrot; ~ *dara* pigeon, dove; ~ *gereja* sparrow; ~ *hantu* owl

busa N foam, lather; **berbusa** ADJ foamy; with a layer of foam

busana N clothing, wear

busuk ADJ rotten

buta ADJ blind; ~ *huruf* illiterate

butik N boutique

butir N grain, counter for small oval objects; *tiga ~ telur* three eggs

butuh V need; **kebutuhan** N need, necessity; **membutuhkan** V to need something

C

cabang N branch; *~ pohon* tree branch

cabé, cabai N chilli; *~ rawit* small, hot red chilli

cabut V to pull out, remove; SL to leave; **mencabut** V to pull out, remove

cacar N pock, pox; *~ air* chicken pox; **cacaran** V to have chicken pox

cacat N fault, defect, flaw; ADJ disabled, handicapped; *orang ~* disabled or handicapped person

caci *~ maki* insults

cacing N worm; **cacingan** ADJ to have (intestinal) worms

cadang *suku ~* spare part; **cadangan** ADJ spare, reserve; stocks

cadel, cedal ADJ to have a speech impediment

cagar N preserve; *~ alam* nature reserve

cahaya N light, shine, glow

cair N flow; **cairan** N liquid; **mencair** V to melt, turn into liquid

cakap ADJ **cakep** SL handsome; SL pretty

cakap: percakapan N conversation

cakar N claw; **mencakar** V to scratch

cakram N disc; discus; *rem ~* disc brakes

calo N ticket scalper, profiteer

calon N candidate; *~ suami* husband-to-be; **mencalonkan** V to nominate someone

camar *burung ~* seagull

camat N sub-district head; **kecamatan** N sub-district

cambuk N whip; **mencambuk** V to whip

campak N measles; *penyakit ~* measles

campur mix; *~ baur* mix with society; *~sari* a blend of traditional and modern Javanese music; *~ tangan* get involved, interfere; **mencampuradukkan** V to mix up, confuse; **campur-an** N mix, mixture; *anak ~* child of mixed descent; **bercampur** ADJ mixed with

canda N joke; *~ gurau* joking, jokes; **bercanda** v to joke

candi N temple, ancient Hindu or Buddhist temple or monument

canggih ADJ sophisticated

cangkir N cup, mug

cangkok graft, transplant; *~ ginjal* liver transplant

cangkul N hoe

cantik ADJ beautiful, pretty; **kecantikan** N beauty

cantum: tercantum ADJ attached, included, inserted

cap N seal; brand, mark; **mengecap** v to brand

cap go méh N 15th day after Chinese New Year

capai, mencapai v to reach, attain; **tercapai** ADJ achieved

capcay, cap cai N chop suey, Chinese vegetables in sauce

capék, capai ADJ tired; **kecapékan** ADJ tired out; N exhaustion

capung N dragonfly

cara N way, style, means; **secara** ADV in a way (used to form adverbs)

cari v to look for, search for, seek; **mencari** v to look or search for, seek; **mencari-cari** v to search repeatedly, everywhere

cas charge; **mengecas** v to charge (electrical equipment)

cat N cét COLL paint; **mengecat** v to paint, dye

catat, mencatat v to note; **catatan** N notes; **tercatat** ADJ noted, registered

catur N chess

cébok to wash your bottom after using the toilet

cebur v to fall into water

cedera, cidera injured, injury; *~ lutut* knee injury

cegah, mencegah v to prevent, fight against

ceguk, cekuk: cegukan N hiccups; v to have the hiccups

cék N cheque, check; *~ kosong* blank cheque

cék, mengecék v to check, confirm

cékér N, SL claw

cekik, mencekik v to strangle

ceking ADJ thin, gaunt, skin and bones

Céko N the Czech Republic

cekung ADJ concave, sunken

celah N gap, crack, crevice

celaka N accident, bad luck, misfortune; **kecelakaan** N accident, disaster

celana N trousers; ~ *pendek* shorts

celémék N apron

céléng, céléngan N piggy bank, savings box

celurit, clurit N crescent-shaped knife, sickle

cemar: mencemari v to dirty, pollute; **pencemaran** N pollution; **tercemar** ADJ polluted

cemara N casuarina (tree)

cemas ADJ worried, anxious

cemberut ADJ bad-tempered, in a bad mood

cemburu ADJ jealous; ~ *buta* blind jealousy

cemerlang ADJ glittering, sparkling, brilliant

cemilan N snack food

cempaka N a white kind of gardenia or magnolia

cempedak N fruit which is cut into slices and fried

cendana *kayu* ~ sandalwood

cendekiawan N intellectual

cenderung v to tend; **kecenderungan** N tendency, trend

céndol N sweet drink of green rice flour, molasses and coconut milk

cendramata, cinderamata N souvenir, keepsake

cengéng ADJ whiny, complaining

cengkéh N cloves

cengkeram v to grip; **cengkeraman** N grip, squeeze; **mencengkeram** v to grip, squeeze

centong ~ *nasi* spoon for serving rice

cepak ADJ shaven-headed

cepat ADJ **cepet** COLL fast, quick; **kecepatan** N speed; **mempercepat** v to speed up, accelerate; **secepat** CONJ as fast as; ~ *mungkin*, **secepat(-cepat)nya** ADV as fast as possible; **tercepat** ADJ fastest

ceplas-ceplos ADV forthright, blunt, straight from the heart (of speech or behavior)

ceplok *telur* ~ fried egg

cerah ADJ clear, sunny

cerai divorce; ~ *mati* widowed; **mencerai(kan)** V to divorce someone; **perceraian** N divorce

ceramah N lecture, talk

cerdas ADJ intelligent, bright; **kecerdasan** N intelligence

cerdik ADJ clever, smart; cunning

cerét, crét: mencrét V to have diarrhea

ceréwét ADJ fussy, finicky, hard to please; talkative

céri *buah* ~ cherry

ceria ADJ happy, in a good mood

cerita, ceritera story, tale; ~ *pendek (cerpen)* short story; ~ *rakyat* folk tale; **bercerita** V to tell (a story); **menceritakan** V to describe, relate

cermai, cermé N small, sour plum

cermin mirror; **mencerminkan** V to reflect

cerna: mencerna V to digest; **pencernaan** N digestion

ceroboh ADJ careless

cerobong N chimney

cerutu N cigar

cét → cat

cétak print; **cétakan** N mold; impression, printing; **mencétak** V to print

céwék N, COLL girl, young woman; ADJ female

cicak, cecak N gecko, house lizard

cicil pay in instalments; **mencicil** V to pay by instalments

cicip taste; **mencicipi** V to try, taste something

cicit N great-grandchild

cidera → cedera

cidomo N horse-drawn cart in Lombok ← **cikar dokar mobil**

ciduk, cédok N dipper

Cik PRON you, Sister (for Chinese women)

Cilé N Chile; *orang* ~ Chilean

cilik ADJ small, little

Cina N China; *bahasa* ~, *orang* ~ Chinese; **Pecinan** N Chinatown

cincang minced

cincau N jelly made from

34

cinchona leaves, used in drinks

cincin N ring

cinderamata, cendramata N souvenir, keepsake

cinta love, like; **bercinta** v to make love; to be in love; **mencintai** v to love someone; **pencinta, pecinta** N lover; **tercinta** ADJ dear, beloved

cipta idea, creativity; **ciptaan** N creation; **mencipta, menciptakan** v to create, make; **tercipta** ADJ created

ciri N characteristic, identifying mark

cita-cita N ideal, dream, ambition

citra N image

cium N kiss; smell; **ciuman** N kiss; **berciuman** v to kiss each other; **mencium** v to smell; to kiss; **tercium** ADJ smelt; found out

coba v, AUX try; please; **cobaan** N trial, ordeal; **mencoba** v to try, attempt; **percobaan** N experiment, test

cobék, coék N pestle for grinding chillies

coblos, mencoblos v to vote, pierce

cocok fit, match, suitable; **mencocokkan** v to match

cokelat, coklat chocolate; *warna* ~ brown

colok v to put in a plug; **colokan** N power point

conték, menconték, menyonték v to copy, cheat

contoh N example, model, sample; *~nya* for example

copét N pickpocket; **kecopétan** ADJ to be pickpocketed, robbed; N pickpocketing; **mencopét** v to pick someone's pocket

copot v to come off (accidentally)

corak N design, pattern, motif, style

corét scratch; **corét-corét** doodle, graffiti; **corétan** N scratch; **mencorét** v to scratch, cross out

corong N funnel, spout

coto N clear meat soup, specialty of Makassar

cuaca N weather

cubit pinch; **mencubit** v to pinch; **secubit** N pinch

cuci v to wash; **cucian** N laundry; **mencuci** v to wash, clean

cucu N grandchild

cuék ADJ uncaring, unfeeling, ignoring; independent

cuka N vinegar

cukup ADJ enough, sufficient; ADV quite; **secukupnya** ADV sufficient, adequate

cukur shave; **mencukur** v to shave

cula N horn

culik, menculik v to kidnap; **penculikan** N kidnapping

cuma, cuman COLL but, only; **cuma-cuma** free, at no cost

cumi, cumi-cumi N squid

curam ADJ steep, sloping, precipitous

curang ADJ dishonest, cheating

curi steal; **curi-curi** surreptitious, secret; **mencuri** v to steal; **pencuri** N thief, burglar

curiga ADJ suspicious; **mencurigakan** ADJ suspicious, suspect

cuti leave; ~ *hamil* maternity leave

D

da, dag, dah GR bye; **da-da** GR (children) bye-bye

d/a *dengan alamat* care of, c/-

dada N breast, chest, bosom; *buah* ~ F breast

dadak: dadakan ADJ sudden; **mendadak** ADJ sudden

dadar *telur* ~ omelet

daérah N region, territory, area; provinces, country(-side); *bahasa* ~ regional language

daftar list, register, roll; **mendaftar** v to register; **mendaftarkan** v to register something; **pendaftaran** N enrolment, registration; **terdaftar** ADJ registered, enrolled

dagang trade; **dagangan** v to sell goods informally; N merchandise; **berdagang** v to trade, do business; **pedagang** N merchant; **perdagangan** N commerce, trade

daging N meat, flesh; ~ *babi* pork; ~ *sapi* beef

dagu N chin

dahak N phlegm, mucus

dahi N forehead

dahulu ADJ before, former(ly); first (more formal than **dulu**); *lebih* ~ first(ly); **mendahului** v to precede, overtake

daki: mendaki v to climb, ascend; ~ *gunung* (to go) mountaineering, bush-walking

dakwa, dakwaan N charge, accusation; **terdakwa** N the accused

dalam PRON in, inside, into; ADJ deep, profound; **celana** ~ underpants; *di* ~ in, inside; *ke* ~ into; **mendalam** ADJ deep; **pedalaman** N inland, hinterland

dalang, dhalang N puppeteer (in shadow puppet plays); mastermind; **mendalangi** v to orchestrate (events)

daluwarsa, kedaluwarsa, kadaluwarsa ADJ expired, overdue

damai peace; **berdamai** v to make peace; **mendamai-kan** v to reconcile, pacify; **perdamaian** N peace, reconciliation

dampak N ill-effect; **berdam-pak** v to have a (negative) effect

damping next to, close; **berdampingan** ADJ side by side; **mendampingi** v to accompany, flank; **pendam-ping** N companion

dan CONJ and

dana N funds, money, grant

danau N lake

dandan v to dress up, put on make-up; **dandanan** N dress, make-up; **berdandan** v to dress, put on make-up; **mendandani** v to decorate, dress, adorn

dangdut N popular Indian-inspired music

dangkal ADJ shallow, super-ficial

dansa N Western-style dance; **berdansa** v to dance

dapat find, get, obtain; be able to, can; **mendapat** v to obtain, receive; **men-dapatkan** v to obtain; discover; **pendapat** N opinion, point of view; **berpendapat** v to have an opinion, believe; **penda-patan** N income, revenue; **sedapatnya** ADV what you can get

dapur N kitchen

darah N blood; **berdarah** v to bleed; **pendarahan** N bleeding

darat N land, shore; **daratan** N mainland; **mendarat** v to land

dari PREP from, of; CONJ from the time; **daripada** CONJ than

darurat ADJ emergency, pressing

dasar N base, basis, foundation; SL all because

dasi N necktie

daster N house-coat, nightgown, nighty

datang v to come, arrive; **kedatangan** N arrival; **mendatang** ADJ coming, next; **mendatangkan** v to bring, import; **pendatang** N immigrant, migrant; newcomer

datar ADJ level, flat; **dataran** N plain; **mendatarkan** v to make flat, level

daun N leaf; **dedaunan** N leaves, foliage

daur N cycle; ~ **ulang** recycling; **mendaur-ulang** v to recycle

dawet N sweet Javanese drink of green rice flour, pink syrup and coconut milk

daya N power, energy

Dayak generic name for indigenous (non-Malay) inhabitants of Kalimantan and Borneo; *orang* ~ Dayak

dayung N oar; **mendayung** v to stroke (an oar); row; to pedal

debar N pulse, beat; **berdebar** v to beat quickly

debat N debate; **berdebat** v to have a debate; **perdebatan** N debate, discussion

débet, débit N debit; **mendé-bet** v to debit

debu N dust; **berdebu** ADJ dusty

dedaunan N leaves, foliage ← **daun**

deg: deg-degan ADJ anxious, worried

déh OK then, well; *Ayo, ~ !* Come on, then! ← **sudah**

dékan N (university) dean

dekat PREP close, near; **berdekatan** ADJ close (of two or more things); **mendekati** V to approach; **pendekatan** N approach; getting to know; **terdekat** ADJ closest, nearest

delapan ADJ eight; ~ *belas* eighteen; ~ *puluh* eighty

délman N two-wheeled horse-drawn carriage

demam N fever

demi CONJ for (the sake of); by

demikian ADV such, so, in this way, thus

démo, démonstrasi N demo, demonstration, protest; **mendémo** V to protest against

démokrasi N democracy; **démokrat** N democrat; **démokratis** ADJ democratic

démonstrasi N demo, demonstration, protest

dénah N plan, map, diagram

denda N fine; *kena* ~ to be fined; **mendenda** V to fine

dendam N revenge; grudge

déndéng N dried meat, jerky

dengan CONJ with

dengar V to hear; **kedengaran, terdengar** ADJ audible; **men-**

dengar V to hear; **mendengarkan** V to listen; **pendengar** N listener; **pendengaran** N hearing

dengkul N knee

dengkur, mendengkur V to snore; to purr (of a cat)

denyut N pulse; throb

déodoran N deodorant

depak, mendepak V to kick something, kick out

depan PREP front; *di* ~ front, in front of; *ke* ~ forward, to the front; *tahun* ~ next year

departemén N department, ministry

derajat N degree, rank

deras ADJ swift; heavy; *hujan* ~ heavy rain

dérék tow (a vehicle); *mobil* ~ tow truck; **mendérék** V to tow

dérét N row, line; **dérétan** N row

dering N ring, chime; **berdering** V to ring, tinkle

derita N suffering; **menderita** V to suffer, endure

dermaga N pier, jetty

dermawan N donor, philanthropist; ADJ charitable

39

désa N village; hometown;
 pedésaan N country(side),
 rural areas
desak push; **mendesak** ADJ
 pressing, urgent; V to press,
 urge, push
Désémber *bulan* ~ December
déterjén N detergent
detik N second
déwa N, M god; **déwa-déwi,**
 déwata N, PL, M & F gods
déwan N council, board
déwasa adult; *orang* ~ adult,
 grown-up
déwata N, PL, M & F gods →
 déwa
déwi N, F goddess → **déwa**
di PREP at; on; in; ~ *atas* above,
 on top of; ~ *dalam* inside; ~
 samping beside
dia PRON he, she, it; him, her
 (often replaced by **–nya** for
 possessive)
diabét, diabétés *(penyakit)*
 ~ diabetes
dialék N dialect
diam silent, not moving;
 diam-diam ADV secretly
diaré N diarrhea
dibikin V, COLL to be made ←
 bikin

dibilang V to be said ← **bilang**
didih: mendidih ADJ boiling
didik educate; **mendidik** V to
 educate, bring up, teach;
 pendidikan N education;
 berpendidikan ADJ educated;
 V to have an education
diét N diet; **berdiét** V to diet,
 go on a diet
difaks V to be faxed ← **faks**
diinfus V to be put on a drip
 ← **infus**
dikontrakkan ADJ for rent,
 lease ← **kontrak**
dikté N dictation
dilarang V to be prohibited;
 ~ *masuk* no entry, no
 admittance; ~ *merokok* no
 smoking ← **larang**
dimengerti V to be understood
 ← **erti, arti**
dinas (to work at a) government office
dinding N (inner) wall
dingin N cold, cool, chilly;
 kedinginan N cold; feeling
 cold
dini ADJ very early, premature
diopname V to be admitted to
 hospital, be hospitalized ←
 opname

dipél v to be mopped, cleaned ← **pél**

dipermak v to be altered, shortened ← **permak**

dipingpong v to be sent here and there, messed about ← **pingpong**

diplomasi N diplomacy; **diplomat** N diplomat

diportal v to be blocked by a barrier, have a barrier lowered ← **portal**

diri N self; ~ *saya* me, myself

diri: berdiri v to stand, get up; **mendirikan** v to build, establish, erect; **sendiri** ADV alone; **PRON** self; **sendirian** ADV alone; single-handedly; **tersendiri** ADJ its own; apart, separate; **terdiri** ~ *atas*, ~ *dari* to consist of, be based or founded on

diserut v to be sharpened ← **serut**

disérvis v to be serviced ← **sérvis**

diskon N discount

diskoték N disco, nightclub

diskriminasi N discrimination; **mendiskriminasi(kan)** v to discriminate against

distrik N district

disunat v to be circumcised ← **sunat**

ditilang v to be fined ← **tilang**

divonis v to be sentenced ← **vonis**

DIY ABBREV *Daerah Istimewa Yogyakarta* Special Region of Yogyakarta

DKI ABBREV *Daerah Khusus Ibukota* Special Capital City Region

dll *dan lain-lain* et cetera

doa N prayer; **berdoa** v to pray, say a prayer; **mendoakan** v to pray for

dobel ADJ double, twice as much

dobrak, mendobrak v to break open, smash

dodol N soft, chewy sweet made from brown sugar or fruit

dok PRON Doc, Doctor (used when addressing a doctor) ← **dokter**

dokar N (two-wheeled horse-drawn) buggy

dokter, dr N doctor, surgeon; ~ *gigi (drg)* dentist; **kedokteran** ADJ medical

dolar N dollar; ~ *Amerika* US dollar

domba N sheep

dompét N purse, wallet; ~ *saya hilang!* I've lost my wallet!

donat N donut, doughnut

dong, donk SL you should know that

dongéng N tale, story, fable

dongkrak N (car) jack, lever

dorong V to push; **mendorong** V to push, encourage; **terdorong** ADJ pushed, shoved

dosa N sin; **berdosa** V to sin, commit a sin

dosén N (university) lecturer

DPR ABBREV *Dewan Perwakilan Rakyat* People's Representative Council

Dr Doktor PRON holder of a Ph.D.

dr *dokter* doctor

drastis ADJ drastic

drg *dokter gigi* dentist

dsb *dan sebagainya* and so on

dua ADJ two; ~ *belas* twelve; ~ *kali* twice; ~ *puluh* twenty; **dua-duanya** ADJ both, the two of them; **berdua** ADJ together, in pairs; **kedua** ADJ second; **kedua(-dua)nya** ADJ both

duda N widower; divorced man

duduk V to sit, be placed; **kedudukan** N position; **menduduki** V to sit on something; to occupy; **penduduk** N inhabitant, citizen, resident; **pendudukan** N occupation

duga, menduga V to suppose, suspect; **dugaan** N suspicion

duit N, SL money, cash, dirt, dosh; *cari* ~ earn a living

duka N sorrow; ~ *cita* grief, sorrow; **berduka** ~ *(cita)* to grieve, be in mourning

duku N small sweet fruit with light brown skin, clear flesh and large dark seed

dukun N traditional or spiritual healer, shaman

dukung support; **dukungan** N support; **mendukung** V to support; **pendukung** N supporter

dulu ADV first, former, before; **duluan** ADV, COLL first, before others ← **dahulu**

dunia N world; ~ *maya* online,

42

Internet
dupa N incense
duri N thorn; **berduri** ADJ
thorny; **durian** N durian,
spiky yellow-skinned fruit
with a strong smell
dus, dos N cardboard box ←
kardus
duta ~ *besar (dubes)* N
ambassador; **kedutaan** ~
(besar) embassy
duyung N seacow
dwi- PREF two; ~*bahasa*
bilingual

E

é EJAC hey (showing recog-
nition, disagreement)
ébi N (dried) shrimp
édisi N edition; **éditor** N editor
égois ADJ egoist, egotistical,
selfish
éja: éjaan N spelling
éjék, mengéjék v to tease,
mock, ridicule
ékonom N economist;
ékonomi N economy
ékor N tail; counter for
animals; **berékor** v to have

a tail
éks- PREF ex-, former →
mantan
éksékutif executive
ékskul N extra-curricular
activities, classes outside
school ← **ékstra kurikulér**
ékspatriat *orang* ~ expatriate
(esp. Caucasian)
ékspor export; **mengékspor** v
to export
éksprés ADJ express
éléktronik ADJ electronic;
éléktronika N electronics
élit, élite [élit] N elite
élpiji N liquid petroleum gas,
LPG
elus stroke, caress; **mengelus**
v to caress, stroke or pat (an
animal)
émail N (tooth) enamel
emak, mak N mother
emas, mas N gold
émbér N bucket, pail
embun N dew; **berembun** ADJ
moist, dewy
emis: mengemis v to beg;
pengemis N beggar
émisi N emission
émosi, émosional ADJ
emotional

43

empat ADJ four; ~ *belas*
fourteen; ~ *puluh* forty;
berempat ADJ in a group
of four; **keempat** ADJ
fourth; **perempat** N quarter;
perempatan, prapatan N
crossroads, intersection;
seperempat N one quarter

emping N chips made from
the melinjo bean

empuk ADJ soft, tender

emut, kemut, mengemut v
to suck on (sweets etc)

énak ADJ nice, tasty, delicious;
pleasant; ~*nya* the good
thing is, ...; ~ *saja*, ~ *aja*
(sarcastically) that's nice!
how dare they!; **énakan**
ADJ, SL better, nicer, tastier;
seénaknya ADV, NEG just how
you like, at will

enam ADJ six; ~ *belas* sixteen;
~ *puluh* sixty; *segi* ~ hexa-
gon; **keenam** ADJ sixth

éncér ADJ liquid, runny,
watery

éncik, cik PRON form of
address to Chinese woman

enggak COLL no, not ← *tidak*

enggan ADJ reluctant,
unwilling

enggang N hornbill

engkau, kau, dikau PRON you

entah who knows

entar soon ← *sebentar*

énténg ADJ light; flippant

Éropa, Éropah N Europe;
orang ~ European

érosi N erosion

érotis ADJ erotic

és N ice; ~ *krim*, ~ *puter*
ice cream; ~ *teler* sweet
dessert with ice; *lemari* ~
refrigerator

ésok ADV ~ *hari* tomorrow;
keésokan ~ *harinya* the next
day → **bésok**

étika N ethics, good manners

étnik, étnis N ethnic group;
ADJ ethnic, non-Western

évakuasi N evacuation →
ungsi

F

fajar N dawn, daybreak

faks N fax, facsimile; **difaks** v
to be faxed

fakultas N faculty

fals ADJ off-key, false (of
music)

falsafah → **filsafat**

famili ADJ related, distant family

fanatik N fan; fanatic

fasih ADJ fluent, eloquent; ~ *berbahasa Indonesia* to speak Indonesian fluently

fatal ADJ very bad; fatal

fatwa N *fatwa*, religious ruling

favorit ADJ favorite; *sekolah* ~ top school

Fébruari *bulan* ~ February

fénoména N phenomenon

féodal, féodalis ADJ feudal, feudalistic; **féodalisme** N feudalism

féri N ferry

fésbuk N Facebook

fiksi N fiction

Filipina N the Philippines

film N film

filsafat, falsafah N philosophy

Finlandia N Finland

firasat N presentiment, foreboding, bad feeling

fisik ADJ physical

fisika N physics

fisiotérapi N physiotherapy

fitnah N slander, libel

flék N blemish, spot (on face)

flu N flu, influenza

fokus N focus; **berfokus** ADJ focused; **memfokuskan** V to focus something

formulir N (blank) form

foto N photo, photograph; **berfoto** V to take, pose for a photo; **fotokopi** N photocopy; **difotokopi** to be photocopied

frustrasi ADJ frustrated

fungsi N function; **berfungsi** V to work, go; to act as

fuyung hai, puyung hai N sweet-and-sour omelet

G

G. *Gunung* Mt (Mount, name of mountain)

gabung connect, join; **gabungan** ADJ joint; **bergabung** V to join together; **menggabungkan** V to connect, combine, fuse

gadai: menggadaikan V to pawn something; **pegadaian** N pawnshop

gadang *rumah* ~ traditional Minangkabau house

gading N tusk, ivory

gadis N girl, maiden, virgin, unmarried woman

gado-gado N cooked salad with peanut sauce; ADJ mixed; *bahasa* ~ mixture of Indonesian and another language

gagah ADJ strong; ~ *perkasa* heroic; handsome

gagak *burung* ~ crow, raven

gagal v to fail; **kegagalan** N failure

gagang N handle; ~ *telepon* handset, telephone cradle

gagap stammer, stutter; ~ *teknologi (gaptek)* technophobe

gagas: gagasan N idea, concept

gagu ADJ mute

gaib ADJ mysterious, invisible

gairah N passion, lust; enthusiasm

gajah N elephant

gaji N (monthly) salary, pay; ~ *bersih* net salary, take-home pay; **menggaji** v to pay, remunerate, employ

galak ADJ fierce, wild, vicious; *anjing* ~ vicious dog

galéri N gallery → **paméran**

gali v to dig; **galian** N excavations, diggings; **menggali** v to dig; **penggalian** N digging

gambar picture, drawing, illustration; **gambaran** N sketch, idea; **bergambar** ADJ illustrated; **menggambar** v to draw, depict; **menggambarkan** v to describe, illustrate

gamelan N traditional orchestra

gampang ADJ, COLL easy → **mudah**

ganas ADJ fierce, wild, ferocious; uncontrolled

ganda double; -fold

gandéng link, join; **bergandéngan** ~ *tangan* to link arms or hands

gandum N wheat; wholemeal

gang N alley, lane

ganggu, mengganggu v to bother, disturb; **gangguan** N disturbance, interference; problem; **terganggu** ADJ bothered, disrupted, disturbed

ganja N marijuana

ganjal v to wedge; to fill a gap

ganjil ADJ uneven, odd

ganteng ADJ, COLL handsome

ganti change, substitute; ~ *baju*, ~ *pakaian* change your clothes; **gantian** v, sl change over; **berganti** v to change; ~*-ganti*, ~*an* in turns; **mengganti** v to change, substitute, replace; **menggantikan** v to substitute or replace someone/something; **pengganti** N replacement, substitute, successor

gantung hang; **menggantung** v to hang, suspend; **tergantung** ADJ depending (on), it depends

gapték N technophobe ← **gagap téknologi**

gapura N (ornamental) gateway, entrance

gara-gara ADV, sl all because of → **goro-goro**

garam N salt

garansi N guarantee (on a product); **bergaransi** ADJ guaranteed

garasi N carport, garage

garing ADJ dry, crisp

garis line, scratch; **bergaris** ADJ lined; **menggarisbawahi** to underline, emphasize; **penggaris** N ruler

garong N robber

garpu N fork

garuda N eagle, national symbol of Indonesia

garuk, menggaruk v to scratch, scrape

gas N gas; ~ *bumi* natural gas

gasing N (spinning) top

gatal ADJ itchy; **gatal-gatal** v to have a rash

gaul v to mix, associate; ADJ, sl trendy; **bergaul** v to mix or associate; **pergaulan** N mixing, social intercourse; association

gaun N (evening) gown

gawang N goal (in field sports); hurdle; *penjaga* ~ goalkeeper

gawat ADJ serious, very bad

gaya energy, strength; style; **bergaya** ADJ stylish, with style

gayung N water dipper; stick

gedé ADJ, coll big, large

gedung N building, public hall

gegar shake, quiver

gegas: bergegas-gegas v to hurry

gejala N symptom, sign

geladak N deck of a ship

47

gelang N bracelet; **pergelang-an** ~ *kaki* ankle; ~ *tangan* wrist

gelanggang N arena, stadium

gelantung hang, suspend

gelap ADJ dark; **kegelapan** N darkness

gelar N title; **bergelar** V titled; **menggelar, menggelarkan** V to hold (an event)

gelatik *burung* ~ kind of bird, finch

gelembung N bubble

géléng: menggéléng to shake your head

geli ticklish; uncomfortable; **menggelikan** ADJ funny, comic; off-putting

gelincir: tergelincir ADJ skidded, slipped

gelisah ADJ nervous, restless

gelitik, menggelitik V to tickle

gelombang N wave; (radio) frequency; **bergelombang** ADJ wavy

gelora N storm, surge, passion; **gelanggang olah raga** sports complex

gema N echo, reverberation; **bergema** V to echo, reverberate

gemar like, enjoy; **kegemar-an** N hobby; **penggemar** N fan, enthusiast

gemas, gemes COLL cute, sweet (often said to children); annoyed

gembira ADJ cheerful, happy, joyous; **bergembira** V to be happy, joyous; **kegembiraan** N joy, happiness; **menggem-birakan** ADJ exciting, happy

gembok N padlock; **meng-gembok** V to padlock

gemetar shiver, tremble; **gemetaran** ADJ shivering, trembling

gemilang glitter, shine; brilliant

gempa N quake, shudder; ~ *bumi* earthquake

gempar clamor, noise, uproar

gemuk ADJ fat, plump, obese; N grease; *jalur* ~ busy route

gén N gene; **génétik** ADJ genetic

genang: genangan N puddle, flood; **tergenang** ADJ flooded

genap ADJ even, complete, exact; *angka* ~ even number

gencat: gencatan ~ *senjata*

ceasefire, truce, armistice
gendang N (kettle) drum
géndong, menggéndong V to carry on the hip
gendut ADJ fat, pot-bellied
géng, génk N gang
genggam fist; **menggenggam** V to grip, grasp
géngsi N prestige, face; **bergéngsi** ADJ prestigious
genit ADJ flirtatious
génsét N generator
genténg N roof tile
gépéng ADJ flat, concave, sunken
gerabah N earthenware pot
gerak move; **gerakan** N movement; **bergerak** V to move; **menggerakkan** V to move, shift something
gerbang N gate, gateway, door
gerbong N carriage
geréja N church
gergaji N saw
gerhana N eclipse
gerigi N, PL teeth, points; **bergerigi** ADJ serrated, jagged
gerilya N guerrilla
gerimis *(hujan)* ~ drizzle
gerobak N cart
gersang ADJ arid

gerutu: menggerutu V to grumble, complain, gripe
gesa: tergesa-gesa ADJ in a hurry or rush
gésék rub; **gésékan** N stroke, scrape; **menggésék** V to rub, scrape
gésér: menggésér V to move aside or over
gesit ADJ nimble, adept, adroit
getah N sap, latex, gum
getar shake, tremor; **getaran** N vibration, shake, tremor
giat: kegiatan N activity
gigi N tooth
gigil: menggigil V to shiver
gigit: menggigit V to bite
gila ADJ crazy, mad, insane
giling *daging* ~ mincemeat
gilir: giliran N turn; **bergilir, bergiliran** ADJ in turns
gimana COLL how; ~ *sih?* what about that? → **bagaimana**
gini ADV, COLL like this, in this way → **begini**
ginjal N kidney
giok *batu* ~ jade
gips N plaster, plaster cast
girang ADJ pleased, glad, happy
gitar N guitar

49

gitu ADV, COLL like that, in that way → **begitu**

gizi N nutrient; *ahli* ~ nutritionist; **bergizi** ADJ nutritious

gladi, geladi ~ *resik*, ~ *bersih* dress-rehearsal

goa, gua N cave, tunnel

goda tempt; **godaan** N temptation; **menggoda** v to tempt; **tergoda** ADJ tempted

golf N golf

golok N machete, chopping knife

golong: golongan N group, category; rank; **tergolong** ADJ to include, be part of or considered

goncang, guncang rock, sway; **goncangan** N shock wave, quake; **menggoncangkan** v to rock or make something move

gondrong (excessively) long hair

gonggong: gonggong, menggonggong v to bark

gonta-ganti v to change constantly → **ganti**

GOR ABBREV *Gelanggang Olah Raga* stadium, sports complex

gordén, hordén N curtain(s)

goréng fry; **goréngan** N fried snacks; **menggoréng** v to fry; **penggoréngan** N wok, frying pan; process of frying

gorés line, scratch; **gorésan** N scratch, stroke; **menggorés** v to scratch, make a stroke; **tergorés** ADJ scratched

gosip gossip

gosok rub; **menggosok** v to rub, polish

gosong ADJ burnt, singed, scorched; *bau* ~ burnt smell

got N roadside drain or ditch

gotong carry; **menggotong** v to carry together

goyang shake, wobble, unsteady; **bergoyang** v to shake, sway; to dance; **menggoyangkan** v to shake or rock something

grup N group (esp business)

gua → **goa**

gubernur N governor

gubuk N hut

gudang N warehouse, shed, store

gugat sue; **gugatan** N lawsuit, accusation; **menggugat** v to sue, accuse

gugup ADJ nervous

gugur V to fall, be killed (in action) or eliminated; **keguguran** N miscarriage

gula N sugar

gulai, gulé N curry; ~ *kambing* goat curry

gulat wrestling; **bergulat** V to wrestle, fight

guling *(bantal)* ~ bolster, Dutch wife

gumpal N clot, lump; **gumpalan** N clot, lump

guna use, benefit; for; **berguna** ADJ useful, worthwhile; **menggunakan** V to use; **pengguna** N user

guna-guna N black magic

guncang, goncang rock, sway; **guncangan** N shock wave, quake; **menggun-cangkan** V to rock or make something move

gundul ADJ bald

gunting N scissors, cut; ~ *kuku* nail clippers; **guntingan** N cutout; **menggunting** V to cut (out)

guntur N thunder

gunung N mountain, mount; remote area; ~ *(ber)api*

volcano; **gunungan** N symbolic mountain used in shadow-puppet plays; **pegunungan** N mountain range

guramé, guraméh, gurami *ikan* ~ large freshwater fish

gurih ADJ tasty, delicious, mouth-watering

gurita *ikan* ~ octopus

guru N teacher; **perguruan** ~ *tinggi* university

gusi N gums

gusur: menggusur V to evict, sweep aside, forcibly remove

H

H. *Haji* title for man who has performed the major pilgrimage to Mecca

habis ADJ finished; empty; ADV entirely; COLL after; **kehabisan** V to run out of (water; food; stock); **menghabiskan** V to finish, use up, spend; **sehabis** CONJ after

hadap face; **berhadapan** *(~ muka)* V face to face; **menghadap** V to face, appear

51

before; **menghadapi** v to
face someone or something;
terhadap conj regarding;
against; with respect to
hadiah n present, gift; prize;
berhadiah adj with prizes
hadir present; available;
kehadiran n presence;
attendance; **menghadiri** v
to attend
hafal, hapal know by heart;
menghafalkan v to learn
by heart
hai sl hi
haid n menstruation
haji n, isl person who has
made the pilgrimage to
Mecca; *Lebaran* ~ Idul
Adha, Feast of the Sacrifice
(performed during the
annual pilgrimage)
hak n right; **berhak** v to have a
right to, be entitled to
hak n heel
hakim n judge
hal n matter, case
halal adj, isl permitted (to eat);
killed according to Islamic
practice
halaman n yard, open area,
page; ~ *rumah* yard

halang: halangan n obstacle;
hindrance; **berhalangan** v
to be prevented; unable;
menghalangi v to hinder,
prevent; **terhalang** adj
blocked; prevented
halte n stop; ~ *bis* bus stop
halus adj fine; soft; refined
HAM abbrev *Hak Asasi*
Manusia Human Rights
hama n pest; plague
hambat, menghambat v to
obstruct, impede, hamper;
hambatan n obstacle
hamil adj pregnant; **kehamilan**
n pregnancy
hampir adv nearly, almost
hancur smashed, crushed;
menghancurkan v to smash,
crush, destroy
handphone n [hénpon; hénfon]
mobile phone, cell phone
handuk n towel
hangat adj warm, hot;
kehangatan n warmth,
friendliness
hangus adj burnt, scorched;
expired
hansip n local security guard;
paramilitary ← **pertahanan**
sipil

52

hantu N ghost

hanya ADV only

hapé, HP N mobile phone, cell phone ← **handphone**

haram ADJ, ISL forbidden, not permitted

harap hope; please; **harapan** N hope, expectation; **berharap** V to hope; **mengharapkan** V to expect

harga N price; value; **berharga** ADJ precious; valuable; **menghargai** V to appreciate; **penghargaan** N appreciation; award

hari N day; ~ *ini* today; ~ *kerja* weekday, working day; ~ *libur* holiday, day off; ~ *ulang tahun (HUT)* birthday, anniversary; **harian** ADJ daily; **berhari-hari** ADV for days; **sehari-hari** ADV every day, daily; **seharian** ADV, COLL all day

harimau N tiger

harta N wealth, belongings

haru emotion; touched; **mengharukan** ADJ moved, touched (emotionally); **terharu** ADJ moved, touched

harum ADJ fragrant; perfumed

harus V must, ought to, have to; **keharusan** N obligation, necessity; requirement; **mengharuskan** V to require; **seharusnya** should

hasil N product; result; **berhasil** V to succeed; **menghasilkan** V to produce

hati N liver; heart; ~ *kecil* conscience; **hati-hati** take care; **memperhatikan** V to notice, pay attention to; **perhatian** N attention

haus ADJ thirsty; **kehausan** ADJ to be thirsty; N thirst

havermut N oatmeal porridge

hawa N air, atmosphere, climate; **berhawa** ~ *sejuk* cool climate

hébat ADJ great; violent; terrific

héboh sensational

héktar N hectare

héla, menghéla V to draw; drag

helai N (counter) sheet; counter for thin flat objects; *se~ kertas* a piece of paper

héli, hélikopter N helicopter

hélm N helmet

hémat ADJ economical, thrifty;

~ *air* save water; **menghémat** v to save on or economize

hembus, embus blow, puff; **menghembus** v to blow

hendak v to will, wish, intend; ~*nya* should; **kehendak** n will; **menghendaki** v to want

hening clear; quiet

henti stop; **berhenti** v to stop, cease; **menghentikan** v to stop something; **memberhentikan** v to stop (a vehicle); to dismiss

héran ADJ astonished, amazed; **menghérankan** ADJ astonishing, astounding

héwan n animal, beast

hias decorative; **hiasan** n decoration; **menghiasi** v to adorn; to decorate something; **perhiasan** n jewellery

hibur: **hiburan** n entertainment; **menghibur** v to entertain; to comfort, console

hidang: hidangan n dish, food served

hidung n nose

hidup live; alive; lively; **kehidupan** n life, existence;

menghidupkan v to bring to life; to start or turn on (a device)

hijau, hijo, héjo ADJ green; ~ *tua* dark green

hijriah, H *tahun* ~ the Islamic calendar

hikmah n wisdom, insight, moral

hilang disappear; lost, missing; **kehilangan** n (feeling of) loss; v to lose something; **menghilang** v to disappear, vanish; **menghilangkan** v to remove

hilir, ilir downstream

hina low, insulting; humble; **hinaan** n insult; **menghinakan** v to humiliate, insult; **penghinaan** n insult, libel (written), slander (spoken)

hindar: menghindar v to steer clear of, avoid; **menghindari** v to avoid something

Hindu *agama* ~ Hinduism; *orang* ~ Hindu

hingga until; **sehingga** CONJ to the point that, as far as, until, so that

hirup inhale; suck; **menghirup** v to breathe in

hitam ADJ black

hitung count; **menghitung** V to count, calculate, reckon; **menghitungkan** V to count or calculate something; **perhitungan** N calculation; **terhitung** ADJ counted, included

Hj. *Hajjah* title for woman who has performed the major pilgrimage to Mecca

hobi N hobby

hoki N good luck or fortune

homo M, SL *(orang)* ~ homosexual, gay

honai N round hut in Papua (Irian Jaya)

Hongaria N Hungary

hong sui, féng sui N feng shui

hordén, gordén N curtain(s)

horé EJAC hooray!

horisontal ADJ horizontal; at one level

hormat respect, honor; **kehormatan** N respect; **menghormat, menghormati** V to honor or respect; **terhormat** ADJ respected

hotél N hotel; ~ *melati* cheap hotel; ~ *(ber)bintang lima*

five-star hotel; **perhotélan** N hotel studies; hospitality

hubung: hubungan N link, connection, relationship; **berhubung** CONJ in connection with, relating to; **berhubungan** V, PL to have a link or connection; **menghubungi** V to contact someone; **menghubung-kan** V to connect, join, link different parts; **perhubungan** N communications, connection; ~ *udara* air route

hujan rain; *musim* ~ rainy season, monsoon; **kehujanan** ADJ caught in the rain

hukum law; punish; **hukuman** N punishment; **menghukum** V to punish, sentence, condemn

hulu N source, beginning

huni: penghuni N occupant, resident

huruf N letter, character

HUT ABBREV *hari ulang tahun* birthday, anniversary

hutan N forest, jungle, wood; ~ *rimba* jungle; **kehutanan** N forestry

55

I

iba pity, compassion
ibadah N worship, religious devotion; **beribadah** v to worship, serve
ibarat CONJ like, as, example
ibu N, PRON, F mother; ~ *angkat* adopted mother; ~ *bapak* parents; ~ *jari* thumb; ~ *kota* capital (city); ~ *rumah tangga* housewife, homemaker; ~ *tiri* stepmother; *bahasa* ~ mother tongue; **ibu-ibu** N, PL ladies
idam: idaman ADJ dream, ideal; **mengidam** v **ngidam** COLL to crave (esp of pregnant woman)
idap: mengidap v to suffer from
idé, ide N idea
idéntik ADJ identical, same
idéntitas N (proof of) identity
idola N idol, star
Idul, Ied ul ISL ~ *Adha* Feast of the Sacrifice; ~ *Fitri* end of fasting celebrations
ijab ~ *kabul* ISL marriage contract

ijazah N certificate, qualification; **berijazah** ADJ certified, qualified
ijin, izin permission; **mengijinkan** v to permit, allow
ikal ADJ curly
ikan N fish; ~ *asin* salty fish; ~ *hiu* shark; **perikanan** N fisheries
ikat tie, knot; weaving, ikat; ~ *pinggang* belt; **ikatan** N alliance, union; **mengikat** v to tie, fasten; **terikat** ADJ bound
iklan N advertisement
iklim N climate
ikut v join in, go along with; ~ *serta* take part, participate; **berikut** ADJ following; **mengikut** v to follow, accompany; **mengikuti** v to follow, join, participate in
ilir → **hilir**
ilmu N science, study; ~ *filsafat* philosophy; ~ *fisika* physics; ~ *kimia* chemistry; ~ *pasti* the physical sciences, mathematics; ~ *sejarah* history; **keilmuan** ADJ scientific
imbal: imbalan N compen-

sation, reward, repayment

imbang balanced; **berimbang** ADJ balanced, proportional; **seimbang** ADJ balanced, well-proportioned; **keseimbangan** N balance

imél N email

imigrasi N immigration

imitasi N fake

Imlék *(Tahun Baru)* ~ Chinese New Year

impi: impian N dream

impor import; **mengimpor** v to import; **pengimpor** N importer

inai N henna

inap stay the night; **menginap** v to stay the night, stay over; **penginapan** N accommodation, hotel

inci N inch

indah ADJ beautiful; **keindahan** N beauty

indera, indra N sense; ~ *penglihatan* sense of sight

India N India; *orang* ~ Indian

Indian *orang* ~ Native American, (South) American Indian

Indo *orang* ~ person of mixed Western and Indonesian descent

Indonésia Indonesia; *Bahasa* ~, *orang* ~ Indonesian

induk mother (animal); ~ *ayam* mother hen

indung mother, home

inféksi N infection; **terinféksi** ADJ infected

info, informasi N information, info

informatika N information technology (IT)

infus N (saline) drip; **diinfus** v to be put on a drip

ingat remember; **ingatan** N memory; **mengingat** v to remember, bear in mind; **mengingatkan** v to remind someone about something; **memperingati** v to commemorate; **peringatan** N warning; commemoration, remembrance

Inggris Britain; England, English; ~ *Raya* Great Britain; *bahasa* ~ English; *orang* ~ English; British

ingin v to wish, desire; **keinginan** N desire, wish

ingkar v to break (a vow etc)

ingus N nasal mucus

57

ini PRON this, these; **begini** ADV like this; **segini** ADJ this much

injak V to tread, pedal; **menginjak** V to step, tread, or stamp on

injil N gospel, Bible

insinyur, Ir N engineer

insya Allah ISL God willing

intan N diamond

interlokal ADJ long-distance (dialing)

intérn ADJ internal

internasional ADJ international

intérnis N specialist (doctor)

interviu, interpiu N interview; **menginterviu** V to interview

inti N core, kernel, nucleus

intim ADJ intimate, close

intip, mengintip V to peep at, spy on

IPA ABBREV *ilmu pengetahuan alam* natural sciences

ipar in-law

IPS ABBREV *ilmu pengetahuan sosial* social sciences

Ir *insinyur* title for holder of a degree in engineering or architecture

Irak N Iraq; *orang* ~ Iraqi

irama N rhythm

Iran N Iran; *orang* ~ Iranian

iri envy; ~ *(hati)* envious

Irian N (West) Papua, Irian; ~ *Jaya* Indonesian province between 1963 & 2000; *orang* ~ Papuan

irigasi N irrigation

iris slice thinly; **irisan** N slice

irit economical; save money

Irlandia N Ireland

Isa N Jesus → **Yesus**

isak sob; **terisak(-isak)** ADJ sobbing

isap V to suck on; **mengisap** V to suck

iseng for fun, not serious; waste or kill time

isi N contents, volume, full; **berisi** V to contain; ADJ full, filled out; **mengisi** V to fill, load

Islam Islam; *agama* ~ Islam; *orang* ~ Muslim

Isra Miraj N, ISL holiday commemorating Muhammad's ascent to Heaven

istana N palace

isteri, istri N wife; **beristeri, beristri** ADJ, M married

istilah N term, word

istiméwa ADJ special

istirahat rest, recreation, break; **beristirahat** v to rest, take a break

istri, isteri N wife; **beristeri, beristri** ADJ, M married

isu N issue, controversy

isya night prayer (during the hours of darkness)

isyarat N signal, sign, gesture

Itali, Italia N Italy

itik N duck

itu PRON that, those; **begitu** ADV like that; **segitu** ADJ that much

iya COLL yes; ~ *ya* it is, isn't it?

izin, ijin permission; **meng-izinkan** v to permit, allow

J

jabat: jabatan N position, work; **berjabat(an)** ~ *tangan* to shake hands; **pejabat** N (government) official

jadi v to become, happen; CONJ so; *tidak* ~ it didn't happen, it fell through; **kejadian** N event, happening; creation;

menjadi v to be or become; **terjadi** v to happen, become

jadwal N timetable, schedule

jaga guard, nightwatchman; **menjaga** v to guard, keep watch

jago N champion; cock, rooster

jagung N corn, maize; ~ *bakar* roasted sweet corn

jahat ADJ bad, wicked, evil; **kejahatan** N crime; **penjahat** N criminal

jahé N ginger

jahit v to sew; *tukang* ~ tailor; **jahitan** N stitches; sewing; **menjahit** v to sew

jajah: jajahan N colony, territory; **menjajah** v to colonize, rule another country; **penjajah** N colonizer, ruler, colonial power

jajan buy cheap goods; *uang* ~ pocket money; **jajanan** N cheap snacks

jaksa N judge

jala N fishing net; *roti* ~ kind of Malay pancake

jalak N starling, mynah

jalan N street, road, way; walk; operate, go; ~ *besar* main

59

road; ~ *keluar* exit, way out; ~ *masuk* entrance; ~ *raya* highway; **jalan-jalan** v to go for a walk; to go out (for fun); **jalanan** N streets, on the road; **berjalan** v to walk, move; **menjalankan** v to operate, run, set in motion; **perjalanan** N journey, trip

jalin: jalinan N net, network; **menjalin** v to forge links, network

jalur N lane, track

jam N hour; clock; ~ *berapa?* what time is it?; ~ *besuk* visiting hours; ~ *buka* opening hours; ~ *karet* rubber time, lack of punctuality; ~ *lima* five o'clock; ~ *tangan* (wrist)watch; **berjam-jam** ADJ for hours and hours

jaman, zaman N age, era, time, period; ~ *dahulu*, ~ *dulu* in the old days, times past

jambu N *(buah)* ~ guava, rose-apple; kind of fruit; ~ *air* rose-apple; ~ *batu*, ~ *biji* guava

jamin, menjamin v to guarantee, promise; **jaminan** N guarantee; **terjamin** ADJ guaranteed

jamrud, zamrud N emerald

jamu N traditional herbal medicine

jamur N mushroom, mold, fungus; **berjamur** ADJ moldy

janda N widow

jangan NEG don't, do not

janggal ADJ odd, strange

janggut, jénggot N beard, goatee; **berjénggot** ADJ bearded

jangka N distance, term; ~ *pendek* short term

jangkar N anchor

jangkrik, jéngkerik N cicada, cricket

janin N fetus, embryo

janji promise; **janjian** v, SL to make a date, promise; **berjanji** v to promise; **menjanjikan** v to promise something; **perjanjian** N agreement, contract

jantan male (animal), manly

jantung N heart, core

Januari *bulan* ~ January

jarak N distance, space

jarang ADJ, ADV seldom, rare, rarely, hardly ever

jari N finger; ~ *kaki* toe; ~ *kelingking* little or baby finger; ~ *manis* ring finger; ~ *telunjuk* forefinger, index finger; ~ *tengah* middle finger

jaring N net, shoal; **jaringan** N network; **menjaring** v to fish with a net; to filter or sift

jarum N needle; hand

jas N coat; ~ *hujan* raincoat

jasa N service, merit

jatah N ration, serve

Jateng N Central Java ← **Jawa Tengah**

jati ~ *diri* identity; **sejati** ADJ genuine, original, real

Jatim N East Java ← **Jawa Timur**

jatuh fall; ~ *cinta* fall in love; ~ *sakit* fall ill; **menjatuhkan** v to fell, let drop; **terjatuh** ADJ (accidentally) fallen

jauh ADJ far; *jarak* ~ long-distance; **kejauhan** ADJ too far

Jawa Java; ~ *Barat (Jabar)* West Java; *bahasa* ~, *orang* ~ Javanese; *pulau* ~ Java

jawab answer, reply; **jawaban** N answer, reply, response;

menjawab v to answer, reply; **terjawab** ADJ answered

jebak: **jebakan** N trap; **menjebak** v to trap; **terjebak** ADJ trapped, caught

jejak N footprint, track; ~ *langkah* footprint

jejaka N bachelor, young single man

jelajah: **menjelajahi** v to travel through or explore a place

jelang: **menjelang** v to approach (usu time)

jelas ADJ clear, obvious; **menjelaskan** v to explain, clarify; **penjelasan** N explanation

jelék ADJ bad, ugly

jemaah, jemaat N congregation, followers of a religion

jembatan N bridge

jempol N thumb

jemput pick up; **jemputan** N vehicle which picks you up; **menjemput** v to pick up

jemur dry (in the sun); **jemuran** N clothes or food drying in the sun; **berjemur** v to sunbathe, sun yourself;

menjemur v to air, dry in the sun
jenazah n dead body, corpse
jendéla n window
jénderal n general
jénggot, janggut n beard; **berjénggot** adj bearded
jéngkél adj annoyed
jéngkol n pungent vegetable
jenis n kind, sort, type; species; ~ *kelamin* sex, gender; *lawan* ~ opposite sex; **sejenis** adj same type or species
jenuh adj fed up, bored; saturated
Jepang n Japan; *bahasa* ~, *orang* ~ Japanese
jepit n tweezers; **jepitan** n clip; tweezers; **terjepit** adj pinched, caught in an uncomfortable situation
jeprét: jeprétan, penjeprét n stapler; **menjeprét** v to snap, staple
jerapah n giraffe
jerawat n pimple; **jerawatan** adj pimply
jerit scream, shriek; **menjerit** v to scream, shriek
Jerman n Germany; *bahasa* ~, *orang* ~ German

jernih adj clear, transparent, pure; *air* ~ clear water
jero: jeroan n innards
jeruk *buah* ~ orange, mandarin; ~ *nipis* lemon
jihad n, isl crusade, holy war
jijik adj disgusting, revolting, filthy; **menjijikkan** adj disgusting, revolting, foul
jika, jikalau conj if, should
jilat lick; **menjilat** v to lick; sl to suck up, flatter
jilbab n, isl (full) veil; **berjilbab** v to wear the veil
jilid n volume
jimat n lucky charm, talisman
jin n spirit
jinak adj tame, domesticated, friendly
jingga adj orange (color)
jinjing *tas* ~ carrybag
jip *mobil* ~ jeep
jiwa n life, soul
Jl(n) *Jalan* street, road
jodoh n life partner, match; m Mr Right; **menjodohkan** v to set up, match
jogét, jogéd (spontaneous) dance; **berjogét** v to dance
jok n seat (in vehicle)
jongkok v to squat

joran N fishing rod

jorok ADJ obscene, disgusting; sloppy; *cerita* ~ dirty story

jual v to sell; ~ *beli* business, buying and selling; **jualan** v to sell informally; **menjual** v to sell; **penjual** N seller, dealer; **penjualan** N sale, sales; **terjual** ADJ sold; *habis* ~ sold out

juang: berjuang v to fight, struggle; **perjuangan** N battle, fight, struggle

juara N champion; ~ *satu* first place; **kejuaraan** N championship

judi v to gamble; *main* ~ to gamble; **berjudi** v to gamble

judul N title; **berjudul** ADJ titled

juga too, also

jujur ADJ honest; **kejujuran** N honesty

Juli *bulan* ~ July

Jumat, Jum'at *hari* ~ Friday; *sholat* ~ Friday prayers

jumlah N amount, total, sum, number; **berjumlah** v to number

jumpa meet; **berjumpa** v to meet

Juni *bulan* ~ June

junior, yunior N junior; student in a younger year level; co-worker of a lower rank

jurang N ravine, gorge

jurnal N journal; **jurnalis** N journalist, reporter → **wartawan**

juru N expert, skilled; ~ *bicara* spokesperson; ~ *masak* cook

jurus: jurusan N direction; major (at university)

jus N juice

justru ADV precisely, exactly

juta N million; *sepuluh* ~ ten million; **jutaan** ADJ millions; **berjuta** v to have millions of; **jutawan** N millionaire

K

KA ABBREV *kereta api* train

kabar N news; ~ *baik* good news; I'm well

kabupatén N regency

kabur ADJ blurry, hazy

kabur v to disappear, vanish

kabut N fog, mist

63

kaca N glass; ~ *mata* glasses, spectacles; ~ *mata hitam* sunglasses, dark glasses

kacang N bean, legume; ~ *kedelai* soybean, soya bean; ~ *tanah* peanut

kacau ADJ disordered, confused, chaotic

kadal N lizard

kadaluwarsa, kedaluwarsa ADJ expired; *tanggal* ~ expiry date, use-by date (food) ← **daluwarsa**

kadang, kadang-kadang, terkadang ADV sometimes, occasionally

kadar N level, degree; **sekadar** ADJ just; ~*nya* as necessary

kafé N café, bar, pub, nightspot

kagét N startled, surprised; **mengagétkan** v to surprise, startle

kagum ADJ admiring; **mengagumi** v to admire

-kah (suffix to make a question) *bisa~?* Can you?

kail N fishing rod

kailan N Chinese broccoli, kailan

kain N cloth; ~ *kebaya* national dress for women

kaisar N, PRON emperor

kait N hook; **kaitan** N relationship, link; **mengaitkan** v to link, connect, join ← **gaét, gait**

kaji: kajian N studies

kaji: mengaji, ngaji v to recite or read the Koran; **pengajian** N Koranic recitation

kak PRON term for older sibling or slightly older person; **kakak** N, PRON elder brother or sister; ~ *laki-laki* elder brother

kakas: perkakas N tool, implement

kakatua N *burung* ~ cockatoo

kakék N, PRON grandfather; old man

kaki N foot, leg

kaku ADJ stiff, frozen

kala N time; CONJ when

kalah lose, be defeated; **mengalahkan** v to conquer, defeat

kalajengking N scorpion

kalang: kalangan N circle, group

kalau CONJ if; **kalau-kalau**

conj in case; **kalaupun conj** even if

Kalbar n West Kalimantan ← **Kalimantan Barat**

kaldu n broth

kalem adj calm, steady

kaléndar, kalénder n calendar

kaléng n tin, can

kali n time, times; *satu* ~, *se*~ once; *dua* ~ twice; **berkali-kali adv** repeatedly, again and again; **sekali adv** once; very; *besar* ~ very large; **sekali-sekali, sesekali adv** every now and then, occasionally; **sekali-kali** *jangan* ~ never (do this); **sekalian adv** all together, all at once; **adv, coll** at the same time; **sekaligus adv** all at once; **sekalipun conj** even though

kali n creek, stream, river

kali coll maybe, perhaps ← **barangkali**

kalian pron, pl you; *anda se*~ all of you

Kalimantan n Kalimantan, Borneo; ~ *Timur (Kaltim)* East Kalimantan

kalimat n sentence

kalkun n turkey

Kalsél n South Kalimantan ← **Kalimantan Selatan**

Kalteng n Central Kalimantan ← **Kalimantan Tengah**

Kaltim n East Kalimantan ← **Kalimantan Timur**

kalung n necklace

kamar n room; **sl** bedroom; ~ *kecil* toilet, lavatory; ~ *mandi* bathroom; ~ *pas* fitting room

kambing n goat, sheep

kamboja *bunga* ~ frangipani

Kamboja n Cambodia

kami pron, excl we, us, our; (very polite) I

Kamis *hari* ~ Thursday

kampanye n campaign

kampung, kampong n village, hometown; ~ *pulang* to go home to the village; **kampungan adj** uneducated, backward, provincial

kampus n university, campus

kamu pron s you (to children and familiars)

kamus n dictionary; ~ *saku* pocket dictionary

kan, 'kan you know; isn't it? ← **bukan**

Kanada n Canada

kanan ADJ right; *ke* ~ to the right; *tangan* ~ right hand

kancil N mouse-deer

kancing N button, stud

kandang N stable, pen

kandung N uterus; bladder; **kandungan** N fetus, unborn child; contents; **mengandung** v to contain, carry; to be pregnant

kangen ADJ long for, miss

kangguru, kanguru N kangaroo

kangkung N water spinach

kanker N cancer; ~ *payudara* breast cancer

kano N canoe

kantin N canteen

kantong, kantung N pocket, pouch

kantor N office; ~ *pos* post office; ~ *pusat* head office; *pergi ke* ~ go to work; **perkantoran** N office block

kantuk: mengantuk, ngantuk ADJ sleepy

kantung → **kantong**

kaos → **kaus**

kapak N ax

kapal N ship, vessel; ~ *terbang* aeroplane, airplane; *awak* ~

crew; **perkapalan** N shipping

kapan INTERROG when; ~ *saja* whenever, any time; **kapan-kapan** ADV one day, some time in the future

kapas N cotton, cotton wool

kapasitas N capacity; **berkapasitas** v with a capacity of

kapsul N capsule

kapuk, kapok N kapok

kapur N lime(stone), chalk

karamél N caramel pudding

karang N coral reef; *batu* ~ coral reef

karang: karangan N essay; **mengarang** v to write, compose; **pengarang** N author, writer, composer

karantina N quarantine

karapan ~ *sapi* Madurese bull races

karat N rust; **karatan, berkarat** ADJ rusty

karat N carat

karburétor, karburator N carburettor

karcis N ticket (of small value); ~ *bis* bus ticket; ~ *masuk* entrance ticket; *loket* ~ ticket office

kardus N cardboard (box)

karé → **kari**

karédok N Sundanese fresh salad with peanut sauce

karena CONJ because, since

karét N rubber; rubber band; ~ *gelang* rubber band; *kebun* ~ rubber plantation; *permen* ~ chewing gum

kari, karé N curry

karton N cardboard

kartu N card; ~ *nama* name card; ~ *pos* postcard; *main* ~ play cards

kartun N cartoon, anime; **kartunis** N cartoonist

karung N sack

karya N works; **karyawan** N (salaried) employee; **karyawati** N, F (salaried) employee

kasar ADJ rough, rude, vulgar; **kekasaran** N coarseness, roughness

kasét N cassette

kasih, kasi V, COLL give; ~ *lihat* show; ~ *pinjam* lend; ~ *tahu* inform, tell

kasih N affection, love; ~ *sayang* love; **kasihan** N pity, feel sorry for; ~ *dia* poor thing!; **kekasih** N darling, sweetheart, beloved

kasir, kassa N cashier

kasuari *burung* ~ cassowary

kasur N mattress

kasus N case

kata N word; ~*nya*, ~ *orang* people say; ~ *sandi* password; **berkata** V to say, speak; **mengatakan** V to say

katak N frog, toad

katédral N cathedral

Katolik Catholic

katrol N pulley

katulistiwa, khatulistiwa N the Equator

katun N cotton

katup N valve

kau PRON, S you (to equals or inferiors) ← **engkau**

kaum N people, community

kaus, kaos N stocking, sock; garment; ~ *kaki* sock; stocking; ~ *tangan* glove, mitten

kawah N crater

kawal N guard; **pengawal** N (body)guard, sentry

kawan N friend; **berkawan** V to have or be friends with

kawas: kawasan N area, region

kawat N wire; ~ *berduri*

67

barbed wire; ~ *listrik* electrical wire

kawin v marry, mate; **kawinan** N, COLL wedding ceremony or reception; **perkawinan** N marriage, wedding

kaya ADJ rich; ~ *raya* very rich; **kekayaan** N wealth, riches

kayak, kaya CONJ, COLL like, as; **kayaknya** it seems, apparently

kayu N wood; ~ *jati* teak; ~ *manis* cinnamon

kayuh: mengayuh v to paddle or pedal something; ~ *sepeda* to ride a bicycle

KB ABBREV *Keluarga Berencana* Family Planning

KBRI ABBREV *Kedutaan Besar Republik Indonesia* Embassy of the Republic of Indonesia

ke PREP to, towards; ~ *atas* up, upwards; ~ *dalam* into; ~ *luar* out; ~ *muka* to the front; ~ *samping* to the side; ~ *tengah* to the middle

keadaan N situation, condition ← **ada**

keadilan N justice ← **adil**

keamanan N safety, security ← **aman**

keanggotaan N membership; *kartu* ~ membership card ← **anggota**

kebakaran N fire; ~ *hutan* forest fire, bushfire; *ada* ~! fire! ← **bakar**

kebaktian N (Protestant) service ← **bakti**

kebangsaan ADJ national ← **bangsa**

kebanyakan N, ADJ too much; most ← **banyak**

kebaya N, F women's blouse worn as national costume

kebenaran N truth ← **benar**

keberangkatan N departure; *pintu* ~ departure gate ← **angkat, berangkat**

keberanian N bravery, courage ← **berani**

keberatan N objection; v to object ← **berat**

kebersihan N cleanliness, hygiene ← **bersih**

kebetulan ADV by chance, accidentally; N coincidence ← **betul**

kebiasaan N habit, custom ← **biasa**

kebijakan N policy ← **bijak**

68

kebisingan N noise, buzz ← **bising**

kebocoran N leak ← **bocor**

kebudayaan N culture, civilization ← **budaya**

kebugaran N health; *pusat* ~ gym, fitness center ← **bugar**

kebuli *nasi* ~ lamb and rice dish of Middle Eastern origin

kebun, kebon N garden, plantation; ~ *binatang* zoo; ~ *raya* botanical garden; *tukang* ~ gardener; **berkebun** v to garden, do gardening; **perkebunan** N plantation, estate; ~ *teh* tea plantation

keburu ADJ, ADV, COLL in time; too early ← **buru**

kebut: mengebut v to speed

kebutuhan N need, necessity ← **butuh**

kecam; mengecam v to criticize; **kecaman** N criticism

kecamatan N sub-district ← **camat**

kecantikan N beauty ← **cantik**

kécap N soy sauce; ~ *asin* soy sauce; ~ *manis* sweet soy sauce

kecapékan ADJ tired out; N exhaustion ← **capék**

kecelakaan N accident, disaster ← **celaka**

kecenderungan N tendency, trend ← **cenderung**

kecepatan N speed ← **cepat**

kecerdasan N intelligence ← **cerdas**

kecéwa ADJ disappointed; **kekecéwaan** N disappointment; **mengecéwakan** v to disappoint; ADJ disappointing

kecil ADJ small, little; young; ~ *hati* disappointed, offended; *orang* ~ the little people, the poor; *dari* ~, *sejak* ~ since youth; **kekecilan** ADJ too small; **mengecilkan** v to make smaller, decrease

kecipratan ADJ be splashed, sprayed accidentally ← **ciprat**

kecolongan ADJ to be robbed; to lose unjustly ← **colong**

kecopétan ADJ to be pickpocketed, robbed; N pickpocketing ← **copét**

kecuali CONJ except; **terkecuali** *tidak* ~, *tanpa* ~ without exception

kecubung *batu* ~ ruby

kecut ADJ sour, acidic

kecut ADJ shrivelled; **pengecut** N coward

kedai N stall, kiosk

kedaluwarsa, kadaluwarsa ADJ expired ← **daluwarsa**

kedamaian N peace ← **damai**

kedap ADJ free from; ~ *air* waterproof; ~ *suara* soundproof; ~ *udara* air-tight

kedatangan N arrival ← **datang**

kedekatan N close relationship ← **dekat**

kedelai, kedelé soy; *susu kacang* ~ soya milk, soymilk

kedengaran ADJ audible ← **dengar**

kedinginan cold; feeling cold ← **dingin**

kedip blink; wink; **berkedip** V to blink (two eyes) or wink (one eye); **berkedip-kedip** ADJ blinking; **mengedipkan** ~ *mata* to blink

kedondong *buah* ~ kind of fruit

kedua ADJ second; **kedua(-dua)nya** ADJ both ← **dua**

kedudukan N position ← **duduk**

kedutaan ~ *(besar)* embassy ← **duta**

keempat ADJ fourth ← **empat**

keénakan ADJ too enjoyable or good ← **énak**

keenam ADJ sixth ← **enam**

keésokan ~ *harinya* the next day ← **ésok, bésok**

kegagalan N failure ← **gagal**

kegelapan N darkness ← **gelap**

kegemaran N hobby ← **gemar**

kegembiraan N joy, happiness ← **gembira**

kegiatan N activity ← **giat**

keguguran miscarry, miscarriage ← **gugur**

kehabisan V to run out of (water, food, stock) ← **habis**

kehadiran N presence, attendance ← **hadir**

kehamilan N pregnancy ← **hamil**

kehangatan N warmth, friendliness ← **hangat**

keharuman N fragrance

keharusan N obligation, necessity, requirement ← **harus**

kehausan to be thirsty; thirst ← **haus**

kehendak N will, wish;
mengehendaki V to wish,
want ← **hendak**

kehidupan N life, existence
← **hidup**

kehilangan (feeling of) loss
← **hilang**

kehormatan N respect ←
hormat

kehujanan ADJ caught in the
rain ← **hujan**

kehutanan N forestry ← **hutan**

keindahan N beauty ← **indah**

keinginan N desire, wish ←
ingin

kejadian N event, happening;
creation ← **jadi**

kejahatan N crime ← **jahat**

kejam ADJ cruel, merciless

kejang N spasm, convulsion

kejap: sejekap N moment,
flash, blink

kejar V chase; **kejar-kejaran** V
chase each other; **mengejar**
V to chase

kejauhan ADJ too far ← **jauh**

kejawén N Javanese traditional mysticism

kéju N cheese

kejuaraan N championship
← **juara**

kejujuran N honesty ← **jujur**

kejut ADJ surprised, startled;
mengejutkan ADJ surprising,
startling; V to surprise
or startle; **terkejut** ADJ
surprised

kekacauan N chaos ← **kacau**

kekasaran N coarseness,
roughness ← **kasar**

kekasih N sweetheart,
beloved, darling ← **kasih**

kekayaan N wealth, riches
← **kaya**

kekebalan N immunity

kekecéwaan N disappointment ← **kecéwa**

kekecilan ADJ too small ←
kecil

kekeliruan N mistake, error
← **keliru**

kekerasan N violence

kekeringan N dryness, aridity
← **kering**

kekosongan N emptiness ←
kosong

kekuasaan N power; authority
← **kuasa**

kekuatan N strength, power
← **kuat**

kekuatiran N worry, fear ←
kuatir

71

kekurangan N shortcoming (of a person); lack; flaw, mistake, defect ← **kurang**

kelab, klab N club; ~ *malam* nightclub

kelabu ADJ gray, cloudy

kelahi: berkelahi V to quarrel, fight, fall out; **perkelahian** N fight, scuffle

kelahiran N birth; ADJ born ← **lahir**

kelakuan N act, behavior ← **laku**

kelalaian N forgetfulness, negligence ← **lalai**

kelamaan ADJ too long (a time) ← **lama**

kelambu N mosquito net

kelamin *jenis* ~ sex, gender

kelapa N coconut; ~ *muda* young coconut; ~ *sawit* oil-palm; *air* ~ coconut milk; coconut juice

kelaparan N hunger, famine, starvation ← **lapar**

kelas N class; ~ *kakap* big-time

keledai N donkey

kelelawar, kelalawar N bat

kelemahan N weakness ← **lemah**

kelembaban N humidity ← **lembab**

keléngkéng *buah* ~ small lychee ← **léngkéng**

kelenjar N gland

kelénténg, klénténg N Chinese temple, pagoda

keléréng N marble; *main* ~ to play marbles

kelihatan ADJ visible; ~*nya* apparently, it seems ← **lihat**

keliling N around; edge, perimeter; **berkeliling** V to go around; **mengelilingi** V to circle, go around

kelinci N rabbit; ~ *percobaan* guinea-pig

kelingking N little or baby finger

kelipatan N multiple ← **lipat**

keliru ADJ wrong, mistaken; **kekeliruan** N mistake, error

kélok N bend, curve

kelola: mengelola V to manage, run; **pengelolaan** N management

kelom, klompen N clogs

kelompok N group

kelontong *toko* ~ shop selling cheap goods

kelopak ~ *mata* eyelid

keluar go out; be issued; PREP

72

out, outside; **mengeluarkan** v to issue, send out, release, publish ← **ke luar**

keluarga N family; **berkeluarga** v to have a family, be married

keluh sigh; **keluhan** N complaint; **mengeluh** v to complain

kelupaan N something forgotten ← **lupa**

kelupas, mengelupas v to peel, come off (of a skin)

kelurahan N administrative unit, village ← **lurah**

kemacetan N (traffic) jam ← **macet**

kémah N tent; **berkémah** v to camp, go camping; **perkémahan** N camping, camp

kemajuan N progress, advance ← **maju**

kemalaman ADV too late (at night); after dark ← **malam**

kemaluan N genital, sex organ ← **malu**

kemampuan N ability, capability ← **mampu**

kemangi N Indonesian mint

kemarahan N anger ← **marah**

kemarau *musim* ~ dry season

kemari here, in this direction

kemarin ADV yesterday; the other day; last; ~ *dulu* the day before yesterday

kemas: kemasan N packaging

kemasyarakatan ADJ social

kematian N death, passing ← **mati**

kemauan N want, will, desire ← **mau**

kembali back, return; again; *(terima kasih)* ~ you're welcome; **kembalian** N small change; **kembalinya** N the return; **mengembalikan** v to give or send back, return

kembang N flower; **berkembang** v to develop, expand; *negara* ~ developing country; **mengembangkan** v to develop something; **perkembangan** N development

kembar N twin

kembung, gembung ADJ filled with air, inflated; bloated

keméja N Western-style shirt (with collar)

kemenangan N victory ← **menang**

kementerian N ministry, department, office ← **menteri**

kemerdékaan N freedom, independence, liberty ← **merdéka**

keméwahan N luxury ← **méwah**

kemih *saluran* ~ urinary tract

kemis, emis: mengemis v to beg; **pengemis** N beggar

kemiskinan N poverty ← **miskin**

kemocéng, kemucing N feather duster

kempés, kempis ADJ deflated, flat; hollow; *ban* ~ flat tire

kemudahan N ease, facility ← **mudah**

kemudi N rudder, steering wheel; **mengemudikan** v to drive, steer; **pengemudi** N driver

kemudian CONJ then

kemuka: terkemuka ADJ prominent ← **ke muka**

kemungkinan N possibility ← **mungkin**

kemut, emut, mengemut v to suck on, chew

kena touch; **kenapa** COLL why, how come; what did you

say?; **mengenai** CONJ about, concerning

kenaikan N rise, raise

kenal v to know, be acquainted with; **kenalan** N acquaintance; **mengenal** v to know, be acquainted with, recognize; **memperkenalkan** v to introduce; **perkenalan** N introduction; **terkenal** ADJ well-known

kenang recall; **kenangan** N memories; **kenang-kenangan** N souvenir, keepsake; **mengenang** v to commemorate, remember

kenapa INTERROG, COLL why, how come; what did you say? ← **kena apa**

kenari *burung* ~ canary

kencan N date; **berkencan** v to go on a date

kencang tight, taut; **mengencangkan** v to tighten

kencing urine; urinate; ~ *manis* diabetes

kencur *beras* ~ traditional Javanese drink

kendali N reins; **mengendalikan** v to control; **terkendali** ADJ controlled

kendang N small drum → **gendang**

kendara: kendaraan N vehicle

kendi N earthen water flask

kendor, kendur ADJ slack, loose

kenduri N feast, celebration

kenék, kernét N bus assistant acting as conductor

kening N forehead, brow

kental ADJ thick, sticky, congealed

kentang N potato; COLL french fries; ~ **goreng** hot potato chips, french fries

kentut fart, break wind

kenyamanan N comfort ← **nyaman**

kenyang ADJ full, not hungry

kenyataan N fact ← **nyata**

kéong N snail

kepada PREP to (someone)

kepal fist; **kepalan** N fist

kepala N head, chief

kepanjangan ADJ too long ← **panjang**

kepariwisataan N tourism industry

kepastian N certainty ← **pasti**

kepedasan ADJ too hot or spicy ← **pedas**

kependékan N abbreviation ← **péndék**

kepéngén, kepingin V, COLL really want to ← **péngén**

kepentingan N importance, interest ← **penting**

keperluan N needs, requirements ← **perlu**

keping N piece (counter for flat objects); splinter

kepiting N crab

kepompong N cocoon

keponakan, kemenakan N niece or nephew; cousin

Kepri (Kepulauan Riau) Riau Archipelago, a province in Sumatra

kepribadian N personality ← **pribadi**

kepulauan N archipelago, chain

kepunyaan N possession, belonging ← **punya**

keputihan N thrush, vaginal itching (white discharge) ← **putih**

keputusan N decision, decree ← **putus**

kera N ape
keracunan ADJ poisoned ← **racun**
keraguan, keragu-raguan N doubt, uncertainty ← **ragu**
kerah N collar
kerajaan N kingdom ← **raja**
kerajinan N crafts ← **rajin**
keram cramp
keramahan N friendliness ← **ramah**
keramaian N noise, din; lively atmosphere ← **ramai**
keramas to wash your hair
keramik ceramic, earthenware
keran N tap, faucet
kerang N shell; mollusc
kerangka N skeleton, framework
keranjang N basket
keras ADJ hard, strong; severe, strict, violent; loud; **bersi-keras** v to maintain, stick to, be obstinate; **kekerasan** N violence; **mengeraskan** v to make something harder, louder; **pengeras** ~ **suara** loudspeaker
kerasan COLL settled, comfortable, feel at home ← **rasa**
keraton, kraton N Javanese palace

kerbau, kebo N buffalo
kerén ADJ, COLL great, cool; trendy
keréta N train; carriage; ~ **api** train
kericuhan N chaos ← **ricuh**
kerikil N gravel, pebble
kerinduan N longing, craving ← **rindu**
kering ADJ dry; **kekeringan** N dryness, aridity; **menge-ringkan** v to dry something
keringat N sweat, perspiration; **keringatan** ADJ sweaty, sweating; **ber-keringat** v to sweat
keripik, kripik N small chip or crisp
keris, kris N traditional dagger, creese
keriting curl, curly
kerja work; job, occupation; ~ **sama** co-operation; **kerjaan** N work, job, things to do; **bekerja** v to work; ~ **sama** to co-operate, work together; **mengerjakan** v to do, carry out; **pekerja** N worker, laborer; **pekerjaan** N work, profession

kernét, kenék N assistant on a bus or truck

kerok traditional treatment for minor illnesses by rubbing the back with a coin; **kerokan** v to be massaged in this way

keroncong, kroncong N traditional songs and music of Portuguese origin

kerongkongan N throat

keropos ADJ eroded, eaten away; *tulang* ~ osteoporosis

keroyok, mengeroyok v to beat savagely in a mob

kertas N paper

kerucut, cerucut N cone

kerudung, kudungan N, ISL veil

kerugian N loss; damage ← **rugi**

keruk dredge; **mengeruk** v to dredge, scrape out

kerupuk, krupuk N large cracker, crisp, chip

kerusakan N damage ← **rusak**

kerusuhan N riot, disturbance ← **rusuh**

kesabaran N patience ← **sabar**

kesadaran N consciousness, awareness ← **sadar**

kesakitan ADJ in pain ← **sakit**

kesaksian N evidence, testimony ← **saksi**

kesal ADJ **kesel** COLL annoyed, in a bad mood

kesalahan N mistake ← **salah**

kesampaian ADJ achieved, reached, realized ← **sampai**

kesan N impression; **berkesan, mengesankan** ADJ impressive; **terkesan** ADJ impressed; seemed

kesasar COLL to lose your way, (get) lost ← **sasar**

kesayangan favorite, pet ← **sayang**

kesedihan N sadness, sorrow ← **sedih**

keséhatan N health ← **séhat**

keseimbangan N balance ← **imbang**

kesejahteraan N welfare ← **sejahtera**

keselamatan N safety; salvation ← **selamat**

keseléo sprain; sprained

keseluruhan *secara* ~ totally, completely ← **seluruh**

kesempatan N opportunity ← **sempat**

kesemutan v to have pins and needles ← **semut**

kesenangan N amusement, hobby ← **senang**

kesenian N art (form) ← **seni**

kesepakatan N agreement ← **pakat**

kesepian N loneliness, solitude ← **sepi**

kesenangan N frequency; too often

kését N door mat

kesetrum v, COLL to receive an electric shock ← **setrum**

kesiangan ADJ late, too late in the day ← **siang**

kesibukan N activity, fuss, bustle, business ← **sibuk**

kesimpulan N conclusion ← **simpul**

kesopanan N manners, politeness ← **sopan**

kesoréan ADV too late ← **soré**

kesukaan N hobby; enjoyment ← **suka**

kesukaran N difficulty ← **sukar**

kesulitan N difficulty, trouble ← **sulit**

kesusahan N trouble, difficulty ← **susah**

ketagihan ADJ addicted to ← **tagih**

ketahuan to be found out ← **tahu**

ketakutan ADJ frightened, terrified, scared ← **takut**

ketan N sticky rice; ~ *bakar* grilled slices of sticky rice

ketapél N catapult

ketat ADJ tight, strict

ketawa v, COLL to laugh → **tawa**

ketéla N yam

ketemu v, COLL to meet ← **temu**

ketentuan N condition, stipulation ← **tentu**

keterangan N explanation ← **terang**

keterlaluan N excess, too much ← **lalu**

keterlambatan N delay ← **lambat**

keterlibatan N involvement, association ← **libat**

kétiak, kéték N armpit

ketiduran v to fall asleep ← **tidur**

ketiga ADJ the third ← **tiga**

ketik v type; **mengetik** v to type

ketika conj when (in past)

ketimbang conj, coll than; instead of ← **timbang**

ketimun → **mentimun**

ketimuran adj Eastern, Oriental ← **timur**

ketinggalan adj left behind ← **tinggal**

ketinggian n altitude, height ← **tinggi**

ketinting n water taxi used on the rivers of Kalimantan

ketok v to knock; panel-beat; ~ *magic* 'magic' panel-beating

ketombé n dandruff

ketoprak n Betawi dish of vegetables in peanut sauce; folk play

ketrampilan n skill ← **trampil**

ketua n chief, chair, president, elder

ketuk, ketok knock; **mengetuk** v to knock

ketularan adj infected, caught something ← **tular**

ketumbar n (ground) coriander

ketupat n coconut fronds woven into a diamond-shape for cooking rice

keturunan n descendant

keuangan n finance ← **uang**

keunikan n unique thing, uniqueness ← **unik**

keuntungan n advantage, profit ← **untung**

kewajiban n obligation, duty ← **wajib**

kewarganegaraan n citizenship ← **warga negara**

keyakinan n belief, conviction, faith ← **yakin**

kg kilogram

khas adj special, specific

khatulistiwa, katulistiwa n the Equator

khawatir, kuatir v to worry, fear; *jangan* ~ don't worry; **kekuatiran** n worry, fear; **menguatirkan** v to worry about something

khayal: khayalan n dream, hallucination

khianat: mengkhianati v to betray someone; **pengkhianat** n traitor

khitan n circumcision; **khitanan** n feast held in honor of a circumcision; **mengkhitan(kan)** v to circumcise

khotbah N sermon

khusus ADJ special, particular; ~*nya* in particular, especially

kian ADV such; increasingly, more and more; **sekian** ADV so much, this much

kibar: berkibar(-kibar) V to wave, flutter; **mengibarkan** V to wave, unfurl

kibor N keyboard

kidal ADJ left-handed

kijang N barking deer, kind of antelope

kikir ADJ stingy, tight, miserly

kikis ADJ scraped; **terkikis** ADJ eaten away, eroded

kilang N refinery, mill; **perkilangan** N refinery

kilap shine; **mengkilap** V to shine, gleam

kilas: sekilas N flash, glance

kilat N lightning

kilau: berkilau ADJ glittering, sparkling

kilir twist; **terkilir** ADJ twisted, sprained

kilo N kilo, kilogram; kilometer; **kiloan** ADV by the kilogram, in kilograms

kimia N chemistry

kimono N kimono; dressing gown

kincir N wheel; ~ *air* waterwheel; ~ *angin* windmill

kini ADV now, nowadays (often when comparing with past)

kios N stall, kiosk; **kiostél, kiospon** N small phone agency, phone kiosk ← **kios télépon**

kipas N fan; ~ *angin*, ~ *listrik* (electric) fan

kiper N (goal)keeper

kira V to think, guess, estimate; **kira-kira** ADV approximately, around, about; **mengira** V to assume, think; **memperkirakan** V to estimate, calculate; **perkiraan** N estimate, guess; **terkira** *tak* ~ unsuspected, not thought of

kiri ADJ left; ~ *kanan* left and right; *belok* ~ turn left

kirim V send; ~ *salam* to send your best wishes; **kiriman** N parcel; **mengirim** V to send; **pengirim** N sender; **pengiriman** N dispatch, forwarding; **terkirim** ADJ sent

kisah N tale, story; **berkisah** V to tell a story

kisar: berkisar v to revolve, rotate, turn

kismis N sultana, currant

kita PRON we, us, our (inclusive); ~ *punya* our

kitab N holy book

kitar: sekitar ADV around; near; PREP around; **sekitarnya** *di* ~ around (a place)

KITAS ABBREV *Kartu Izin Tinggal Sementara* temporary residence permit for foreigners

KKN ABBREV *korupsi, kolusi, nepotisme* corruption (collusion and nepotism)

klakson N horn

klasik ADJ classic, classical

klénténg, kelénténg N Chinese temple, pagoda

klép, kelép N valve, catch

klik v to click (a mouse)

klinik N clinic

klosét N cistern (of toilet)

klub N (sports) club

km *kamar* room (in a hotel); kilometer

knalpot N exhaust pipe, muffler

koalisi N coalition

koboi N cowboy

kocok *mie* ~ kind of noodles; **mengocok** v to shake, shuffle

kode N code; ~ *pos* postcode

kodok N frog

kok you know (emphasizing contrary argument); *tidak apa-apa* ~ really, it's OK; INTERROG how come, why

koki N cook

kokoh, kukuh ADJ strong, robust

kokpit N cockpit

kol N cabbage

kolaborasi N collaboration

kolak N sweet fruit stew

kolam N pond, pool

koléga N colleague

koléksi N collection

kolintang N large wooden xylophone from Minahasa

Kolombia N Colombia

kolonél N, PRON colonel

kolong N space under a large object; ~ *meja* under the table

kolor N drawstring shorts

kolot ADJ old-fashioned, out of date; conservative

koma N comma

komandan N commander

kombinasi N combination

81

koméntar N comment; **ber-koméntar** v to (make a) comment

komik *(buku)* ~ comic (book); **komikus** N comic book author or artist

komisaris N commissioner

komisi N committee, commission

komité N committee → **panitia**

kompas N compass

komplék, kompléks, kom-pléx N housing complex, compound

komplét, komplit ADJ complete

kompor N stove, cooker

komprés N compress, pack

kompromi N compromise

komputer N computer

komunis ADJ, N communist; **komunisme** N communism

konci → **kunci**

kondéktur N conductor, guard (on a train or city bus)

kondisi N condition

kondom N condom

konéksi N connections, contacts (at an institution)

konferénsi, konperénsi N conference

konfrontasi N confrontation; Indonesian aggression towards Malaysia in the 1960s

Kong Hu Cu Confucius, Confucian, Confucianism

kongkol: persekongkolan N plot, intrigue

konglomerat N wealthy financier

kongrés N congress, convention

konséling N counselling; **konsélor** N counsellor

konsén, konséntrasi ADJ focused, concentrating

konsép N concept, draft

konsér N concert

konsul N consul; **konsulat** N consulate; ~ *jenderal (konjen)* consulate-general

konsumén N consumer

kontak contact

kontés N contest

kontra ADJ against, opposing, anti

kontrak N contract; **kontrakan** N rented (house); **dikon-trakkan** ADJ for rent, lease

konyol ADJ silly, foolish

koper N suitcase, baggage

koperasi N co-operative, co-op

kopi N coffee; ~ *susu* white or milk coffee; ~ *tubruk* ground coffee

kopi N copy → **fotokopi**

kopyor *es* ~ sweet drink made from this coconut

koran N newspaper

korban N victim; **berkorban** v to make sacrifices, do without; **mengorbankan** v to sacrifice

Koréa N Korea; ~ *Selatan (Korsel)* South Korea; ~ *Utara* North Korea; *bahasa* ~, *orang* ~ Korean

korék ~ *api* matches; **mengorék** v to scrape, scratch

koréksi N correction; **mengoréksi** v to correct

korma, kurma N date

Korsél N South Korea ← **Koréa Selatan**

kortsléting, korsléting N short-circuit

korup ADJ corrupt; **korupsi** N corruption; ADJ corrupt; ~ *kolusi dan nepotisme (KKN)* corruption; **koruptor** N corrupt person

Korut N North Korea ← **Koréa Utara**

kos board, lodging; **kos-kosan** N boarding-houses, rooms for board

kosa ~ *kata* vocabulary

kos-kosan N boarding-houses, rooms for board ← **kos**

kosong ADJ empty, blank; hollow; zero; **kekosongan** N emptiness; **mengosongkan** v to empty

kota N town, city; **perkotaan** N metropolitan area; **kotamadya** N municipality

kotak N box; square; **kotak-kotak** ADJ checked pattern

kotamadya N municipality ← **kota**

kotor ADJ dirty, filthy; gross; **kotoran** N excrement; dirt

kraton, keraton N Javanese palace

krédit N credit; *kartu* ~ credit card

kriminal ADJ criminal

kring sound of telephone ringing

kripik, keripik N small chip or crisp

krisis N crisis

kristal crystal

Kristen ADJ Christian, Protestant; *gereja* ~ Protestant church

Kristus *Yesus* ~ Jesus Christ

krupuk → **kerupuk**

ksatria, kesatria N knight, warrior; ADJ chivalrous

KTP ABBREV *Kartu Tanda Penduduk* national identity card

ku, -ku PRON I, my, mine; *rumah*~ my home

kuah N soup, sauce, gravy (accompanying a food)

kualitas, kwalitas N quality; **berkualitas** ADJ quality

kuas N brush (for art or cosmetics); paintbrush

kuasa N power; **berkuasa** ADJ powerful, mighty; **kekuasaan** N power; authority; **menguasai** v to control, have power over

kuat ADJ strong; **kekuatan** N strength, power; **menguatkan** v to strengthen

kuatir, khawatir v to worry, fear; *jangan* ~ don't worry; **kekuatiran** N worry, fear; **menguatirkan** v to worry about something

Kuba N Cuba

kubik ADJ cubic

kubis N cabbage

kubu N block, faction

kubur N grave, tomb; **kuburan** N cemetery, graveyard; **menguburkan** v to bury; **terkubur** ADJ buried in an accident

kucing N cat

kuda N horse; ~ *laut* seahorse; ~ *nil* hippo, hippopotamus; **berkuda** v to ride a horse, go (horse-)riding

kudéta N coup, coup d'etat

kudung, kerudung N loose veil

kudus ADJ, CHR holy

kué N cake, pastry

kuil N, CH, HIND temple

kuis N quiz

kuku N nail (of people), claw (of animals); *cat* ~ nail polish

kukuh, kokoh ADJ strong, robust

kukus steam; **mengukus** v to steam (food)

kuliah N lecture; v, COLL to study at university or college

kulit N skin, hide (of animals);

leather; peel, rind (of fruit); **berkulit** to have skin, -skinned

kulkas N refrigerator, fridge

kuman N germ, bacteria

kumat, komat relapse

kumbang N beetle; bumblebee

kumis N mustache

kumpul v to get together, gather; **kumpulan** N collection; group; **berkumpul** v to assemble, meet; **mengumpulkan** v to collect, gather; **ngumpul** v, SL to get or come together; **perkumpulan** N association, club; assembly

kumuh ADJ dirty, slummy

kumur *obat* ~ mouthwash; **berkumur(-kumur)** v to gargle

kunang-kunang N firefly

kunci key; lock; fastener; **mengunci** v to lock (up)

kuncup N bud

kuning ADJ yellow; COLL light brown; N saffron, turmeric; ~ *telur* yolk; **kuningan** N brass

kunjung: kunjungan N visit, excursion; **berkunjung** v to visit, pay a visit to; **mengun-**

jungi v to visit a place

kuno ADJ ancient, historic; old-fashioned, out-of-date, conservative

kunyit, kunir, kuning N saffron; turmeric

kupas peel; **mengupas** v to peel; to analyze

kuping N ear; **menguping** v to eavesdrop, listen in

kupu: kupu-kupu N butterfly

kura-kura N tortoise

kurang ADJ, ADV less, lacking; **berkurang** v to decrease, diminish, subside; **kekurangan** N shortcoming (of a person); lack; flaw, mistake, defect; **mengurangi** v to take from, subtract, minus; **sekurang(-kurang)nya** ADV at least

kurban, qurban N, ISL sacrifice, usu goats or cattle

kurir N courier

kurma, korma N date

kurs N exchange rate

kursi N chair, seat; ~ *roda* wheelchair

kursus course

kurung cage; **mengurung** v to cage, put in a cage, lock up

85

kurus ADJ thin, skinny

kusén, kosén N frame (of door or window)

kusut ADJ tangled, tousled, unkempt; complicated

kutak, utak: mengutak-ngatikkan v to work on or tinker with

kutik: mengutik v to tinker with; to touch on

kutil N wart

kutip, mengutip v to quote, cite an extract; **kutipan** N extract, quotation

kutu N louse, flea

kutub N pole; ~ *selatan* the South Pole; *beruang* ~ polar bear

kutuk curse; **kutukan** N curse; **mengutuk** v to curse; **terkutuk** ADJ cursed, accursed

kwalitas → **kualitas**

kwétiau, kwétiauw N large Chinese egg noodles

kwitansi, kuitansi N bill, receipt

L

laba: laba-laba N spider

laboratorium, lab N laboratory

labu N gourd, pumpkin, squash

labuh: pelabuhan port, harbor

lacak: melacak v to trace

laci N drawer; chest of drawers, dresser

lacur: pelacur N prostitute

lada N pepper

ladang N field; area of opportunity

lafal N pronunciation; **melafalkan** v to pronounce

laga N fight; *film* ~ action film

lagi SL in the act of; ~ *makan* eating → **sedang**

lagi ADV again; more; **lagipula** N furthermore, moreover

lagu N song, music; ~ *anak-anak* children's song; ~ *daerah* song or music from a certain region; ~ *kebangsaan* national anthem

-lah added after a word to soften the message; *baik*~

OK then; *mari–* let us go
lahan N ground, land, terrain
lahar N lava
lahir born; external; **kelahiran** N birth; ADJ born; **melahirkan** v to give birth to; to create; **terlahir** ADJ born
lain ADJ other, different; *~ lagi* different again; **melainkan** CONJ rather, instead; **selain** except, apart from
lajang ADJ single, unmarried
laju fast, rapid, quick; rate
lajur lane (one of many); *~ kiri* left lane → **jalur**
laki ADJ, SL male; N, SL husband; **lelaki** ADJ, N male; **laki-laki** ADJ, N male; *saudara ~* brother; *anak ~* son
lakon N play; act
laksa N Malay dish of vermicelli noodles with chicken in coconut sauce
laku ADJ popular, in vogue; salable; **berlaku** ADJ effective, valid; v to behave; **kelakuan** N act, behavior; **melakukan** v to do, perform, carry out
lalai ADJ careless, negligent; **kelalaian** N forgetfulness, negligence

lalap, lalapan N raw vegetables, eaten as a side-dish
lalat, laler N fly
lalu CONJ then; ADJ last; *~ lintas* traffic; **melalui** v to pass through; CONJ through, via; **selalu** ADV always; **terlalu** ADV too; **keterlaluan** ADJ too much, overly, unacceptable
lama ADJ long; old, former; **lama-lama** ADJ too long; **kelamaan** ADJ too long (a time); **selama** CONJ for, during, as long as; **selamanya** ADV always, forever
laman N webpage, website
lamar, melamar v to apply; **lamaran** N application; proposal
lambai: melambaikan v to wave something; *~ tangan* to wave (goodbye)
lamban ADJ slow
lambang N symbol; **berlambang** v to have a symbol
lambat ADJ slow, late; **melambatkan** v to slow down; **selambat-lambatnya** ADV at the latest; **terlambat** ADJ (too) late, delayed; **keterlambatan** N delay

87

lambung N stomach

lambung: melambung V to bounce

laminasi N laminating

lampion N paper lantern

lampir: lampiran N attachment, appendix; **melampirkan** V to attach, enclose; **terlampir** ADJ attached, enclosed

lampu N light, lamp; ~ *lalu lintas*, ~ *merah* traffic light

lampung: pelampung N floater; flotation device

lamun: melamun V to daydream, fantasize

lancang ADJ impudent, impolite, shameless

lancar ADJ smooth, fluent; **selancar** *papan* ~ surfboard; **berselancar** V to surf, go surfing

lancip ADJ pointed, pointy

landak N porcupine, echidna

landas N base, ground; *lepas* ~ take-off

langgan: langganan N subscription; regular customer; **berlangganan** V to subscribe to; **pelanggan** N subscriber, customer

langgar: melanggar V to disobey, offend

langgeng ADJ everlasting, eternal

langit N sky; **langit-langit** N palate, roof of your mouth; ceiling

langka ADJ rare

langkah N step; **melangkah** V to step

langsing ADJ slim, slender

langsung ADJ direct, straight; **berlangsung** V to take place

lanjur: terlanjur ADV too late, already

lanjut ADJ advanced, further; **melanjutkan** V to continue something; **selanjutnya** ADV then, after that

lansia ADJ elderly ← **lanjut usia**

lantai N floor (of building), story (of house)

lantar: terlantar, telantar ADJ neglected, abandoned

lantik: pelantikan N inauguration

lap N rag, cloth; **mengelap** V to wipe, mop

lapang ADJ wide, spacious; **lapangan** N field; ~ *tenis*

tennis court; ~ *terbang*, ~
udara (lanud) airfield, airport
lapar ADJ hungry; **kelaparan** N
hunger, famine, starvation
lapis layer, fold, lining;
lapisan N coat, layer
lapor, melapor V to report;
laporan N report; **melaporkan** V to report, inform
lapuk rotten, decayed
larang: melarang V to ban,
prohibit, forbid; **dilarang** V
prohibited; ~ *masuk* no entry,
no admittance; ~ *merokok* no
smoking; **larangan** N ban,
prohibition; **terlarang** ADJ
forbidden, banned
larat: melarat ADJ miserable,
poor; poverty-stricken
lari run; **berlari** V to run;
melarikan V to run off with,
abduct, kidnap; **pelari** N
runner
laron N flying white ant
larut dissolve; **larutan** N
solution
las weld; **mengelas** V to weld
laskar N army, troops
latar N base; ~ *belakang*
background
latih, melatih V to train;

latihan N training, practice,
exercise; **pelatih** N coach,
trainer; **pelatihan** N training
lauk *(~) pauk* side-dish
laut N sea; **lautan** N ocean; ~
Hindia the Indian Ocean;
pelaut N sailor, seaman
lawak: pelawak N comedian,
comic, clown
lawan N opponent, adversary,
opposite; **melawan** V to
oppose, resist; **perlawanan** N
opposition, resistance
layak, laik ADJ proper, suitable
layan: layanan N service;
melayani V to serve; **pelayan**
N attendant, M waiter, F waitress; **pelayanan** N service
layang: layang-layang kite
layar sail; **berlayar** V to sail;
pelayaran N voyage
layat: melayat V to visit a
house in mourning, pay your
respects
lebah N bee
lébar ADJ wide, broad; **lébarnya** N width; **melébarkan** V
to widen
Lebaran N Idul Fitri, first two
days after the Ramadan fast
lébarnya N width ← **lébar**

89

lebat ADJ thick, dense

lebih ADV more; ~ *baik*, ~ *bagus* better; **berlebihan** ADJ excessive; **kelebihan** N extra, excess; **melebihi** V to exceed, surpass

lécét sore, blister

léci N lychee

ledak: ledakan N explosion; **meledak** V to explode

lédék, melédék V to tease, provoke

lédéng, léding *tukang* ~ plumber

lega ADJ relieved

légal ADJ legal; **melégalisasi**, **melégalisir** V to legalize

légénda N legend, myth; **légéndaris** ADJ legendary

légong *tari* ~ Balinese trance dance performed by young girls

léhér N neck

lekas ADJ fast, quick, speedy; *(semoga)* ~ *sembuh* get well soon

lekat: melekat V to stick; **pelekat** *bahan* ~ adhesive

lelah ADJ tired, weary; **melelahkan** ADJ tiring

lelaki, laki-laki ADJ male; N

man, male

lélang N auction

lelap ADJ sound, fast, completely; *tidur* ~ sound asleep

lélé *ikan* ~ catfish

léléh melt, run; **meléléh** V to drip, run

leluhur N ancestor → **luhur**

lém N glue

lemah ADJ weak; **kelemahan** N weakness

lemak N fat; grease

lemari N cupboard, closet, shelf; ~ *baju* wardrobe

lemas, lemes ADJ weak, drained

lembab, lembap ADJ humid, damp, moist; **kelembaban** N humidity; **pelembab, pelembap** N moisturizer

lembaga N institute, foundation, board

lembah N valley

lembap → **lembab**

lembar N sheet (of paper), page

lembék ADJ soft, weak, flimsy

lembur V to work overtime, stay late

lembut ADJ soft, gentle

lémpar, melémpar V to

throw; **lémparan** N throw; **terlémpar** ADJ thrown, flung

lemper N sweet cake of sticky rice with a meat filling

léncéng: meléncéng V to deviate, go out of your way

lendir N mucus

lengan N arm, sleeve

lengkap ADJ complete; **melengkapi** V to furnish, supply; **pelengkap** N an accessory; **perlengkapan** N outfit, equipment

léngkéng, keléngkéng N (buah) ~ small lychee

léngkét ADJ sticky, close

lénsa N lens; ~ kontak contact lenses

lentur ADJ elastic, pliable

lenyap ADJ disappeared, gone, vanished

lepas loose, free; escape; **melepaskan** V to release, let free

léréng N slope

lés (to attend) a private class or course

lésbi lesbian

lését: melését V to slip, skid; to miss the target; **terpelését** ADJ slipped

lesu ADJ tired, weary

letak place, location; **letaknya** N the location, position; **meletakkan** V to put in place, set down; **terletak** ADJ situated, located

letih ADJ tired

létnan N lieutenant

letus: letusan N eruption; **meletus** V to erupt

léwat PREP past; via; jam empat ~ lima five past four; **meléwati** V to pass or go through

lezat ADJ delicious, tasty

lho you know (used to emphasize a statement, often denying something); EJAC well!

liang N hole, passage

liar ADJ wild, untamed; unregulated

Libanon N Lebanon

libat: melibatkan V to involve, include; **terlibat** ADJ involved, implicated; **keterlibatan** N involvement, association

libur be free, on holiday (from school or work); **liburan** N holiday; **berlibur** V to go or be on holiday

91

licik ADJ cunning, tricky
licin ADJ smooth; slippery
lidah N tongue
lidi N palm-leaf rib
liga N (football) league
lihat v to see; **kelihatan** ADJ visible; ~**nya** apparently, it seems; **melihat** v to see, look; **melihat-lihat** v to look around, have a look
lilin N candle; wax
lilit turn, twist; **terlilit** ADJ caught up, twisted
lima ADJ five; ~ **belas** fifteen; ~ **puluh** fifty; **ke**~ fifth
lincah ADJ nimble, deft, agile; **kelincahan** N agility
lindas: melindas v to run over, squash; **terlindas** ADJ run over
lindung: berlindung v to (take) shelter; **melindungi** v to protect, shelter; **pelindung** N protective device; **perlindungan** N protection
lingkar N ring, circle, circumference; **lingkaran** N circle; **melingkari** v to circle or surround
lingkung: lingkungan N environment, surroundings, circle

lintah N leech
lintang across, latitude; **melintang** ADJ horizontal, across
lipat fold; *dua kali* ~ double, twice; **lipatan** N fold; **kelipatan** N multiple; **melipat** v to fold
lipstik N lipstick
liput: liputan N coverage, reporting; **meliputi** v to include, cover
lisan ADJ oral, verbal
listrik electric, electricity
liter N liter, litre
lobak N radish
logam N metal
logat N accent
logika N logic
lohor ISL the midday prayer
lok, lokomotif N locomotive
lokakarya N seminar, workshop
lokasi N location
loket N counter, desk, ticket window or office
lokomotif, lok N locomotive
lolong howl; **melolong** v to howl (of dogs)
lolos v to escape; succeed, progress

92

lomba N race, competition, contest; **berlomba** v to compete, race

lombok N chilli

lompat jump, leap; **melompat** v to jump, leapfrog

loncat jump (over something); **meloncat** v to spring, jump

loncéng N bell

longgar ADJ loose, wide

longsor slip; *tanah* ~ landslide

lonjong ADJ oval

lontar throw; **melontarkan** v to throw

lontong N cooked, solid slab of rice

loper N newspaper delivery boy

lorong N path; lane, alley

losmén N guest house, accommodation, cheap hotel

loték N a dish of fresh vegetables with peanut sauce

loténg N attic, loft

lotot → **melotot, pelotot**

lowongan ADJ wanted, vacancy

loyang N cake tin, tray, mould

Lt. *lantai* floor, level

lu SL you

luang ADJ free, empty; **peluang** N chance, opportunity

luap: meluap v to overflow, swell, wash

luar out, external; ~ *biasa* outstanding, extraordinary; ~ *negeri* overseas, abroad; **keluar** go out; be issued; prep out, outside; **mengeluarkan** v to issue, publish, send out, release

luas wide, broad; space; **luasnya** N width; area

lubang, lobang N hole, passage; ~ *hidung* nostril

lubuk N deep pool

lucu ADJ cute, sweet; funny; odd; **lelucan** N joke

ludah N saliva, spit; **meludah** v to spit

lugu ADJ naive, gullible

luhur ADJ lofty, noble, esteemed; **leluhur** N ancestor

luka N wound; injured; **melukai, melukakan** v to hurt or wound

lukis v to paint, draw; **lukisan** N painting, picture, portrait (of a person); **melukis** v to paint, draw; **pelukis** N painter, artist

lulus v to pass; **lulusan** N graduate

lumas: pelumas N lubricant

lumayan ADV, ADJ quite, not bad, fairly

lumba-lumba N dolphin, porpoise

lumpang N pestle, rice pounder

lumpia N spring rolls

lumpuh ADJ paralysed, lame

lumpur N mud

lumur smear; **berlumuran** ADJ smeared, stained

lumut N moss

lunak ADJ soft

lunas ADJ paid off, in full

luncur: meluncurkan V to launch, set in motion

luntur fade, lose color, run

lupa V to forget; **kelupaan** N something forgotten; **melupakan** V to forget something; **terlupakan** tak ~ unforgettable

lurah N head of a *kelurahan*, village chief; **kelurahan** N administrative unit, village

lurus ADJ straight; **pelurusan** N straightening

lusa ADV the day after tomorrow; *besok* ~ tomorrow or the day after

lusin N dozen, twelve; **selusin** N a dozen

lutut N knee; **berlutut** to kneel (down)

M

M *Masehi* Christian calendar

m meter

maaf sorry; *minta* ~ apologize, say you're sorry; **memaafkan** V to forgive, pardon

maag, mag N, COLL stomach (disorder); *sakit* ~ weak stomach, gastric pain

mabuk ADJ drunk; ill; motion sickness

macam N kind, sort, model; **macam-macam** ADJ, NEG all sorts; **bermacam-macam** ADJ various; **semacam** ADJ a kind or type of

macan N large spotted cat; N, COLL tiger

macet, macét jammed, blocked; traffic jam; **kemacetan** N (traffic) jam

madrasah N, ISL boarding school, college

madu N honey

madya ADJ medium, middle

magang (do) work experience, apprentice

magrib, maghrib N sunset; sunset (prayer)

mahal ADJ expensive, dear

mahasiswa N (university or college) student; **mahasiswi** N, F (female) student

mahir ADJ expert, skilled

mahkota N crown, crest

main V to play, do (a sport); **main-main** V to joke around, not be serious; **mainan** N toy; **bermain** V to play; **memainkan** V to play something; **pemain** N player, actor; **permainan** N game, match

majalah N magazine

majikan N employer

maju go forward, advance, progress, improve; **kemajuan** N progress, advance

maka CONJ therefore, so, then; **makanya** CONJ that's why, so

makam N grave; **memakamkan** V to bury; **pemakaman** N funeral, burial

makan V to eat; ~ *dulu* said when eating first before others; ~ *malam* (eat or have) dinner; **makanan** N food; **memakan** V to eat, consume, take

makanya CONJ that's why, so ← **maka**

makhluk, mahluk N creature

maki, mencaci-maki V to insult, abuse; **memaki, memaki-maki** V to insult, heap abuse on

makin ADV increasingly; ~ *lama*, ~ *besar* the longer, the bigger; **semakin** ADV even more

maklum V to know, be aware

makmur ADJ prosperous

makna N meaning

maknit, magnét N magnet

maksimal maximal(ly); **maksimum** N maximum

maksud N purpose, intention, meaning; **bermaksud** V to intend; **dimaksud(kan)** V to be meant or intended

mal, mol N shopping center, mall

malah, malahan instead, rather, on the other hand

Malaka, Melaka N Malacca

malam N night, evening; ~ *Jumat* Thursday night; *Jumat* ~ Friday night; **malam-malam** ADV late at night; **bermalam** V to spend or stay the night; **kemalaman** ADV too late (at night); after dark; **semalam** ADV last night

malang ADJ unlucky

malas ADJ lazy, can't be bothered; **bermalas-malas(an)** V to lie or laze around, be lazy

Malaysia N Malaysia; *bahasa* ~, *orang* ~ Malaysian

maling N thief

malu ADJ shy, ashamed, embarrassed; **malu-malu** ADJ shy; **kemaluan** N genital, sex organ; **memalukan** ADJ embarrassing

mam, mam-mam V, CH eat

mampet ADJ stuck, blocked, jammed

mampir V to drop in, call on

mampu ADJ able, capable; ADJ well-off; **kemampuan** N ability, capability

mana PRON where, which; ~ *saja* whichever; *dari* ~ from where; *di* ~ where; *ke* ~ where; **mana-mana** *di* ~, *ke* ~ everywhere

mancing → **pancing**

mancung ADJ straight (of noses)

mancur *air* ~ fountain ← **pancur**

mandek, mandeg stop, cease, get stuck, stagnate

mandi bathe, take a bath, wash (the body); **memandikan** V to wash someone

manfaat N benefit, use; **bermanfaat** ADJ useful, of benefit; **memanfaatkan** V to take advantage of, (draw) benefit from

mangga N mango

manggis N mangosteen

mangkok, mangkuk N bowl

mangsa N prey

manik: manik-manik N beads

manis ADJ sweet; pretty; nice; **manisan** N sweets, candy; sugared snacks; **pemanis** ~ *buatan* artificial sweetener

manja spoilt; **memanjakan** V to spoil someone

mantan ADJ former (of people); ~ *Presiden* former President

mantap ADJ stable, steady

mantel N (long) coat, raincoat

mantu N son- or daughter-in-law; v to marry off a son or daughter → **menantu**

manula N old person, senior citizen → **manusia lanjut usia**

manusia N human (being); humanity

map N folder

mapan ADJ settled, comfortable

marah ADJ angry; **marah-marah** frequently angry; in a bad mood; **kemarahan** N anger; **memarahi** v to scold, be angry with

Maret *bulan* ~ March

marga N (Batak) family name

mari let's go, come on; please (said when someone begs leave); ~*lah* let us

marinir N Marines

markas N office, headquarters

markisa N kind of passionfruit

marmer N marble

marmot, marmut N guinea pig, marmot

Maroko, Marokko N Morocco

martabak N large fried snack with filling

mas, emas N gold

Mas PRON, M address for elder brother, male person slightly older than yourself, or worker in service industry

masa N time, period

masa, masak no! I can't believe it! it's not possible (expression of disbelief)

masak ADJ cook; cooked; **masakan** N food, cooking, dish; **memasak** v to cook

masalah N problem; ~*nya* the problem is; **bermasalah** ADJ problem, troublesome

masam, masem ADJ sour; acid

masih ADV still, yet

masing: masing-masing PRON each, respectively

masinis N train driver, engineer

masjid, mesjid N mosque

masker N surgical mask

massa N the masses, the public; **massal** ADJ mass

masuk v to come in, enter; **memasukkan** v to put in, insert, import, enter; **termasuk** ADJ including

masyarakat N society

mata N eye; **mata-mata** N spy

matahari N sun; *bunga* ~ sunflower; ~ *terbenam* sunset; ~ *terbit* sunrise

mata-mata N spy ← **mata**

matang ADJ ripe, cooked, mature

matématika N mathematics, maths

matéri N material; **matérial** ADJ material

mati die; go out, be extinguished; ~ *lampu* blackout; **kematian** N death, passing; **mematikan** v to kill, extinguish, put out

mau v to want, will; **kemauan** N want, will, desire

maya *dunia* ~ cyberspace

mayat N corpse

Mbak PRON, F address for elder sister, female person slightly older than yourself, or worker in service industry

Mbok PRON, F mother; address for female servants

mébel, meubel N furniture

medali, médali N medal

megah ADJ glorious, luxurious, grand

Méi *bulan* ~ May

méja N table

Mekah, Mekkah N Mecca

mekar v to blossom

Méksiko N Mexico

melacak v to trace ← **lacak**

melafalkan v to pronounce ← **lafal**

melahirkan v to give birth to; to create ← **lahir**

melainkan CONJ rather, instead

Melaka, Malaka N Malacca

melakukan v to do, perform, carry out ← **laku**

melalui v to pass through; CONJ through, via ← **lalu**

melamar v to apply ← **lamar**

melambaikan v to wave something; ~ *tangan* to wave goodbye ← **lambai**

melambatkan v to slow down ← **lambat**

melambung v to bounce ← **lambung**

melampirkan v to attach, enclose

melamun v to day-dream, fantasize ← **lamun**

melanggar v to disobey, offend ← **langgar**

melangkah v to step ← **langkah**

98

melanjutkan v to continue something ← **lanjut**

melapor v to report; **melaporkan** v to report, inform ← **lapor**

melarang v to ban, prohibit, forbid ← **larang**

melarikan v to run off with, abduct, kidnap ← **lari**

melati N jasmine

melatih v to train ← **latih**

melawan v to oppose, resist ← **lawan**

melayani v to serve ← **layan**

melayat v to visit a house in mourning, to pay your respects ← **layat**

Melayu Malay; Indonesian; *bahasa ~, orang ~* Malay

melébarkan v to widen ← **lébar**

melebihi v to exceed, surpass ← **lebih**

meledak v to explode ← **ledak**

melédék N to tease, provoke ← **lédék**

melégalisasi, melégalisir v to legalize ← **légalisasi**

melék awake, eyes open

melekat v to stick ← **lekat**

melelahkan ADJ tiring ← **lelah**

meléléh v to drip, run ← **léléh**

melémpar v to throw ← **lémpar**

melénceng v to deviate, go out of your way ← **léncéng**

melengkapi v to furnish, supply ← **lengkap**

melepaskan v to release, let free ← **lepas**

melését v to slip, skid; to miss the target ← **lését**

meletakkan v to put in place, set down ← **letak**

meletus v to erupt ← **letus**

meléwati v to pass or go through ← **léwat**

melibatkan v to involve, include ← **libat**

melihat v to see, look; **melihat-lihat** v to look around, have a look ← **lihat**

melindas v to run over, squash ← **lindas**

melindungi v to protect, shelter ← **lindung**

melingkari v to circle or surround ← **lingkar**

melintang ADJ horizontal, across ← **lintang**

melipat v to fold ← **lipat**

meliputi v to include, cover ← **liput**

melolong v to howl (of dogs) ← **lolong**

melompat v to jump, leapfrog ← **lompat**

mélon N rockmelon, cantaloupe

meloncat v to spring, jump (over something) ← **loncat**

melontar, melontarkan v to throw ← **lontar**

melotot v to stare or gape at, with bulging eyes ← **lotot**

meluap v to overflow, swell, wash ← **luap**

meludah v to spit ← **ludah**

melukai, melukakan v to hurt or wound ← **luka**

melukis v to paint, draw ← **lukis**

meluncurkan v to launch, set in motion ← **luncur**

melupakan v to forget something ← **lupa**

memaafkan v to forgive, pardon ← **maaf**

memadukan v to combine, unite ← **padu**

memahami v to understand, comprehend ← **paham**

memahat v to sculpt, chisel ← **pahat**

memainkan v to play something ← **main**

memakai v to wear; to use ← **pakai**

memakamkan v to bury ← **makam**

memakan v to eat, consume, take ← **makan**

memaki, memaki-maki v to insult, heap abuse on ← **maki**

memaksa v to force ← **paksa**

memalsukan v to falsify, forge ← **palsu**

memalukan ADJ embarrassing ← **malu**

memanaskan v to heat (up) ← **panas**

memancing v to fish (with hook and line) ← **pancing**

memandang v to view, consider ← **pandang**

memandikan v to wash someone ← **mandi**

memandu v to guide ← **pandu**

mémang CONJ **émang** COLL indeed

memanggang v to roast,

bake, toast ← **panggang**

memanggil v to call ← **panggil**

memanjakan v to spoil someone ← **manja**

memanjat v to climb

memantau v to observe, watch ← **pantau**

memar ADJ bruised

memarahi v to scold, be angry with ← **marah**

memasak v to cook ← **masak**

memasang v to put up, attach, fix ← **pasang**

memastikan v to confirm, make sure, ascertain ← **pasti**

memasukkan v to put in, insert, import, enter ← **masuk**

mematahkan v to break ← **patah**

mematikan v to kill, extinguish, put out ← **mati**

mematuhi v to obey ← **patuh**

membaca v to read ← **baca**

membagi v to divide, distribute ← **bagi**

membahas v to discuss, debate ← **bahas**

membaik v to improve ← **baik**

membajak v to hijack; to copy illegally ← **bajak**

membajak v to plough ← **bajak**

membakar v to burn ← **bakar**

membalap v to race ← **balap**

membalas v to reply, respond ← **balas**

membalik v to return, reverse, turn over; **membalikkan** v to turn something over ← **balik**

membandingkan v to compare something ← **banding**

membangun v to build or create

membangunkan v to wake someone up ← **bangun**

membantah v to deny, dispute ← **bantah**

membantai v to slaughter, kill viciously ← **bantai**

membanting v to throw down (with a bang) ← **banting**

membantu v to help (someone) ← **bantu**

membasahi v to moisten, wet ← **basah**

membatalkan v to cancel, repeal ← **batal**

membatik N to apply wax onto fabric ← **batik**

membawa v to take, bring, carry; conduct ← **bawa**

membayar v to pay ← **bayar**

membédakan v to discriminate, differentiate between, consider as different ← **béda**

membeku v to freeze ← **beku**

membéla v to defend ← **béla**

membelah v to split in two ← **belah**

membeli v to buy, purchase ← **beli**

membélok v to bend, turn ← **bélok**

membenarkan v to confirm, verify; justify ← **benar**

membenci v to hate ← **benci**

membentuk v to form, set up something (eg. committee) ← **bentuk**

memberantas v to wipe out, fight against ← **berantas**

memberéskan v to clear up, make ready ← **bérés**

memberhentikan v to stop (a vehicle); dismiss

memberi v to give ← **beri**

memberitahu v to advise, inform, tell ← **beri tahu**

memberitakan v to report ← **berita**

memberontak v to rebel, revolt ← **berontak**

membersihkan v to clean; wipe out (eg. disease) ← **bersih**

membesarkan v to bring up, raise (children) ← **besar**

membetulkan v to correct, repair ← **betul**

membiarkan v to let, allow, permit ← **biar**

membicarakan v to discuss ← **bicara**

membilas v to rinse ← **bilas**

membimbing v to lead, guide, coach ← **bimbing**

membina v to build up, found ← **bina**

membingungkan ADJ confusing ← **bingung**

membintangi v to star (in) ← **bintang**

membisik v to whisper ← **bisik**

membius v to drug, anesthetize ← **bius**

memblokir v to block ← **blokir**

membocorkan v to leak something ← **bocor**

membohong v to lie ← **bohong**

memboikot v to boycott something ← **boikot**

membolos v skip, be absent, play truant, wag, skive ← **bolos**

membongkar v to pull apart, dismantle; to unpack; to unearth ← **bongkar**

memborong v to buy up, buy in bulk ← **borong**

membosankan ADJ boring, tiresome ← **bosan**

membuang v to throw out; to waste; to exile ← **buang**

membuat v to make ← **buat**

membubarkan v to break something up ← **bubar**

membujuk v to coax ← **bujuk**

membuka v to open ← **buka**

membuktikan v to prove ← **bukti**

membumihanguskan v to conduct a searched-earth policy

membungkus v to wrap; ~ *kado* wrap a gift ← **bungkus**

membunuh v to kill ← **bunuh**

membunyikan v to sound, ring something ← **bunyi**

memburu v to hunt, chase ← **buru**

membutuhkan v to need something ← **butuh**

memecah ~ *belah* to break into fragments, cause division; **memecahkan** v to break; to solve ← **pecah**

memecat v to fire, dismiss ← **pecat**

memedulikan v to care or be bothered about ← **peduli**

memegang v to hold, grasp ← **pegang**

memelésétkan v to up-end, send off-course; change ← **pelését**

memelihara v to take care of, look after, cultivate ← **pelihara**

memeluk v to hug or embrace ← **peluk**

memencét v to press (a button, key) ← **pencét**

memengaruhi v to influence, affect ← **pengaruh**

memenjara, memenjarakan v to put in prison, imprison ← **penjara**

memensiunkan v to pension off ← **pénsiun**

103

mementingkan v to make important, emphasize ← **penting**

memenuhi v to fulfill, meet requirements ← **penuh**

memerankan v to portray, play the role of ← **peran**

memeras v to squeeze; press; to blackmail, extort ← **peras**

memercayai v to trust someone; **memercayakan** v to entrust with ← **percaya**

memeriahkan v to liven up, enliven ← **meriah**

memeriksa v to examine or investigate ← **periksa**

memerkosa v to rape ← **perkosa**

memerlukan v to need, require ← **perlu**

memesan v to order ← **pesan**

memetik v to pick; to strum ← **petik**

memfokuskan v to focus something ← **fokus**

memicu v to trigger, set off ← **picu**

memijat v to massage ← **pijat**

memikirkan v to think about ← **pikir**

memilih v to choose or select;

to elect or vote (for) ← **pilih**

memiliki v to own, possess ← **milik**

memimpikan v to dream of ← **mimpi**

memimpin v to lead ← **pimpin**

memindahkan v to move, transfer ← **pindah**

meminjam v to borrow; **meminjami** v to lend someone; **meminjamkan** v to lend something ← **pinjam**

meminta v to ask for, request; **meminta-minta** v to beg, ask for money ← **minta**, **pinta**

memisahkan v to separate something ← **pisah**

memompa v to pump ← **pompa**

memotong v to cut, deduct; to slaughter, amputate; to interrupt ← **potong**

memotrét v to photograph ← **potrét**

mempelai ~ *pria* groom; ~ *wanita* bride

mempelajari v to study something in depth ← **ajar**

memperbaiki v to repair, fix ← **baik**

memperbesar v to enlarge something ← **besar**

memperboléhkan v to allow, permit ← **boléh**

mempercepat v to speed up, accelerate ← **cepat**

memperhatikan v to notice, pay attention to ← **hati**

memperingati v to commemorate ← **ingat**

memperkenalkan v to introduce ← **kenal**

memperkirakan v to estimate, calculate ← **kira**

memperoléh v to obtain, get ← **oléh**

memperpanjang v to extend, make longer ← **panjang**

mempersatukan v to unite various things ← **satu**

mempersembahkan v to offer (up), present ← **sembah**

mempersiapkan v to prepare something, get something ready ← **siap**

mempersilakan v to invite someone to do something ← **sila**

mempersoalkan v to question, discuss ← **soal**

mempertahankan v to defend or maintain ← **tahan**

mempertanggungjawabkan v to account for ← **tanggung jawab**

mempertanyakan v to query ← **tanya**

mempertimbangkan v to consider ← **timbang**

mempraktékkan v to put into practice ← **prakték**

memprihatinkan ADJ worrying ← **prihatin**

memprioritaskan v to prioritize ← **prioritas**

memproduksi v to produce ← **produksi**

mempromosikan v to promote ← **promosi**

memprotés v to (make a) protest ← **protés**

mempunyai v to have, own, possess ← **punya**

memuaskan ADJ satisfactory ← **puas**

memuat v to contain ← **muat**

memuja v to worship ← **puja**

memuji v to praise

memukul v to hit, beat, strike ← **pukul**

memulai v to start or begin something ← **mula, mulai**

memulangkan v to give back; to send back, repatriate ← **pulang**

memungkinkan ADJ conducive; v to enable, make possible ← **mungkin**

memungut v to pick up, collect ← **pungut**

memusatkan v to focus ← **pusat**

memusuhi v to fight against, antagonize, make an enemy of ← **musuh**

memutar v to wind; to rotate; **perputaran** N rotation ← **putar**

memutuskan v to terminate or break; to decide ← **putus**

menabrak v to collide with ← **tabrak**

menabuh v to beat (a drum) ← **tabuh**

menabung v to save or deposit money ← **tabung**

menahan v to bear, endure; to detain ← **tahan**

menaiki v to ride, mount, get on; **menaikkan** v to raise, hoist ← **naik**

menakutkan v, ADV frightening; to frighten or scare ← **takut**

menambah v to add to or increase; **menambahi** v to increase something; **menambahkan** v to add something to ← **tambah**

menambal v to mend, patch, darn ← **tambal**

menampar v to slap ← **tampar**

menanam v to plant or grow; to invest ← **tanam**

menandai v to mark ← **tanda**

menandatangani v to sign something ← **tanda tangan**

menang v to win; **kemenang-an** N victory; **pemenang** N winner, victor

menangani v to handle ← **tangan**

menanggapi v to respond, reply ← **tanggap**

menanggung v to guarantee, be responsible ← **tanggung**

menangis v to cry ← **tangis**

menangkap v to catch, capture ← **tangkap**

menanjak ADJ rising, climbing, steep ← **tanjak**

menantang v to challenge; ADJ challenging ← **tantang**

menanti-nanti v to wait for a long time; **menantikan** v to wait for ← **nanti**

menantu N son- or daughter-in-law → **mantu**

menanyakan v to ask about ← **tanya**

menara N tower; minaret (of a mosque)

menari v to dance, perform a traditional dance; **menari-nari** v to dance about ← **tari**

menarik v to pull or draw; ADJ interesting, attractive ← **tarik**

menaruh v to put (away) ← **taruh**

menasihati v to advise ← **nasihat**

menawar v to bargain; **menawarkan** v to offer or bid ← **tawar**

mencabut v to pull out, remove ← **cabut**

mencair v to melt, turn into liquid ← **cair**

mencakar v to scratch ← **cakar**

mencalonkan v to nominate someone ← **calon**

mencambuk v to whip ← **cambuk**

mencampuradukkan v to mix up, confuse ← **campur**

mencapai v to reach, attain ← **capai**

mencari v look or search for, seek; **mencari-cari** v to search repeatedly, everywhere ← **cari**

mencatat v to note (down) ← **catat**

mencegah v to prevent, fight against ← **cegah**

mencekik v to strangle ← **cekik**

mencemari v to dirty, pollute ← **cemar**

mencengkeram v to grip, squeeze ← **cengkeram**

mencerai, menceraikan v to divorce someone ← **cerai**

menceritakan v to describe, relate ← **cerita**

mencerminkan v to reflect ← **cermin**

mencerna v to digest ← **cerna**

mencetak v to print ← **cetak**

mencicil v to pay by instalments ← **cicil**

mencicipi v to try, taste something ← **cicip**

mencintai v to love someone ← **cinta**

mencipta, menciptakan v to create, make ← **cipta**

mencium v to smell; to kiss ← **cium**

mencoba v to try, attempt ← **coba**

mencoblos v to vote, pierce ← **coblos**

mencocokkan v to match ← **cocok**

mencopét v to pick someone's pocket ← **copét**

mencorét v to scratch, cross out ← **corét**

méncrét v to have diarrhea

mencubit v to pinch ← **cubit**

mencuci v to wash, clean ← **cuci**

mencukur v to shave ← **cukur**

menculik v to kidnap ← **culik**

mencuri n to steal ← **curi**

mencurigakan ADJ suspicious, suspect ← **curiga**

mendadak ADJ sudden ← **dadak**

mendaftar v to register; **mendaftarkan** v to register something ← **daftar**

mendahului v to precede, overtake ← **dahulu**

mendaki v to climb, ascend; ~ *gunung* (to go) mountaineering, bushwalking ← **daki**

mendalam ADJ deep ← **dalam**

mendalangi v to orchestrate (events) ← **dalang**

mendamaikan v to reconcile, pacify ← **damai**

mendampingi v to accompany, flank ← **damping**

mendandani v to decorate, dress, adorn ← **dandan**

mendapat v to obtain, receive; **mendapatkan** v to obtain; discover ← **dapat**

mendarat v to land ← **darat**

mendatang ADJ coming, next; **mendatangkan** v to bring, import ← **datang**

mendatarkan v to make flat, level ← **datar**

mendaur-ulang v to recycle ← **daur ulang**

mendayung v to stroke (an oar), row; to pedal ← **dayung**

mendébet v to debit ← **débet**

mendekati v to approach ← **dekat**

mendémo v to protest against ← **démo**

mendenda v to fine ← **denda**

mendengar v to hear; **mendengarkan** v to listen ← **dengar**

mendengkur v to snore; to purr (of a cat) ← **dengkur**

menderita v to suffer, endure ← **derita**

mendesak ADJ pressing, urgent; v to press, urge, push ← **desak**

mendidih ADJ boiling ← **didih**

mendidik v to educate, bring up, teach ← **didik**

mending, mendingan ADJ, COLL better, better off

mendirikan v to build, establish, erect ← **diri**

mendiskriminasi, mendiskriminasikan v to discriminate against ← **diskriminasi**

mendoakan v to pray for ← **doa**

mendorong v to push, encourage ← **dorong**

menduduki v to sit on something; to occupy ← **duduk**

mendukung v to support ← **dukung**

mendung ADJ cloudy, overcast

menebak v to guess ← **tebak**

menebang v to fell, cut down ← **tebang**

menegakkan v to erect; to uphold or maintain ← **tegak**

menegangkan ADJ tense, stressful ← **tegang**

menegaskan v to clarify, point out, affirm ← **tegas**

meneguk v to gulp or guzzle ← **teguk**

menegur v to speak to, address; to warn, rebuke, tell off ← **tegur**

menekan v to press; **menekankan** v to stress, emphasize ← **tekan**

menelan v to swallow something ← **telan**

menélépon v to ring (up), call, (tele)phone ← **télépon**

menemani v to accompany ← **teman**

menémbak v to shoot ← **témbak**

menembus v to pierce, stab ← **tembus**

menempati v to occupy, take a place ← **tempat**

109

menémpél v to stick or adhere to; **menémpélkan** v to stick, paste or glue something ← **témpél**

menempuh v to endure, go through; to take on, take up ← **tempuh**

menemui v to meet up with, arrange to meet; **menemu-kan** v to discover ← **temu**

menenangkan v to calm someone (down) ← **tenang**

menendang v to kick ← **tendang**

menengah ADJ intermediate ← **tengah**

menéngok v to look or see; to look in on someone ← **téngok**

menentang v to oppose, resist ← **tentang**

menénténg v to carry dangling from the hand ← **ténténg**

menentukan v to decide, determine, stipulate ← **tentu**

menenun v to weave ← **tenun**

menerangkan v to explain ← **terang**

menerapkan v to apply something ← **terap**

menerbangkan v to fly something ← **terbang**

menerbitkan v to publish, issue ← **terbit**

menerima v to receive, accept ← **terima**

menerjemahkan v to trans-late (writing); to interpret (speaking) ← **terjemah**

menertawakan v to laugh at ← **tawa**

menertibkan v to keep order, discipline ← **tertib**

meneruskan v to continue, keep doing something ← **terus**

menetap v to stay; **menetap-kan** v to appoint, fix, stipu-late ← **tetap**

menéwaskan v to kill someone ← **téwas**

mengacaukan v to mix or mess up ← **kacau**

mengadakan v to create, organize, make available; ~ *kampanye* to run a campaign ← **ada**

mengadu v to complain, report ← **adu**

mengaduk v to stir, mix ← **aduk**

mengagumi v to admire ← **kagum**

mengaitkan v to link, connect, join ← **kait**

mengajak v to invite, ask out; to urge; ~ *jalan-jalan* to ask out; ~ *kawin*, ~ *nikah* to ask someone to marry you ← **ajak**

mengajar v to teach; **menga-jari** v to teach someone ← **ajar**

mengaji v to recite or read the Koran ← **kaji**

mengakhiri v to end, finish something ← **akhir**

mengaku v to admit, confess, acknowledge; to claim; ~ *salah* to admit guilt ← **aku**

mengalahkan v to conquer, defeat ← **kalah**

mengalami v to experience ← **alam**

mengalir v to flow ← **alir**

mengamankan v to make safe, restore order; to place in custody ← **aman**

mengambil v to take, get, fetch ← **ambil**

mengamén v **ngamén** COLL to sing in the street for money, busk ← **amén**

mengamuk v to run amok, go berserk ← **amuk**

mengancam v to threaten, intimidate ← **ancam**

mengandung v to contain, carry; to be pregnant ← **kandung**

mengangguk v to nod ← **angguk**

mengangkat v to lift or pick up, raise; to appoint; to remove, amputate ← **angkat**

menganjurkan v to suggest, propose ← **anjur**

mengantar v to take, escort, accompany; **mengantar-kan** v to take someone or something ← **antar**

mengantri v to queue ← **antré, antri**

mengantuk ADJ sleepy ← **kantuk**

menganut v to follow ← **anut**

menganyam v to weave, plait, braid ← **anyam**

mengapa why ← **apa**

mengapung v to float, be suspended ← **apung**

mengarang v to write, compose ← **karang**

111

mengatakan v to say ← **kata**
mengatasi v to overcome ← **atas**
mengatur v to arrange, organize, regulate ← **atur**
mengawasi v to supervise ← **awas**
mengawinkan ~ *anak* to marry off a son or daughter ← **kawin**
mengayuh v to paddle or pedal something; ~ *sepeda* to ride a bicycle ← **kayuh**
mengebom v to bomb something ← **bom**
mengecap v to brand ← **cap**
mengecas v to charge (electrical equipment) ← **cas, charge**
mengecat v to paint, dye ← **cat**
mengecék v to check, confirm ← **cék**
mengecéwakan v to disappoint; ADJ disappointing ← **kecéwa**
mengecilkan v to make smaller, decrease ← **kecil**
mengéjék v to tease, mock, ridicule ← **éjék**
mengejutkan ADJ surprising, startling; v to surprise or startle ← **kejut**
mengékspor v to export ← **ékspor**
mengelap v to wipe, mop ← **lap**
mengelas v to weld ← **las**
mengelilingi v to circle, go around ← **keliling**
mengelola v to manage, run ← **kelola**
mengeluarkan v to issue, send out, release ← **keluar**
mengeluh v to complain ← **keluh**
mengelupas v to peel, come off (of a skin) ← **kelupas**
mengelus v to caress, stroke or pat (an animal) ← **elus**
mengembalikan v to give or send back, return ← **kembali**
mengembangkan v to develop something ← **kembang**
mengemis v to beg ← **emis, kemis**
mengemudikan v to drive, steer ← **kemudi**
mengemut v to suck on (sweets etc) ← **emut, kemut**
mengenai CONJ about, over, on, concerning ← **kena**

mengenal v to know, be acquainted with, recognize; **memperkenalkan** v to introduce ← **kenal**

mengencangkan v to tighten ← **kencang**

mengendalikan v to control ← **kendali**

mengepak v to pack ← **pak**

mengepél v to mop (up) ← **pél**

mengeraskan v to make something harder, louder ← **keras**

mengerém v to brake ← **rém**

mengerikan ADJ terrifying, horrifying ← **ngeri**

mengeringkan v to dry something ← **kering**

mengerjakan v to do, carry out ← **kerja**

mengeroyok v to beat savagely in a mob ← **keroyok**

mengerti v to understand; **dimengerti** v to be understood; **pengertian** N understanding ← **arti**

mengesahkan v to validate, ratify, legitimize, legalize ← **sah**

mengesankan ADJ impressive ← **kesan**

mengetahui v to know something, have knowledge of ← **tahu**

mengetik v to type ← **ketik**

mengetuk v to knock ← **ketuk**

menggabungkan v to connect, combine, fuse ← **gabung**

menggadaikan v to pawn something ← **gadai**

menggaji v to pay, remunerate, employ ← **gaji**

menggali v to dig ← **gali**

menggambar v to draw, depict; **menggambarkan** v to describe, illustrate ← **gambar**

mengganggu v to bother, disturb ← **ganggu**

mengganti v to change, substitute, replace; **menggantikan** v to substitute or replace someone/something ← **ganti**

menggantung v to hang, suspend ← **gantung**

menggaruk v to scratch, scrape ← **garuk**

menggelar, menggelarkan v to hold (an event) ← **gelar**

menggéléng to shake your head ← **géléng**

menggelikan ADJ funny, comic; off-putting ← **geli**

menggelitik v to tickle ← **gelitik**

menggembirakan ADJ exciting, happy ← **gembira**

menggembok v to padlock ← **gembok**

menggenggam v to grip, grasp ← **genggam**

menggerakkan v to move, shift something ← **gerak**

menggésék v to rub, scrape ← **gésék**

menggésér v to move aside or over ← **gésér**

menggigil v to shiver ← **gigil**

menggigit v to bite ← **gigit**

menggoda v to tempt ← **goda**

menggoncangkan v to rock or make something move ← **goncang**

menggoréng v to fry ← **goréng**

menggorés v to scratch, make a stroke ← **gorés**

menggosok v to rub, polish ← **gosok**

menggotong to carry together ← **gotong**

menggoyangkan v to shake or rock something ← **goyang**

menggugat v to sue, accuse ← **gugat**

menggunakan v to use ← **guna**

mengguncangkan v to rock or make something move ← **guncang**

menggunting v to cut (out) ← **gunting**

menggusur v to evict, sweep aside, forcibly remove ← **gusur**

menghabiskan v to finish, use up, spend ← **habis**

menghadap v to face, appear before; **menghadapi** v to face someone or something ← **hadap**

menghadiri v to attend ← **hadir**

menghafalkan v to learn by heart ← **hafal**

menghambat v to obstruct, impede, hamper ← **hambat**

menghancurkan v to smash, crush, destroy ← **hancur**

mengharapkan v to expect ← **harap**

114

menghargai v to appreciate ← **harga**

mengharukan ADJ moved, touched (emotionally) ← **haru**

menghasilkan v to produce ← **hasil**

menghéla v to draw, drag ← **héla**

menghémat v to save on or economize ← **hémat**

menghembus v to blow ← **hembus**

menghendaki v to want ← **hendak**

menghentikan v to stop something ← **henti**

menghérankan ADJ astonishing, astounding ← **héran**

menghiasi v to adorn, decorate something ← **hias**

menghibur v to entertain; to comfort, console ← **hibur**

menghidupkan v to bring to life, start or turn on (a device) ← **hidup**

menghilang v to disappear, vanish; **menghilangkan** v to remove ← **hilang**

menghinakan v to humiliate,

insult ← **hina**

menghindar v to steer clear, avoid; **menghindari** v to avoid something ← **hindar**

menghirup v to breathe in ← **hirup**

menghitung v to count, calculate, reckon; **menghitungkan** v to count or calculate something ← **hitung**

menghormat, menghormati v to honor or respect

menghubungi v to contact someone; **menghubungkan** v to connect, join, link different parts ← **hubung**

menghukum v to punish, sentence, condemn ← **hukum**

mengidam v to crave (esp of pregnant woman) ← **idam**

mengijinkan v to permit, allow ← **ijin, izin**

mengikat v to tie, fasten ← **ikat**

mengikut v to follow, accompany; **mengikuti** v to follow, join, participate in ← **ikut**

mengimpor v to import ← **impor**

115

menginap v to stay the night, stay over ← **inap**

mengingat v to remember, bear in mind; **mengingatkan** v to remind someone about something ← **ingat**

menginjak v to step, tread, or stamp on ← **injak**

menginterviu v to interview ← **interviu**

mengintip v to peep at, spy on ← **intip**

mengira v to assume, think ← **kira**

mengirim v to send ← **kirim**

mengisap v to suck; to smoke ← **isap**

mengisi v to fill, load ← **isi**

mengizinkan v to permit, allow ← **izin, ijin**

mengkhianati v to betray someone ← **khianat**

mengkilap v to shine, gleam ← **kilap**

mengobati v to treat, cure ← **obat**

mengobral v to put on sale ← **obral**

mengobrol v to chat ← **obrol**

mengolés v to grease, spread, lubricate; **mengoléskan** v to smear with something ← **olés**

mengomél v to complain, grumble, whinge, whine ← **omél**

mengompol v to wet your pants, the bed ← **ompol**

mengorbankan v to sacrifice ← **korban**

mengorék v to scrape, scratch

mengoréksi v to correct ← **koréksi**

mengosongkan v to empty ← **kosong**

menguap v to yawn ← **kuap**

menguasai v to control, have power over ← **kuasa**

menguatirkan v to worry about something ← **kuatir**

mengubah v to change or alter ← **ubah**

menguburkan v to bury ← **kubur**

mengucap, mengucapkan v to say or express something ← **ucap**

menguji v to examine or test ← **uji**

mengukir v to carve or engrave ← **ukir**

mengukur v to measure ← **ukur**

mengukus v to steam (food) ← **kukus**

mengulang v to repeat, do again; **mengulangi** v to repeat something ← **ulang**

mengumpat v to curse, swear ← **umpat**

mengumpet v to hide or conceal yourself ← **umpet**

mengumpulkan v to collect, gather ← **kumpul**

mengumumkan v to announce or declare ← **umum**

mengunci v to lock (up) ← **kunci**

mengundang v to invite (formally) ← **undang**

mengundi v to conduct a draw or lottery ← **undi**

mengundurkan v to postpone ← **undur**

mengungkap v to uncover; **mengungkapkan** v to express ← **ungkap**

mengungsi v to evacuate or flee ← **ungsi**

mengunjungi v to visit a place ← **kunjung**

menguntungkan v to profit; ADJ profitable ← **untung**

mengupas v to peel; to

analyze ← **kupas**

menguping v to eavesdrop, listen in ← **kuping**

mengurangi v to take from, subtract, minus ← **kurang**

mengurung v to cage, put in a cage, lock up ← **kurung**

mengurus v to arrange, organize, manage ← **urus**

mengurut v to massage ← **urut**

mengusahakan v to try, endeavor to ← **usaha**

mengusir v to drive away or out, chase away, expel ← **usir**

mengusulkan v to propose or suggest ← **usul**

mengutak-atik, mengutak-ngatikkan v to work on or tinker with ← **kutak, utak-atik**

mengutamakan v to give preference or priority to ← **utama**

mengutip v to quote, cite an extract ← **kutip**

mengutuk v to curse ← **kutuk**

menidurkan v to put to sleep ← **tidur**

menikah v to marry, get

117

married; **menikahi** v to
marry someone ← **nikah**

menikam v to stab ← **tikam**

menikmati v to enjoy ←
nikmat

menilai v to evaluate, appraise

menimbulkan v to give rise,
bring to the surface ←
timbul

menindaklanjuti v to take a
step or measure ← **tindak
lanjut**

meninggal ~ *(dunia)* to die;
meninggalkan v to leave
(behind), abandon ← **tinggal**

meningkat v to rise, increase,
improve; **meningkatkan** v to
increase or raise the level of
something ← **tingkat**

meninjau v to observe, view
← **tinjau**

menipu v to trick, deceive
← **tipu**

meniru v to copy or imitate
← **tiru**

menit N minute

menitip v to leave in someone's care, entrust ← **titip**

meniup v to blow ← **tiup**

menjadi v to be or become
← **jadi**

menjaga v to guard, keep
watch ← **jaga**

menjahit v to sew ← **jahit**

menjajah v to colonize, rule
another country ← **jajah**

menjalankan v to operate,
run, set in motion ← **jalan**

menjalin v to forge links,
network ← **jalin**

menjamin v to guarantee,
promise ← **jamin**

menjanjikan v to promise
something ← **janji**

menjaring v to fish with a
net; to filter or sift ← **jaring**

menjatuhkan v to fell, let
drop ← **jatuh**

menjawab v to answer, reply
← **jawab**

menjebak v to trap ← **jebak**

menjelajahi v to travel
through or explore a place
← **jelajah**

menjelang v to approach (usu
time) ← **jelang**

menjelaskan ADJ to explain,
clarify ← **jelas**

menjemput v to pick up ←
jemput

menjemur v to air, dry in the
sun ← **jemur**

118

menjeprét v to snap, staple ← **jeprét**

menjerit v to scream, shriek ← **jerit**

menjijikkan ADJ disgusting, revolting, foul ← **jijik**

menjilat v to lick; SL to suck up, flatter ← **jilat**

menjodohkan v to set up, match ← **jodoh**

menjual v to sell ← **jual**

menodong v to threaten or hold up at knifepoint ← **todong**

menolak v to refuse, reject ← **tolak**

menolong v to help or assist ← **tolong**

menonjok v to punch, hit ← **tonjok**

menonjol v to stick out, protrude; ADJ prominent ← **tonjol**

menonton v to watch, look on ← **tonton**

méns COLL period, menstruation

mensukséskan v to make something succeed ← **suksés**

mensyukuri v to appreciate, be thankful ← **syukur**

mentah ADJ raw, uncooked, not ripe

méntal, méntalitas N way of thinking, mentality

mentéga N butter

menteri N minister; **kementerian** N ministry, department, office

mentimun, timun N cucumber

mentraktir v to invite out, shout, treat, pay for another ← **traktir**

menuding v to accuse, point the finger ← **tuding**

menuduh v to accuse ← **tuduh**

menugaskan v to assign someone, give a task to ← **tugas**

menuju v to approach, go towards ← **tuju**

menukar v to change; **menukarkan** v to change something ← **tukar**

menular v to infect; ADJ contagious, infectious ← **tular**

menulis v to write ← **tulis**

menumpahkan v to spill something ← **tumpah**

menumpang v to make use of someone else's facilities; to get a lift or ride ← **tumpang**

menunda v to delay, put off, postpone; **menundakan** v to delay or postpone something ← **tunda**

menunduk v to bow your head; **menundukkan** v to bow or lower something; to defeat ← **tunduk**

menunggang v to ride ← **tunggang**

menunggu v to wait for something; **menunggu-nunggu** v to wait a long time for ← **tunggu**

menunjuk v to indicate, point out, refer to; **menunjukkan** v to show, point out ← **tunjuk**

menuntut v to claim or demand ← **tuntut**

menurun v to fall, drop, decline; **menurunkan** v to lower or reduce ← **turun**

menurut CONJ according to ← **turut**

menutup v to close or shut; **menutupi** v to cover (up) ← **tutup**

menyadari v to realize, be aware of ← **sadar**

menyahut v to answer, reply, respond ← **sahut**

menyajikan v to serve, present, offer ← **saji**

menyakiti v to hurt, treat badly; **menyakitkan** ADJ painful ← **sakit**

menyaksikan v to witness ← **saksi**

menyala v to burn, blaze; **menyalakan** v to light, set fire to ← **nyala**

menyalami v to greet ← **salam**

menyalin v to copy ← **salin**

menyalip v overtake, slip past ← **salip**

menyamar v to be in disguise ← **samar**

menyambung v to join, continue; **menyambungkan** v to connect to (something else) ← **sambung**

menyambut v to welcome or receive ← **sambut**

menyampaikan v to deliver, hand over, pass on ← **sampai**

menyandar v to lean ← **sandar**

menyangka v to suspect,

suppose, presume; *tidak* ~ never thought ← **sangka**

menyanyi v to sing; **menyanyikan** v to sing something ← **nyanyi**

menyapu v to sweep or wipe ← **sapu**

menyarankan v to suggest ← **saran**

menyatakan v to declare, state, certify ← **nyata**

menyatukan v to unite various things ← **satu**

menyayangi v to love ← **sayang**

menyebabkan v to cause ← **sebab**

menyebalkan ADJ annoying, tiresome ← **sebal**

menyebarkan v to spread something ← **sebar**

menyeberang v to cross ← **seberang**

menyebut v to mention, name, say ← **sebut**

menyediakan v to prepare, get ready ← **sedia**

menyedihkan ADJ depressing, sad ← **sedih**

menyedot v to suck (up) ← **sedot**

menyegarkan ADJ refreshing ← **segar**

menyelam v to dive ← **selam**

menyelamatkan v to save, rescue ← **selamat**

menyelenggarakan v to run, hold, organize ← **selenggara**

menyelesaikan v to finish, end, settle ← **selesai**

menyelidiki v to investigate ← **selidik**

menyelundupkan v to smuggle (in) ← **selundup**

menyembah v to pay homage to, worship ← **sembah**

menyembelih v to slaughter, butcher ← **sembelih**

menyembuhkan v to cure, heal ← **sembuh**

menyembunyikan v to hide or conceal something ← **sembunyi**

menyempit v to (become) narrow ← **sempit**

menyemprot v to spray; **menyemprotkan** v to spray with something ← **semprot**

menyenangkan ADJ pleasing, agreeable ← **senang**

menyengat v to sting ← **sengat**

121

menyénggol v to bump, brush, tweak ← **sénggol**

menyentuh v to touch ← **sentuh**

menyépak v to kick (out) ← **sépak**

menyepakati v to agree to ← **sepakat, pakat**

menyerah v to surrender, give in, give up; **menyerahkan** v to hand over ← **serah**

menyerang v to attack ← **serang**

menyerap v to absorb, soak up ← **serap**

menyérét v to drag ← **sérét**

menyerobot v to push in front ← **serobot**

menyesal v to regret; **menyesalkan** v to feel bad about, regret (another's action) ← **sesal**

menyesatkan ADJ misleading, confusing ← **sesat**

menyesuaikan v to adapt, bring into line ← **sesuai**

menyetél v to tune, set, adjust ← **setél**

menyetir v to drive ← **setir**

menyetor v to pay in, deposit ← **setor**

menyetrika v to iron ← **setrika**

menyetujui v to agree to, approve, ratify ← **tubuh, setubuh**

menyéwa v to rent, hire; **menyéwakan** v to let (a house), hire out, lease ← **séwa**

menyiapkan v to prepare something, get something ready ← **siap**

menyikat v to brush ← **sikat**

menyiksa v to torture ← **siksa**

menyimpan v to keep, save up, store ← **simpan**

menyimpulkan v to conclude or summarize ← **simpul**

menyindir v to insinuate, allude ← **sindir**

menyinggung v to touch on ← **singgung**

menyingkatkan v to abbreviate, shorten ← **singkat**

menyingkirkan v to remove, brush aside ← **singkir**

menyiram v to pour, water (plants) ← **siram**

menyisir v to comb, check thoroughly ← **sisir**

menyobék v to tear off ← **sobék**

menyogok v to bribe ← **sogok**

menyonték v to copy, cheat ← **conték, sonték**

menyoroti v to light up, illuminate, focus on ← **sorot**

menyuap v to feed by hand; to bribe ← **suap**

menyucikan v to purify, cleanse ← **suci**

menyudutkan v to push into a corner, deflect ← **sudut**

menyukai v to like ← **suka**

menyulam v to embroider ← **sulam**

menyulap v to conjure up; to make something vanish or change ← **sulap**

menyumbang v to contribute, make a donation ← **sumbang**

menyumbat v to plug, stop ← **sumbat**

menyunatkan v to have someone circumcised ← **sunat**

menyuntik v to inject or vaccinate ← **suntik**

menyupir v to drive ← **supir**

menyurati v to write a letter to ← **surat**

menyuruh v to command,

order ← **suruh**

menyusahkan v to bother, make difficult ← **susah**

menyusui v to feed ← **susu**

menyusul v to follow, go after ← **susul**

menyusun v to heap or pile; to arrange, organize, compile ← **susun**

mépét ADJ tight, squeezed

meraba v to feel or grope something ← **raba**

meracuni v to poison ← **racun**

meradang v to become inflamed ← **radang**

meragukan v to doubt something ← **ragu**

mérah ADJ red; ~ *jambu* pink

merahasiakan v to keep secret ← **rahasia**

merajut v to knit; to crochet ← **rajut**

merak N peacock

merakit v to assemble ← **rakit**

meralat v to correct a mistake ← **ralat**

meramaikan v to liven up, enliven ← **ramai**

meramal v to tell fortunes; **meramalkan** v to predict, foretell ← **ramal**

merampok v to rob, hold up ← **rampok**

merancang v to plan, design ← **rancang**

merangkak v to crawl ← **rangkak**

merantai v to chain up ← **rantai**

merasa v to think, feel; **merasakan** v to feel something ← **rasa**

meratakan v to level, flatten ← **rata**

merawat v to nurse, care for; to maintain, look after ← **rawat**

merayakan v to celebrate ← **raya**

merayap v to crawl, creep ← **rayap**

merayu v to tempt, flatter, seduce ← **rayu**

mercon N fireworks

mercu ~ *suar* lighthouse

merdéka ADJ free, independent; **kemerdékaan** N freedom, independence, liberty

merdu ADJ sweet, melodious, honeyed

merebus v to boil (in) water ← **rebus**

merebut v to snatch, capture; **merebutkan** v to snatch something ← **rebut**

mérek N brand, label (clothes), make (vehicle); **bermérek** v to have a label, branded

meréka PRON, PL they, them, their; ~ *punya* theirs

merekam v to record ← **rekam**

merekrut v to recruit ← **rekrut**

merem be asleep, eyes shut

merembes v to seep in, leak, ooze ← **rembes**

meréméhkan v to belittle, treat as unimportant ← **réméh**

merencanakan v to plan ← **rencana**

merendahkan v to lower; to humiliate ← **rendah**

meréngék v to whimper, whine ← **réngék**

merenggut v to snatch, tug ← **renggut**

merenung v to daydream ← **renung**

merépotkan v to make someone busy or go to some trouble ← **répot**

meresap v to be absorbed, penetrate, seep into ← **resap**

meresépkan v to write a prescription for a drug ← **resép**

meresmikan v to formalize, make official ← **resmi**

merestui v to agree to, give your blessing to ← **restu**

meriah ADJ merry, lively; **memeriahkan** v to liven up, enliven

meriam N cannon

merica N pepper

merinding v to have goosebumps or an eerie feeling, be spooked ← **rinding**

merindukan v to miss, long for ← **rindu**

mérk → **mérek**

merobék v to tear up, shred ← **robék**

merokok v to smoke ← **rokok**

merombak v to pull down, demolish; to reorganize ← **rombak**

merosot v fall down, descend, plummet ← **rosot**

merpati N pigeon, dove

mertua N parents-in-law

merubah → **mengubah**

merugikan v to hurt, harm, injure ← **rugi**

meruntuhkan v to destroy overthrow ← **runtuh**

merupakan v to be, form, constitute ← **rupa**

merusak v to spoil, damage; **merusakkan** v to destroy, break ← **rusak**

méses N chocolate sprinkles

mesin N machine, engine

mesjid, masjid N mosque

meski, meskipun CONJ although, even though

mesra ADJ intimate, close

mesti, musti v, AUX should; ~*nya* should; **semestinya** should have (been)

méter N meter; metre; **méteran** N tape measure

meterai, méterai N seal

métode N method

méwah N luxurious; **keméwahan** N luxury

mewakili v to represent ← **wakil**

mewarisi v to inherit ← **waris**

mewarnai v to color (in) ← **warna**

mewawancarai v to interview ← **wawancara**

mewujudkan v to make something real, realize something ← **wujud**

meyakini v to convince someone; **meyakinkan** ADJ convincing, believable ← **yakin**

mi, mie N noodles; ~ *goreng* fried noodles

migrasi N migration

migrén N migraine

mik, mikrofon N microphone, mike

mili, miliméter N millimeter

miliar, milyar N billion → **milyar**

milik N property, possession; **memiliki** v to own, possess; **pemilik** N owner

milis N mail list

militér N military

milyar, miliar N billion; **milyarder** N billionaire

mimbar N pulpit, platform, forum

mimisan nose bleed, blood nose

mimpi dream; **bermimpi** v to dream; **memimpikan** v to dream of → **impi**

min → **minus**

minal aidin (wal faidzin) greeting at Idul Fitri

Minang, Minangkabau ethnic group of West Sumatra

minder to lack confidence, low self-esteem; to feel inferior

minggir v, COLL move to one side, pull over (on the road) → **pinggir**

minggu N week; Sunday; *malam* ~ Saturday night; **berminggu-minggu** ADV for weeks; **seminggu** ADJ a week

miniatur ADJ miniature

minoritas N minority

minta v to ask, beg, request; to apply for; **minta-minta** v to beg (alms); **meminta** v to ask for, request; **permintaan** N request

minum drink; **minuman** N drink

minyak N oil; ~ *wangi* perfume; **berminyak** ADJ oily, greasy; **perminyakan** N oil and gas

miring ADJ sloping, slanting; not straight

misa N, CATH mass

misal N example; **misalnya, misalkan** for example, for

126

instance

miskin ADJ poor, lacking in; **kemiskinan** N poverty

mistéri N mystery; **mistérius** ADJ mysterious

mistik, mistis ADJ mystical

mitos N myth

mitra N partner, friend

mobil N car

mode N fashion, trend

moga: moga-moga, semoga may, hopefully

mogok strike; break down

mohon v to request, ask, beg; please; **permohonan** N request, application → **pohon**

molék ADJ pretty, charming

molor stretch, become longer

Monas N National Monument in Central Jakarta ← **Monumén Nasional**

moncong N muzzle, nose

mondar-mandir v to go back and forth, to and fro

mondok v, COLL to board, stay ← **pondok**

montir N mechanic

monumén N monument

monyét N monkey; DEROG term of abuse

motif N design, pattern, motif; **bermotif** v to have a design

moto N MSG, monosodium glutamate ← **Ajinomoto**

moto N motto, chant

motor N motorcycle, (motor) bike

-mu PRON, POSS, S your; *buku~* your book → **kamu**

mua N eel

muak loathe; disgusted, fed up

mual ADJ nauseous, queasy, sick

muara N mouth (of a river); **bermuara** v to have a mouth, empty into

muat contain; **muatan** N load, cargo; **memuat** v to contain

muda ADJ young; *hijau ~* light green; **pemuda** N youth; young man

mudah ADJ easy; **mudah-mudahan** ADV hopefully; **kemudahan** N ease, facility

mudik v to go upstream, back to the village

muka N face, front, surface; *ke ~* to the front, forward; **terkemuka** ADJ prominent; **bermuka** v to have a face; *~*

dua two-faced; **permukaan** N surface

mukim: permukiman N housing, residential area

mula beginning, start; **bermula** v to start, begin; **memulai** v to start or begin something; **pemula** N beginner; **semula** ADV originally

mulai v to begin, start; **memulai** v to start or begin something ← **mula**

mulas (stomach) cramp

mulia ADJ honorable, noble

mulus ADJ smooth, flawless

mulut N mouth

mumpung v to make the most of, capitalize on

muncrat v to spurt, spray

muncul v to appear, turn up

mundur v to go backwards, reverse, retreat; to resign → **undur**

mungkin CONJ maybe, possibly; **kemungkinan** N possibility; **memungkinkan** ADJ conducive; v to enable, make possible

muntah v to vomit, throw up

mur N nut

murah ADJ cheap

murid N pupil, student

murni ADJ pure; only

murung ADJ gloomy, despondent

musang N civet cat

mushola, musholla, mushalla N, ISL small prayer-house

musibah N disaster, calamity

musik N music; **pemusik, musikus, musisi** N musician

musim N season; *~ bunga, ~ semi* spring; *~ dingin* winter; *~ gugur* autumn, fall; *~ panas* summer

musium, muséum N museum

Muslim ADJ, ISL Muslim ← **Islam**

musnah ADJ destroyed

mustahil ADJ impossible

musuh N enemy; **memusuhi** v to fight against, antagonize, make an enemy of

musyawarah: bermusyawarah v to deliberate, discuss

mutakhir ADJ modern, latest

mutiara N pearl

mutu N quality; **bermutu** ADJ quality

Myanmar N Myanmar, Burma

N

nabati ADJ vegetable, plant

nabi N, ISL, CHR prophet

nada N note, tone, sound; ~ *dering* ringtone

nadi N pulse

nafas, napas N breath, breathe; **bernafas** V to breathe; **bernafaskan** V with a breath of; **pernafasan** N breathing, respiration

nafsu N desire; **bernafsu** ADJ passionate, lusty

naga N dragon

nah, na well, well then; look!

naik go up, climb, rise, ascend; ~ *haji* to go on the pilgrimage to Mecca; ~ *pesawat* to board, boarding; **kenaikan** N rise, raise; **menaiki** V to ride, mount, get on; **menaikkan** V to raise, hoist

nakal ADJ naughty

naluri N instinct

nama N name; ~ *depan* first name; ~ *kecil* everyday name, nickname; **bernama**

ADJ named; **menamakan** V to call, name; **ternama** ADJ famous, well-known

nampak → tampak

namun CONJ however, yet

nanah N pus

nanas, nenas N pineapple

nangka N jackfruit

nanti ADV later; **menanti** V to wait; **menanti-nanti** V to wait for a long time; **menantikan** V to wait for

napas, nafas N breath, breathe; **bernapas** V to breathe; **bernapaskan** V with a breath of; **pernapasan** N breathing, respiration

narkoba N (illegal) drugs, narcotics and other banned substances ← **narkotik, psikotropika dan obat terlarang**

nasabah N (bank) customer

naséhat → nasihat

nasi N (cooked) rice; ~ *goreng* fried rice

nasib N fate, lot, destiny

nasihat, naséhat N advice; **menasihati** V to advise; **penasihat** N adviser

nasional N national; **nasionalis**

N nationalist; **nasionalisme N** nationalism

naskah N manuscript, original (text); *penulis ~* script writer

Natal Christmas; **natalan v, COLL** to celebrate Christmas

ndak, nggak, enggak COLL no, not ← **tidak**

negara N state, country; **negarawan N** statesman

negeri N country, land

nékad, nékat reckless; stubborn; **kenékatan N** determination, resolve, recklessness

nelayan N fisherman

nenas → **nanas**

nénék N, PRON grandmother; great-aunt; female relative of grandmother's generation

népotisme N nepotism

neraka N hell

nétral ADJ neutral

ngaji v, COLL to recite or read the Koran ← **kaji**

ngantor v, COLL to go to work ← **kantor**

ngantuk ADJ, COLL sleepy ← **antuk**

ngarang v, COLL to make something up (off the top of your head) ← **karang**

ngeri ADJ terrified; **mengerikan ADJ** terrifying, horrifying

ngetrén, ngetrénd ADJ, COLL trendy, fashionable ← **trénd**

ngetwit v to tweet (on Twitter)

nggak, enggak, ndak COLL no, not → **tidak**

ngilu ADJ painful (of teeth), smarting; *rasa ~* pain

ngobrol v, COLL to chat ← **obrol**

ngomong v, COLL to speak, talk; **ngomong-ngomong ADV** by the way

ngompol v, COLL to wet your pants, the bed ← **ompol**

ngorok v, COLL to snore; to sleep

niaga N commerce; **perniagaan N** commerce, trade, business

niat N intention; **berniat v** to intend

nikah POL marry; **menikah v** to marry, get married; **menikahi v** to marry someone; **pernikahan N** wedding

nikmat ADJ enjoyable, delicious; **menikmati v** to enjoy

nilai N value, worth; mark, grade (at school); **menilai** v to evaluate, appraise

ninabobo lullaby; sing to sleep

nir- PREF without; **nirlaba** ADJ non-profit, not for profit

nisan N headstone, gravestone

noda N stain

nol ADJ zero, nil

nomor, nomer N number; event, match; **menomersatukan** v to put first, give priority

non- PREF not; non-; **nonaktif** ADJ not in active service; **menonaktifkan** v to release from active service, non-activate

Non, Nona PRON Miss

nonaktif ADJ not in active service

nongkrong → **tongkrong**

nonton v, COLL to watch, look on ← **tonton**

Nopémber → **November**

norit N diarrhea tablets, made from black carbon

Norwégia N Norway

notaris N notary

Novémber, Nopémber *bulan* ~ November

nuansa N touch, nuance

nuklir ADJ nuclear

numpang → **tumpang**

nurani ADJ inner

nuri *burung* ~ parrot

nusa N island; ~ *Tenggara* the Lesser Sunda Islands; **Nusantara** N Indonesia

Ny. ABBREV *Nyonya* Madam, title for married woman, especially a non-Indonesian

-nya SUF, POSS added to words to indicate possession; the

nyala flame, blaze, burn; **menyala** v to burn, blaze; **menyalakan** v to light, set fire to

nyaman ADJ comfortable, pleasant; **kenyamanan** N comfort

nyamuk N mosquito

nyanyi sing; **nyanyian** N song; **bernyanyi, menyanyi** v to sing; **menyanyikan** v to sing something; **penyanyi** N singer, vocalist

nyaring ADJ clear, loud, shrill

nyata ADJ clear, obvious, plain; **kenyataan** N fact; **menyatakan** v to declare,

131

state, certify; **pernyataan** N statement, declaration

nyawa N soul, life

nyekar v, COLL to strew flower petals on a grave; to visit a grave → **sekar**

nyenyak ADJ sound asleep

Nyepi N Balinese Day of Seclusion

nyeri N pain

nyiur N coconut palm

nyonya PRON, F term of address for a married woman, Madam; Mrs

O

o EXCL oh; ~ *ya* oh yes, by the way

obat N medicine; **berobat** v to go to the doctor, seek medical advice; **mengobati** v to treat, cure; **pengobatan** N treatment

obral N sale; **mengobral** v to put on sale

obrol: mengobrol v **ngobrol** COLL to chat; **obrolan** N chat

obyék N object; ~ *wisata* tourist destination, sight

obyék: mengobyék, ngobyék v, COLL to have a job on the side, moonlight

odol N, ARCH toothpaste

ogah ADJ, SL unwilling, reluctant

ojék, ojég N motorcycle taxi

oké SL okay, OK

oksigén N oxygen

Oktober *bulan* ~ October

olah: olahan ADJ processed; **pengolahan** v processing

olahraga v sport; **berolahraga** v to do or play sport; **olahragawan** N, M sportsman

oléh CONJ by, through; **oléh-oléh** N souvenir; **memperoléh** v to obtain, get; **peroléhan** N acquisition

oléng ADJ on a lean, leaning to one side

olés: olésan N smear; **mengolés** v to grease, spread, lubricate; **mengoléskan** v to smear with something

oli, olie N (engine) oil

Olimpiade N the Olympics, the Olympic Games

Om, Oom PRON Uncle; term of address to extended family, parents' friends, friends'

parents etc

ombak N wave; **berombak** ADJ wavy

omél: mengomél V to complain, grumble, whinge, whine ← **omél**

omong chat, talk, speak; **omongan** N chat; gossip; **ngomong** V, COLL to speak, talk; **ngomong-ngomong** by the way

ompol: mengompol V to wet the bed, wet your pants

ompong ADJ toothless

oncom N fermented soybean cake

ondé: ondé-ondé N small round cakes made of green peanuts, covered in sesame seeds

onderdil N (automotive) spare part

ongkos N cost (for a service), expense, charge

ons N ounce

operasi N operation

opini N opinion

opname go into hospital, hospitalization; **diopname** V to be admitted to hospital, be hospitalized

opor ~ *ayam* chicken in coconut sauce

optik N optician; optical

orang N person, human; ~ *Barat* Westerner; ~ *Cina*, ~ *Tionghoa* (ethnic) Chinese; ~ *gila* tramp; mentally-ill person; ~ *Islam* Muslim; ~ *kulit putih* white person; ~ ~ *tua* parents; **perorangan** ADJ personal, individual; **seorang** a (person); counter for people; **perseorangan** ADJ individual; **seseorang** N a certain person, somebody

oranye ADJ orange

orgel, organ N organ

orkés N orchestra

ormas N social or people's organization ← **organisasi masyarakat**

orok N (newborn) baby

oséng: oséng-oséng N stir-fried vegetables

otak N brain

otak: otak-otak N steamed fish cakes, baked in banana leaves

otda N regional autonomy ← **otonomi daérah**

otomatis ADJ automatic

133

otomotif ADJ automotive

otonomi N autonomy

otorita, otoritas N authority

otot N muscle; **berotot** ADJ muscular

oven N oven, kiln

overdosis, OD overdose

oya, o ya oh yes, by the way

P

pabrik factory

pacar N boyfriend, girlfriend; **pacaran** V, COLL to be going out, to go out, date

pada PREP in, at, on (expressing time); to

pada COLL, PL pluralizing word *sudah ~ pulang* everybody's going home

padahal CONJ whereas, however

padam put out, extinguish; **pemadam** *pasukan ~ kebakaran* fire brigade

padang N field, plain

padat ADJ dense, full, crammed

padi N (unhusked) rice

padu: memadukan V to combine, unite; **terpadu** ADJ integrated

pagar N fence; hedge

pagi N morning; **pagi-pagi** ADV (very) early

paha N thigh

pahala N reward, merit

paham, faham V to understand, know; **memahami** V to understand, comprehend

pahat chisel; **memahat** V to sculpt, chisel

pahit ADJ bitter

pahlawan N hero

pai N pie

pajak tax

pajang: pajangan N display

pak: mengepak V to pack

Pak, Bapak PRON Father; term of address to older, respected men

pakai, paké SL wear; use; **pakaian** N clothes, dress; *~ dalam* underwear; **berpakaian** ADJ dressed in; **memakai** V to wear; to use; **pemakai** N user; **pemakaian** N use, usage; **terpakai** ADJ used, in use

pakar N expert, authority

pakat: sepakat V to agree; **kesepakatan** N agreement; **menyepakati** V to agree to

pakét N packet, package, promotion

pakis N fern

paksa force; **memaksa** V to force; **terpaksa** ADJ forced

paku N nail

pala *buah* ~ nutmeg

palang N barrier, bar, cross; ~ *Merah* Red Cross

palem N palm

Palestina N Palestine

paling ADV most; at the most; ~ *baik* the best

palsu ADJ false, forged; **memalsukan** V to falsify, forge

paman N uncle, male relative of parents' generation

pamér show off; **paméran** N exhibition

pamit, pamitan, berpamit V to take leave

panah N bow; **panahan** N archery; **pemanah** N archer

panas ADJ hot, warm; hot and dry; **kepanasan** N heat; ADJ too hot; **memanaskan** V to heat (up)

panca ADJ five; **Pancasila** N Indonesian state philosophy of five principles

pancaroba N change of season

Pancasila N Indonesian state philosophy of five principles

panci N saucepan, pan

pancing: memancing V to fish (with hook and line); **terpancing** ADJ hooked, caught up; involved

pancur: pancuran, pancoran N fountain; shower

pandai ADJ clever; ~ *besi* smith

pandan *daun* ~ pandanus leaf, used for green coloring in food

pandang see, gaze; **pandangan** N view, sight; **memandang** V to view, consider; **pemandangan** N view

pandu guide, scout, pilot; **memandu** V to guide

panén N harvest, windfall

pangan N food

pangéran N prince

panggang N roast, bake, toast; *ayam* ~ roast chicken; **memanggang** V to roast, bake, toast; **pemanggangan** N spit

panggil call; **panggilan** N call, summons; **memanggil** V to call

135

panggul N hip

panggung N stage

pangkal N base; **pangkalan** N terminal, base; ~ *udara (lanud)* air base

pangkas cut; ~ *rambut* barber

pangkat N rank, class; to the power of; **berpangkat** v to have the rank of

pangku lap; **pangkuan** N lap

panglima N commander

pangsit N wonton, dumpling

panik N panic

panitia N committee, board

panjang ADJ long; ~*nya* length; ~ *lebar* detailed; *(empat) persegi* ~ rectangle; ~ *umur* long life; **kepanjangan** ADJ too long; **memperpanjang** v to extend, make longer; **sepanjang** CONJ, ADJ as long as

panjat climb; **memanjat** v to climb; **memanjatkan** v to send up

pantai N beach, coast; ~ *batu* pebble beach

pantas ADJ proper, decent, right; **sepantasnya** ADV proper, rightly

pantat N bottom, backside

pantau: pantauan N observation; **memantau** v to observe, watch; **pemantau** N observer, monitor

panti N building; ~ *asuhan* orphanage

pantul: memantulkan v to reflect something

pantun N traditional poem (of four lines)

papan N plank, board, bench; ~ *tulis* blackboard, whiteboard

papaya → **pepaya**

paprika N red or green pepper, paprika

Papua Nugini N Papua New Guinea, PNG

para pluralizes the following word; ~ *pemirsa* viewers

parabola N satellite dish; parabola; *TV* ~ satellite TV

paraf N initials

parah ADJ grave, serious, bad

parang N chopper, machete

parasut N parachute → **payung**

parau ADJ hoarse

paré, paria, peria N kind of bitter gourd or squash

parfum N perfume

paria → **paré**

parit N (roadside) ditch

pariwisata N tourism

parkir park (a vehicle); *tempat* ~ car park, parking lot

parkit *burung* ~ parakeet

parpol N (political) party ← **partai politik**

partai N party; ~ *politik (parpol)* political party

paru, paru-paru N lung

paruh, paro N half, part; *kerja* ~ *waktu* work part-time; **separuh** N half

paruh N bill, beak

parut grater

pas exact, just (as); fit; *kamar* ~ changing room

pasal N, LEG paragraph, section

pasang N pair, couple; **pasang-an** N pair; **sepasang** N a pair of

pasang, memasang V to put up, attach, fix; **pemasangan** N installation

pasang ~ *surut* rise and fall, ebb and flow

pasar N market, bazaar; **pemasaran** N marketing

pasca PREF [pasca, paska] after, post-; **pascasarjana** ADJ post-graduate

pasfoto N passport(-sized) photo

pasién N patient

pasir N sand

Paskah N Easter

pasok: pasokan N supply

paspor N passport

pasrah ADJ accepting, fatalistic; **kepasrahan** N submission

pasta N paste; pasta, spaghetti; ~ *gigi* toothpaste

pastél N samosa, small pasty containing vegetables, egg and vermicelli noodles

pasti sure, certain, definite; **kepastian** N certainty; **memastikan** to confirm, make sure, ascertain

pastor N, CATH priest

pasuk: pasukan N troops

patah break, fracture (of bones); **mematahkan** V to break

patok: patokan N standard, peg

patri solder

patroli N patrol

patuh ADJ loyal, obedient; **mematuhi** V to obey

137

patung N statue, figurine; **pematung** N sculptor

patungan v to pay together; to work together

patut ADJ decent, proper, deserving

paus *ikan* ~ whale

Paus Pope

paut: terpaut ADJ fastened, bound; separated

pavilyun, paviliun N smaller house attached to a larger one

payah ADJ difficult, serious; tired

payudara N, F breast

payung N umbrella; parachute

Pébruari → **Fébruari**

pecah break, smash; curdled (of milk); **pecahan** N piece, fragment, fraction; **memecahkan** v to break; to solve

pecat sacked, dismissed, fired; **memecat** v to fire, dismiss

pecel ~ *lele* catfish with rice and side-dishes; *nasi* ~ rice and salad with peanut sauce

péci N black, flat-topped cap worn by men, also with national dress

Pecinan N Chinatown ← **Cina**

pecinta N lover ← **cinta**

pedagang N merchant ← **dagang**

pedanda N Balinese priest

pedang N sword

pedas ADJ spicy, hot; **kepedasan** ADJ too hot or spicy

pédé, PD SL self-confidence; ← **percaya diri**

pedésaan N country(side), rural areas ← **désa**

pedih, perih smart, sting

pédikur N pedicure

peduli v **perduli** COLL to care, bother; **memedulikan** v to care or be bothered about

pegadaian N pawnshop ← **gadai**

pegal ADJ sore, cramped, stiff

pégang, pegang hold, grip, grasp; **berpegang** v to hold onto; **memegang** v to hold, grasp

pegas N spring

pegawai N official, employee; ~ *negeri* public or civil servant

pegunungan N mountain range ← **gunung**

pejabat N (government)

138

official ← **jabat**

pekan N week; market; *akhir* ~ weekend

pekat ADJ thick, strong, concentrated; **kepekatan** N thickness viscosity

pekerja N worker, laborer; **pekerjaan** N work, profession ← **kerja**

pél *kain* ~ rag for mopping the floor; **mengepél** v to mop (up); **dipél** v to be mopped, cleaned

pelabuhan port, harbor ← **labuh**

pelacur N prostitute ← **lacur**

pelajar N pupil, student; **pelajaran** N lesson ← **ajar**

pelampung N floater, flotation device ← **lampung**

pelan, perlahan: pelan-pelan, perlahan-lahan ADV slowly, softly

pelana N saddle

pelanggan N subscriber, customer ← **langgan**

pelangi N rainbow

pelan-pelan ADV slowly, softly ← **pelan**

pelantikan N inauguration ← **lantik**

pelari N runner ← **lari**

pelat N plate; ~ *polisi* (vehicle) number plate, license plate

pelatih N coach, trainer; **pelatihan** N training ← **latih**

pelaut N sailor, seaman ← **laut**

pelawak N comedian, comic, clown ← **lawak**

pelayan N waiter; M waitress; F attendant; **pelayanan** N service ← **layan**

pelayaran N voyage ← **layar**

pelbagai, berbagai ADJ all kinds or sorts of, various ← **bagai**

pélek N rim of wheel ← **vélg**

pelekat *bahan* ~ adhesive ← **lekat**

pelembab, pelembap N moisturizer ← **lembab**

pelését: memelésétkan v to up-end; to send off-course; **terpelését** ADJ slipped, skidded; tripped ← **lését**

pelihara take care of; **peliharaan** *hewan* ~ pet; **memelihara** v to take care of, look after; to cultivate; **pemeliharaan** N care, maintenance, cultivation; **terpelihara** ADJ well cared-for, well-maintained → **piara**

pelindung N protective device ← **lindung**

pelipis N temple (on head)

Pélni N National Shipping Line, state passenger shipping service ← **Pelayaran Nasional Indonésia**

pelopor N pioneer, leader, forerunner

pelosok N remote place

pelotot: melotot V to stare, have bulging eyes ← **lotot**

peluang N opportunity; **berpeluang** V to have an opportunity, a chance ← **luang**

peluit, pluit N whistle

peluk hug; **pelukan** N embrace; **memeluk** V to hug or embrace; **pemeluk** N follower, adherent

pelukis N painter, artist ← **lukis**

pelumas N lubricant ← **lumas**

peluntur N laxative ← **luntur**

peluru N bullet

pemadam *pasukan ~ kebakaran* fire brigade ← **padam**

pemain N player, actor ← **main**

pemakai N user; **pemakaian** N

use, usage ← **pakai**

pemakaman N funeral, burial ← **makam**

pemandangan N view ← **pandang**

pemanggangan N spit ← **panggang**

pemanis ~ *buatan* artificial sweetener ← **manis**

pemasangan N installation ← **pasang**

pemasaran N marketing ← **pasar**

pematung N sculptor ← **patung**

pembaca N reader ← **baca**

pembalut N sanitary pad ← **balut**

pembangunan N development ← **bangun**

pembantu N servant, maid; assistant ← **bantu**

pembayaran N payment ← **bayar**

pembelian N purchase V beli

pemberitahuan N announcement, notice ← **beri tahu**

pemberontakan N rebellion, revolt, mutiny ← **berontak**

pembersih N cleaning agent ← **bersih**

pembicaraan N discussion ← **bicara**

pembohong N liar ← **bohong**

pemborong N developer, contractor ← **borong**

pembuat N producer; maker; **pembuatan** N production, manufacture ← **buat**

pembunuh N murderer, killer; **pembunuhan** N murder, killing ← **bunuh**

pemburu N hunter ← **buru**

Pémda N Regional Government → **Pemerintah Daérah**

pemeliharaan N care, maintenance, cultivation ← **pelihara**

pemeluk N follower, adherent ← **peluk**

pemenang N winner, victor ← **menang**

pementasan N staging, production ← **pentas**

pemeriksa N examiner; **pemeriksaan** N examination, investigation ← **periksa**

pemesanan N order, request ← **pesan**

pemicu N trigger ← **picu**

pemikir N thinker; **pemikiran** N thinking, consideration

← **pikir**

pemilihan N election; ~ *umum (pemilu)* general election ← **pilih**

pemilik N owner ← **milik**

pemilu N general election ← **pemilihan umum**

pemimpin N leader ← **pimpin**

pemindahan N transfer, shifting, removal ← **pindah**

pemirsa N television audience, viewer ← **pirsa**

permohonan N request, application ← **mohon**

pémpék, mpék mpék N fried fish-cakes, a specialty of Palembang

pemuda N youth; young man ← **muda**

pemugaran N restoration, renovation ← **pugar**

pemula N beginner ← **mula**

pemusik N musician ← **musik**

pemutih N bleach ← **putih**

péna N (fountain) pen, quill

penakut N coward ← **takut**

penampilan N performance ← **tampil**

penangkapan N capture, arrest ← **tangkap**

penari N dancer ← **tari**

penasaran ADJ curious, inquisitive, impatient

penasihat N adviser ← **nasihat**

penawaran N offer, bid ← **tawar**

pencahar N laxative ← **cahar**

pencak ~ **silat** traditional self-defense

pencemaran N pollution ← **cemar**

pencernaan N digestion ← **cerna**

pencét press; **memencét** V to press (a button, key); **terpencét** ADJ accidentally pressed

pencil: terpencil ADJ isolated, remote

pencinta N lover ← **cinta**

penculikan N kidnapping ← **culik**

pencuri N thief, burglar ← **curi**

pendaftaran N enrollment, registration ← **daftar**

pendamping N companion ← **damping**

pendapat N opinion, point of view; **pendapatan** N income, revenue ← **dapat**

pendarahan N bleeding ← **darah**

pendatang N immigrant, migrant; newcomer ← **datang**

péndék ADJ short; ~ **kata** in short; ~**nya** in a word; **kepéndékan** N abbreviation; **meméndékkan** V to shorten

pendekatan N approach; getting to know ← **dekat**

pendengar N listener; **pendengaran** N hearing ← **dengar**

pendéta N, CHR minister, clergyman, vicar; HIND priest

pendopo, pendapa N traditional large roofed verandah in front of an official residence

penduduk N inhabitant, citizen, resident; **penduduk-an** N occupation ← **duduk**

pendukung N supporter ← **dukung**

penebangan N logging; ~ **liar** illegal logging ← **tebang**

peneliti N researcher; **penelitian** N research ← **teliti**

penémbak N marksman, gunman ← **témbak**

penemu N inventor,

discoverer; **penemuan** N invention, discovery ← **temu**

penerbang N pilot, aviator; **penerbangan** N flight; aviation ← **terbang**

penerbit N publisher ← **terbit**

penerjemah N translator; **penerjemahan** N translation ← **terjemah**

penerjun ~ *(payung)* parachutist, sky diver ← **terjun**

penerus N successor; someone who continues another's work ← **terus**

penetapan N appointment ← **tetap**

pengacara N lawyer, solicitor ← **acara**

pengadilan N court of justice or law; trial ← **adil**

pengaduan N complaint; *surat* ~ letter of complaint ← **adu**

pengait N catch

pengajar N teacher ← **ajar**

pengalaman N experience ← **alam**

pengamat N observer; **pengamatan** N observation, monitoring ← **amat**

pengamén N street singer, busker ← **amén**

pengangguran N unemployment, unemployed person ← **anggur**

pengantin, pengantén N, F bride; N, M (bride)groom; marrying couple; ~ *baru* newlyweds; ~ *pria* (bride) groom; ~ *wanita* bride

penganut N follower, believer ← **anut**

pengap ADJ stuffy; stale, musty

pengarang N author, writer, composer ← **karang**

pengaruh N influence; ~ *obat* effect of medicine or drugs; **berpengaruh** ADJ influential; **memengaruhi** V to influence, affect; **terpengaruh** ADJ affected or influenced

pengasuh N carer; ~ *anak* nursemaid, babysitter ← **asuh**

pengawal N (body)guard, sentry ← **kawal**

pengecut N coward ← **kecut**

pengelolaan N management ← **kelola**

pengemudi N driver ← **kemudi**

péngén, pingin, kepéngén, kepingin V, COLL to really want to

143

pengeras ~ *suara* loudspeaker ← **keras**

pengertian N understanding ← **erti, arti**

pengetahuan N knowledge ← **tahu**

penggalian N digging ← **gali**

pengganti N replacement, substitute, successor ← **ganti**

penggaris N ruler ← **garis**

penggemar N fan, enthusiast ← **gemar**

penggoréngan N wok, frying pan; process of frying ← **goréng**

pengguna N user ← **guna**

penghargaan N appreciation, award ← **harga**

penghasil N producer ← **hasil**

penghinaan N insult, libel (written), slander (spoken) ← **hina**

penghuni N occupant, resident ← **huni**

pengimpor N importer ← **impor**

penginapan N accommodation, hotel ← **inap**

pengirim N sender; **pengiriman** N dispatch, forwarding ← **kirim**

pengkhianat N traitor ← **khianat**

pengobatan N treatment ← **obat**

pengolahan V processing ← **olah**

penguji N examiner ← **uji**

pengukuran N measuring, measurement ← **ukur**

pengumuman N notice, announcement ← **umur**

pengunduran N postponement, delay ← **undur**

pengungsi N refugee, evacuee; **pengungsian** N evacuation ← **ungsi**

pengurus N manager, organizer ← **urus**

pengusaha N, M businessman; F businesswoman ← **usaha**

penindasan N oppression ← **tindas**

pening ADJ dizzy

peningkatan N rise, increase ← **tingkat**

peninjau N observer ← **tinjau**

penipu N con man, trickster; **penipuan** N deception ← **tipu**

peniti N safety-pin; brooch

penitipan N care ← **titip**

penjahat N criminal

penjajah N colonizer, ruler, colonial power ← **jajah**

penjara N prison, jail; **memenjara(kan)** v to put in prison, imprison

penjelasan N explanation ← **jelas**

penjual N seller, dealer; **penjualan** N sale, sales ← **jual**

penolakan N refusal, rejection ← **tolak**

penonton N spectator, audience ← **tonton**

pénsil N pencil

pénsiun pension, retired; **pénsiunan** N pensioner **meménsiunkan** v to pension off

pentas stage; **pementasan** N staging, production

péntil N valve

penting ADJ important; **kepentingan** N importance, interest

pentol: pentolan N boss, big shot

penuh ADJ full; **memenuhi** v to fulfill, meet requirements; **sepenuhnya** ADV fully, completely; **terpenuhi** ADJ satisfied, fulfilled

penulis N author, writer ← **tulis**

penumpang N passenger ← **tumpang**

penutup N stopper, lid; end ← **tutup**

penutur N speaker ← **tutur**

penyair N poet ← **syair**

penyakit N disease, illness, complaint ← **sakit**

penyanyi N singer, vocalist ← **nyanyi**

penyebab N cause ← **sebab**

penyeberangan N crossing ← **seberang**

penyelam N diver ← **selam**

penyelamatan N rescue (operation) ← **selamat**

penyelenggara N organizer ← **selenggara**

penyelesaian N solution, settlement ← **selesai**

penyelidik N investigator, detective; **penyelidikan** N investigation ← **selidik**

penyerahan N handing over, handover ← **serah**

penyiar N announcer ← **siar**

penyidikan N investigation ← **selidik**, **sidik**

penyihir N wizard, witch, sorcerer ← **sihir**

pényok, péyot, péot ADJ dented

penyu N turtle

penyulap N magician, conjurer ← **sulap**

penyulihan ~ *suara* dubber

penyunting N editor ← **sunting**

penyusun N compiler, author ← **susun**

pepatah N proverb, saying

pepaya, papaya N pawpaw, papaya

peperangan N battle ← **perang**

pépés method of cooking by steaming or roasting in banana leaves

pér N spring

perabot N tools; **perabotan** N furnishings

peraga N visual aid; **peragawati** N, F model

perahu N (sail) boat

perajin N craftsman, artisan ← **rajin**

pérak N silver; silver coin; *seratus* ~ one hundred rupiah

perakitan N assembly ← **rakit**

peralatan N equipment ← **alat**

perampok N robber; **peram-**

pokan N robbery ← **rampok**

peran N part, role; **berperan** v to play the role or part; **memerankan** v to portray, play the role of; **pemeran** N actor, actress

peranakan ADJ of mixed Chinese and Indonesian blood, Straits Chinese ← **anak**

perancang N designer, planner ← **rancang**

Perancis, Prancis N France

perang N war; ~ *Dunia Kedua* World War II; ~ **perang-perangan** N war games; paintball; **berperang** v to wage war, go to war; **peperangan** N battle

perangkap N trap; **terperang-kap** ADJ trapped, caught

perangko, prangko N (postage) stamp

perang-perangan N war games; paintball ← **perang**

perantara N broker, intermediary, go-between ← **antara**

peranti, piranti N apparatus, equipment; ~ *lunak* software

perapian N fireplace, oven ← **api**

peras, memeras v to press,

squeeze; to blackmail, extort

perasaan N feeling ← **rasa**

peraturan N rule, regulation ← **atur**

perawan N virgin

perawat N nurse, sister; **perawatan** treatment; maintenance, upkeep ← **rawat**

perayaan N celebration ← **raya**

perbaikan N repair, improvement ← **baik**

perban N bandage, dressing; **diperban** V to be bandaged

perbandingan N comparison, ratio ← **banding**

perbankan ADJ banking

perbatasan N border, frontier ← **batas**

perbédaan N difference ← **béda**

perbelanjaan *pusat* ~ shopping center, mall ← **belanja**

perbuatan N act, deed ← **buat**

percakapan N conversation ← **cakap**

percaya trust, believe; **kepercayaan** N belief, faith; **memercayai** V to trust someone; **memercayakan** V to entrust with; **terpercaya** ADJ trusted, reliable

perceraian N divorce ← **cerai**

percobaan N experiment, test ← **coba**

percuma in vain

perdagangan N commerce, trade ← **dagang**

perdamaian N peace, reconciliation ← **damai**

perdana ADJ first, starter; ~ *Menteri* Prime Minister

perdebatan N debate, discussion ← **debat**

perekat N glue, adhesive → **rekat**

perempat N quarter; **perempatan** N crossroads, intersection ← **empat**

perempuan N woman, female

perenang N swimmer ← **renang**

peresmian N formal ceremony, inauguration ← **resmi**

pergaulan N mixing, social intercourse; association ← **gaul**

pergelangan ~ *kaki* ankle; ~ *tangan* wrist ← **gelang**

pergi go, leave; **bepergian** V to travel, be away; **kepergian** N departure

perguruan ~ *tinggi* university ← **guru**

perhatian N attention ← **hati**

perhiasan N jewelery ← **hias**

perhitungan N calculation ← **hitung**

perhotélan N hotel studies, hospitality ← **hotél**

perhubungan N communications, connection ← **hubung**

peri- PREF concerning; **perihal** N subject; CONJ about, concerning

peri N fairy godmother

perih, pedih smart, sting

perihal N subject; CONJ about, concerning

perikanan N fisheries ← **ikan**

periksa investigate, check; **memeriksa** V to examine or investigate; **pemeriksa** N examiner; **pemeriksaan** N examination, investigation

perincian N details, detailed explanation ← **rinci**

perintah order, command; **pemerintah** N government

perintis N pioneer ← **rintis**

perisai N shield

peristiwa N incident, occurrence, happening

periuk N cooking pot

perjalanan N journey, trip ← **jalan**

perjanjian N agreement, contract ← **janji**

perjuangan N battle, fight, struggle ← **juang**

perkakas N tool, instrument

perkantoran N office block ← **kantor**

perkapalan N shipping ← **kapal**

perkara N matter, case, affair

perkasa ADJ powerful; manly, virile

perkawinan N marriage, wedding ← **kawin**

perkedél N (potato) patty, croquette; ~ *jagung* corn patty

perkémahan N camping, camp ← **kémah**

perkembangan N development ← **kembang**

perkenalan N introduction ← **kenal**

perkiraan N estimate, guess ← **kira**

perkosa: memerkosa V to rape, violate; **perkosaan** N rape

perkotaan N metropolitan area ← **kota**

perkumpulan N association, club; assembly ← **kumpul**

perkutut *burung* ~ turtledove

perlahan, pelan, perlahan-lahan, pelan-pelan ADV slowly, softly

perlawanan N opposition, resistance ← **lawan**

perlengkapan N outfit, equipment ← **lengkap**

perlindungan N protection ← **lindung**

perlu need, necessary; **keperluan** N needs, requirements; **memerlukan** v to need, require

permadani N carpet

permainan N game, match ← **main**

permak, vermak alteration to clothes; **dipermak** ADJ altered, shortened

permén N sweet, lolly, candy

permintaan N request; *atas* ~ by request ← **minta**

perminyakan N oil and gas ← **minyak**

permisi excuse me

permohonan N request, application ← **mohon**

permukaan N surface ← **muka**

permukiman N housing, residential area ← **mukim**

pernafasan, pernapasan N breathing, respiration ← **nafas**

pernah ADV ever; once; have + past perfect form of verb; ~ *makan bebek?* Have you ever eaten duck?

pernikahan N wedding ← **nikah**

pernis N varnish

pernyataan N statement, declaration ← **nyata**

peroléhan N acquisition ← **oléh**

perompak N pirate ← **rompak**

péron N platform

perona ~ *mata* eyeshadow; ~ *pipi* rouge ← **rona**

perosotan N (children's) slide ← **rosot**

perpisahan N parting, fare-well ← **pisah**

perpustakaan N library ← **pustaka**

pérs N press, media

persaingan N competition ← **saing**

149

persalinan N childbirth ← **salin**

persamaan N similarity, likeness, resemblance; equation ← **sama**

persatuan N union, association ← **satu**

persediaan N stock, supply ← **sedia**

persegi ADJ square; sided → **segi**

perselingkuhan N affair ← **selingkuh**

persembunyian N hiding place, hideout ← **sembunyi**

persén N percent; *seratus ~* one hundred percent; **persénan** N tip; **perséntase, proséntase** N percentage

perserikatan N federation ← **serikat**

perséro ADJ proprietary limited (Pty Ltd) ← **séro**

persetujuan N agreement, approval ← **tuju, setuju**

persiapan N preparations ← **siap**

persimpangan N intersection ← **simpang**

persis ADV exactly

persoalan N problem, issue, matter ← **soal**

personalia, personél ADJ personnel, staff

pertahanan N defense

pertama ADJ first; **pertama-tama** ADV first of all

pertambahan N increase ← **tambah**

pertambangan N mining ← **tambang**

Pertamina N state-run national oil and gas company

pertandingan N contest, competition, match ← **tanding**

pertanian N agriculture ← **tani**

pertanyaan N question ← **tanya**

pertempuran N battle ← **tempur**

pertemuan N meeting ← **temu**

pertengkaran N quarrel ← **tengkar**

pertigaan N T-junction ← **tiga**

pertimbangan N consideration ← **timbang**

pertokoan N shopping center or complex, mall ← **toko**

pertolongan N help,

assistance, aid ← **tolong**

pertukaran N exchange ← **tukar**

pertumbuhan N growth, development ← **tumbuh**

pertunangan N engagement ← **tunang**

pertunjukan N show, performance ← **tunjuk**

perubahan N change, alteration ← **ubah**

perumahan N housing (complex) ← **rumah**

perundingan N discussion ← **runding**

perunggu N bronze

perusahaan N company ← **usaha**

perut N stomach, belly

perwakilan N representation, delegation ← **wakil**

perwira N officer

pesan message, instruction, order; **pesanan** N order; **memesan** v to order; **pemesanan** N order, request

pesantrén N Islamic boarding school → **santri**

pesat ADJ fast, rapid

pesawat N machine; ~ *(terbang)* aeroplane, airplane

pésék ADJ flat-nosed

peserta N participant ← **serta**

pesiar N trip, cruise; *kapal* ~ cruise ship, pleasure craft

pesindén N, F singer accompanying a gamelan orchestra

pesing *bau* ~ stink of urine

pesisir N coast

pésta N party, celebration; ~ *perkawinan*, ~ *pernikahan* wedding reception; **berpésta** v to (have a) party

pesuruh N messenger, errand boy ← **suruh**

peta N map, chart; ~ *dunia* world map; *buku* ~ atlas; *buku* ~ *jalan* road atlas, street directory

petani N farmer ← **tani**

petas: petasan N firecracker, fireworks

peté, petai N stinkbean

peténis N tennis player ← **ténis**

peternakan N cattle farm, ranch ← **ternak**

peti N chest, case, box; ~ *es* ice-box

petik pluck; **petikan** N extract, quotation; **memetik** v to pick; to strum

petinju N boxer ← **tinju**

petir N thunder, lightning

petis *tahu* ~ fried tofu with a spicy sauce

pétromaks *lampu* ~ kerosene lantern

petunjuk N instruction, direction ← **tunjuk**

pewarna N dye, stain ← **warna**

péyot, péot, pényok ADJ dented

piala N trophy, cup

piano N piano; **pianis** N pianist

picu N trigger; **memicu** v to trigger, set off; **pemicu** N trigger

pidato N speech, address; **berpidato** v to make a speech, give an address

pigura N picture frame

pihak N party; side; **berpihak, sepihak** ADJ unilateral

pijak: pijakan N foothold, something to stand on

pijar *lampu* ~ light bulb

pijat, pijit massage; **memijat** v to massage

pikir, fikir v to think; **pikiran** N thought, idea; **berpikir** v to think; **memikirkan** v to think about; **pemikir** N thinker; **pemikiran** N thinking, consideration

piknik N picnic

pikun ADJ senile, dotty

pil N (contraceptive) pill, tablet

pilek sniffle, have a cold or runny nose

pilem → **film**

pilih choose; **pilihan** N choice, selection; ADJ select; **memilih** v to choose or select; to elect or vote (for); **pemilihan** N election; ~ *umum (pemilu)* general election

pimpin, memimpin v to lead; **pemimpin** N leader

pincang ADJ crippled, lame

pindah move; change; **berpindah** v to move; **memindahkan** v to move, transfer; **pemindahan** N transfer, shifting, removal

pinggang N waist

pinggir N edge, border; **pinggiran** N edges, outskirts; **minggir** V, COLL to move to the side, pull over; **terpinggirkan** ADJ cast aside, marginalized

pingpong N table tennis,

pingpong; **dipingpong** v
to be sent here and there,
messed about
pingsan faint, collapse;
unconscious
pinisi, phinisi *kapal* ~
Buginese cargo boat
pinjam borrow; **pinjaman**
N loan; **meminjam** v to
borrow; **meminjami** v to lend
someone; **meminjamkan** v to
lend something
pinsét N tweezers
pinta: (me)minta v to
request, ask for; **(me-)
minta-minta** v to beg, ask
for money; **permintaan** N
request; *atas* ~ by request
pintar ADJ pinter COLL clever
pintu N door, gate; ~ *darurat*
emergency exit; ~ *keluar*
exit; ~ *masuk* entrance
pipa N pipe, tube
pipi N cheek
pipis N, CH wee, pee, go to
the toilet
pirang ADJ, M blond, F blonde,
fair-haired
piranti, peranti N apparatus,
equipment; ~ *lunak* software
piring N plate, dish; *mencuci* ~

to wash the dishes; **piringan**
N plate-shaped object
pirsa: pemirsa N television
audience, viewer
pisah separate, split; ~ *ranjang* separate (of a couple);
berpisah v to part, separate;
memisahkan v to separate
something; **perpisahan** N
parting, farewell; **terpisah**
ADJ separated
pisang N banana
pisau N knife
pita N ribbon
piton N *(ular)* ~ python
piyama N pyjamas, pajamas
plafon N ceiling
plagiat N plagiarism; **plagiator**
N someone who copies or
commits plagiarism
plakat N placard, poster
plastik ADJ plastic; N plastic
bag, carrier bag
platina N platinum
pléster N sticking plaster,
bandaid
plong ADJ relieved
PLTA ABBREV *Pembangkit Listrik
Tenaga Air* hydro-electric
power station
pluit → **peluit**

plus ADJ plus, added; *kacamata* ~ long-sighted glasses

PMI ABBREV *Palang Merah Indonesia* Indonesian Red Cross

PNG ABBREV *Papua Nugini* Papua New Guinea

poci N teapot

poco-poco N line dance from North Sulawesi

pohon N tree

poin N point, mark

pojok N corner; **pojokan** N, SL corner

pokok main; ~*nya* basically, the main thing is; *gaji* ~ base salary

pola N pattern

Polandia N Poland

Polda N Regional Police ← **Polisi Daérah**

polés polish

poligami N polygamy

poliklinik, poli N polyclinic, doctor's surgery; ~ *umum* GP's surgery, doctor's surgery

polisi N police; ~ *wanita (polwan)* policewoman; *kantor* ~ police station

politik N politics; **politikus** N **politisi** PL politician; **politis**

ADJ political

polos ADJ plain, unpretentious; smooth; *baju* ~ plain shirt

Polri N Indonesian police force

polsék N local police station ← **polisi séktor**

polusi N pollution; ~ *udara* air pollution

Polwan N policewoman ← **polisi wanita**

pompa pump; ~ *bensin* petrol station, gasoline pump, service station; **memompa** V to pump

pon N pound

pondok N hut, cottage; **mondok** V, COLL to board, lodge, stay

poni N fringe, bangs

popok N napkin, diaper

populér ADJ popular; **popularitas** N popularity

porno ADJ pornographic; **pornoaksi** N pornographic actions; **pornografi** N pornography

porsi N serve, portion

portal N iron gateway into a building complex; barrier blocking access into a complex; **diportal** V to be

154

blocked by a barrier, have a barrier lowered

Portugal, Portugis N Portugal

pos N post; ~ *penjagaan*, ~ *satpam* security post; ~ *udara* airmail

pose N pose (for a photograph); **berpose** v to pose for a photograph

posisi N position

positif ADJ positive; *berpikir* ~ to think positive

posko N post (for a political party or fund-raising effort) ← **pos koordinasi**

posyandu N all-in-one government administrative office ← **pos pelayanan terpadu**

pot N pot, vase; ~ *bunga* vase (indoors), flowerpot (outdoors)

potong piece, cut; ~ *rambut* cut your hair, get your hair cut; hairdresser, barber (for men); **potongan** N discount, reduction; cut (of clothes); **memotong** v to cut, deduct; to slaughter, amputate; to interrupt; **terpotong** ADJ cut (off)

potrét N portrait; photograph of a person; **memotrét** v to photograph

PP ABBREV *pulang pergi* there and back, shown on public transport

PR ABBREV *pekerjaan rumah* homework

pra- PREF pre-, before; ~*sangka* prejudice

prajurit N soldier

prakték, praktik N practice; practical; **mempraktékkan** v to put into practice; **praktis** ADJ practical

pramugara N, M steward; cabin crew; **pramugari** N, F stewardess, air hostess; cabin crew

Pramuka N Scouts

prapatan, perapatan N, COLL crossroads, intersection

prasangka N prejudice

prasmanan ADJ buffet-style

préman N thug

préséntasi N (oral) presentation

présiden N president

préstasi N performance, achievement; **berpréstasi** ADJ prestigious; successful

pria N male, man

pribadi N self, individual, personality; **kepribadian** N personality

pribumi N **pri** COLL native inhabitant, indigenous Indonesian; **non-pri** COLL ethnic Chinese

prihatin concerned, worried; **memprihatinkan** ADJ worrying

prinsip N principle

prioritas N priority; **memprioritaskan** V to prioritize

priyayi N upper class, esp in colonial era

problém, problim N problem

produk N product; **produksi** N production; **memproduksi** V to produce

profési N profession; **profésional** ADJ professional

profil N profile, outline

proklamasi N proclamation (of independence)

promosi N promotion; **mempromosikan** V to promote

propinsi N province

prosédur N procedure; **prosédural** ADJ procedural

prosés N process; court case; **mmemproséskan** V to process

protés N protest; **memprotés** V to (make a) protest

Protéstan N Protestant → **Kristen**

provokasi N provocation; **provokator** N trouble-maker, provocateur

proyék N project, scheme

psikiater N [sikiater] psychiatrist → **jiwa**

psikolog [sikolog] N psychologist; **psikologi** N psychology → **jiwa**

puas ADJ satisfied, content; **memuaskan** ADJ satisfactory

puber N puberty

pucat ADJ pale; ADJ, COLL scared

pucuk N shoot, sprout

pudar faded, washed-out; **memudar** V to fade

puding N pudding, dessert

pugar: pemugaran N restoration, renovation

puing N ruins; rubble

puisi N poetry (esp Western); **puitis** ADJ poetic

puja worship; **pujaan** N something worshipped or idolized; **memuja** V to

worship

pujaséra N food court, collection of food stalls ← **pusat jajan serba rasa**

puji praise; **pujian** N praise; **memuji** v to praise; **terpuji** ADJ highly-praised

pukul strike; FORM hour; ~ *tiga belas* 1 pm; **pukulan** N strike, beat, hit; **memukul** v to hit, beat, strike; **terpukul** ADJ hard-hit

pula ADV also, too; again

pulang v to go home, return; ~ *hari* to return on the same day, not stay overnight; ~ *pergi (PP)* there and back, both ways; **memulangkan** v to give back; to send back, repatriate

pulau N island; ~ *Seribu* the Thousand Islands; **kepulauan** N archipelago, chain

pulih recovered

pulpén N fountain pen

pulsa N credit (for a telephone)

puluh *dua* ~ twenty; **puluhan** N dozens; *tahun delapan* ~ the eighties; **sepuluh** N ten

pun emphasizing particle; too, also; even; then

punah ADJ extinct

puncak N peak, summit, top

pundak N shoulder

pundi piggybank, purse

punggung N back

pungut pick up (off ground); **memungut** v to pick up, collect

puntung ~ *rokok* cigarette butt

punya have, own; *yang* ~ the owner; **kepunyaan** N possession, belonging; **mempunyai** v to have, own, possess

pupuk N fertilizer

pura N Balinese or Hindu temple

pura-pura pretend, fake

purba ADJ ancient; **purbakala** N ancient times

puri N palace, castle

purna- PREF post-, after

pus N, COLL pussycat

pusaka N heirloom, inheritance

pusar N navel, belly button; **pusaran** N vortex; ~ *angin* whirlwind; **berpusar** v to revolve, whirl

pusat N center; **berpusat** ~ *pada* to focus or center on;

memusatkan v to focus

pusing ADJ dizzy; ~ *kepala* headache

puskésmas N clinic, public health center ← **pusat keséhatan masyarakat**

pustaka N, LIT book; *daftar* ~ list of references; **perpustakaan** N library; **pustakawan** N librarian

putar turn around, rotate; **putaran** N round, revolution; **berputar** v to rotate, turn; **memutar** v to wind; to rotate; **seputar** ADJ around, about

putih ADJ white; ~ *telur* albumen, egg white; *merah* ~ red and white; **keputihan** N thrush, vaginal itching (white discharge); **memutihkan** v to whiten, bleach; **pemutih** N bleach

puting N nipple

putra, putera N, POL son; ~ *mahkota* crown prince; ~*-putri* children, sons and daughters

putri, puteri N, POL daughter

putus broken off; ~ *asa* give up hope; **keputusan** N

decision, decree; **memutus** v to break; **memutuskan** v to terminate or break; to decide; **terputus** ADJ cut off; **terputus-putus** v to keep cutting out

puyuh *burung* ~ quail

puyung hai → **fuyung hai**

Q

Quran *al-*~ the Koran

R

raba: meraba v to feel or grope something

Rabu, Rebo *hari* ~ Wednesday

rabun ADJ blurry; ~ *jauh* shortsighted

racik: racikan N blend, concoction; prescription

racun N poison (not from animals); **beracun** ADJ poisonous, containing poison; **keracunan** ADJ poisoned; **meracuni** v to poison

rada ADV, COLL quite, rather

radang ADJ inflamed;
meradang V to become
inflamed

radio N radio; ~ *Republik
Indonesia (RRI)* Indonesian
state radio

rafia *tali* ~ plastic twine

raga N body; **peraga** N visual
aid; **peragawati** N, F model

ragam N manner, way; kind;
beragam ADJ various; **seragam** N uniform

ragu doubt, doubtful; **ragu-
ragu** ADJ doubtful, unsure;
keragu(-ragu)an N doubt,
uncertainty; **meragukan** V to
doubt something

rahang N jaw

rahasia N secret, mystery;
merahasiakan V to keep
secret

rahim N uterus, womb

raib vanished, disappeared

raja N king; **kerajaan** N
kingdom

rajaléla: merajaléla V to be
out of control; to act
violently

rajin ADJ diligent, hard-
working, industrious; **kera-**

jinan N crafts; **perajin** N
craftsman, artisan

rajungan N kind of small
edible crab

rajut: rajutan N knitting,
crochet work; **merajut** V to
knit; to crochet

rak N shelf; ~ *buku* bookshelf

rakét N racquet, racket

rakit N raft; **merakit** V to
assemble; **perakitan** N
assembly

raksasa giant

rakus ADJ greedy

rakyat N people

ralat N correction, errata;
meralat V to correct a
mistake

Ramadan Muslim fasting
month

ramah ADJ friendly; **keramahan** N friendliness

ramai, ramé ADJ busy, lively;
crowded; **ramai-ramai** ADV in
a group, together; **keramaian**
N noise, din; lively atmosphere; **meramaikan** V to
liven up, enliven

ramal: ramalan N prediction,
prophecy, forecast; **meramal**
V to tell fortunes; **meramal-**

159

kan v to predict, foretell

rambut N hair; **rambutan** N rambutan, fruit with hairy red skin; **berambut** ADJ hairy; v to have hair

ramé → **ramai**

rami N hemp, jute

ramping ADJ slender

rampok, merampok v to rob, hold up; **perampok** N robber; **perampokan** N robbery

ramu: ramuan N mixture

rancang: rancangan N plan, design; **merancang** v to plan, design; **perancang** N designer, planner

rangka N skeleton, framework ← **kerangka**

rangkai: rangkaian N combination, series

rangkak: merangkak v to crawl

rangkap multiple; *tiga* ~ three copies, in triplicate

ranjang N bed

ranjau N mine

ransel N backpack

rantai N chain; **merantai** v to chain up

rantau N abroad, across the sea

rapat ADJ close to; tight

rapat meeting, meet

rapi N neat, tidy, organized

rapot, rapor N (school) report

ras N breed; pure-bred

rasa N feel, feeling; sense; taste; ~*nya* it appears, it seems; **kerasan** COLL feel at home; **merasa** v to think, feel; **merasakan** v to feel something; **perasaan** N feeling; **terasa** v to be felt

rata ADJ flat, even, level; **rata-rata** ADV equally; on average; **meratakan** v to level, flatten

ratu N queen

ratus *dua* ~ two hundred; **seratus** ADJ one hundred, a hundred

raut: rautan ~ *pensil* pencil sharpener

rawa N swamp, marsh

rawan ADJ vulnerable, troubled, unsafe

rawat: merawat v to nurse, care for; to maintain, look after; **perawat** N nurse, sister; **perawatan** N treatment; maintenance, upkeep

rawon N black meat soup from East Java

raya ADJ great, greater; *hari ~* holiday, feast day; Idul Fitri: *Indonesia ~* the national anthem; **merayakan** v to celebrate; **perayaan** N celebration

rayap N termite, white ant; *kena ~, dimakan ~* eaten by termites; **merayap** v to crawl, creep

rayu: merayu v to tempt, flatter, seduce

razia N raid, spot-check

réaksi N reaction; **beréaksi** v to react

rebab N two-stringed musical instrument

rebana N tambourine

rebus v boil, boiled; **merebus** v to boil in water

rebut, merebut v to snatch, capture; **rebutan** v fighting for something; **berebut** v to fight for; **berebutan** v to fight each other for; **merebutkan** v to snatch something

redaksi N editors, editorial staff; **redaktur** N editor

redup dim, go out

réformasi N reform (esp after 1998); **réformis** ADJ reformist, pro-reform

rejeki, rezeki, rizki N fortune, luck; livelihood, living

rekam: rekaman N recording; **merekam** v to record

rekan N colleague, partner, associate; **rekanan** N regular service provider

rekat: perekat N glue, adhesive

rékayasa N engineering

rékening N (bank) account

réklamasi N reclamation

rékoméndasi N recommendation

rékor N record; *~ dunia* world record

rékréasi N recreation, relaxing, fun

rekrut recruit; **merekrut** v to recruit

réktor N vice-chancellor, rector; **réktorat** N vice-chancellor's office

rél N rail; *~ kereta api* railway line, railroad, train tracks

réla, réd(h)a, ridha, ridho willing; **relawan** N volunteer

rélatif ADJ relative

rém N brake; **mengerém** v to brake

remaja N teen, adolescent, young single person, youth

rématik N rheumatism

rembes: merembes V to seep in, leak, ooze

réméh ADJ small, unimportant, trifling; **meréméhkan** V to belittle, treat as unimportant

rempah N spice; **rempah-rempah** N spices

rempéyék, péyék N peanut crisps

renang swimming; **berenang** V to swim; **perenang** N swimmer

rencana N plan, program, draft; **berencana** V to plan; **merencanakan** V to plan

rénda N lace

rendah ADJ low, humble; ~ *hati* humble; **merendahkan** V to lower; to humiliate; **terendah** ADJ lowest

rendam soak; **terendam** ADJ inundated, flooded, soaked

rendang N meat cooked in coconut milk

réngék: meréngék V to whimper, whine

renggut: merenggut V to snatch, tug

renta ADJ worn

rentak: serentak ADJ all at once, simultaneous, at the same time

rentan ADJ susceptible

renung: renungan N reflection, musing, contemplation; **merenung** V to daydream

renyah ADJ crisp, crispy

réog N trance dance, most famously in Ponorogo, East Java

réparasi N repair(s) ← **baik**

répot very busy; bothered; **répot-répot** V to go to great trouble; **merépotkan** V to make someone busy or go to some trouble

reruntuhan, runtuhan N ruins → **runtuh**

resah ADJ restless

resap: meresap V to be absorbed; to penetrate, seep into

résénsi, risénsi N review

resép N recipe; prescription; **meresépkan** V to write a prescription for a drug

resépsi N reception; ~ *perkawinan*, ~ *pernikah-*

162

an wedding reception;
resépsionis N receptionist

resérse N detective, forensic

resik ADJ clean

resmi ADJ official, formal;
meresmikan V to formalize,
make official; **peresmian** N
formal opening, inauguration

résto N up-market restaurant

réstoran N restaurant

réstorasi N restoration

restu N blessing; **merestui**
V to agree to, give your
blessing to

retak ADJ cracked; **retakan** N
crack, fissure

réuni N (school) reunion

révolusi N revolution

réwél ADJ fussy, troublesome,
difficult

RI ABBREV *Republik Indonesia*
Republic of Indonesia

riam N (river) rapids

rias *meja* ~ dressing table;
riasan N make-up

ribu N thousand; *sepuluh* ~ ten
thousand; **beribu(-ribu)** ADJ
thousands of; **seribu** ADJ one
thousand, a thousand

ribut noise; noisy

ricuh ADJ chaotic, out of

control; **kericuhan** N chaos

rilék, riléks, rélaks relax,
relaxed

rimba N jungle, forest

rinci detail; **rincian** N details;
perincian N details, detailed
explanation

rindang ADJ leafy, shady

rinding: merinding V to have
goose-bumps or an eerie
feeling, be spooked

rindu longing; **kerinduan** N
longing, craving; **merindukan** V to miss, long for

ring N (boxing) ring

ringan ADJ light, easy

ringgit N ringgit, Malaysian
currency (100 cents)

ringkas: ringkasan N summary, synopsis

rintang: rintangan N obstacle; barricade

rintis: perintis N pioneer

risau ADJ uneasy, anxious

risét N research

risih, risi, résé feel uncomfortable

risik: berisik ADJ noisy, loud;
V to rustle

risiko N risk; **berisiko** ADJ risky

risték N research and technol-

163

ogy ← **risét dan téknologi**

riwayat N story, tale

robah, rubah → ubah

robék ADJ torn (of cloth), holey; **merobék** V to tear up, shred

roboh, rubuh collapse; **merobohkan** V to knock down, demolish

roda N wheel; **beroda** ADJ wheeled

rogoh: merogoh V to grope around, search for (inside something else)

roh N spirit, ghost; **rohani** ADJ spiritual, religious

rok N skirt; dress; ~ *mini* miniskirt

rokok N cigarette; **merokok** V to smoke

romansa N romance; **romantik** ADJ romantic

Romawi, Rumawi ADJ Roman; *huruf* ~ Roman letters or numerals

rombak: merombak V to pull down, demolish; to reorganize

rombong: rombongan N group, party

romo, Romo N, PRON, CATH (Catholic) priest, Father

rompak: perompak N pirate

rompi N waistcoat, vest

rona N color, shade; **perona** ~ *mata* eyeshadow; ~ *pipi* rouge

ronda patrol; ~ *malam* night watch, night patrol

rondé *wedang* ~ Javanese warm drink

rongga N cavity, hollow, hole

rongkong → kerongkongan

ronsen → rontgen

ronta: meronta(-ronta) V to struggle, squirm to get loose

rontak → berontak

rontgen [ronsen], **ronsen** N x-ray; **dironsen** V to be x-rayed

rontok fall out, shed

rosot: merosot V to fall down, descend, plummet; **perosotan** N (children's) slide

rotan N rattan

roti N bread, bun; ~ *gandum* (brown or wholemeal) bread

Rp. *rupiah* rupiah, Indonesian currency

RRC ABBREV *Republik Rakyat Cina* People's Republic of China

164

RS ABBREV *rumah sakit* hospital

RT/RW ABBREV *Rukun Tetang--ga/Rukun Warga* neighborhood association/citizens' association

ruang N space, room; ~ *makan* dining room; **ruangan** N room; hall

ruas N space between joints

rubuh collapse, fall down ← **roboh**

rudal N guided missile ← **peluru kendali**

rugi loss, lose out; **kerugian** N loss; damage; **merugikan** V to hurt, harm, injure

rujak N fruit salad with spicy sauce

rujuk: rujukan N reference

rukan N office with a dwelling upstairs, shophouse ← **rumah kantor**

ruko N shophouse ← **rumah toko**

rukun ADJ harmonious

rukun N pillar, principle

rumah N house; ~ *makan* restaurant; ~ *sakit* hospital; *di* ~ at home; ~ *tangga* household, family; **perumahan** N housing

(complex)

rumpun: serumpun ADJ related, of one family; *bahasa* ~ languages related to Indonesian

rumput N grass, lawn

rumus N formula

runcing ADJ sharp, pointed; *bambu* ~ bamboo spear

runding: perundingan N discussion

runtuh fall down, collapse; **runtuhan, reruntuhan** N ruins; **meruntuhkan** V to overthrow

rupa shape, appearance, look; ~*nya* it seems, appears; **rupa-rupa** ADJ all kinds of; **berupa** ADJ in the shape or form of; **merupakan** V to be; to form, constitute; **serupa** ADJ similar

rupiah N rupiah, Indonesian currency

rusa N deer

rusak ADJ broken, damaged, destroyed, spoilt; ~ *parah* badly damaged; **kerusakan** N damage; **merusak** V to spoil, damage; **merusakkan** V to destroy, break

Rusia N Russia; *bahasa ~, orang ~* Russian

rusuh restless, disturbed; **kerusuhan** N riot, disturbance

rute N route

ruwet ADJ complicated

S

saat N moment, time

sabar ADJ patient; **bersabar** V to be patient; **kesabaran** N patience

sabit N sickle

sablon N screen-printed cloth banner; screen-printing

Sabtu *hari ~* Saturday

sabuk N belt, sash

sabun N soap; *~ cuci piring* dishwashing liquid

sabung *~ ayam* cock fighting

sabut *~ kelapa* coconut fiber

sadar conscious, aware; **kesadaran** N consciousness, awareness; **menyadari** V to realize, be aware of

sado N two-wheeled horse carriage

safir *batu ~* sapphire

sagu N sago

sahabat N friend; **bersahabat** ADJ to be friends

saham N share

sahur, saur N, ISL meal before dawn during fasting month

sahut, menyahut V to answer, reply, respond

saing: bersaing V to compete; *harga ~* competitive price; **persingan** N competition

saja, aja ADV only, just; -ever; *itu ~* just that ← **sahaja**

sajadah, sejadah N, ISL prayer mat or rug

sajak N rhyme; poem

saji serve; **sajian** N dish; offering; **sesajén** N ritual offering; **menyajikan** V to serve, present, offer; **penyajian** N presentation

Saka *Tahun ~* Balinese calendar

saking CONJ, COLL all because of, due to, as a result of

sakit sick, ill; pain, ache; *~ perut* stomach ache, upset stomach; *~~sakitan* often ill, frequently unwell; **kesakitan** ADJ in pain; **menyakiti** V to hurt, treat badly; **menyakit-kan** ADJ painful; **penyakit** N disease, illness, complaint

sakral ADJ holy, sacred

saksi witness; **kesaksian** N evidence, testimony; **menyaksikan** v to witness

sakti ADJ magically or supernaturally powerful

saku N pocket

salah ADJ wrong, mistaken, faulty; ~ *satu* one of; **ber-salah** ADJ guilty; **kesalahan** N mistake

salak *buah* ~ fruit with a hard brown skin like a snake, snakefruit

salam peace; ~ *alaikum* ISL peace be upon you; ~ *hormat* respectfully yours, yours sincerely; ~ *saya* best wishes, regards; **menyalami** v to greet

saldo N balance; ~ *terakhir* current balance

saléh → soléh

salep N ointment, cream

salib N cross

salin copy, duplicate; *baju* ~ change of clothes, spare clothes; **salinan** N

copy; **bersalin** v to give birth; **menyalin** v to copy; **persalinan** N childbirth

saling PRON each other, mutual; ~ *mencintai* to love each other

salip, menyalip v overtake, slip past

salju N snow; **bersalju** ADJ snowy, snow-covered

salon N beauty salon, hairdresser's

salto N somersault

salur: saluran N channel

salut v, COLL to admire, salute

sama ADJ, ADV same, both; ~ *sekali* NEG completely; **sama-sama** you're welcome; ADV both, equally; **bersama** ADV together; jointly; **persamaan** N similarity, likeness, resemblance; equation; **sesama** ADJ fellow, another

sama-sama you're welcome; ADV both, equally ← **sama**

sambal, sambel N chilli sauce

sambil v, AUX while, at the same time; ~ *lalu* in passing

sambung connect; **sambung-menyambung** ADJ continuously; **sambungan** N con-

167

nection; **bersambung** ADJ in parts; to be continued; **menyambung** v to join, continue; **menyambungkan** v to connect to (something else); **tersambung** ADJ connected

sambut welcome; **sambutan** N reception, welcome; **bersambut, menyambut** v to welcome or receive

sampah N rubbish, garbage, trash, waste; *tempat* ~ rubbish bin, garbage can, trashcan; *tukang* ~ garbage man

sampai, sampé arrive, reach; until; ~ *jumpa,* ~ *nanti* see you later; **kesampaian** ADJ achieved, reached, realized; **menyampaikan** v to deliver, hand over, pass on

samping N side; *di* ~ next to, beside(s); **sampingan** N side-job, extra work; **bersampingan** ADJ next to each other

sampo N shampoo; ~ *anti-ketombe* anti-dandruff shampoo

sampul N cover, folder, envelope

samudera, samudra N ocean; ~ *Hindia,* ~ *Indonesia* Indian Ocean

sana ADV yonder, over there (far from speaker and listener); *di* ~ over there (far from both speaker and listener); ~-*sini* here and there

sandal N sandals (open-toed shoes); ~ *jepit* thongs, flip flops

sandar: sandaran N support, prop; **bersandar, menyandar** v to lean

sandera N hostage

sandi N code, cipher; *kata* ~ password

sandiwara N drama, play

sangat ADV very, extremely

sanggar N workshop, studio

sanggul N bun (worn with women's national costume)

sanggup v, AUX to be able to, to be capable of

sangka v to guess, suspect; **sangkaan** N suspicion; **bersangka** v to suspect or think; **menyangka** v to suspect, suppose, presume; *tidak* ~ never thought; **tersangka** N *(yang)* ~ suspect

sangkar N cage

sangkut ~ *paut* connection, link; **bersangkutan** ADJ concerned, involved; **tersangkut** ADJ involved; caught, snagged

sanksi N disciplinary action, sanction

santai ADJ relaxed, easy-going, informal

santan N coconut milk (used in cooking)

santer ADJ strong, rife

santri N student at an Islamic school (esp a boarder); strict Muslim; **pesantrén** N Islamic boarding school

santun ADJ polite, well-mannered; **santunan** N benefit, compensation (from insurance)

sapa greet; **sapaan** N greeting

sapi N cow; *susu* ~ cow's milk

sapu broom; ~ *tangan* hand-kerchief, hanky; **menyapu** v to sweep or wipe

saput: tersaput ~ *awan* clouded over

SARA ADJ communal, sectarian; related to ethnicity, religion, race or socio-economic group ← **suku agama ras antargolongan**

saraf N nerve

saran N suggestion; **menyarankan** v to suggest

sarana N facility, means; ~ *umum* public amenity; *pra*~ infrastructure

sarang N nest

sarap: sarapan N breakfast

sardin, sardén *ikan* ~ sardine

sari N essence, extract; flower; ~ *bunga* pollen

sariawan, seriawan (mouth) ulcer, have an ulcer

saring filter; **saringan** N filter, sieve

sarjana N university graduate; ~ *muda* undergraduate

sarung N sarong; cover, case; ~ *bantal* pillowcase, pillowslip

Sasak ethnic group of Lombok

sasando N harp-like musical instrument from Timor

sasar: sasaran N target; **kesasar** v, COLL to lose your way, (get) lost

sastra N literature; ~ *Indonesia* Indonesian literature; **sastrawan** N literary figure

169

sate, satai N satay, kebab;
~ *ayam* chicken satay; ~
kambing goat satay

satpam N security guard ←
satuan pengamanan

satu ADJ one; **satu-satu** ADV
one by one, individually;
satuan N unit; **bersatu** V to
be united; **menyatukan,
mempersatukan** V to unite
various things; **pemersatu** N
unifying agent, unifier; **persatuan** N union, association

satwa N animal, fauna

saudara N family (member);
sibling, brother, sister;
PRON you; brother, sister; ~
perempuan sister; **bersaudara** V to be related; to have
brothers and sisters; **saudari**
PRON, F you, sister; *saudara-~*
brothers and sisters

sauh N anchor

sauna N sauna; small steaming
box in a salon

saung N open-air restaurant by
a fish-pond, esp in West Java

saus N sauce, gravy; ~ *tomat*
tomato sauce

sawah N (irrigated or wet) rice
paddy, ricefield

sawi N bok choy, mustard
greens; green leafy vegetable

sawo N brown, sweet fruit;
sapodilla

saya PRON I, me, my; ~ *sendiri*
I (myself); *kepada* ~ to me

sayang pity, regret; love; PRON
darling; *~ku* my darling;
~ *sekali* what a pity;
kesayangan favorite, pet;
menyayangi V to love

sayap N wing; **bersayap** ADJ
winged

sayat: sayatan N slice

sayembara N contest,
competition

sayur N vegetable; ~ *asem*
sour vegetable soup; ~ *mayur*
(all kinds of) vegetables;
sayur-sayuran N vegetables

SD ABBREV *Sekolah Dasar* pri-
mary/elementary school

seadanya ADJ what's there
← **ada**

seandainya CONJ supposing,
if ← **andai**

sebab N reason, cause; CONJ
because; *~nya* the reason is,
the reason being; **menyebabkan** V to cause; **penyebab**
N cause

sebagai CONJ like, as

sebagian N some, a section of ← **bagi**

sebaiknya ADV preferably, it's best if ← **baik**

sebal ADJ fed up, annoyed, cheesed off; **menyebalkan** ADJ annoying, tiresome

sebaliknya ADV on the contrary, on the other hand ← **balik**

sebar: menyebarkan V to spread, distribute

sebelah PREP next to; N half, side; *(di)* ~ *kanan* on the right (side) ← **belah**

sebelas ADJ eleven ← **belas**

sebelum PREP before; **sebelumnya** ADV previously, before(hand) ← **belum**

sebenarnya ADV in fact, actually ← **benar**

sebentar N a moment, minute, while

seberang across, other side; **menyeberangi** V to cross; **penyeberangan** N crossing

sebetulnya ADV in fact, actually ← **betul**

sebisanya, sebisa-bisanya ADV as well as you can, to the best of your ability ← **bisa**

sebuah ADJ a, one (generic counter); ~ *kursi* a chair ← **buah**

sebut mention; ~ *saja* take (for instance); **sebutan** N mention; **menyebut** V to mention, name, say; **tersebut** ADJ (afore)mentioned, said

secara ADV in a way; used to form adverbs ← **cara**

secepat CONJ as fast as; ~ *mungkin*, **secepat-(-cepat) nya** ADV as fast as possible ← **cepat**

secukupnya ADV sufficient, adequate ← **cukup**

sedak: tersedak ADJ choking

sedang ADJ medium, moderate

sedang AUX while, -ing; ~ *tidur* sleeping; **sedangkan** CONJ whereas, while

sedap ADJ delicious, tasty

sedapatnya ADV what you can get ← **dapat**

sedekah N alms, charity, handout

sederhana ADJ simple, plain

sedia ready, prepared; willing; **bersedia** V to be prepared or willing; **menyediakan** v to prepare, get ready; **persediaan** N stock, supply; **tersedia** ADJ available, prepared

sedih ADJ sad; **bersedih** v to be or feel sad; **kesedihan** N sadness, sorrow; **menyedihkan** ADJ depressing, sad

sedikit ADJ a little, a few, a bit

sedot suck; **sedotan** N straw; **menyedot** v to suck (up)

sedu sob

seénaknya ADV, NEG just how you like, at will ← **énak**

segala ADJ all, every; **segala-galanya** N everything, the lot

segan ADJ reluctant, averse

segar ADJ fresh; ~ *bugar* fit and healthy; **menyegarkan** ADJ refreshing

ségel seal, stamp

segera ADV immediately, directly; soon; *dengan* ~ express, immediately

segi N side, angle; point of view; ~ *empat* square, rectangle; ~ *tiga* triangle; **persegi** ADJ square, rectangular

segini ADJ this much ← **ini**

segitu ADJ that much ← **itu**

sehabis CONJ after ← **habis**

sehari-hari ADV every day, daily; **seharian** ADV, COLL all day ← **hari**

seharusnya should ← **harus**

séhat ADJ healthy; **keséhatan** N health

sehingga CONJ until, to the point that, as far as; so that ← **hingga**

seimbang ADJ balanced, well-proportioned ← **imbang**

sejahtera ADJ prosperous; **kesejahteraan** N welfare

sejak CONJ since, from the time when

sejarah N history; **bersejarah** ADJ historic, historical

sejati ADJ original, genuine, real ← **jati**

sejenis ADJ of the same type or species ← **jenis**

sejuk ADJ cool

sekadar ADJ just; ~*nya* as necessary ← **kadar**

sekali ADV very; *indah* ~ very beautiful

sekali ADV once; *jangan* ~-*kali* never (do this); **sekali-sekali,**

sesekali ADV every now and then, occasionally

sekalian ADV all together, all at once; ADV, COLL at the same time ← **kali**

sekaligus ADV all at once ← **kali**

sekalipun CONJ even though ← **kali**

sekali-sekali ADV every now and then, occasionally ← **kali**

sekarang ADV now, at present

sekat bar, block, partition

sekejap N moment, flash, blink ← **kejap**

sekian ADV so much, this much ← **kian**

sekilas N flash, glance ← **kilas**

sekitar PREP around; ADV around; near; **sekitarnya** *di* ~ around (a place) ← **kitar**

sékjén N secretary-general ← **sékretaris jénderal**

sekolah N school; institute of learning; ~ *Dasar (SD)* primary school, elementary school; *menengah* secondary school, high school; **berse-kolah** V to go to school

sekongkol, persekongkolan N plot, intrigue, conspiracy ← **kongkol**

sekop, skop N spade, shovel; spades (in cards)

sékretariat N secretariat; **sékretaris** N secretary

sekrup N screw

séks N sex; *hubungan* ~ sexual relations, sexual intercourse; **seksi** ADJ sexy; **séksual** ADJ sexual

séksi N section

séksi ADJ sexy ← **seks**

sékte N sect

séktor N sector

sekurangnya, sekurang-kurangnya ADV at least ← **kurang**

sekutu N partner, ally; **persekutuan** N alliance, partnership

sél N cell

sela N gap, pause

selada, salada, salat N salad; lettuce

selai N jam; ~ *jeruk* marmalade; ~ *kacang* peanut butter

selain CONJ except, besides, apart from ← **lain**

selalu ADV always ← **lalu**

selam diving; **menyelam** v to dive; **penyelam** n diver

selama conj during, as long as; **selamanya** adv always, forever ← **lama**

selamat safe; congratulations; ~ *datang* welcome; ~ *jalan* goodbye; bon voyage, have a safe trip; ~ *malam* good evening; ~ *sore* good afternoon; **selamatan** n (thanksgiving) feast; **keselamatan** n safety; salvation; **menyelamatkan** v to save, rescue; **penyelamatan** n rescue (operation)

selambat-lambatnya adv at the latest ← **lambat**

selancar *papan* ~ surfboard; **berselancar** v to surf, go surfing ← **lancar**

Sélandia Baru n New Zealand

selang n interval; ~ *sehari* every other day, every second day

selang n hose

selanjutnya adv then, after that ← **lanjut**

Selasa *hari* ~ Tuesday

selat n strait

selatan adj south

sélébritis, séléb n celebrity

selédri n celery

seléndang, sléndang n shawl; sash worn over the shoulder with women's national costume

selenggara: menyelenggarakan v to run, hold, organize; **penyelenggara** n organizer

seléra n appetite, taste

selesai finished, over; **menyelesaikan** v to finish, end, settle; ~ *masalah* to overcome a problem; **penyelesaian** n solution, settlement

selesma, selésma having a cold; cold

selidik: menyelidiki v to investigate; **penyelidik** n investigator, detective; **penyelidikan** n investigation

selimut n blanket

selingkuh, berselingkuh v to have an affair; **perselingkuhan** n affair

selip: terselip adj fallen or slipped into

selisih n difference

174

selok: selokan N ditch, trench
selonjor sit with legs sticking out in front
selop N slipper
sélotip N sellotape, adhesive or sticky tape
seluk ~ *beluk* ins and outs, details
selundup: selundupan *barang* ~ contraband, smuggled goods; **menyelundupkan** v to smuggle (in)
seluruh ADJ entire, whole; **seluruhnya** ADV completely; ADJ all; **keseluruhan** *secara* ~ totally, completely
selusin N a dozen ← **lusin**
semak N shrub, bush
semakin ADV even more ← **makin**
semalam ADV last night ← **malam**
semangat N spirit, enthusiasm; **bersemangat** ADJ spirited, enthusiastic
semangka N watermelon
sembah N homage, tribute, respect; **menyembah** v to pay homage to, worship; **mempersembahkan** v to offer (up), present

sembahyang pray, prayer; **bersembahyang** v to pray, perform a prayer
sembako N nine daily necessities ← **sembilan bahan pokok**
sembarang ADJ any, whichever; **sembarangan** ADJ arbitrary, random
sembelih: menyembelih v to slaughter, butcher
sembelit constipation, constipated
sembilan ADJ nine; ~ *belas* nineteen; ~ *puluh* ninety
semboyan N motto, slogan
sembuh recovered, better; *cepat* ~ get well soon; **menyembuhkan** v to cure, heal
sembunyi hide, conceal; **sembunyi-sembunyi** ADV secretly, in secret; **bersembunyi** v to hide (yourself); **menyembunyikan** v to hide or conceal something; **persembunyian** N hiding place, hideout
semenanjung N peninsula
sementara CONJ during; ADJ temporary; ~ *itu* in the meantime, meanwhile

175

semestinya should have (been) ← **mesti**

seminggu ADJ a week ← **minggu**

semir polish; ~ *sepatu* shoe polish

semoga may, hopefully ← **moga**

sempat chance, opportunity; **kesempatan** N opportunity

sempit ADJ narrow; **menyempit** v to (become) narrow

semprot squirt; spurt; **semprotan** N spray-gun; **menyemprot** v to spray; **menyemprotkan** v to spray with something

sempurna ADJ perfect, complete

semrawut ADJ haphazard, uncontrolled

semua ADJ all; *~nya* all, everyone

semula ADV originally ← **mula**

semut N ant; **kesemutan** v to have pins and needles

sén cent

senam N gymnastics, aerobics; exercise; ~ *hamil* pre-natal exercises; ~ *pagi* morning exercise; *baju* ~ leotard

senang ADJ happy, content; v to like; **bersenang-senang** v to enjoy yourself, have fun; **kesenangan** N amusement, hobby; **menyenangkan** ADJ pleasing, agreeable

senapan N rifle

senda ~ *gurau* joke; **bersenda** ~ *gurau* to joke around

sendawa: bersendawa v to burp, belch

sendi N joint

sendiri ADV alone; PRON self; **sendirian** ADV alone, single-handedly; **tersendiri** ADJ its own; apart, separate ← **diri**

séndok N spoon; ~ *garpu* spoon and fork

séng N zinc

sengaja ADV deliberately, on purpose; *tidak* ~ unintentionally

sengat sting; **sengatan** N sting, bite; **menyengat** v to sting

sénggol brush, bump; **menyénggol** v to bump, brush, tweak; **tersénggol** ADJ bumped, brushed

176

sengkéta N dispute; *tanah ~* disputed land

sengsara N misery

seni N art; *~ lukis* painting; **kesenian** N art (form); **seniman** N, M **seniwati** N, F artist

Senin, Senén *hari ~* Monday

sénior N person in higher class or of higher position

senja N twilight, dusk

senjata N weapon; *~ api* firearm, gun; **senjata** ADJ armed

sénsor N censor; *kena ~, disensor* censored

sénsus N census

sénter N *(lampu) ~* flashlight, torch

sénti N centimeter, centimetre; *berapa ~* how many centimeters, how long ← **séntiméter**

sentil: sentilan N flick, nudge

sentiméter, sénti N centimeter, centimetre

séntral central

sentuh touch; **sentuhan** N touch; **menyentuh** v to touch; **tersentuh** ADJ touched

senyap ADJ quiet, still

senyum, tersenyum v to smile

seorang a (person); counter for people; *~ Arab* an Arab ← **orang**

sépak kick; *~ bola* soccer, football; *~ takraw* game played with a rattan ball; **menyépak** v to kick (out)

sepakat v to agree; **kesepakatan** N agreement; **menyepakati** v to agree to ← **pakat**

sepanjang CONJ, ADJ as long as ← **panjang**

séparatis separatist

separo, separuh N half ← **paruh**

sepasang N a pair of ← **pasang**

sepatu N shoe(s); *~ sandal* sandals; **bersepatu** ADJ in shoes

sepéda N bicycle, (push)bike; *~ motor* motor bike; *naik ~* to ride a bike; **bersepéda** v to ride a bicycle

sepenuhnya ADV fully, completely ← **penuh**

seperempat N one quarter ← **empat**

seperti CONJ like; *~nya* it seems

sepertiga ADJ one-third ← **tiga**

sepi ADJ quiet, still, lonely; **kesepian** N loneliness, solitude

sepihak ADJ unilateral ← **pihak**

sepoi: sepoi-sepoi *angin* ~ breeze, zephyr

seprei, seprai N (bed)sheet

Séptémber *bulan* ~ September

sepuluh N ten ← **puluh**

sepupu N cousin

sepur N, COLL railway (line); rail; platform

seputar ADJ around, about ← **putar**

seragam n uniform ← **ragam**

serah hand over, transfer; **menyerah** v to surrender, give in, give up; **menyerahkan** v to hand over; **penyerahan** N handing over, hand-over; **terserah** ADJ it depends; up to you

serai, séréh N lemon grass, citronella

serak ADJ hoarse

serakah ADJ greedy

seram ADJ weird, creepy

serambi N verandah

serang, menyerany v to attack; **serangan** N attack

serangga N insect, bug

serap absorb; **menyerap** v to absorb, soak up

serat N fiber, fibre

seratus ADJ one hundred, a hundred ← **ratus**

serba ADJ all kinds of, various

serbét N serviette, table napkin

serbu: menyerbu v to attack (as a group), charge, invade

serbuk N powder

séréal N (breakfast) cereal

séréh, serai N lemon grass, citronella

serentak ADJ all at once, simultaneous, at the same time

sérét, menyérét v to drag

seri N draw, tie

séri N series

seribu ADJ one thousand, a thousand ← **ribu**

serigala N wolf

serikat union, united; **perserikatan** N federation

sérius ADJ serious

séro: perséroan N company

serobot push in front;

menyerobot v to push in front

sérong ADJ on an angle, oblique

serpih, serpihan N shred, bit, piece; ~ *kayu* wood chip

serta CONJ (together) with; **beserta** CONJ along with, and; **peserta** N participant

seru ADJ exciting, great

seruling, suling N flute

serumpun ADJ related, of one family; *bahasa* ~ related languages ← **rumpun**

serupa ADJ similar ← **rupa**

sérvis N repairs, service, maintenance; **disérvis** v to be serviced

sesajén N ritual offering ← **saji**

sesak ADJ close, dense, crowded

sesal regret; **menyesal** v to regret; **menyesalkan** v to feel bad about, regret (another's action)

sesama ADJ fellow, another ← **sama**

sesat lost; **menyesatkan** ADJ misleading, confusing; **tersesat** ADJ lost

sesekali ADV every now and then, occasionally ← **kali**

seseorang N somebody, a certain person ← **orang**

sesuai ADJ in accordance with, appropriate; **menyesuaikan** v to adapt, bring into line ← **suai**

sesuatu N something ← **suatu**

sesudah PREP after; ~ *itu*, **sesudahnya** after that, then ← **sudah**

sesungguhnya ADV actually, really ← **sungguh**

setahu CONJ as far as is known ← **tahu**

sétan, syaitan N devil, demon

setasiun, stasiun, setasion N (railway) station

setél N set; **setélan** N set, suit

setél, menyétél v to tune, set, adjust; ~ *mesin mobil* to tune an engine

setelah PREP after ← **telah**

setempat ADJ local ← **tempat**

setengah ADJ half; *jam* ~ *dua* half past one; **setengah-setengah** ADV half-heartedly ← **tengah**

seterusnya ADV after that, henceforth ← **terus**

setia ADJ faithful

setiap ADJ each, every; ~ *saat* any time ← **tiap**

setidaknya, setidak-tidaknya ADV at least ← **tidak**

setinggi ADJ as high as ← **tinggi**

setir: menyetir V to drive

setop: setopan N, COLL traffic lights

setor: setoran (make a) deposit; **menyetor** V to pay in, deposit

setrika, seterika iron; **setrikaan** N (clothes for) ironing; **menyetrika** V to iron

setrip, strip N (diagonal) slash; strip; section of a mobile phone battery symbol

setrum N current; **kesetrum** V, COLL to receive an electric shock

setuju agree, agreed; **menyetujui** V to agree to, approve, ratify; **persetujuan** N agreement, approval ← **tuju**

seumpamanya CONJ for instance ← **umpama**

seumur ADJ the same age; lifelong ← **umur**

séwa hire, rent; **menyéwa** V to rent, hire; **menyéwakan** V to let (a house), hire out, lease

shio N Chinese horoscope, based on year born

sholat, shalat, solat ISL (perform) one of the five daily prayers

si PREF used before the name of a familiar third party

sia: sia-sia ADJ pointless, useless

siaga ADJ alert, on guard, ready

sial unlucky; **sialan** EJAC damn! hell!

siang N day; late morning, early afternoon (usu between 10 am and 3 pm); *makan* ~ lunch; **kesiangan** ADJ late, too late in the day

siap ready; **bersiap** V to get ready; **bersiap-siap** V to make preparations; **meny-iapkan, mempersiapkan** V to prepare something, get something ready; **persiapan** N preparations

siapa INTERROG, PRON who; ~ *namanya?* what's your name?; ~ *saja* anybody;

siapa-siapa PRON, NEG nobody

siar: siaran N telecast, broadcast; **penyiar** N announcer

siar: pesiar N trip, cruise; *kapal* ~ cruise ship; pleasure craft

sia-sia ADJ pointless, useless

sibuk ADJ busy; engaged (of phones); **kesibukan** N activity, fuss, bustle, business

sidang N session, meeting; hearing

sidik ~ *jari* fingerprints; **penyidikan** N investigation ← **selidik**

sifat N quality, nature, character; **bersifat** V to have the quality of

sih used as a filler; *saya* ~ *tidak keberatan* I myself have no objection

sihir N spells, witchcraft; **penyihir** N wizard, witch, sorcerer

sikap N attitude; **bersikap** V to display an attitude

sikat N brush; **menyikat** V to brush

siklus N cycle

siksa torture; **menyiksa** V to torture; **tersiksa** ADJ tortured

siku N elbow; bracket

sila: silakan, silahkan please (when offering); ~ *masuk* please come in; **mempersilakan** V to invite someone to do something

silang cross, across

silat N traditional self-defense

silaturahmi N good relations, friendship; **bersilaturahmi** V to maintain good relations, visit or meet friends

silau ADJ blinded, dazzled

silét N razor, scalpel

silsilah N family tree, pedigree (of an animal)

SIM N driver's license, driving license ← **Surat Izin Mengemudi**

simpan V to keep, put; **simpanan** N something kept; *uang* ~ savings, deposit; **menyimpan** V to keep, save up, store

simpang cross; ~ *tiga* T-junction; **persimpangan** N intersection

simpul N knot; **kesimpulan** N conclusion; **menyimpulkan** V

to conclude or summarize

sinar N ray, beam; **bersinar** V to shine, gleam

sindir, menyindir V to insinuate, allude; **sindiran** N allusion, insinuation

sinéas N cinematographer; **sinétron** N local TV comedy or drama ← **sinéma éléktronik**

singa N lion

Singapura N Singapore

singgah V to drop by, call at, stop over

singgung, menyinggung V to touch on; **tersinggung** ADJ offended, hurt

singkat ADJ short, brief, concise; *~nya* in brief; **singkatan** N abbreviation; **menyingkatkan** V to abbreviate, shorten

singkir: menyingkirkan V to remove, brush aside; **tersingkir** ADJ eliminated, swept aside

singkong N cassava

sini ADV here; *di ~* here ← **ini**

sinsé, sin shé N Chinese doctor, practitioner of Chinese medicine or acupuncture

sinyal N signal

siomay, sio may N fishcakes eaten with peanut sauce

sipil ADJ civil

sipit ADJ narrow, slanting (of eyes)

siput N snail

siram V to pour; **siraman** N bathing ceremony before a wedding; **menyiram** V to pour, water (plants)

siréne N siren

sirih N betel; *makan ~* chew betel

sirip N fin

sirkuit N (racing) circuit, race track

sirkus N circus

sirop N syrup, cordial

sirsak N soursop, greenskinned fruit with white fleshy interior

sisa N rest, remainder, remains; **tersisa** ADJ leftover

sisi N side

sisik N scale (of fish)

sisir N comb; hand (of bananas); *se~ pisang* a bunch of bananas; **menyisir** V to comb, check thoroughly

sistém, sistim N system

siswa N pupil; **siswi** N, F pupil

situ *di ~* there (close to listener) ← **itu**

situasi N situation

situs N site; *~ internet* website

siul: bersiul v to whistle

skala N scale; **berskala** v to be on a scale

skétsa N sketch

skor N score

Skotlandia N Scotland

SLI ABBREV *Sambungan Langsung Internasional* international direct dialling

SLJJ ABBREV *Sambungan Langsung Jarak Jauh* long-distance direct dialling

SMA ABBREV *Sekolah Menengah Atas* Senior High School

SMP ABBREV *Sekolah Menengah Pertama* Junior High School

soal N question, issue, problem, matter; CONJ on the topic of; *~nya* the problem is; **mempersoalkan** v to question, discuss; **persoalan** N problem, issue, matter

sobat N friend, comrade

sobék torn (esp of paper); **menyobék** v to tear

soda air *~* soda water; **bersoda** ADJ carbonated;

minuman ~ carbonated drink

sofbol N softball

sogok *uang ~* bribe; **sogokan** N bribe; **menyogok** v to bribe

sohun, so'un N vermicelli noodles

sok COLL pretend; as if; *~ tahu* be a know-all

sol *~ sepatu* (shoe) sole

solar N diesel fuel

soléh, saléh ADJ pious, religious

solusi N solution

sombong ADJ arrogant, stuck-up

songkét N *(kain)* ~ woven cloth, often with gold thread

sop N (western-style) soup

sopan ADJ polite, well-mannered; **kesopanan** N manners, politeness; **kesopan-santunan** N manners, etiquette

sorak cheer, shout; applause; **bersorak** v to cheer, shout

soré (late) afternoon, early evening; *~ hari* late in the day; **kesoréan** ADV too late

sorot N beam of light; **sorotan** N focus; **menyoroti** v to light

183

up, illuminate, focus on

sosial ADJ social

sosis N sausage

sosok N figure

soto N clear soup; ~ *ayam* chicken soup

sotong *ikan* ~ cuttlefish, squid

spanduk N large banner

Spanyol N Spain

spasi N space, spacing

spérma N sperm

spidol N felt-tip marker or pen, texta; whiteboard marker

spion N spy

spontan ADJ spontaneous

srikaya, serikaya N custard-apple

stabil ADJ stable

stabilo N highlighter, fluorescent marker

stadion N (sports) stadium

stadium N stage (of an illness); ~ *tiga* advanced

status N (marital) status

stémpel, setémpel N official stamp

stopkontak N power point, electricity socket

stréng ADJ strict, harsh, disciplinarian

strés, setrés stress(ed)

stupa N stupa, bell-shaped dome covering a Buddha statue

suai: sesuai ADJ in accordance or keeping with; **menyesuaikan** V to adapt

suaka N asylum; *pencari* ~ asylum seeker

suami N husband; **bersuami** ADJ, F married

suap N mouthful; bribe; **suapan** N bribe; **menyuap** V to feed by hand; to bribe

suara N voice

suasana N atmosphere

suatu ADJ a (certain); ~ *hari* one day; **sesuatu** N something

subuh N, ISL dawn

subur ADJ fertile

subyék N subject

suci ADJ pure, holy; **menyucikan** V to purify, cleanse

sudah AUX **udah** COLL already; indicates past time; **sesudah** PREP after; **sesudahnya** after that, then

sudut N corner, angle, perspective; point of view; **menyudutkan** V to push into a corner, deflect

184

suguh: suguhan N something offered or presented

suhu N temperature

suit whistling sound; **suitan** N whistle

suka V to like; **ADV** often; **kesukaan** N hobby; enjoyment; **menyukai** V to like

sukar ADJ difficult, hard; **kesukaran** N difficulty

sukaréla ADJ voluntary; **sukarélawan** N volunteer ← **réla**

suksés N success; *semoga ~* good luck, every success; **mensukséskan** V to make something succeed

suku N tribe; part; *~ bangsa* ethnic group

sulam: sulaman N embroidery; **menyulam** V to embroider

sulang: bersulang V to toast, drink to

sulap magic, conjure; **sulapan** N conjuring, magic; **menyulap** V to conjure up; to make something vanish or change; **penyulap** N magician, conjurer

Sulawési, Sulawesi *(pulau) ~* Sulawesi, Celebes

sulit ADJ difficult, hard

Sulsel N South Sulawesi ← **Sulawési Selatan**

Sulteng N Central Sulawesi ← **Sulawési Tengah**

Sultra N Southeast Sulawesi ← **Sulawési Tenggara**

Sulut N North Sulawesi ← **Sulawési Utara**

Sumatera, Sumatra *(pulau) ~* Sumatra

sumbang: sumbangan N contribution, donation; **menyumbang** V to contribute, make a donation

Sumbar N West Sumatra ← **Sumatera Barat**

sumbat plug; cork, stopper; **menyumbat** V to plug, stop

sumber N source; well

sumpah curse; oath; **bersumpah** V to swear

sumpek ADJ crowded, stuffy

sumpit N chopsticks

Sumsel N South Sumatra ← **Sumatera Selatan**

sumsum N bone marrow

sumur N well

Sumut N North Sumatra ← **Sumatera Utara**

sun peck on the cheek, kiss

sunat: sunatan N circumcision (celebration); **disunat** V to be circumcised; **menyunatkan** V to have someone circumcised

Sunda *bahasa* ~, *orang* ~ Sundanese

sungai N river

sungguh ADJ real, true; **sungguh-sungguh** ADJ serious; **sesungguhnya** ADV actually, really

suntik: suntikan N vaccination, injection; needle; **menyuntik** V to inject or vaccinate

sunting: penyunting N editor

sunyi ADJ lonely, still, quiet

supaya CONJ in order that, so (used before nouns)

supir, sopir N driver, chauffeur; **menyupir** V to drive

suram ADJ gloomy, dark

surat N letter; certificate, card; ~ *kabar* newspaper; **menyurati** V to write a letter to

surga, syurga, sorga N heaven, paradise

Suriah N Syria; *orang* ~ Syrian

Suriname N Surinam

suruh order, ask; tell; **suruhan** N messenger, errandboy; **menyuruh** V to command, order; **pesuruh** N messenger, errand boy

surut V to recede; *air* ~ low tide

surya *tenaga* ~ solar energy

susah difficult; trouble, sorrow; **kesusahan** N trouble, difficulty; **menyusahkan** V to bother, make difficult

suster N nurse(maid); N, CATH nun

susu N milk; N, SL breast; ~ *kaleng* condensed milk; **menyusui** V to feed

susul: menyusul V to follow, go after

susun heap, pile; *rumah* ~ (*rusun*) block of flats, apartment block; **susunan** N arrangement, organization, system; **menyusun** V to heap or pile; to arrange, organize, compile; **penyusun** N compiler, author

sutera, sutra N silk

sutradara N director

swa- PREF self-; ~*layan* self-serve, supermarket

Swédia N Sweden

Swis N Switzerland

switer N jumper, pullover, sweater

syair N poem; **penyair** N poet

syal N shawl, scarf

syarat, sarat N condition, terms; *dengan ~* on condition; **bersyarat** ADJ conditional

syariah *hukum ~* Islamic law

syukur, sukur thanks, thanksgiving; thank goodness; **bersyukur** ADJ grateful; **mensyukuri** v to appreciate, be thankful

T

taat ADJ obedient; religious

tabel N table, chart

tabir N curtain, screen; *~ surya* sunscreen, sunblock

tabrak collide; **tabrakan** N collision, accident; **menabrak** v to collide with; **tertabrak** ADJ to be hit

tabu taboo

tabuh N drum; drumstick; **menabuh** v to beat (a drum)

tabung N container, tube; **tabungan** N savings; **menabung** v to save or deposit money

tabur scatter, sprinkle; **bertaburan** ADJ scattered over

tadi ADV just now; *~nya* originally, at first; *~ pagi* this morning; *~ malam* last night

tagih: tagihan N amount due, bill; **ketagihan** ADJ addicted to

tahan bear, stop, last; *tidak ~* can't bear; **tahanan** N prisoner, detainee; custody, detention; **menahan** v to bear, endure; to detain; **mempertahankan** v to defend or maintain; **pertahanan** N defense; **tertahan** ADJ held back, prevented

tahap N stage, phase; **bertahap** ADJ in stages

tahi N shit, feces; *~ lalat* mole

tahu v [tau] to know; **tahu-tahu** ADV suddenly, unexpectedly; **ketahuan** v to be found out; **mengetahui** v to know something, have knowledge of; **pengetahuan**

N knowledge; **setahu** CONJ as far as is known

tahu N tofu

tahun N year; ~ *Baru* New Year; ~ *Baru Cina*, ~ *Baru Imlek* Chinese New Year; **tahunan** ADJ annual, yearly

tahu-tahu ADV suddenly, unexpectedly ← **tahu**

Taiwan N Taiwan

tajam ADJ sharp

taji N spur (of a cock)

tajuk N crown; editorial

tak no, not; ~ *kan*, ~*kan* will not, won't ← **tidak**

takar: takaran N measuring container or spoon

takkan will not, won't ← **tak kan**

takraw N small rattan ball

taksi N taxi

takut ADJ scared, afraid; *rasa* ~ fear; **ketakutan** ADJ frightened, terrified, scared; **menakutkan** V, ADV frightening; to frighten or scare; **penakut** N coward

talang N (roof) gutter

talenan N chopping or cutting board

tali N rope, cord, tie; ~ *sepatu* shoelace

taman N garden, park; ~ *budaya* cultural center; ~ *kanak-kanak (TK)* kindergarten

tamasya N view; spectacle; excursion

tamat end, finish; ~ *sekolah* graduate; **tamatan** N graduate

tambah add; **tambahan** N addition, increase; **bertambah** V to increase; **menambah** V to add to or increase; **menambahi** V to increase something; **menambahkan** V to add something to; **pertambahan** N increase

tambak N dam, pond; dike, levee, embankment

tambal N patch; ~ *ban* tire repair; **tambalan** N patch, darn (on a sock); **menambal** V to mend, patch, darn

tambang N mine; ~ *emas* gold mine; **pertambangan** N mining

tambat tie up, tether

tambur N drum

taméng N shield

tampak visible, appear

188

tampan ADJ, M handsome

tampang N appearance; COLL face

tampar slap, smack; **menampar** v to slap

tampil v to appear; **penampilan** N performance

tamu N guest, visitor; *ruang* ~ front room, living room; room for receiving guests

tanah N earth, ground, land, soil; country; ~ *air* Indonesia; *minyak* ~ kerosene

tanam: tanaman N plant; **menanam** v to plant or grow; to invest

tancap *layar* ~ open-air makeshift cinema; ~ *gas* step on the gas, accelerate

tanda N sign, mark, symbol; ~ *tangan* signature; **bertanda** ADJ marked; **menandatangani** v to sign something; **menandai** v to mark

tanding N match, equal; **bertanding** v to compete, play; **pertandingan** N contest, competition, match

tanduk N horn

tandus ADJ infertile, barren

tangan N hand, arm; sleeve; **menangani** v to handle

tangga N ladder, stair(case)

tanggal N date; ~ *lahir* date of birth; **tertanggal** ADJ dated

tanggap: tanggapan N response, reaction; **menanggapi** v to respond, reply

tanggul N dike, levee, embankment

tanggung ADJ guaranteed; ~ *jawab* responsibility; **bertanggung jawab** v to be responsible; **mempertanggungjawabkan** v to account for; **tanggungan** N dependent; responsibility; **menanggung** v to guarantee, be responsible

tangis *isak* ~ crying; **tangisan** N weeping, crying; **menangis** v to cry

tangkai N stem, stalk

tangkap, **menangkap** v to catch, capture; **penangkapan** N capture, arrest; **tertangkap** ADJ caught

tangkas ADJ agile, adroit, deft

tangki N tank

tani N farmer; **petani** N farmer; **pertanian** N agriculture

189

tanjak: tanjakan N rise, ascent, climb; **menanjak** ADJ rising, climbing, steep

tanjung N cape; **semenanjung** N peninsula

tanpa PREP, CONJ without

tantang challenge; **tantangan** N challenge; **menantang** v to challenge; ADJ challenging

tante PRON, POL term of address to a familiar but unrelated woman, esp of mother's generation, in Westernized circles

tanya ask; **bertanya** v to ask; **bertanya-tanya** v to wonder, ask yourself; **menanyakan** v to ask about; **mempertanyakan** v to query; **pertanyaan** N question

tapak, telapak ~ *kaki* sole; footprint; ~ *tangan* palm

tapal ~ *kuda* horseshoe

tapé, tapai N fermented rice

tapi → **tetapi**

taplak ~ *meja* tablecloth

tar, tart *kue* ~ (birthday) cake

taraf N standard, level

tari N (traditional) dance; ~*tarian* traditional dancing; **tarian** N (traditional) dance;

menari v to dance, perform a traditional dance; **menari-nari** v to dance about; **penari** N dancer

tarif, tarip N tariff, fare, rate

tarik pull; **menarik** v to pull or draw; ADJ interesting, attractive; **tertarik** ADJ attracted, interested

taring N tusk; fang

taruh v to place, put; **taruhan** bet, wager; **bertaruh** v to bet; **menaruh** v to put (away)

tas N bag; ~ *pinggang* bum bag; ~ *tangan* handbag

tato N tattoo

tauco, taoco N brown sauce made from fermented soybeans

taugé, taogé, togé N bean sprouts

tawa laugh, laughter; **tawaan** N object of fun; **ketawa** COLL **tertawa** v to laugh or smile; **menertawakan** v to laugh at

tawan: tawanan N prisoner of war (POW), detainee

tawar bargain; **menawar** v to bargain; *tawar-*~ bargaining; **menawarkan** v to offer or bid; **penawaran** N offer, bid

tawon N bee

tawur: tawuran gang or street fight, often among schoolboys

tayang: tayangan N program, telecast; ~ *langsung* live telecast

téater N theatre (building), theater; drama group

tebak guess; **tebakan** N guess; **menebak** v to guess

tebal ADJ thick

tebang fall, be cut down (of trees); **menebang** v to fell, cut down; **penebangan** N logging; ~ *liar* illegal logging

tebing N cliff, gorge, steep bank

tebu N sugarcane

teduh ADJ shady; quiet, still; **berteduh** v to take shelter

téga v to have the heart to, dare to; ~*nya* how could you have the heart

tegak ADJ upright, erect; **menegakkan** v to erect; to uphold or maintain

tegang ADJ tense, stressed, strained; **ketegangan** N tension; **menegangkan** ADJ tense, stressful

tegas ADJ clear, distinct; **menegaskan** v to clarify, point out, affirm

tégel N, ARCH (floor) tile ← **ubin**

teguh ADJ firm, fast, strong, solid

teguk N gulp, swallow, draft; **tegukan** N swallow, gulp; **meneguk** v to gulp or guzzle

tegur speak; rebuke; ~ *sapa* say hello; **teguran** N warning, rebuke; greeting; **menegur** v to speak to, address; to warn, rebuke, tell off

téh N tea; ~ *tawar* black tea no sugar; *kantong* ~, *celup* ~ teabag

tékad will, determination

tekan press; **tekanan** N pressure, stress; **menekan** v to press; **menekankan** v to stress, emphasize; **tertekan** ADJ stressed, pushed, pressured

teka-teki N riddle, puzzle

téken v to sign, initial

téknik, téhnik N engineering; ADJ technical

téknis ADJ technical; **téknisi** N technician

téko N kettle, teapot

téks N text; subtitle

tekuk ~ *lutut* bend your knee

tekun ADJ hard-working

teladan N example, model

telaga N lake

telah ADV already; **setelah** CONJ after

telan v to swallow; **menelan** v to swallow something; **tertelan** v accidentally swallowed

telanjang ADJ naked, nude, bare

telanjur ADV too late, already ← **lanjur**

telantar, terlantar ADJ neglected, abandoned

telapak, tapak ~ *kaki* sole; footprint; ~ *tangan* palm

telat ADV, COLL (too) late

telatén ADJ patient, persevering

teledor ADJ careless

téléfon → **télepon**

télékomunikasi N telecommunications; *warung* ~ *(wartel)* small office where you can make calls and send faxes

telentang ADJ on your back, prone ← **lentang**

télepon, télépon, téléfon telephone; ~ *seluler (ponsel)* mobile phone; **menélépon** v to ring (up), call, (tele)phone

téler ADJ drunk, intoxicated; exhausted

télévisi, tévé, tivi N television, TV

telinga N ear

teliti ADJ accurate, careful, meticulous; **peneliti** N researcher; **penelitian** N research

teluk N bay, gulf

telur, telor N egg; ~ *ayam* egg

téma N theme

teman N friend; **berteman** v to be friends; **menemani** v to accompany

tembaga N copper

témbak shoot, fire; **témbakan** N shot, shooting; **menémbak** v to shoot; **penémbak** N marksman, gunman; **tertémbak** ADJ shot (accidentally)

tembakau N tobacco

témbok N (concrete or outer) wall

192

tembus pierce, penetrate; **menembus** v to pierce, stab

tempat N place; ~ *lahir* birthplace, place of birth; ~ *tidur* bed; ~ *tinggal* home, residence; **menempati** v to occupy, take a place; **setempat** ADJ local

témpé N unrefined soybean curd

témpél stick to; **menémpél** v to stick or adhere to; **menémpélkan** v to stick, paste or glue something

témpo N time, pace; ~ *hari* the other day, recently

tempuh: menempuh v to endure, go through; to take on, take up; ~ *ujian* to do an exam

tempur fight, combat; *pesawat* ~ fighter; **pertempuran** N battle

tempurung N coconut shell

temu find, locate; **temuan** N find, discovery; **bertemu** v to meet; *sampai* ~ *lagi* see you later, so long; **ketemu** v, coll to meet; **menemui** v to meet up with, arrange to meet; **menemukan** v to discover;

penemu N inventor, discoverer; **penemuan** N invention, discovery; **pertemuan** N meeting

tenaga N energy, power

tenang ADJ calm, still, quiet; **menenangkan** v to calm someone (down)

tenar ADJ well-known, popular

ténda N tent

tendang kick; **tendangan** N kick; **menendang** v to kick

tengah middle, in the middle of, half; **tengah-tengah** PREP middle; **menengah** ADJ intermediate; *kaum* ~ middle class; **setengah** ADJ half; *jam* ~ *dua* half past one; **setengah-setengah** ADV half-heartedly

tenggara ADJ southeast

tenggelam sink, sunken; drown

tenggiling N anteater

tenggiri *ikan* ~ mackerel

tenggorok, tenggorokan N throat

tengkar: bertengkar v to quarrel; **pertengkaran** N quarrel

tengkorak N skull

193

tengkurap, tengkurup ADV on your front or face

téngok, menéngok V to look or see; to look in on someone

ténis N tennis; **peténis** N tennis player

ténsi N blood pressure

tentang CONJ about, concerning; **bertentangan** ADJ contradictory, contrary, opposing; **menentang** V to oppose, resist

tentara N soldier

ténténg, menénténg V to carry dangling from the hand

tentu ADJ certain, sure, definite; ~*nya*, ~ *saja* of course; **ketentuan** N condition, stipulation; **menentukan** V to decide, determine, stipulate; **tertentu** ADJ definite, fixed, certain

tenun *kain* ~ woven cloth; **tenunan** N weaving, woven fabric; **menenun** V to weave

tepat ADJ precise, exact

tepi edge, side; ~ *jalan* side of the road; ~ *laut* seaside

tepuk ~ *tangan* applause,

clap; **bertepuk tangan** V to applaud, clap

tepung N flour; ~ *beras* rice flour; ~ *terigu* flour

ter- PREF (before adjectives) the most; **terbaik** ADJ the best; **tertinggi** ADJ the highest

tér N tar

terakhir ADJ last, final, latest ← *akhir*

terang ADJ clear; **terang-terangan** ADJ frank, open; **keterangan** N explanation; **menerangkan** V to explain

terap: terapan ADJ applied; **menerapkan** V to apply something

térapi N therapy; *fisio*~ physiotherapy

téras N balcony, terrace

terasa V to be felt ← *rasa*

terasi N shrimp paste

teratai *(bunga)* ~ lotus

teratur ADJ organized, regular ← *atur*

terbaik ADJ the best ← *baik*

terbakar ADJ burnt ← *bakar*

terbalik ADJ overturned, upside-down, opposite ← *balik*

terbang V fly; **menerbangkan**

v to fly something; **penerbang** n pilot, aviator; **penerbangan** n flight; aviation

terbaru ADJ latest, newest ← **baru**

terbatas ADJ limited ← **batas**

terbayang ADJ imagine, conceivable ← **bayang**

terbentuk ADJ formed, shaped, created ← **bentuk**

terbesar ADJ largest, biggest ← **besar**

terbit v to rise, appear; **terbitan** n publication, edition; **menerbitkan** v to publish, issue; **penerbit** n publisher

terbuka ADJ open ← **buka**

terbukti ADJ proven ← **bukti**

terbunuh ADJ killed ← **bunuh**

terburu-buru ADJ in a hurry ← **buru**

tercantum ADJ attached, included, inserted ← **cantum**

tercapai ADJ achieved ← **capai**

tercatat ADJ registered; *surat ~* registered mail ← **catat**

tercemar ADJ polluted ← **cemar**

tercepat ADJ fastest ← **cepat**

tercinta ADJ dear, beloved ← **cinta**

terdaftar ADJ registered, enrolled ← **daftar**

terdakwa n the accused ← **dakwa**

terdekat ADJ closest, nearest ← **dekat**

terdiri *~ atas*, *~ dari* to consist of, be based or founded on ← **diri**

terdorong ADJ pushed, shoved ← **dorong**

terendah ADJ lowest ← **rendah**

terendam ADJ inundated, flooded, soaked ← **rendam**

terganggu ADJ bothered, disrupted, disturbed ← **ganggu**

tergantung ADJ depending (on), it depends; **ketergantungan** n dependency ← **gantung**

tergelincir ADJ skidded, slipped ← **gelincir**

tergenang ADJ flooded ← **genang**

tergesa-gesa ADJ in a hurry or rush ← **gesa**

tergoda ADJ tempted ← **goda**

tergolong ADJ to include, be part of or considered ← **golong**

tergorés ADJ scratched ← **gorés**

terhadap CONJ regarding, against, with respect to ← **hadap**

terhalang ADJ blocked, prevented ← **halang**

terharu ADJ moved, touched ← **haru**

terhormat ADJ respected ← **hormat**

teriak scream, yell; **berteriak** v to scream or shout

terigu N wheat

terima menerima v to accept, ~ *kasih* thank you, thanks; **berterima kasih** v to be grateful or thankful

teripang, tripang N sea slug, sea cucumber, *trepang*

terisak, terisak(isak) ADJ sobbing ← **isak**

terjadi v to happen, become ← **jadi**

terjal ADJ very steep, precipitous

terjamin ADJ guaranteed ← **jamin**

terjatuh ADJ (accidentally) fallen ← **jatuh**

terjawab ADJ answered ← **jawab**

terjebak ADJ trapped, caught ← **jebak**

terjemah: terjemahan N translation; **menerjemahkan** v to translate (writing); to interpret (speaking); **penerjemah** N translator; **penerjemahan** N translation

terjepit ADJ pinched, caught in an uncomfortable situation ← **jepit**

terjual ADJ sold; *habis* ~ sold out ← **jual**

terjun dive, fall; go down; **penerjun** ~ *(payung)* parachutist, sky diver

terkecuali *tidak* ~, *tanpa* ~ without exception ← **kecuali**

terkejut ADJ surprised ← **kejut**

terkenal ADJ well-known ← **kenal**

terkendali ADJ controlled ← **kendali**

terkesan ADJ impressed; seemed ← **kesan**

terkilir ADJ twisted, sprained ← **kilir**

terkira *tak* ~ unsuspected, not thought of ← **kira**

terkirim ADJ sent ← **kirim**

terkubur ADJ buried in an

accident ← **kubur**

terkutuk ADJ cursed, accursed ← **kutuk**

terlahir ADJ born ← **lahir**

terlalu ADV too; **keterlaluan** N excess, too much ← **lalu**

terlambat ADJ (too) late, delayed; **keterlambatan** N delay ← **lambat**

terlampir ADJ attached, enclosed ← **lampir**

terlanjur, telanjur ADJ too late, already ← **lanjur**

terlarang ADJ forbidden, banned ← **larang**

terlémpar ADJ thrown, flung ← **lémpar**

terletak ADJ situated, located ← **letak**

terlibat ADJ involved, implicated; **keterlibatan** N involvement, association ← **libat**

terlilit ADJ caught up, twisted ← **lilit**

terlindas ADJ run over ← **lindas**

terlupakan *tak* ~ unforgettable ← **lupa**

termasuk ADJ including ← **masuk**

términal N (bus) terminal, bus station

ternak N cattle, livestock; **peternakan** N cattle farm, ranch

ternama ADJ famous, well-known ← **nama**

terobos break through; pierce; **terobosan** N breakthrough

terompét N trumpet

térong, térung, terung N eggplant, aubergine

teropong N telescope, binoculars

terowong: terowongan N tunnel, shaft

terpadu ADJ integrated ← **padu**

terpakai ADJ used, in use ← **pakai**

terpaksa ADJ forced ← **paksa**

terpancing ADJ hooked, caught up; involved ← **pancing**

terpaut ADJ fastened, bound; separated ← **paut**

terpelajar ADJ educated ← **ajar**

terpelését ADJ slipped, skidded; tripped ← **pelését**

terpelihara ADJ well cared-for, well-maintained ← **pelihara**

197

terpencét ADJ accidentally pressed ← **pencét**

terpencil ADJ isolated, remote ← **pencil**

terpengaruh ADJ affected or influenced ← **pengaruh**

terpenuhi ADJ satisfied, fulfilled ← **penuh**

terperangkap ADJ trapped, caught ← **perangkap**

terpercaya ADJ trusted, reliable ← **percaya**

terpisah ADJ separated ← **pisah**

terpotong ADJ cut (off) ← **potong**

terpuji ADJ highly-praised ← **puji**

terpukul ADJ hard-hit ← **pukul**

terputus ADJ cut off; **terputus-putus** V to keep cutting out ← **putus**

tersambung ADJ connected ← **sambung**

tersangka N *(yang)* ~ suspect

tersangkut ADJ involved; caught, snagged ← **sangkut**

tersaput ~ *awan* clouded over ← **saput**

tersebut ADJ (afore-)mentioned, said ← **sebut**

tersedia ADJ available, prepared ← **sedia**

terselip ADJ fallen or slipped into ← **selip**

tersendiri ADJ its own; apart, separate ← **diri**, **sendiri**

tersénggol ADJ bumped, brushed ← **sénggol**

tersentuh ADJ touched ← **sentuh**

tersenyum V to smile ← **senyum**

terserah ADJ it depends; up to you ← **serah**

tersesat ADJ lost ← **sesat**

tersiksa ADJ tortured ← **siksa**

tersinggung ADJ offended, hurt ← **singgung**

tersingkir, tersingkirkan ADJ eliminated, swept aside ← **singkir**

tersisa ADJ leftover ← **sisa**

tertabrak ADJ hit ← **tabrak**

tertahan ADJ held back, prevented ← **tahan**

tertanggal ADJ dated ← **tanggal**

tertarik ADJ attracted, interested ← **tarik**

tertawa V to laugh; **menertawakan** V to laugh at ← **tawa**

tertekan ADJ stressed, pushed, pressured ← **tekan**

tertelan ADJ accidentally swallowed ← **telan**

tertémbak ADJ shot (accidentally) ← **témbak**

tertentu ADJ definite, fixed, certain ← **tentu**

tertib ADJ orderly, organized, disciplined; **menertibkan** v to keep order, discipline

tertidur ADJ fallen asleep ← **tidur**

tertolong ADJ saved, rescued ← **tolong**

tertukar ADJ changed by accident ← **tukar**

tertunda v delayed, postponed ← **tunda**

tertutup ADJ closed ← **tutup**

terulang ADJ repeated ← **ulang**

terumbu N coral

terungkap ADJ expressed, revealed ← **ungkap**

terus ADV straight on; continuous, constant; **terusan** N extension; canal; **terus-terusan** ADV constantly, continuously; **meneruskan** v to continue, keep doing

something; **penerus** N successor; someone who continues another's work; **seterusnya** ADV after that, henceforth

terutama ADV especially, particularly ← **utama**

tetangga N neighbor

tetap ADJ fixed, definite, constant; ADV still; **menetap** v to stay; **menetapkan** v to appoint, fix, stipulate; **penetapan** N appointment

tetapi, tapi CONJ but

tétés drip, drop; **tétésan** N drip, drop, droplet

tetumbuhan → **tumbuh**

tévé, tivi N TV ← **télévisi**

téwas v to be killed; die; killed in action; **menéwaskan** v to kill someone

Thai *bahasa* ~, *orang* ~ Thai; **Thailand** N Thailand

tiada no; there isn't any, there aren't any ← **tidak ada**

tiang N pillar, pole, mast; ~ *bendera* flagpole

tiap, setiap ADJ each, every; ~ *saat* any time

tiba v to arrive or come; **tiba-tiba** ADV suddenly

tidak, tak, ndak, nggak, enggak no, not; *~ pasti* uncertain; **setidak-(tidak)nya** ADV at least

tidur sleep; asleep; **tiduran** V to lie down, rest; **ketiduran** V to fall asleep; **menidurkan** V to put to sleep; **tertidur** ADJ fallen asleep

tifa N large drum from Papua

tifus, tipus N typhoid (fever)

tiga ADJ three; *~ belas* thirteen; **bertiga** ADJ in threes; **ketiga** ADJ the third; **sepertiga** ADJ one-third; **pertigaan** N T-junction

tikai: bertikai V to quarrel or disagree

tikam stab; **tikaman** N stab; **menikam** V to stab

tikar N mat

tikét N (relatively expensive) ticket; *~ kereta api* (long-distance) train ticket

tikung: tikungan N bend, curve

tikus N (small) mouse, (large) rat; *~ besar* rat; **tikusan** N (computer) mouse

tilang N traffic fine; **ditilang** V to be fined ← **bukti**

pelanggaran

tim N team

tim *nasi ~* steamed rice with chicken

timah N tin; *~ putih* tin

timbang: timbangan N scales; **ketimbang** CONJ, COLL compared with; **mempertimbangkan** V to consider; **pertimbangan** N consideration

timbel, timbal N lead

timbul emerge; **menimbulkan** V to give rise, bring to the surface

timbun N pile, heap

Timteng N the Middle East ← **Timur Tengah**

Timtim N, ARCH East Timor, Timor Loro Sae ← **East Timor**

timun, mentimun N cucumber ← **mentimun**

timur ADJ east; *~ laut* northeast; **ketimuran** ADJ Eastern, Oriental

tindak act, deed; *~ lanjut* follow-up; **menindaklanjuti** V to take a step or measure; **tindakan** N action, measure, step

200

tindas: penindasan N oppression

tinggal V to live, stay, remain; **meninggal ~ (dunia)** to die; **meninggalkan** V to leave (behind), abandon

tinggi ADJ high, tall; **~nya** height; **ketinggian** N altitude, height; **setinggi** ADJ as high as

tingkah action

tingkat N level, floor, story, grade; **tingkatan** N grade, degree, level; **bertingkat** ADJ having different levels; **meningkat** V to rise, increase, improve; **meningkatkan** V to increase or raise the level of something

tinjau: tinjauan N review; **meninjau** V to observe, view; **peninjau** N observer

tinju N boxing; fist; **bertinju** V to box; **petinju** N boxer

tinta N ink

Tionghoa ADJ, POL Chinese

tipe N type, sort

tipék, tipéks: ditipéks V to white-out, be corrected

tipis ADJ thin

tipu trick, cheat; **menipu** V to trick, deceive; **penipu** N con man, trickster; **penipuan** N deception

tipus, tifus N typhoid (fever)

tirai N curtain

tiri ADJ step-; **adik ~, kakak ~** stepbrother or stepsister

tiru, meniru V to copy or imitate; **tiruan** N imitation, fake

tisu N tissue; **~ basah** wipe

titik N dot, point; full stop, period

titip, menitip V to leave in someone's care, entrust; **titipan** N parcel, something sent with another person; **penitipan** N care

tiup blow; **meniup** V to blow

tivi, tévé N TV ← *télévisi*

TK ABBREV *Taman Kanak-kanak* kindergarten, preschool

TKI ABBREV *Tenaga Kerja Indonesia* Indonesian worker migrant

TNI ABBREV *Tentara Nasional Indonesia* Indonesian National Army/Armed Forces

toalét, toilét N toilet, washroom

todong, menodong v to threaten or hold up at knifepoint

toké̆k n large gray house gecko

toko n shop, store; **pertokoan** n shopping center or complex, mall

tokoh n figure, character

tol n toll; *jalan* ~ toll road

tolak v to refuse, reject; **menolak** v to refuse, reject; **penolakan** n refusal, rejection

tolong help; please; *minta* ~ please help me; **menolong** v to help or assist; **pertolongan** n help, assistance, aid; **tertolong** ADJ saved, rescued

tomat n tomato

tombak n spear

tombol n knob, button

tong n drum, barrel, bin

tongkat n stick, cane

tongséng n goat and cabbage curry

tonjok, menonjok v to punch, hit

tonjol: menonjol v to stick out, protrude; ADJ prominent

tonton: tontonan n show, performance; **menonton, nonton** v to watch, look on; **penonton** n spectator, audience

topéng n mask

topi n hat; ~ *pet* cap

tosérba n general store; department store ← **toko sérba ada**

tradisi ADJ tradition (not *adat*); **tradisional** ADJ traditional

traktir, mentraktir v to invite out, shout, treat, pay for another

trampil ADJ skilled; **ketrampilan** n skill

transaksi n (bank) transaction

transisi n transition

transmigrasi n transmigration (from Java to other islands)

trén, trénd n trend, fashion; **ngetrén** ADJ, COLL trendy, fashionable

trompét n trumpet

tropis ADJ tropical

trotoar n pavement, sidewalk

truk n truck

tua ADJ old; dark (of colors); **ketua** n chair(person); chief

tuan, Tn PRON master, sir (esp for foreigners)

tuang v to pour

tubuh N body

tuding: tudingan N accusation; **menuding** v to accuse, point the finger

tuduh: tuduhan N charge, accusation; **menuduh** v to accuse

tugas N task, duty, function; **menugaskan** v to assign someone, give a task to

tugu N monument, column

Tuhan N, PRON God, Allah; **tuhan** N god

tuju: tujuan N direction, destination; aim, goal; **menuju** v to approach, go towards; **setuju** agree, agreed; **menyetujui** v to agree to, approve, ratify; **persetujuan** N agreement, approval

tujuh ADJ seven; ~ *belas* seventeen; ~ *puluh* seventy

tukang N (unskilled) worker, handyman; ~ *sepatu* cobbler, shoemaker

tukar v to exchange; ~-*menukar* barter; **menukar** v to change; **menukarkan** v to change something;

pertukaran N exchange; **tertukar** ADJ changed by accident

tulang N bone

tular: ketularan ADJ infected, caught something; **menular** v to infect; ADJ contagious, infectious

tuli ADJ deaf

tulis v to write; **tulisan** N writing, script; **menulis** v to write; **penulis** N author, writer

tulus ADJ sincere

tumbang fall, fallen

tumbuh v to grow; **tetumbuhan, tumbuh-tumbuhan** N plants; **tumbuhan** N a growth; plant; **pertumbuhan** N growth, development

tumis v to stir-fry, sautée

tumpah spill, spilt; **menumpahkan** v to spill something

tumpang: menumpang v to make use of someone else's facilities; to get a lift or ride; **penumpang** N passenger

tumpuk N heap, pile; **bertumpuk** v to be in piles

tumpul ADJ blunt

tuna- PREF without

tunai N cash

tunang: tunangan N, F fiancée; N, M fiancé; V, COLL to be engaged; **pertunangan** N engagement

tunda delay; **menunda** V to delay, put off, postpone; **menundakan** V to delay or postpone something; **tertunda** ADJ delayed, postponed

tunduk V to bow to, submit, obey; **menunduk** V to bow your head; **menundukkan** V to bow or lower something; to defeat

tunggal ADJ single, sole

tunggang: menunggang V to ride; ~ *kuda* to ride a horse

tunggu V to wait; **menunggu** V to wait for something; **menunggu-nunggu** V to wait a long time for

tunjang: tunjangan N allowance, bonus

tunjuk, menunjuk V to indicate, point out, refer to; **menunjukkan** V to show, point out; **pertunjukan** N show, performance; **petunjuk** N instruction, direction

tuntas ADJ complete, total

tuntut claim; **tuntutan** N claim, charge; **menuntut** V to claim or demand

tupai N squirrel

tur N tour; **turis** N tourist

Turki N Turkey

turun V to descend, fall, come down; **keturunan** N descendant; **menurun** V to fall, drop, decline; **menurunkan** V to lower or reduce

turut V to take part, join; ~ *berduka cita* express your condolences; **berturut-turut** ADJ consecutive, successive; **menurut** CONJ according to

tusuk skewer, needle; poke; ~ *sate* satay stick

tuts N key, button

tutul ADJ spotted

tutup lid, cover; closed, shut; ~ *botol* bottle-cap; **menutup** V to close or shut; **menutupi** V to cover (up); **penutup** N stopper, lid; end; **tertutup** ADJ closed

tutur speak; **penutur** N speaker

TV ABBREV *teve, tivi, televisi* television

TVRI ABBREV *Televisi Republik Indonesia* Indonesian state-owned television

U

uang N money; ~ *kembali* change; **keuangan** N finance

ubah change; **berubah** v to change; **mengubah** v to change or alter; **perubahan** N change, alteration

uban N (strand of) gray or white hair

ubi N edible tuber or root; sweet potato, yam

ubin N (floor) tile

ubur-ubur N jellyfish

ucap say; **ucapan** N greetings; **mengucap, mengucapkan** v to say or express something

udah → **sudah**

udang N shrimp

udara N air, atmosphere

udik → **mudik**

ujar speak, say

uji test; **ujian** N test, exam(-ination); **menguji** v to examine or test; **penguji** N examiner

ujung N point, end

ukir, mengukir v to carve or engrave; **ukiran** v carving

ukur measure; **ukuran** N size, measurement; **mengukur** v to measure; **pengukuran** v measuring, measurement

ulang repeat; ~ *tahun* birthday, anniversary; **ulangan** N test; **berulang** v to happen again, recur; **berulang-ulang** ADV again and again, repeatedly; **mengulang** v to repeat, do again; **mengulangi** v to repeat something; **terulang** ADJ repeated

ular N snake

ulat N worm, caterpillar

ultah N birthday, anniversary ← *ulang tahun*

umat N people (of one faith)

umbi N tuber; **umbi-umbian** N tubers

umpama N example; ~*nya* for example; **seumpamanya** CONJ for instance

umpan N bait

umpat, mengumpat v to curse swear; **umpatan** N oath, swear word

umpat, umpet: umpet-umpetan N, COLL hide and seek; **mengumpet** V to hide or conceal yourself

umum ADJ general, public, common; *(pada) ~nya* generally, in general; **mengumumkan** V to announce or declare; **pengumuman** N notice, announcement

umur N age; **berumur** ADJ aged; **seumur** ADJ the same age; lifelong

undang, mengundang V to invite (formally); **undangan** N invitation; formal event

undang: undang-undang N law, act; *~ Dasar* constitution

undi N lot; **undian** N lottery; **mengundi** V to conduct a draw or lottery

undur, mundur V to reverse, go back; **mengundurkan** V to postpone; **pengunduran** N postponement, delay

unggul ADJ superior

unggun *api ~* (camp)fire

ungkap V to express, reveal; **ungkapan** N expression; **mengungkap** V to uncover;

mengungkapkan V to express; **terungkap** ADJ expressed, revealed

ungsi: mengungsi V to evacuate or flee; **pengungsi** N refugee, evacuee; **pengungsian** N evacuation

ungu ADJ purple

uni N union

unik ADJ unique; **keunikan** N unique thing, uniqueness

univérsitas N university

unjuk *~ rasa* demonstration

unsur N element

unta, onta N camel; *burung ~* ostrich

untai N string; counter for string-like objects; **untaian** N string, chain

untuk PREP for

untung advantage, gain, profit; luck; **beruntung** ADJ lucky, fortunate; **keuntungan** N advantage, profit; **menguntungkan** V to profit; ADJ profitable

upacara N ceremony

upah N wage, wages

upaya N effort

upil N snot, bogey, nasal mucus

urap N vegetable salad with grated coconut

urat N tendon, vein; muscle; ~ *saraf* nerve

urus organize, arrange; **urusan** N arrangement, dealing, affair; **berurusan** v to have dealings with, deal with; **mengurus** v to arrange, organize, manage; **pengurus** N manager, organizer

urut order in a series; **urutan** N order, sequence

urut massage, rub; **mengurut** v to massage

urutan N order, sequence ← **urut**

usah *tidak* ~ not necessary

usaha N effort; **berusaha** v to try, make an effort; **mengusahakan** v to try, endeavor to; **pengusaha** N, M businessman; N, F businesswoman; **perusahaan** N company

usia N, POL age; ~ *lanjut* old age; **berusia** v to be (aged)

usir, mengusir v to drive away or out, chase away, expel

usul propose, suggest; motion; **mengusulkan** v to propose

or suggest

usus N intestine

utak ~*atik* fiddle or tinker with ← **kutak-katik**

utama ADJ main; **mengutamakan** v to give preference or priority to; **terutama** ADV especially, particularly

utang, hutang N debt; **berutang** v to owe

utara ADJ north

utuh ADJ whole, complete, untouched

V

vaksin N vaccine; **vaksinasi** N vaccination

vakum N vacuum

valas N foreign currency ← **valuta asing**

valuta N currency

vanili N vanilla

vas N vase

vélg, véleg, pélek N wheel rim

verboden, perboden no entry

vérsi N version

véspa N moped, motor scooter

vétsin N MSG (monosodium glutamate)

Viétnam N Vietnam

vihara, wihara N Buddhist temple or monastery

vila N villa, holiday house, summer cottage

vital ADJ vital; *alat* ~ vital organs; genitals

vocer, voucer N credit voucher (for mobile phones)

vokal ADJ vocal, outspoken; **vokalis** N vocalist

voli *bola* ~ volleyball

volume N volume, size, bulk

vonis N ruling; sentence; **divonis** v to be sentenced

W

wabah N epidemic, plague

waduk N reservoir; dam

wafat v, POL to pass away or die; ~ *1970* died 1970

wagub N deputy governor ← **wakil gubernur**

wah EXCL wow! oh! ADJ amazing, outstanding; fantastic, wonderful

wahana N vehicle, means

Waisak, Wésak N Buddhist New Year

wajah N, POL face

wajan N wok

wajar ADJ natural

wajib compulsory; must, obliged; **kewajiban** N obligation, duty

wajik N diamonds (card suit); diamond-shaped cake of sticky rice

wakil N representative, substitute; ADJ vice; **mewakili** v to represent; **perwakilan** N representation, delegation

waktu N time, hours; CONJ when; *pada ~nya* in due time, at the right time

walaikum ISL ~ *salam* and upon you be peace (said in response to *salam alaikum*)

walau, walaupun CONJ although

walét *burung* ~ swift

-wan SUF, M -man, one who does something

wangi fragrant; perfume; **wangi-wangian, wewangian** N scents, perfumes

208

wanita N woman

waprés N vice-president ← **wakil présidén**

waras ADJ sane, healthy

warga N citizen; **warganegara** N citizen, national; **kewarganegaraan** N citizenship

waris: warisan N inheritance; **mewarisi** V to inherit

warna N color; ~ *putih* white; ~*-warni* colorful, multicolored; **berwarna** ADJ colored; **mewarnai** V to color (in); **pewarna** N dye, stain

warnét N Internet café ← **warung internét**

warpostél N office where you can make calls, and send post and faxes ← **warung pos dan télékomunikasi**

warta N news; M **wartawan**, F **wartawati** journalist, reporter

warteg N small, cheap food stall ← **warung Tegal**

wartél N small office where you can make calls and send faxes ← **warung télékomunikasi**

warung N stall, small local shop; ~ *kopi* coffee stall

waserai N (commercial) laundry

wasir N hemorrhoids

wasit N umpire, referee

waslap N washcloth, flannel

waspada ADJ on guard, careful, cautious

wassalam ISL and upon you be peace

wastafel N basin, sink (in bathroom)

watak N nature, character

-wati SUF, F -woman, one who does something

wawancara N interview; **mewawancarai** V to interview

wawas: wawasan N outlook, view, concept

wayang N puppet; ~ *golek* wooden, three-dimensional puppet; ~ *kulit* shadow puppet (performance)

WC N [wé sé] toilet, bathroom, lavatory

wédang N warm Javanese beverage

wéker N alarm; *jam* ~ alarm clock; *memasang* ~ to set the alarm

wenang: kewenangan, wewenang N authority;

209

sewenang-wenang ADV tyrannically, arbitrarily

wewangian → **wangi**

wewenang N authority ← **wenang**

WIB ABBREV *Waktu Indonesia Barat* Western Indonesian time

wihara, vihara N Buddhist temple or monastery

wilayah N area, territory

windu N eight-year cycle

wingko ~ *babat* small coconut slice, a specialty of Semarang

wira-: wirausaha N business; **wiraswasta** N, M businessman F businesswoman

wisata N tourism, travel; *biro* ~ travel agent; **wisatawan** N tourist

wiski N whisky, whiskey

wisma N house, building

wisuda graduate

WIT ABBREV *Waktu Indonesia Timur* Eastern Indonesian time

WITA ABBREV *Waktu Indonesia Tengah* Central Indonesian time

WNA ABBREV *warga negara asing* foreign national

WNI ABBREV *warga negara Indonesia* Indonesian national

wol N wool

wortel N carrot

wujud N existence; **mewujudkan** V to make something real, realize something

wulan *catur* ~ trimester, term

X

X *sinar* ~ X-ray

Y

ya, iya yes

ya EJAC oh, O

Yahudi ADJ Jewish; *orang* ~ Jewish, Jew

yaitu CONJ namely, that is

yakin ADJ sure, convinced; **keyakinan** N belief, conviction, faith; **meyakini** V to believe, be convinced; **meyakinkan** ADJ convincing, believable

Yaman N Yemen

yang CONJ that, which, who; ~ *biru* the blue one; ~ *lalu* in the past

yatim N orphan, fatherless child; ~ *piatu* orphan

yayasan N foundation (not for profit)

Yordania N Jordan

yth. *yang terhormat* the respected, used when addressing letters

yuk → **ayo**

Yunani N Greece

yunior junior (at work or school)

Z

zaitun N olive

zakat, jakat N alms

zaman, jaman N age, era, time, period

zamrud, jamrud N emerald

zat, jat N element, substance

ziarah N pilgrimage, visit to a holy place or cemetery; **berziarah** V to make a pilgrimage, visit a holy place

English–Indonesian

A

a ART satu, suatu, se~; per, tiap;
~ *dog* seekor anjing → **ékor**;
~ *house* sebuah rumah →
buah; ~ *man* seorang lelaki
→ **orang**

abacus N sempoa

abandon V mengabaikan,
menelantarkan; **abandoned**
V, ADJ terabaikan, telantar

abattoir N [abatuar] pejagalan

abbreviate V menyingkatkan,
memendekkan; **abbreviation**
N singkatan, kependekan

abdomen N perut

ability N [abiliti] kemampuan,
kesanggupan, kepandaian
← **able**

able ADJ [ébel] bisa, mampu,
sanggup

abnormal ADJ tidak normal,
tidak biasa

aboard ADJ di atas kendaraan

abolish V menghapus,
meniadakan

Aborigine N [Aborijini] orang
Aborijin, penduduk asli

Australia; **aboriginal** ADJ, N
orang Aborijin

abortion N pengguguran,
aborsi

about PREP tentang, mengenai,
seputar (sebuah topik);
sekitar, keliling (sebuah
tempat); kurang lebih, kira-
kira (jumlah)

above PREP [abav] (di) atas;
lebih daripada

abridged ADJ singkat

abroad ADV luar negeri, negeri
orang

abrupt ADJ tiba-tiba; kasar,
kurang sopan

absence N ketidakhadiran;
absent ADJ tidak hadir

absolute ADJ mutlak, total;
absolutely ADV secara mutlak,
betul

absorb V menyerap; **absorp-
tion** N serapan, absorpsi;
penyerapan

abstract ADJ abstrak; tidak
konkret

absurd ADJ gila, tidak masuk
akal

abundant ADJ berlimpah (ruah)

abuse N [abyus] penganiayaan, penyalahgunaan; kekerasan; v [abyuz] menganiaya, menyalahgunakan, memperlakukan dengan kasar

academic ADJ akademis; N akademisi; **academy** N akademi, sekolah tinggi

accelerator N (pedal) gas

accent [aksént] N logat, aksen, nuansa

accept v menerima; **acceptable** ADJ layak, dapat diterima

access N akses; v mendapat, memakai

accessory: accessories N, PL aksesoris, variasi (pada mobil), perlengkapan

accident N [aksidént] kecelakaan; **accidental** ADJ kebetulan, tidak disengaja

accommodation N penginapan, akomodasi

accompany v menemani, mengantarkan, mengiringi

accomplice N [akamplis] kaki tangan, antek

accomplishment N prestasi

accord N persepakatan, persetujuan; **according** ~ *to* menurut

account N rekening (bank); pertanggungjawab; laporan, cerita; **accountant** N akuntan

accurate ADJ teliti, cermat, tepat

accusation N tuduhan; **accuse** v menuduh, menuding

accustomed ADJ terbiasa

ace N (kartu) as; ADJ, COLL mahir, hebat

ache N [ék] sakit, pegal; *tooth*~ gigi ngilu; v sakit

achieve v mencapai, meraih; **achievement** N prestasi

acid N asam; ADJ pahit

acknowledgment N pengakuan; ucapan terima kasih

acne N, PL [akni] jerawat

acquaintance N kenalan

acquire v memperoleh; **acquisition** N perolehan, barang yang diperoleh

acre N [éker] ukuran tanah (0.46 hektar)

acrobat N akrobat, pesenam

across PREP (di) seberang, melintang, lintas; mendatar

act N perbuatan; babak,

214

lakon (dalam pertunjukan);
undang-undang; v berbuat,
bertindak; **action** n perbuatan, aksi; proses; **activate**
v menghidupkan, meng-
gerakkan; **active** ADJ giat,
rajin, sibuk, aktif; hidup
(telepon genggam); **activist**
n aktivis; **activity** n kegiatan,
kesibukan; **actor** n, m aktor,
pemain (film); **actress** n, f
aktris, pemain (film); **actual**
ADJ **actually** ADV sebenarnya
acupuncture n tusuk jarum
adapt v menyesuaikan;
adaptable ADJ mudah
menyesuaikan diri, supel
add v bertambah, menambah,
menambahkan
addict n pecandu
addition n tambahan, penam-
bahan, jumlah; **additional**
ADJ tambahan, ekstra ← **add**
address n alamat, adres;
pidato; v mengalamatkan
(surat); berpidato; menegur,
menyapa
adequate ADJ cukup, memadai
adjoining ADJ berdampingan
adjust v menyetel, mencocokkan, mengatur,

menyesuaikan
administration n; **administrative** ADJ pemerintahan;
pemerintah; pelaksanaan;
pemberian; **administrator**
n pemerintah, pelaksana,
pengurus
admirable ADJ mengagumkan,
patut dikagumi ← **admire**
admiral n laksamana
admiration n kekaguman;
admire v mengagumi
admission n penerimaan, izin
masuk; pengakuan; **admit**
v menerima, mengizinkan
masuk; mengakui
adopt v mengangkat atau
memungut anak; mengambil
adorable ADJ lucu, mengge-
maskan, manis, jelita; **adore**
v memuja; sangat mencintai,
gila akan
adult ADJ dewasa; n orang
dewasa
adultery n zinah
advance n kemajuan; uang
muka; v maju; memajukan,
mempercepat
advantage n untung,
keuntungan
adventure n petualangan

215

adverb N kata keterangan (pada kata kerja)

advertise V mengiklankan, memasangiklan; **advertisement** N iklan, pariwara, reklame

advice N [advais] nasihat, saran; **advise** V [advaiz] menasihati; **advisor** N penasihat

aerial N [érial] antena; ADJ angkasa, udara

aeronautical ADJ, N aeronautika, ilmu penerbangan

affair N perkara, hal, soal, urusan; perselingkuhan, cerita cinta

affect V mempengaruhi; **affection** N rasa kasih sayang; **affectionate** ADJ memperlihatkan kasih sayang

afford V mampu (membayar dll); **affordable** ADJ terjangkau (harganya)

afraid ADJ takut

Africa N Afrika; **African** ADJ, N orang Africa

Afro-American N orang Amerika berkulit hitam (keturunan Afrika); orang Negro

after PREP, CONJ, ADV kemudian; PREP setelah, sesudah; **afternoon** N sore, petang; sesudah jam 12 siang sampai dengan matahari terbenam; *good* ~ selamat siang (jam 12–15); selamat sore (jam 15–19); **afterwards** PREP sesudahnya, kemudian

again ADV (sekali) lagi; *then* ~ tapi

against PREP terhadap; berlawanan, bertentangan

agate N [aget] batu akik

age N umur, usia

agency N agen, perwakilan; *news* ~ kantor berita ← **agent**

agenda N agenda, acara, rencana

agent N agen, wakil

aggressive ADJ galak, bersifat menyerang, agresif

ago ADV lalu, lampau, silam

agony N kesakitan, penderitaan; sakratulmaut

agree V setuju, bersepakat; menyetujui, mengiyakan; **agreement** N persetujuan, kesepakatan, perjanjian

agricultural ADJ berkaitan dengan pertanian; **agri-**

culture N pertanian
AH ABBREV *after hours* r, rmh (rumah)
ahead ADV [ahéd] di depan, di muka, terlebih dahulu ← **head**
aid N bantuan, pertolongan; *first* ~ pertolongan pertama
AIDS (Acquired Immune Deficiency Syndrome) N AIDS
aim N sasaran, maksud, tujuan; v membidik, mengincar, menuju
air N udara; angin; ~ *mail* pos udara; v menjemur, menganginkan; **aircraft** N pesawat terbang, kapal terbang; **air crew** N awak kabin; **air force** N angkatan udara; **airline** N perusahaan penerbangan, maskapai penerbangan; **airplane** N pesawat terbang; **airport** N bandara, bandar udara; **air raid** N serangan udara; **airtight** ADJ kedap udara
aisle N [ail] lorong
alarm N weker; tanda bahaya; rasa kaget
albatross N elang laut

alcohol N alkohol, minuman keras; **alcoholic** ADJ beralkohol
alert N tanda (bahaya); v memperingatkan; ADJ siaga, waspada
algebra N aljabar
Algeria N Aljazair
alien N [élien] makhluk asing, orang asing; ADJ asing
alike ADJ serupa, mirip ← **like**
alive ADJ (dalam keadaan) hidup ← **live**
all ADJ [ol] semua, seantero; sekalian, seluruh; ~ *day* sepanjang hari, seharian; ~ *over* habis; di mana-mana; ~ *right* baiklah; ~ *of us* kita semua; *not at* ~ sama sekali tidak; **all-round** ADJ umum
allergic ADJ mempunyai alergi; **allergy** N alergi
alley N [ali] lorong, gang
alligator N [aligétor] buaya (bermoncong pendek)
allow v mengizinkan, memperbolehkan, memperkenankan; **allowance** N tunjangan, uang harian, uang saku
alloy N logam campuran
almighty ADJ [olmaiti] maha

kuasa

almond N kacang almond, buah badam

almost ADV [olmost] hampir, nyaris

alone ADJ, ADV sendiri, seorang diri; hanya, saja

along PREP sepanjang; **alongside** ADJ di sisi, di tepi

aloud ADJ dengan suara keras, dengan suara nyaring

alphabet N abjad, aksara, alfabet

already ADV [olrédi] sudah, telah

also ADV [olso] juga, pula, pun

alter v mengubah; memperbaiki

alternate v berselang-seling, menyelang-nyeling; **alternative** N pilihan lain, alternatif

although CONJ [oltho] meskipun, walaupun

altitude N ketinggian, tinggi

altogether ADJ [oltogéther] semuanya, secara keseluruhan; neg sama sekali

aluminium, aluminum N aluminium

always ADV selalu, senantiasa

am ABBREV *ante meridiem* pagi, siang (jam 0.00–12.00)

amateur ADJ, N [amater] amatir; tidak profesional

amaze v mengherankan, menakjubkan, mengagumkan

ambassador N duta besar

ambition N ambisi, cita-cita; **ambitious** ADJ berambisi, mempunyai cita-cita tinggi

ambulance N ambulans

ambush N serangan mendadak, penyergapan; v menyerang secara mendadak, menyergap

Amen EJAC amin

amendment N pembetulan; amandemen

amenities N, PL fasilitas, sarana

America N Amerika (Serikat); **American** N orang America

amethyst N batu kecubung

amiable ADJ [émiabel] ramah, baik hati

among [amang], **amongst** PREP di tengah, di antara

amount N jumlah, banyaknya; v berjumlah, menjadi

amuse v menghibur; **amused** ADJ terhibur, tertawa;

amusement N hiburan, kesenangan; **amusing** ADJ lucu, menyenangkan

an ART (sebelum huruf vokal) satu, suatu, se~; per, tiap; ~ *apple* sebuah apel → **buah**; ~ *owl* seekor burung hantu → **ekor**

anal ADJ → *sex* sodomi ← **anus**

analysis N analisa, analisis, uraian; **analyze** V menganalisa, meneliti

ancestor N leluhur, nenek moyang

anchor N [anker] sauh, jangkar; V membuang sauh, berlabuh

ancient ADJ [énsyent] kuno, zaman purbakala

and CONJ dan, serta, bersama; ~ *so on* dan lain sebagainya

anecdote N lelucon, cerita, anekdot

anesthetic N obat bius

angel N [énjel] malaikat

anger N [angger] kemarahan, murka; V membuat marah

angle N [anggel] sudut

angry ADJ marah, murka ← **anger**

animal N binatang, hewan, satwa

animation N semangat; kartun animasi, anime

ankle N [angkel] pergelangan kaki

annexe, annex N pavilyun

anniversary N (hari) ulang tahun, hari jadi; hari peringatan

announce V mengumumkan, memberitahukan; **announcer** N penyiar; **announcement** N pengumuman, maklumat

annoy V mengganggu, mengusik; **annoying** ADJ mengganggu, menjengkelkan

annual ADJ tahunan; **annually** ADV setiap tahun

anonymous ADJ tanpa nama, anonim; ~ *letter* surat kaleng

another N, ADJ satu lagi, yang lain

answer N [anser] jawaban, jalan keluar (dari masalah); V menjawab, membalas (surat)

ant N semut; *white* ~s rayap

Antarctic ADJ berasal dari Antartika; *the* ~, **Antarctica** N Antartika, Kutub Selatan

antenna N antena

anthem N lagu wajib; *national*

219

~ lagu kebangsaan

anthology N kumpulan, antologi, bunga rampai

anthropologist N antropolog; **anthropology** N ilmu antropologi

antics N, PL tingkah lucu, kelucuan

antidote N penawar ← **anti**

antique N barang kuno, barang antik; ADJ kuno, antik

anus N [énus] dubur

anxiety N [angzayeti] kecemasan, kegelisahan, kekuatiran; **anxious** ADJ [angsyes] gelisah, cemas

any ADJ [éni] sesuatu, beberapa, sembarang; NEG sedikit pun; **anybody, anyone** N siapa pun, siapa saja; **anyhow** ADV bagaimanapun; **anything** N apa saja, apa pun; **anywhere** N di mana saja; ADV ke mana saja

apart ADV terpisah; ~ *from* selain, kecuali

apartment N apartemen, rumah susun

ape N kera, siamang

apologize v minta maaf; **apology** N permintaan maaf

app N aplikasi

apparent ADJ nyata, jelas, kentara; **apparently** ADV tampaknya, ternyata ← **appear**

appeal N permohonan, permintaan, seruan; banding; v naik banding

appear v tampak, muncul, timbul, menghadap; **appearance** N tampang, penampilan

appendix N lampiran; usus buntu

appetite N selera, nafsu makan

apple N buah apel

appliance N peranti, pesawat, alat

applicant N pelamar, pemohon; **application** N (surat) lamaran; penerapan, pemakai; **apply** v berlaku; menerapkan, menggunakan

appreciate v [aprisyiét] berterima kasih; menghargai, menilai; mengerti

apprentice N [apréntis] murid

approach N pendekatan; v mendekati, menuju (tempat); menjelang (waktu)

appropriate ADJ patut, layak,

pantas, sesuai

approval N [apruval] izin, persetujuan; **approve** V memperkenankan, mengizinkan, menyetujui

approximate ADJ kira-kira, kurang lebih; **approximately** ADV kira-kira, kurang lebih

April N [Épril] bulan April

aqua ADJ biru toska

aquarium N akuarium, kolam ikan

aquatic ADJ [akuotik] berhubungan dengan air atau laut

aqueduct N jalan air (di atas tanah)

Arab N orang Arab; *Saudi* ~ Arab Saudi; **Arabic** N [Arabik] bahasa Arab

arch N garis lengkung; busur; **archer** N pemanah; **archery** N panahan

archeologist N ahli purbakala; **archeology** N ilmu purbakala

archipelago N [arkipélago] kepulauan, gugusan pulau

architect N [arkitekt] arsitek; **architecture** N arsitektur

archive, archives N [arkaiv] arsip

Arctic ADJ Arktik, Artik,

berasal dari kawasan Kutub Utara

are V, PL → **be**

area N [éria] daerah, wilayah, kawasan

Argentina N [Arjentina] Argentina; **Argentinian** N orang Argentina

argue V [argyu] berdebat, bertengkar; memperdebatkan, membantah; **argument** N pertengkaran; alasan, dalih

arid ADJ gersang, kering

aristocracy N kaum ningrat; **aristocrat** N orang ningrat, bangsawan

arithmetic N ilmu berhitung

arm N lengan, tangan (baju)

arm N senjata; V mempersenjatai

armchair N kursi sofa, kursi tamu

armor N baju baja

armpit N ketiak

army N tentara, bala tentara; angkatan darat

aroma N bau harum, aroma; **aromatic** ADJ berbau harum

around PREP sekeliling, sekitar, seputar; dekat; ADJ kira-kira

221

arrange v mengurus, menata, mengatur; mengaransemen (lagu); **arrangement** N penataan, pengaturan, perjanjian; aransemen

arrest N penahanan, penangkapan; v menahan, menangkap

arrival N kedatangan; **arrive** v datang, tiba

arrogant ADJ sombong, angkuh

arrow N (anak) panah

art N seni lukis; kesenian; **arts** N kesenian; sastra (jurusan)

artery N pembuluh nadi, arteri

arthritis [arthraitis] encok, radang sendi

article N barang, benda; pasal, bab(hukum); kata sandang

artificial ADJ buatan, palsu

artist N seniman, seniwati; artis (seni peran); **artistic** ADJ artistik, indah ← **art**

as ADV, CONJ sama, se-; seperti; karena, sebab; ~ *big* ~ *a house* sebesar rumah; ~ *for me* kalau saya; ~ *if* seolah-olah

asbestos N asbes

ash N abu

ashamed ADJ malu

ashore ADJ di darat; *to go* ~ naik ke darat ← **shore**

ashtray N asbak

Asia N Asia; *Southeast* ~ Asia Tenggara

aside ADV di sebelah; ~ *from* selain dari ← **side**

ask v bertanya, minta, memohon

asleep ADJ sedang tidur

assassinate v membunuh tokoh terkenal; **assassination** N pembunuhan tokoh terkenal

assemble v berkumpul, berhimpun, bersidang; mengumpulkan; merakit; **assembly** N perkumpulan, perhimpunan, sidang; perakitan; apel (di sekolah)

assess v menaksir, menilai; **assessment** N taksiran, penilaian

asset N aset, modal

assignment N tugas

assist v menolong, membantu; **assistance** N pertolongan, bantuan; **assistant** N pembantu, asisten

associate N kawan, mitra,

222

rekan; v bergaul; meng-
aitkan, menghubungkan;
association N gabungan,
persatuan, asosiasi
assorted ADJ bermacam jenis
assume v menganggap;
assumption N asumsi,
prasangka
asterisk N tanda bintang
asthma N (penyakit) asma,
sesak dada
astonish v mengherankan,
menakjubkan; **astonished**
ADJ heran
astound v **astounding** ADJ
mengejutkan, mengherankan
astrologer N [astrolojer]
peramal; **astrology** N nasib
menurut bintang, astrologi
astronomer N astronom, ahli
bintang; **astronomy** N (ilmu)
astronomi, ilmu bintang
asylum N [asailum] suaka,
tempat perlindungan;
~-*seeker* pencari suaka
at PREP di; pada; ~ *all* sama
sekali; ~ *home* di rumah;
betah; ~ *last* akhirnya; ~
least paling tidak; ~ *once*
sekarang juga
atheist N [éthiest] ateis

athlete N [athlit] atlet, olahragawan; pelari; **athletic** ADJ
[athlétik] kuat, berotot, fit;
athletics N cabang atletik,
lari
atlas N atlas, buku peta
ATM ABBREV *automated teller
machine* ATM (anjungan
tunai mandiri)
atmosphere N suasana; hawa,
udara; angkasa, atmosfer
atoll N pulau karang, atol
atom N atom; **atomic** ADJ
berkaitan dengan atom,
nuklir
attach v menambat, melekatkan, mengaitkan,
melampirkan; **attached** ADJ
terlampir; berpasangan;
sayang; **attachment** N
lampiran; rasa sayang
attack N serangan; v
menyerang
attempt N usaha, percobaan;
v mencoba, berusaha
attend v hadir; menghadiri;
attendance N kehadiran;
attendant N pelayan
attention N perhatian;
attentive ADJ penuh perhatian
attic N loteng

attitude N sikap, pendirian; SL keberanian

attorney N [atérni] pengacara

attract V menarik atau memikat(hati); **attraction** N daya tarik, daya pikat; atraksi; **attractive** ADJ menawan

auction N lelang

audible ADJ kedengaran, terdengar

audience N para penonton, tamu, hadirin

August N bulan Agustus

aunt N [ant] **aunty, auntie** SL bibi, tante

Australia N [Ostrélia] Australia

authentic ADJ asli, otentik

author N pengarang, penulis

authority N otoritas, kekuasaan; yang berwajib, instansi; ahli, pakar; **authorization** N kewenangan; **authorize** V mengizinkan

autism N [otizem] autisme; **autistic** ADJ autis

autobiography N otobiografi

automatic ADJ otomatis, dengan sendirinya

autonomous ADJ otonom;

autonomy N otonomi

autopsy N otopsi, bedah mayat

autumn N [otum] musim gugur

Av, Ave *Avenue* Jl (Jalan)

available ADJ tersedia

avenge V membalas dendam (terutama atas kematian)

avenue N [avenyu] jalan

average N, ADJ rata-rata

aviary N [éviari] kandang burung yang besar

avocado N alpukat

awake N **awoke awoken** bangun; ADJ dalam keadaan bangun; **awaken** V bangun ← **wake**

award N penghargaan; V memberi penghargaan

aware ADJ sadar akan, menyadari; **awareness** N kesadaran

away ADV tidak di sini, tidak ada; dari tempat itu; *go ~!* pergilah!

awe N [o] perasaan kagum; **awful** ADJ dahsyat, mengerikan

awkward ADJ kikuk, canggung

ax, axe N kapak

axis N poros, sumbu

axle N as roda

B

babble v berceloteh, mengoceh; bicara tanpa kendali

babe N, sl [béb] bayi; cewek; **baby** N bayi; ADJ anak; *a ~ elephant* anak gajah; *~sit* v menjaga anak; **babysitter** N penjaga anak

bachelor N bujangan, jejaka; *~'s degree* S1 (Strata Satu)

back N belakang, punggung, balik; ADJ di belakang; ADV ke belakang, mundur; *~ seat* jok belakang; v mendukung, mendanai; **background** N latar belakang; **backing** N sokongan, dukungan; **backside** N, sl pantat; **backstroke** N gaya punggung; **backward, backwards** ADJ, ADV ke belakang, mundur

bacon N irisan daging babi asap

bacteria N, PL bakteri, kuman

bad ADJ jelek, buruk, kurang baik; *~ dream* mimpi buruk

badge N lencana, pin

baffled ADJ bingung

bag N tas, karung

baggage N [bagej] bagasi, koper, tas

baggy ADJ kendor, kebesaran

bail N uang jaminan

bait N umpan

bake v membakar; **baker** N tukang memasak roti; **bakery** N toko roti

balance N keseimbangan; neraca, timbangan; FIN saldo; v menimbang; **balanced** ADJ berimbang

balcony N balkon, teras, beranda

bald ADJ botak, gundul, plontos

ball N bola; N pesta berdansa

ballerina N pebalet, penari balet; **ballet** N [balé] balet

balloon N balon

bamboo N bambu

ban N larangan; v melarang; **banned** ADJ dilarang

banana N pisang

band N gerombolan, geng, kawanan; grup (band); gelang

bandage N [bandej] perban; v memerban, membalut

bank N bank; tepi, sisi (sungai); **banker** N bankir

banner N spanduk

225

baptism N permandian; **baptist** N pembaptis; **baptize** v mempermandikan, membaptis

bar N palang pintu, batang, halangan, rintangan; tempat minum, kafe

barb N duri

barbecue, barbeque, BBQ N acara memanggang daging di luar rumah

barber N tukang cukur

bare ADJ telanjang, polos; hanya; **barefoot** ADJ dengan kaki telanjang; **barely** ADJ hampir tidak

bargain N [bargen] pembelian yang murah; v tawar-menawar, menawar

bark N kulit kayu

barn N gudang (tempat menyimpan jerami, rumput kering dsb)

barricade N [barikéd] rintangan, barikade; v memblokir, merintangi

barrier N palang, penghalang, rintangan

barter N niaga tukar-menukar barang, barter; v tukar-menukar barang, barter, membarter

base N markas, dasar; v berdasar, mendasarkan

basic ADJ asasi, pokok

basin N baskom, wastafel

basket N keranjang, bakul, basket; ~*ball* bola basket

bat N alat pemukul (dalam olahraga); v memukul bola (dalam kriket, bisbol dsb)

bat N kelelawar, kampret, kalong

batch N sejumlah; seri (keluaran barang)

bath N (bak) mandi; ~*robe* kimono; ~*tub* badkip; **bathe** v [béth] mandi; **bathroom** N kamar mandi

battery N baterai

battle N pertempuran, peperangan; perjuangan; v bertempur, berjuang

bay N teluk; ~ *leaf* daun salam

bazaar N [bezar] pasar kaget

be v was been menjadi, adalah

beach N pantai, pesisir; v mendamparkan diri

bead N manik-manik; tetesan

beam N balok; sinar (cahaya); v bersinar, tersenyum lebar

bean N buncis, kacang

bear N beruang; *polar* ~ beruang putih

bear v **bore, born** memikul, menahan; bersalin; melahirkan

beard N [bird] jenggot

beast N binatang

beat N pukulan; irama, ritme; v **beat, beaten** memukul; mengalahkan

beautiful ADJ [byutiful] cantik (perempuan), asri (pemandangan), bagus, indah; **beauty** N kecantikan, keindahan; wanita cantik

became v, PF → **become**

because CONJ [bikoz] (oleh) karena, sebab

become v [bikam] **became become** menjadi

bed N tempat tidur, ranjang; **bedroom** N kamar (tidur); **bedspread, bedcover** N selimut

bee N lebah, tawon, kumbang

beef N daging sapi

beehive N sarang lebah ← **bee**

beer N bir

beetle N kumbang

before PREP di muka, depan; sebelum; ADV sebelum

beg v meminta-minta, mengemis; memohon; ~ *your pardon* maaf; **beggar** N pengemis

begin v **began begun** mulai, memulai; **beginning** N awal, permulaan

behave v berkelakuan (baik); **behavior** N perilaku

behind N [behaind] belakang; SL pantat; PREP di belakang, ke belakang; ADV tertinggal, ketinggalan

being N makhluk; keadaan → **be**

Belgium N [Béljum] Belgia

belief N **beliefs** pendapat, kepercayaan, iman, agama; **believe** v percaya, berpendapat

bell N bel, lonceng, genta

belly N (bagian bawah) perut

belong v milik, termasuk kepunyaan; **belongings** N, PL barang milik

beloved N [belovéd] ADJ yang dicintai, yang disayangi

below PREP di bawah, ke bawah

belt N ikat pinggang, sabuk; *seat* ~ sabuk pengaman

bench N bangku, tempat duduk

227

bend N belokan; v **bent bent** membelok, melengkung

beneath PREP di bawah

benefit N manfaat, untung; v menguntungkan

bent v, PF → **bend**; ADJ bengkok, tidak lurus

beside PREP di sisi, di dekat; kecuali, di luar, selain dari; **besides** ADV, PREP lagipula, ditambah lagi

best ADJ paling bagus, paling baik, terbaik

bet N taruhan; v **bet bet** bertaruh

betray v mengkhianati; **betrayal** N pengkhianatan

better ADJ lebih baik; sembuh

between PREP (di) antara, di tengah

beverage N minuman (terutama yang panas)

beware ADJ awas, berhati-hati

beyond PREP (di) sebelah, lebih (jauh), melampaui, melebihi

BH ABBREV *business hours* k, ktr (kantor)

bias N [bayas] kecenderungan; **biased** ADJ tidak berimbang

Bible N [baibel] Injil, Alkitab

bicycle N [baisikel] sepeda

big ADJ besar, gemuk; raksasa; ~ *toe* jempol kaki

bike N sepeda (motor); v naik sepeda; **biker** N penggemar sepeda motor

bilingual ADJ [bailingguel] dwibahasa

bill N bon, rekening, nota; wesel, daftar; paruh (pada burung); v menagih

billiards N, PL bilyar

billion N satu milyar (1 000 000 000); **billionaire** N milyarder

bin N tempat sampah, tong

bind v [baind] **bound bound** menjilid; mengikat; **binder** N map; **binding** N penjilidan

binoculars N, PL teropong, binokular

biography N biografi, riwayat hidup

biologist N [bayolojist] ahli biologi; **biology** N ilmu biologi

bird N burung

birth N kelahiran; ~*day* hari ulang tahun, hari jadi

biscuit N [bisket] biskuit, kue kering

bishop N uskup

bit N sedikit, sepotong; V, PF → **bite**

bite N gigitan; V **bit bitten** menggigit

bitter ADJ pahit

black ADJ hitam, gelap; **blackmail** N pemerasan; V memeras

bladder N kandung kemih

blade N mata pisau

blame N kesalahan; V menyalahkan, menyalahi (orang)

blank N tempat kosong; peluru kosong; ADJ kosong, hampa

blanket N selimut; V menyelimuti

blast N angin kencang, letupan, tiupan

blaze N kebakaran; V menyala; blazing ADJ menyala

blazer N jas (setengah resmi)

bleach N pemutih; V memutihkan (baju)

bleak ADJ suram, gelap

bleed *nose~* mimisan; V **bled** berdarah; **bleeding** ADJ berdarah

blend N campuran; V berbaur, mencampur

bless V memberkati; **blessing** N pemberkatan; doa restu

blew V, PF → **blow**

blind N [blaind] horden, penutup jendela, kerai; *~ed* silau; N buta; **blindly** ADJ membabi buta, tanpa melihat atau berpikir

blink N kedipan mata, kejapan mata; V mengedip, mengejapkan mata

blister N lecet, lepuh; V menjadi lecet, melepuhkan

block N balok; blok; V merintangi, membatasi, menghambat; *~ed* tersumbat, mampet

blog/blogger N blog/penulis blog

blond ADJ, M **blonde** F (berambut) pirang

blood N darah; **bloodstain** N bekas darah; **bloody** ADJ berdarah

blossom N bunga; V berbunga

blouse N [blauz] blus

blow N pukulan, tamparan; tiupan; V **blew blown** bertiup; meniup; *~ your nose* membuang ingus, bersin; **blowpipe** N sumpitan

blue ADJ biru

blunder N [blander] kesalahan

besar; v berbuat salah

blunt ADJ tumpul

blur N kabur; **blurred, blurry** ADJ kabur, kurang jelas

blush v memerah (muka); **blusher** N pemerah pipi, perona pipi

board N papan; karton, kertas tebal, kardus; dewan; v naik pesawat; mondok, kos; **boarder** N anak kos; **boarding** ~ *house* rumah kos, asrama (sekolah); ~ *pass* N pas naik pesawat

boast N bualan; v membual

boat N kapal, perahu

bob v membungkuk; turun naik

body N badan, tubuh; organisasi, himpunan; **bodyguard** N pengawal pribadi

bog N rawa, payau; v terhenti (kendaraan)

boil N bisul; v mendidih; merebus; **boiler** N ketel (kukus)

bold ADJ berani

bolt N baut, slot; v mengunci; kabur

bomb N [bom] bom; v mengebom; **bomber** N pesawat

pengebom; **bombing** N pengeboman

bond N pengikat; ikatan; kewajiban

bone N tulang; gading

book N buku, kitab, novel; v memesan; ~*case*, ~*shelf* lemari buku; **booking** N pemesanan, buking; **booklet** N buku kecil, buklet; **bookshop** N toko buku

boot N sepatu (bot), sepatu lars; v menghidupkan (komputer)

booth N loket, gerai

border N tepi, sisi; perbatasan, tapal batas; v berbatasan dengan; membatasi

bore V, PF → bear

boring ADJ membosankan, menjemukan

born V, PF dilahirkan, lahir, terlahir → bear

borrow v pinjam, meminjam

boss N pemimpin, bos; **bossy** ADJ suka menyuruh

both ADJ kedua, kedua(-kedua)nya; *both ... and ...* baik ... maupun ...

bother N repot, kesusahan; v merepotkan, menyusahkan;

mengganggu

bottle N botol

bottom N bawah, pantat, alas;
ADJ bawah

bought V, PF [bot] → **buy**

bounce N lambungan;
semangat; V melambung,
memantul

bound V melompat, berlari-
lari; V, PF → **bind**

boundary N (tapal) batas

bow N [bau] tundukan; V
membungkukkan badan,
menunduk; menyerah

bow N [bo] busur

bowels N, PL [bauls] usus,
pencernaan

bowl N [bol] mangkuk, pinggan

bowling N boling

box N kotak, dus, peti; tinju;
V bertinju; meninju; **boxer** N
petinju; **boxing** N tinju

boy N anak lelaki

boycott N boikot; V memboikot

boyfriend N, M pacar

bracelet N [bréslét] gelang
(berantai)

bracket N tanda kurung

brag V membual, men-
yombong

brain N otak, benak;
brainwash V mencuci otak

brake N rem; *hand~* rem
tangan; V mengerem

branch N cabang; bagian

brand N cap, merek

brandy N brendi

brass N kuningan

brave ADJ berani; **bravery** N
keberanian

brawl N tawuran, pertikaian; V
tinju, bergumul

Brazil N Brasil; **Brazilian** N
orang Brasil

bread N [bréd] roti

break N [brék] istirahat,
rehat, jeda; patah, putus; V
broke broken memecahkan,
mematahkan; **breakdown**
N perincian; kegagalan,
kerusakan; **breakfast** N, V
[brékfast] sarapan, makan
pagi

breast N [brést] dada, payudara; SL susu, tetek; ~ *milk*
ASI (air susu ibu)

breath N [bréth] nafas, napas;
breathe V [brith] bernafas,
menarik nafas

breed N ras; V bred bred
mengembangbiakkan;

231

mendidik; **breeder** N peternak; **breeding** N trah, nenek moyang; sopan santun

breeze N angin sepoi-sepoi

bribe N uang sogok, uang suap; V menyogok, menyuap; **bribery** N suapan, sogokan

brick N batu bata

bridal ADJ berkaitan dengan acara pernikahan; **bride** N, F pengantin wanita, mempelai wanita; **bridegroom** N, M pengantin pria

bridge N jembatan; V menjembatani, mempertemukan

brief ADJ pendek, ringkas, singkat; **briefing** N rapat pendek, penyebaran informasi

brigade N [brigéd] regu, pasukan; *fire* ~ pasukan pemadam kebakaran

bright N [brait] terang, gemilang; cerdik, cemerlang, pandai

brilliant ADJ gemilang, berseri

bring V **brought brought** [brot] membawa; ~ *up* membesarkan

Britain N [Briten] Britania COLL Inggris

broad ADJ lebar, luas

broadcast N siaran; V **broadcast broadcast** menyiarkan

broccoli N brokoli

broke, broken V, PF → **break** ADJ rusak

broker N makelar, calo, perantara

bronze N perunggu

brooch N [broc] bros

broom N sapu

brother N [brather] kakak atau adik lelaki; saudara; **brotherhood** N persaudaraan

brought V, PF → **bring**

brown ADJ (warna) coklat

bruise N [bruz] memar; **bruised** ADJ memar, bengkak

brush N sikat, kuas (alat seni); V menyikat

brutal ADJ brutal, bengis, kasar

bubble N gelembung

buck N rusa jantan; SL dolar

bucket N ember

Buddha N Budha; **Buddhist** N orang Budha

budget N [bajét] anggaran; V menganggarkan

budget airline N maskapai penerbangan bertarif rendah

buffalo N kerbau

buffet N [bafé] bufet, prasmanan

bug N serangga, kumbang, kutu

buggy N kereta atau kendaraan kecil

build v [bild] **built built** mendirikan, membangun, membina; **builder** N pemborong; **building** N gedung, bangunan

bulb N lampu pijar, bola lampu, bohlam

bull N sapi jantan

bullet N peluru

bulletin N selebaran, berita kilat

bully N orang yang menakut-nakuti atau mengejek orang lain; v menakut-nakuti orang lain

bump N pukulan, tonjokan; v menabrak; **bumpy** ADJ tidak rata, bergelombang

bun N roti berbentuk bola, biasanya manis

bunch N tandan, gugus, segenggam; segerombolan

bundle N [bandel] berkas, paket; v membungkus

bunk N ranjang yang sempit

bunny N, SL kelinci

buoy N [boi] pelampung

burden N beban; muatan, tanggungan; v membebani, memberatkan

bureau N [byuro] kantor, biro; meja tulis; **bureaucrat** N birokrat

burglar N maling; **burglary** N kemalingan

burial N [bérial] pemakaman ← **bury**

burn N luka terkena panas, luka bakar; v **burned burnt** menyala; membakar; **burner** N sumbu

burst v **burst burst** meletus; menyembur

bury v [béri] mengubur, menanam

bus N bis

bush N semak belukar

business N pekerjaan; perkara, urusan; perdagangan, perniagaan; perusahaan; N, M **businessman**; N, F **businesswoman** pengusaha, wiraswasta

busy ADJ [bizi] sibuk

but CONJ tetapi, tapi, namun; kecuali

butcher N [bucer] jagal, tukang potong, tukang daging; toko daging

butter N mentega

butterfly N kupu-kupu; gaya kupu-kupu

button N kancing

buy N [bai] pembelian; v **bought bought** [bot] membeli; **buyer** N pembeli

by PREP oleh, dengan

bye EJAC selamat jalan, selamat tinggal; ~~ CHILD selamat jalan, selamat tinggal

C

c *cent* sen

cab N bagian depan truk; ~ *driver* supir taksi

cabbage N [kabej] kol, engkol, kubis

cabin N bagian depan truk; ~ *crew* awak kabin

cabinet N kabinet; lemari

cable N [kébel] kabel

cactus N cacti kaktus

café, cafe N kafe, warung kopi

cage N sangkar, kurungan; v mengurung

cake N kue

calculate v menghitung-hitung, memperhitungkan, menaksir; **calculator** N kalkulator

calendar N kalender, almanak; penanggalan

calf N [kaf] anak sapi

call N [kol] panggilan, seruan; percakapan telepon; kunjungan; v memanggil; menelepon; **caller** N penelepon; tamu

calligrapher N [kaligrafer] orang yang bisa membuat tulisan tangan indah; **calligraphy** N tulisan tangan yang indah

calm N [kam] ketenangan, keteduhan; ADJ tenang, teduh

Cambodia N Kamboja

came v, PF → **come**

camel N [kamel] unta

camera N kamera

camp N perkemahan, kamp; v berkemah

can N kaleng

can AUX, v could/was able, been able dapat, bisa

Canada N Kanada

234

canal N terusan

cancel V membatalkan, mencoret, menghapus

cancer N kanker

candidate N calon, kandidat

candle N lilin

candy N permen, kembang gula

cane N tongkat

canoe N [kanu] kano

cantaloupe N [kantalop] melon, blewah

canteen N kantin

canyon N ngarai

cap N topi pet; tutup

capable ADJ bisa, mampu, dapat

capacity N daya tampung, kapasitas

cape N tanjung

capital N modal; huruf besar; *~ (city)* ibukota

capitol N ibukota

captain N kapten, nahkoda; kapitan

capture N penangkapan; V menangkap

car N mobil; gerbong; *~ park* tempat parkir; *~~sharing* berbagi mobil, Uber

caramel N gula bakar, permen rasa karamel

caravan N kafilah; karavan

carbon N karbon, zat arang

card N kartu; kardus

cardboard N karton, kertas tebal

care N pemeliharaan, perawatan; V peduli, memedulikan; *child ~* penitipan anak-anak; *to take ~* berhati-hati, jaga diri; *to take ~ of* memelihara, mengurus

career N karir

careful ADJ hati-hati; **careless** ADJ teledor, lalai ← **care**

carer N perawat, penjaga anak ← **care**

caretaker N penjaga ← **care**

cargo N muatan kapal

carnival N pesta, pasar malam, karnafal

carpenter N tukang kayu

carpet N permadani, karpet

carport N garasi, atap untuk perlindungan mobil

carriage N [karijj] kereta; gerbong ← **carry**

carrot N wortel; insentif

carry V mengangkut, membawa

cart N kereta, pedati, gerobak

235

cartoon N (film) kartun; komik

cartridge N [kartrij] pelor, peluru; isi pulpen, kartrid

carve V mengukir

case N peti, koper; kasus, perkara, hal, perihal

cash N uang kontan, uang tunai

cashew N kacang mede

cashier N [kasyir] kasir, kassa ← **cash**

cast N pemain-pemain sandiwara; V **cast cast** melempar, melontar; menuangkan; memilih untuk peran; ~ *iron* besi tuang

castle N [kasel] puri, benteng, istana

casual ADJ santai

casualty N korban kecelakaan

cat N kucing

catalog N katalog, daftar; V mendokumentasi

catch N angkapan, hasil; jepitan, gesper; V **caught caught** [kort] menangkap; terkena, terjangkit (penyakit)

category N kategori, golongan

cater V melayani; menyediakan makanan; **caterer** N perusahaan jasa boga; **cater-**

ing N jasa boga

caterpillar N ulat

cathedral N [kathidral] katedral

Catholic (orang) Katolik

cattle N sapi, ternak

caught V, PF → **catch**

cauliflower N [koliflauer] kembang kol

cause N [coz] sebab; V menyebabkan, mengakibatkan

caution N sikap hati-hati, kewaspadaan; V mengingatkan

cave N gua

cavity N rongga, lubang (gigi)

ceiling N [siling] langit-langit, plafon

celebrate V [sélébrét] merayakan; **celebration** N perayaan

celebrity N selebriti

celery N seledri

cell N sel; bilik penjara; ~ *phone* telepon seluler (ponsel), telepon genggam

cement N semen, beton

cemetery N kuburan, tempat pemakaman umum (TPU)

censor N sensor; V menyensor

census N sensus

center N pusat; **central** ADJ pusat, tengah, pokok

centimeter N senti, sentimeter

centipede N [sentipid] kaki seribu, lipan

century N abad

cereal N [sirial] sereal

ceremony N upacara

certain ADJ [serten] tentu, pasti, yakin; **certainly** ADJ tentu saja

certificate N sertifikat, ijazah

chain N rantai; kalung; serangkaian; V merantai

chair N kursi; ketua; **chairman** N, M **chairperson** N ketua

chalk N kapur

challenge N tantangan; V menantang

chamber N [cémber] kamar

champagne N [syampéin] sampanye

champion N juara

chance N kesempatan, peluang

change N perubahan; uang kembali; V menukar, mengubah

channel N saluran, selat

chant V bernyanyi; menyanyikan (berulang-ulang)

chapter N bab, pasal

character N [karakter] sifat; peran; huruf; **characteristic** N ciri; ADJ khas

charcoal N arang

charge N muatan; ongkos, harga; serangan, serbuan; tuduhan; V menyerang; meminta bayaran, menagih; (me)ngecas

charity N amal

charm V memesonakan, menarik hati; menyihir

chart N grafik; peta

charter N piagam; V mencarter

chase N pengejaran; V mengejar

chat N percakapan; V mengobrol; **chatter** N celotehan, obrolan; V berceloteh, mengobrol; **chatting** N kegiatan berkomunikasi lewat internet

chauffeur N [syofer] supir, sopir

cheap ADJ murah

cheat N penipu; V menipu; curang; **cheating** N curang, kecurangan

check, cheque N cek

check N pemeriksaan, uji, cek; V memeriksa, menguji, mengecek

cheek N pipi; **cheeky** ADJ berani, nakal

cheer N kegembiraan; sorak; v memberi semangat, bersorak; mendukung; **cheerful** ADJ gembira, senang hati

cheese N keju

chef N [syéf] juru masak

chemical N [kémikel] bahan kimia; ADJ kimiawi; **chemist** N ahli kimia, apoteker; **chemistry** N ilmu kimia

cherry N buah ceri

chess N catur

chest N dada; peti, kopor

chew v mengunyah

chicken N (rasa) ayam; ~ *pox* cacar air

chief N **chiefs** kepala (suku), pemimpin; ADJ utama, pokok; **chiefly** ADV terutama, pertama-tama

child N [caild] **children** [cildren] anak, putra; **childish** ADJ kekanak-kanakan

Chile N [Cili] Cile

chill N udara dingin

chilli N cabe; ~ *sauce* (saus) sambal

chilly ADJ sejuk, dingin ← **chill**

chimney N **chimneys** cerobong asap

chimpanzee N simpanse

chin N dagu

China N [Caina] (negeri) Cina; **china** N, ADJ porselen; **Chinatown** N Pecinan; **Chinese** N orang Cina, orang Tionghoa; ADJ Cina, Tionghoa; ~ *New Year* (Tahun Baru) Imlek

chip N keping; keripik; *hot ~s* kentang goreng; v pecah

chocolate N, ADJ coklat

choice N pilihan, terpilih ← **choose**

choir N [kuaier] koor

choke v mencekik

cholera N kolera

cholesterol N kolesterol

choose v **chose chosen** memilih

chop N potong; steik yang bertulang; v memotong, mencincang

chopsticks N, PL sumpit

chose, chosen v, PF ← **choose**

Christ N [Kraist] (Yesus) Kristus; **christening** N permandian; **Christian** N orang Kristen atau Katolik; ADJ Kristiani, Nasrani,

Masehi; **Christmas** N (hari) Natal

chubby ADJ gemuk, berlebihan berat badan

chunky ADJ berisi, berat

cigar N [sigar] cerutu; **cigarette** N [sigarét] rokok

cinema N [sinema] (gedung) bioskop

cinnamon N kayu manis

circle N [serkel] lingkaran, bulatan; kawasan, lingkungan; V melingkari; mengedari

circular ADJ [serkyuler] bulat, bundar; **circulate** V beredar; mengedarkan; **circulation** N peredaran, sirkulasi

circumcision N [sirkumsisyen] sunatan

circus N sirkus

citizen N [sitizen] warganegara

city N [siti] kota

civil ADJ sipil; sopan; **civilian** N orang sipil; **civilization** N [sivilaizésyen] peradaban

claim N tuntutan; tagihan; pengakuan; V menuntut; menagih; mengaku; meminta

clam N kerang

clan N suku bangsa, kaum, marga

clap N tepuk; V bertepuk tangan; **clapper** N anak lonceng

clarify V [klarifai] menjelaskan, menerangkan

clarinet N klarinet

clash N bentrokan; V bentrok

clasp N jepitan, gesper; pelukan

class N kelas; pelajaran; golongan; **classify** V menggolongkan; **classroom** N ruang kelas

class N mutu, kualitas (tinggi); **classic** ADJ klasik

clause N ayat, klausa; syarat; anak kalimat

claw N cakar, jepit

clay N tanah liat

clean ADJ bersih; V membersihkan; **cleaning** N pembersihan

clear ADJ terang, jernih; jelas; nyaring, nyata; V membereskan

clever ADJ [klever] pandai, cerdas, pintar

client N [klaient] nasabah, pelanggan, tamu, klien

cliff N tebing

climate N [klaimet] iklim

climax N [klaimaks] puncak, klimaks, orgasme

239

climb N [klaim] perjalanan naik; v memanjat; menaiki

clinic N klinik, pusat kesehatan masyarakat (puskesmas)

clip N jepitan; v menjepit, menggunting, memotong; **clippers** N gunting (kuku)

clock N jam; *alarm ~* weker; *three o'~* jam tiga; v mencatat waktu

close v [kloz] menutup

close ADJ [klos] dekat, akrab

closet N [klozet] lemari baju

cloth N kain, bahan; **clothes** N, PL pakaian, baju

cloud N awan; **cloudy** ADJ berawan

clove N cengkeh

clown N badut, pelawak; v melucu

club N perhimpunan, klub, kelab; **clubbing** N pergi ke diskotek

clue N tanda, petunjuk

clumsy ADJ canggung, kikuk

cluster N gugus, tandan; v berkerumun

clutch N genggam; kopling

cm *centimeter* cm (sentimeter)

coach N pelatih; bis pariwisata; v melatih

coal N batu bara

coarse ADJ [kors] kasar

coast N pantai, pesisir

coaster N alas gelas

coat N mantel, jas; lapisan; kulit atau bulu binatang; v melapisi

coax v membujuk

cobra N kobra, ular sendok

cobweb N sarang laba-laba

cock N ayam jantan; **cocky** ADJ arogan

cockatoo N [kokatu] burung kakatua

cockpit N kokpit

cockroach N kecoa

cocktail N sejenis minuman keras, koktil

cocoa N [koko] (biji) coklat

coconut N (buah) kelapa

code N sandi, kode

coffee N kopi; *white ~*, *milk ~* kopi susu

coffin N peti mati

coil N gulungan, gulung; v bergelung

coin N uang logam, koin

coincidence N [koinsidens] kebetulan

cold N masuk angin, pilek; rasa dingin; ADJ dingin

240

collaborator N orang yang bekerja sama

collapse N keruntuhan, kerobohan; V runtuh, ambruk, roboh

collar N kerah, leher baju

colleague N [kolig] rekan, kolega, teman kantor

collect V mengumpulkan, memungut; **collection** N kumpulan, koleksi; **collector** N kolektor

college N [kolej] sekolah, kolese; perguruan tinggi, universitas

collide V bertabrakan, menabrak; **collision** N [kolisyen] tabrakan

colon N titik dua

colonel N [kernel] kolonel

colonial ADJ kolonial, penjajah; **colonize** V menjajah, menduduki; **colony** N jajahan

color N [kaler] warna; V mewarnai; **colorful** ADJ berwarna-warni

coma N koma, mati suri

comb N [koom] sisir; V menyisir

combination N gabungan, kombinasi; **combine** V menggabungkan, memadukan

come V [kam] **came come** datang, tiba, sampai; ~ *from* berasal dari, datang dari; ~ *in* masuk; ~ *out* keluar; **comeback** N kembali

comet N bintang berekor

comfort N [kamfert] V menghibur; **comfortable** ADJ, **comfy** SL nyaman

comic N pelawak; ADJ lucu ← **comedy**

coming N [kaming] kedatangan; ADJ mendatang ← **come**

comma N koma

command N perintah; komando; V memimpin

commemorate V memperingati, merayakan; **commemoration** N peringatan, perayaan

commence V mulai, memulai

comment N komentar; V berkomentar, memberi komentar; mengomentari

commerce N perdagangan, perniagaan; **commercial** N, ADJ dagang, perniagaan; komersial

commission N pesan; komisi

commit v berjanji; melakukan

committee N [komiti] panitia, komite

common ADJ biasa, umum; bersama; rendah

communicate v berkomunikasi; memberitahu, menghubungi; **communication** N komunikasi, perhubungan

communism N komunisme

community N masyarakat, umat, komunitas ← **commune**

commuter N pelaju

compact ADJ kompak; padat

companion N kawan, teman; **company** N [kampeni] kawan-kawan; perusahaan, maskapai (penerbangan)

compare v membandingkan; **comparison** N perbandingan

compass N [kampas] pedoman, kompas; jangka

compete v [kompit] bersaing, bertanding

competent ADJ mampu, kompeten

competition N persaingan; pertandingan; **competitive** ADJ (suka) bersaing; **com-**

petitor N pesaing, saingan ← **compete**

complain v mengadu, mengeluh

complete ADJ lengkap, komplit; v menyelesaikan; **completely** ADJ, NEG sama sekali

complex N kompleks; ADJ rumit, ruwet

complicate v mempersulit; **complication** N kesulitan; komplikasi (penyakit)

compliment N pujian; v memuji

component N unsur, komponen, suku cadang

compose v menyusun, membentuk, mengarang; **composer** N komponis

compound N kompleks (perumahan)

comprehend v mengerti, memahami; **comprehension** N pengertian, pemahaman

compromise N [kompromaiz] kompromi; v mencari jalan tengah, berkompromi

compulsory ADJ paksa, wajib

computer N komputer

comrade N [komrad] kawan, teman; kamerad

242

concave ADJ cekung
conceal V menyembunyikan
conceited ADJ sombong, angkuh
concentrate V memusatkan (perhatian), konsen; **concentration** N pemusatan, konsentrasi
concern N perkara, hal; perhatian; perusahaan
concert N konser
concession N izin, kelonggaran; konsesi ← **concede**
concise ADJ pendek, ringkas, singkat
conclude V menyimpulkan; memutuskan; **conclusion** N kesimpulan; akhir
concrete N [konkrit] semen, beton; ADJ nyata
condemn V [kondém] menghukum; menghakimi, mengutuk
condition N keadaan, kondisi; syarat; conditional ADJ dengan syarat
condolences our ~ kami ikut berduka cita, kami ucapkan belasungkawa
condom N kondom
conduct N kelakuan, cara;

conductor N dirigen (musik); kondektur (angkutan umum); penghantar
cone N kerucut; marka jalan
confess V mengaku; **confession** N pengakuan
confetti N guntingan kertas yang dilempar saat berpesta, hujan kertas
confidence N kepercayaan; **confident** ADJ berani, percaya diri
confine V membatasi, mengurung; memingit
confirm V menegaskan, memastikan; **confirmation** N kepastian, penegasan, konfirmasi
conflict N perselisihan, pertikaian, percekcokan, konflik; perang; V bertentangan
confront V menghadapi; menentang, melawan; **confrontation** N konfrontasi
confuse V membingungkan
congratulations N, PL ucapan selamat; EJAC selamat
connect V menyambung, menghubungkan; **connection** N hubungan, sambungan;

koneksi

conquer v [konker] mengalahkan, menaklukkan, merebut

conscience N [konsyens] hati nurani; **conscientious** ADJ rajin

conscious ADJ [konsyus] sadar

consecutive ADJ berturut-turut

consequence N akibat, dampak; **consequently** ADV oleh karena itu, maka

conservation N perlindungan, pemeliharaan; **conservative** ADJ kolot, konservatif

consider v menganggap, mengindahkan; mempertimbangkan; **considerable** ADJ cukup banyak; **considering** CONJ mengingat

consist v terdiri atas, terdiri dari

consistent ADJ konsekuen, tetap

console v menghibur

consonant N huruf mati, konsonan

conspiracy N [konspirasi] komplotan, persekongkolan

constant ADJ tetap, selalu

constellation N gugus

bintang, konstelasi

constipated ADJ sembelit

constitution N undang-undang dasar (UUD), konstitusi

construct v membangun, membuat, membentuk; **construction** N bangunan, pembangunan (gedung), konstruksi; ~ *site* proyek

consul N konsul, wakil; **consulate** N konsulat

consult v menanyakan, mencari pendapat, berkonsultasi; **consultation** N perundingan, konsultasi

consume v memakan, menghabiskan; memakai; **consumer** N pengguna, pemakai, konsumen; **consumption** N pemakaian

contact N hubungan, kontak; v menghubungi

contagious ADJ menular, menjangkit

contain v berisi, memuat, mengandung; **container** N tempat; ~ *ship* kapal barang

contamination N kontaminasi

contemporary ADJ modern, kini, kontemporer

contempt N penghinaan

244

content N [kéntént] kepuasan
content N [kontént] isi, bahan;
  contents N, PL isi, muatan
contest N pertandingan, lomba; v bertanding; memperjuangkan; contestant N
  peserta
continent N benua
continuation N terusan, lanjutan, sambungan; continue
  v terus; melanjutkan, meneruskan; continuous ADJ terus-
  menerus
contraceptive N, ADJ kon-
  trasepsi; ~ pill pil KB
contract N kontrak, surat
  perjanjian; contraction N
  kontraksi; contractor N
  kontraktor, pemborong
contradict v membantah,
  menyanggah
contrast N perbedaan, kontras;
  v berbeda; membandingkan
contribute v menyumbang,
  memberikan; contribution N
  sumbangan, kontribusi
control N kendali, kontrol; v
  mengendalikan
controversial ADJ kontrover-
  sial
convenience N kesempatan;

kemudahan; convenient ADJ
  enak; dekat
convention N seminar,
  rapat, konvensi; kebiasaan;
  conventional ADJ biasa ←
  convene
conversation N percakapan,
  pembicaraan
conversion N perubahan;
  convert v masuk agama baru;
  mengubah
convex ADJ cembung
convey v [konvé] membawa,
  mengangkut; menyampaikan
convict N narapidana; v
  menghukum
conviction N keyakinan,
  kepercayaan
convince v meyakinkan
convoy N iring-iringan, konvoi
cook N juru masak, koki; v
  memasak; cookery N cara
  memasak; cookie N kue
  kering yang keras
cool ADJ sejuk, dingin; v
  menyejukkan
coolie N kuli
co-operate, cooperate v
  bekerja sama; co-operation N
  kerja sama
cope v menghadapi, hidup

245

dengan (kesulitan)

copper N tembaga

copy N salinan, kopi; V menya-lin, meniru; memfotokopi; **copyright** N hak cipta

coral N karang

cord N tali

core N inti, hati

coriander N ketumbar

cork N gabus; sumbat

corn N jagung

corner N sudut, penjuru

corporal N kopral

corporate ADJ berkaitan dengan perusahaan; **corpora-tion** N perusahaan, perkum-pulan, persekutuan, grup

corpse N [korps] mayat (manusia)

correct ADJ benar, betul; V membetulkan, memperbaiki

correspond V surat-menyurat; sesuai dengan; **correspond-ent** N orang yang menulis surat atau artikel; wartawan

corridor N lorong

corrupt ADJ korup, dapat disuap; **corruption** N korupsi, suap

cosmetics N, PL alat-alat kecantikan (seperti lipstik,

perona pipi dsb)

cost N harga (barang), ongkos (perjalanan), biaya (jasa); V **cost cost** berharga

costume N pakaian, busana, kostum

cosy, cozy ADJ enak, mungil

cottage N pondok, bungalo

cotton N, ADJ kapas, katun

cough N, V [kof] batuk

could V [kud] bisa, dapat, mampu; PF → **can**

council N dewan; pemerintah setempat (seperti kecamatan)

counsellor N konselor

count N penghitungan; V berhitung; menghitung

counter N loket

country N [kantri] negeri, negara; tanah air; **country-side** N pedesaan, pedalaman

couple N [kapel] pasang, pasangan

coupon N kupon

courage N [karej] keberanian; **courageous** ADJ [karéjus] berani

courier N kurir

course N [kors] kursus; jalan, arah

court N [kort] pengadilan

court N [kort] jalan buntu; taman; lapangan main

courtesy N [kertesi] kesopanan, sopan-santun

cousin N [kazen] (saudara) sepupu

cover N [kaver] tutup, penutup; sampul (buku); sarung (bantal); perlindungan; v menutup; meliputi

cow N sapi, lembu

coward N pengecut, penakut; **cowardly** ADJ penakut, pengecut

crab N kepiting, rajingan

crack N retak; bunyi; v retak, pecah dengan bunyi gemeretak; **cracker** N petasan; biskuit kering

craft N kerajinan tangan; ketrampilan; **craftsman** N perajin, tukang

cramp N kejang

crash N tabrakan, ambruknya; v bertabrakan, menubruk; jatuh (pesawat terbang)

crate N peti kayu

crater N kawah

crawl v merangkak, merayap

crayon N krayon, kapur tulis lilin

crazy ADJ gila

cream N krim, kepala susu

create v [kriét] menciptakan, membuat; **creation** N ciptaan, kreasi; **creature** N makhluk

credit N penghargaan; kredit; ~ *card* kartu kredit

creep v merangkak, merayap, menjalar; **creepy** ADJ angker, mengerikan

cremation N kremasi, pembakaran mayat

crescent N jalan yang melingkar

crew N awak kapal; regu, kru

cricket N jangkrik, belalang; semacam olahraga seperti kasti

crime N kejahatan; **criminal** N penjahat; ADJ jahat

crisis N [kraisis] krisis

crisp ADJ garing; segar

criteria N, PL syarat; patokan, norma

critical ADJ kritis, genting; **criticism** N kritik; **criticize** v mengritik

crocodile N buaya

crooked ADJ bengkok

crop N panen; v memotong

cross N silang; salib; persim-

pangan, persilangan; v me-
lintasi, menyeberangi;
crossing N penyeberangan; **crossroads** N simpang,
perempatan; **crossword** N
teka-teki silang (TTS)
crouch v berjongkok
crow N [kro] burung gagak
crowd N orang banyak, gerombolan orang, kerumunan
orang
crown N mahkota; ubun-ubun
crude ADJ kasar, mentah;
primitif
cruel ADJ bengis, kejam
cruise N [kruz] pelayaran
pesiar
crunchy ADJ garing
crusader N orang yang
memperjuangkan sesuatu
crust N kerak, kulit
crutch N; **crutches** PL kruk
cry N [krai] teriak, pekik;
tangis; v berteriak, memekik;
menangis
crystal N, ADJ hablur, kristal
Cuba N Kuba
cube N kubus
cucumber N [kyukamber]
timun, mentimun
cuddle N [kadel] pelukan; v

memeluk, mengemong
cuisine N [kuisin] santapan,
masakan
cultivate v memelihara,
menanam; **cultivation** N
pemeliharaan, penanaman
cultural ADJ **culture** N
kebudayaan, budaya
cunning N, ADJ cerdik, licik
cup N cangkir, cawan; piala;
cupboard N [kaberd] lemari;
cupcake N kue kecil
cure N obat, pengobatan; v
mengobati (sampai sembuh)
curfew N jam malam
curiosity N penasaran, keing-
intahuan; **curious** ADJ
penasaran, ingin tahu; aneh
currant N kismis (kecil,
berwarna hitam)
currency N mata uang
current N arus; ADJ kini; berlaku
curry N kari, gulai
curse N kutukan; umpatan,
makian; v mengutuk;
mengumpat, memaki
curtain N [kerten] horden,
gorden, tirai
curve N lengkung; v
melengkung
cushion N [kusyen] bantal

custard N sejenis puding
custom N adat, kebiasaan;
  customer N langganan,
  nasabah (bank)
customs N bea cukai, pabean
cut N potongan; v **cut cut**
  memotong, menggunting
cute ADJ lucu; mungil, manis
cyberspace N dunia maya
cycle N [saikel] daur, siklus;
  v bersepeda, naik sepeda;
  cyclist N pengendara sepeda;
  pembalap sepeda
cyclone N [saiklon] angin
  topan, siklon
cylinder N silinder
Czech ADJ Ceko

D

Dad N, SL Pak; **Daddy** N, SL,
  CHILD Papa
dagger N keris
daily N harian; ADV tiap hari
dairy N perusahaan susu
dam N bendungan; v
  membendung
damage N [damej] kerusakan;
  rugi, kerugian; v merugikan,
  merusak

damn v mengutuk; ADJ terkutuk; EJAC persetan
damp N kelembaban, iklim
  lembab; ADJ lembab
dance N tari, tari-tarian;
  dansa; v menari; berdansa;
  dancer N penari
dandruff N ketombe
danger N [dénjer] bahaya;
  dangerous ADJ berbahaya
dare N tantangan; v menantang; ADJ berani; **daring** N
  keberanian; ADJ berani
dark N gelap, kegelapan; ADJ
  gelap; ~ *green* hijau tua;
  darkness N kegelapan
darling N sayang, buah hati;
  ADJ tersayang
dash N garis datar; v berlari
dashboard N dasbor, panel
  peralatan
data N data; **database** N bank
  data
date N korma
date N tanggal; kencan; v
  mengencani, memacari
daughter N, F [doter] anak
  perempuan, putri
dawn N dini hari, fajar;
  permulaan
day N hari; siang; *all* ~ sepan-

249

jang hari; *one* ~ sekali waktu; *during the* ~ siang hari; **daybreak** N dini hari, fajar; **daydream** N lamunan, khayalan; **daylight** N siang; sinar matahari; **daytime** N, ADJ siang hari

daze N keadaan pusing

dazzle V menyilaukan, memesonakan

dead ADJ mati; sunyi senyap; ~ *end* jalan buntu; **deadline** N batas waktu; **deadly** ADJ mematikan; sungguh-sungguh → **die**

deaf ADJ [déf] tuli

deal N persetujuan; V **dealt** **dealt** [délt] membagi (kartu); ~ *in* jual-beli; ~ *with* memperlakukan, menghadapi; **dealer** N pedagang; **dealings** N, PL urusan, transaksi

dear N yang baik, yang terhormat (*in letters*); *my* ~ sayangku; adj mahal

death N [déth] kematian

debate N perdebatan; V berdebat; memperdebatkan

debt N [dét] hutang

decay N kerusakan, kebusuk-

an; V melapuk, membusuk

deceased ADJ telah meninggal, mangkat, wafat

deceitful ADJ penuh tipu daya, bersifat menipu; **deceive** V menipu; ~*d* tertipu

December N bulan Desember

decent ADJ sopan, patut, layak

deception penipuan ← **deceit**

decide V memutuskan, menentukan, menetapkan

decision N [desisyen] keputusan ← **decide**

deck N geladak, dek

declaration N pernyataan, pengumuman, maklumat, deklarasi; **declare** V menyatakan, mengumumkan

decline N kemunduran, kemerosotan; V mundur, menjadi kurang; menolak

decorate V menghiasi; **decoration** N hiasan, perhiasan; tanda kehormatan

decrease N pengurangan, penurunan; V berkurang; mengurangi, menurunkan

dedicate V mempersembahkan, mengabdikan; **dedication** N pengabdian,

persembahan

deduct v memotong, mengurangi; **deduction** N potongan, pengurangan

deduction N kesimpulan; pengurangan ← **deduce**

deep ADJ dalam; **deepen** v mendalam; memperdalam

deer N rusa, menjangan

default v gagal; lalai membayar

defeat N kekalahan; v mengalahkan, menggagalkan

defect N [difékt] cacat, cela, kerusakan; **defective** ADJ rusak, cacat ← **defect**

defend v membela, mempertahankan; **defendant** N tergugat; **defender** N pembela; bek; **defense** N pertahanan, pembelaan, perlawanan; **defensive** ADJ bersikap bertahan, defensif

defiant ADJ bersifat menentang, bersifat melawan

define v menentukan, menetapkan, mengartikan; **definite** ADJ tertentu, pasti; **definition** N definisi

deflate v kempes; mengempeskan

deforestation N deforestasi, penebangan hutan

deformed ADJ cacat

degree N (suhu) derajat; gelar sarjana

dehydrated ADJ [dihaidréted] dehidrasi, kurang minum

delay N keterlambatan, penundaan; v menunda, memperlambat

delegate N wakil, utusan; v menyerahkan; mengutus; **delegation** N delegasi, perwakilan

delete v menghapus, mencoret

deliberate ADJ (dengan) sengaja

delicate ADJ halus; sering sakit

delicious ADJ [delisyus] enak, sedap, lezat

delight N [delait] kesenangan, kegembiraan; **delightful** ADJ menyenangkan, membahagiakan

deliver v mengirim, menghantarkan, memberi; membidani; melahirkan; **delivery** N penyerahan, pengiriman; ~ *boy* kurir

demand N tuntutan; persediaan; v menuntut, minta

251

democracy N demokrasi, kerakyatan; **democrat** N demokrat; **democratic** ADJ demokratis

demolish V membongkar, merobohkan

demonstration N pertunjukan; demonstrasi, demo, unjuk rasa

dengue [déngi] ~ *fever* demam berdarah

dense ADJ padat, rapat, lebat; SL bodoh; **density** N kepadatan

dentist N dokter gigi

deny V [denai] menyangkal, memungkiri, menolak

depart V berangkat, pergi; **departure** N keberangkatan

department N departemen; bagian; ~ *store* toko serba ada (toserba)

depend V bergantung, tergantung

deposit N deposito, simpanan; endapan

deputy N wakil

derail V anjlok, keluar dari rel

descend V turun; **descendant** N keturunan, anak cucu; **descent** N jalan turun; keturunan

describe V melukiskan, menggambarkan; **description** N penggambaran, deskripsi

desert N [désert] gurun, padang pasir

deserted ADJ sunyi (senyap)

deserve V berhak mendapat, patut (menerima)

design N rancangan, contoh, gambar, desain; V merancang, mendesain

designer N perancang, desainer ← **design**

desire N keinginan, nafsu, hasrat; V ingin, menginginkan, mendambakan

desk N meja (tulis); bangku (di sekolah)

desperate ADJ sudah putus asa

despite PREP meskipun, kendati

dessert N [desert] pencuci mulut, puding

destination N tujuan, jurusan

destiny N nasib, takdir

destroy V menghancurkan, memusnahkan, membinasakan; **destruction** N kerusakan, kehancuran, pemusnahan, pembinasaan;

destructive ADJ merusak, membinasakan

detail N rinci, perincian, seluk-beluk; V merincikan

detective N reserse, detektif

detention N penahanan, penawanan ← **detain**

detergent N sabun, obat, deterjen

deteriorate V [detioriorét] memburuk, merosot

determination N tekad bulat; **determine** V menetapkan, menentukan, memutuskan

detest V membenci

devastate V menghancurkan; **devastation** N penghancuran

develop V mengembangkan, membangun, membina; mencuci (film); **developer** N pengembang, pemborong; **development** N pembangunan, perkembangan; pengembangan, pembinaan

device N alat

devil N setan, iblis

devoted ADJ tekun

devout ADJ soleh, beriman ← **devote**

dew N embun

diabetes N [daiabitis] penyakit gula, kencing manis

diagnose V mendiagnosa, menentukan; **diagnosis** N diagnosa

diagonal ADJ sudut-menyudut, diagonal

diagram N denah, bagan

dial V memencet (nomor telepon)

dialect N dialek

diameter N garis tengah, diameter

diamond N berlian, intan

diaper N popok

diarrhoea, diarrhea N [daiaria] mencret, sakit perut, diare

diary N [daiari] buku harian

dice N, PL dadu

dictate V mendikte; **dictation** N dikte, imla

dictator N diktator

dictionary N kamus

did V, PF → **do**

die V [dai] **died died** mati, meninggal, wafat; gugur, wafar (dalam perang)

diesel N [disel] minyak solar; mesin diesel

diet N [daiet] diet; makanan; V mengikuti diet, membatasi

makan

differ v berbeda; **difference** N beda, perbedaan; **different** ADJ beda, lain, berbeda

difficult ADJ susah, sulit, sukar; **difficulty** N kesulitan, kesusahan

dig v **dug dug** menggali

digit N [dijit] angka; jari; **digital** ADJ digital

dignified ADJ [dignifaid] bermartabat, mulia; **dignity** N martabat

dike N pematang, bendung, tanggul

dilemma N pilihan sulit, dilema

diligent ADJ rajin, telaten

dim v meredup; meredupkan; ADJ redup, suram

dine v bersantap (malam)

dining N santapan ← **dine**

dinner N makan malam; makan siang

dinosaur N [dainosor] dinosaurus

diploma N ijazah, diploma

diplomat N pegawai kedutaan, diplomat; **diplomatic** ADJ diplomatik, berkaitan dengan kedutaan

direct ADJ langsung; serta merta; terus terang; v memimpin, mengarahkan, memerintahkan, menunjukkan; menyutradarai; **direction** N arah, petunjuk; **directly** ADV secara langsung, serta merta, segera; **director** N direktur, pemimpin; sutradara

directory N buku alamat, buku daftar

dirt N kotoran, debu; tanah; **dirty** ADJ kotor, dekil

disabled ADJ cacat; orang cacat

disadvantage N rugi, kerugian

disagree v tidak setuju; **disagreement** N percekcokan, perbedaan pendapat

disappear v hilang, lenyap

disappoint v mengecewakan; **disappointment** N kekecewaan, rasa kecewa

disapprove v tidak menyetujui, tidak suka, menolak

disaster N musibah, malapetaka, bencana; **disastrous** ADJ malang, celaka

disc, disk N cakram

discipline N disiplin, tata

254

tertib, ketertiban

discount N potongan (harga), diskon, korting; V memotong harga, mendiskon

discourage V [diskarej] mengecilkan hati, tidak menganjurkan

discover V menemukan, mendapat; **discovery** N penemuan

discriminate V membedakan, mendiskriminasikan; **discrimination** N pembedaan, diskriminasi

discuss V [diskas] berembuk membicarakan; **discussion** N pembicaraan, diskusi

disease N penyakit

disgrace N aib, malu; V mencoreng muka, memalukan; **disgraceful** ADJ memalukan

disguise N [disgaiz] samaran

disgust N rasa muak; V menjijikkan, memuakkan

dish N piring, pinggan; sajian, hidangan; *~cloth* lap piring

dishwasher N mesin pencuci piring ← **dish**

dislike N ketidaksukaan; V tidak suka

dismay N kecemasan; V mencemaskan

dismiss V menolak; membubarkan, memecat; **dismissal** N pembubaran, pemecatan

disobedient ADJ tidak patuh, nakal; **disobey** V melawan, tidak mematuhi

dispensation N kelonggaran, dispensasi

dispenser N alat atau mesin dengan persediaan

displace V menggantikan

display N pameran, pertunjukan; V memperlihatkan, mempertunjukkan, memamerkan

disposal N persediaan; pembuangan

disprove V [dispruv] membantah, menyangkal; membuktikan salah

dispute N perselisihan, percekcokan; V membantah; mempermasalahkan

disqualified ADJ dinyatakan tidak berhak atau keluar, dibatalkan

dissatisfaction N ketidakpuasan, kekecewaan

dissolve v larut; melarutkan

distance N jarak, kejauhan; **distant** ADJ jauh

distinct ADJ jelas, kentara; **distinction** N perbedaan; nilai unggul

distorted ADJ berubah; diubah

distract v mengalihkan perhatian; menyesatkan; **distraction** N selingan; gangguan, kesesatan

distress N kesulitan, kesusahan; ~ed menderita

distribute v menyebarluaskan, membagikan, menyalurkan, mendistribusikan; **distribution** N penyebarluasan, pembagian; penyaluran, pendistribusian; **distributor** N penyalur, pengecer

district N, ADJ distrik, daerah

disturb v mengganggu; **disturbance** N kekacauan, kegaduhan, gangguan

ditch N selokan, parit

dive v menyelam, terjun; **diver** N penyelam; **diving** N selam; loncat indah

diverse ADJ berbagai (macam), aneka, pelbagai; **diversity** N keanekaragaman

divide N jurang, kesenjangan; v membagi

division N pembagian; bagian; divisi

divorce N perceraian; v bercerai

DIY ABBREV *do it yourself* barang yang dirakit atau dikerjakan sendiri

dizzy ADJ pusing (kepala), pening, bingung

do v [du] did done berbuat, bikin; membuat, melakukan, mengerjakan

dock N galangan, dok; **dockyard** N galangan

doctor N dokter; doktor (S3)

document N surat, dokumen; **documentary** N film dokumenter; **documentation** N catatan, dokumentasi

dodge v mengelakkan, menghindar

dog N anjing

doing N [duing] perbuatan

doll N **dolly** CHILD boneka

dollar N dolar; *US* ~ dolar AS

dolphin N [dolfin] lumba-lumba

dome N kubah

domestic ADJ dalam negeri,

domestik

dominant ADJ berkuasa, berpengaruh, dominan; **dominate** v menguasai, mendominasi; **domination** N penguasaan, dominasi

donate v menyumbangkan; **donation** N sumbangan

done v, PF [dan] → **do**

donkey N keledai

donor N pemberi, donor; *blood ~* donor darah ← **donate**

don't v jangan ← **do**

donut N donat

door N pintu

dorm, dormitory N asrama

dot N titik, noktah, percik

double ADJ [dabel] ganda; kembaran; v melipatganda-kan; *~ bed* tempat tidur untuk dua orang

doubt N [daut] ragu, keraguan; v menyangsikan, meragukan; **doubtful** ADJ sangsi, ragu-ragu

dough N [do] adonan; **doughnut** → **donut**

dove N [dav] burung merpati

down ADV di bawah, ke bawah; **downstairs** ADV di lantai bawah; **downtown** (di) pusat kota; **downward, downwards** ADV ke bawah

doze N tidur sebentar, tidur ayam

dozen N [dazen] lusin; *~s* berpuluh-puluh, puluhan

draft N rancangan; v merancang

drag v menyeret, menarik

dragon N naga

dragonfly N capung

drain N saluran, parit, got; kali; aliran; v menguras, mengalirkan, mengeringkan; **drainage** N pengaliran, drainase

drama N seni peran, drama, sandiwara

drank v, PF → **drink**

draw v **drew drawn** meng-gambar; menarik; **drawback** N kekurangan, sisi buruk; **drawer** N laci; **drawing** N lukisan, gambar

dreadful ADJ menakutkan, dahsyat

dream N mimpi, impian; v mimpi; bermimpi, mengim-pikan

dress N rok; pakaian, baju, kostum; v berpakaian, men-

257

genakan pakaian; menghiasi; **dressing** N perban; saus (untuk salada)

drew V, PF → **draw**

drift N arus, aliran, arah; V terbawa arus, terhanyut

drill N bor; V mengebor

drink N minuman; V **drank drunk** minum, meminum; **drinker** N peminum

drip N tetes, tetesan; V menetes

drive N semangat, dorongan; V **drove driven** [driven] membawa (mobil), mengemudikan, menyupir; **driver** N supir, sopir, pengemudi, pengendara (mobil); kusir, sais (kendaraan berkuda); **driveway** N jalanan masuk halaman untuk mobil; **driving** ADJ mendorong

driverless car N mobil tanpa pengemudi

drizzle N, V hujan rintik-rintik

drop N titik, tetes; V jatuh, turun, terjun; menjatuhkan, menurunkan

drought N [draut] masa kering tanpa hujan

drove V, PF → **drive**

drown V tenggelam; menenggelamkan

drowsy ADJ mengantuk

drug N obat (bius), obat-obatan; V membius

drum N gendang, tambur; V mengetuk

drunk N mabuk; V, PF → **drink**

dry ADJ kering, haus; membosankan; V menjemur, mengeringkan; ~-*cleaning* binatu, waserai; ~ *season* musim kemarau; **dryer** N alat atau mesin pengering

duck N itik, bebek; V berjongkok menghindari; **duckling** N anak itik

due ADJ jatuh tempo; perlu, wajib

dug V, PF → **dig**

dull ADJ bodoh, dungu

dumb ADJ bisu; bodoh

dummy N, ADJ tiruan

dump N *(rubbish)* ~ tempat pembuangan sampah, tempat pembuangan akhir (TPA); V membuang

dumpling N pangsit

dune N bukit pasir

duplicate N rangkap kedua, salinan, kopi, duplikat

duration N lamanya

during CONJ, PREP selama, sementara

dusk N senja

dust N abu, debu; v membersihkan, menghilangkan debu; **dustbin** N tempat sampah; **duster** N lap debu, penyapu; **dusty** ADJ berdebu

Dutch N bahasa Belanda

dutiful ADJ patuh, menurut; **duty** N kewajiban; pekerjaan, tugas; bea

dwarf N katai, cebol

dye N zat pewarna; v mencelupkan, mengecat (rambut)

dynamic ADJ dinamis, hidup

dynamite N dinamit, bahan peledak

E

each ADJ masing-masing; tiap-tiap, saban; ~ *other* saling, satu sama lain

eager ADJ ingin sekali, pengen

eagle N burung rajawali

ear N telinga, kuping; **eardrum** N gendang telinga

early ADJ [érli] pagi-pagi, dini

earn v [érn] mendapat gaji, memperoleh

earnings N, PL pendapatan, gaji, upah ← **earn**

earring N anting ← **ear**

earth N [érth] bumi, dunia; tanah, debu; *on* ~ di dunia; **earthquake** N gempa bumi

east ADJ timur; ~ *Timor* Timor Loro Sae

Easter N Paskah

eastern ADJ (daerah) timur ← **east**

easy ADJ mudah, gampang

eat v ate eaten makan

echo N [éko] gema, gaung, kumandang; v bergema, bergaung, berkumandang

eclipse N gerhana

ecological ADJ berkaitan dengan ekologi; **ecology** N ekologi

economic ADJ berkaitan dengan ekonomi; **economical** ADJ hemat, ekonomis; **economist** N ekonom; **economy** N ekonomi, dunia usaha; kehematan

ecstasy N kegembiraan, kebahagiaan; ekstasi; **ecstatic** ADJ sangat gembira atau bahagia

edge N [éj] pinggir, sisi, tepi; mata (pisau); on ~ tegang

edible ADJ dapat dimakan

edit V menyunting, mengedit; **edition** N terbitan, keluaran, edisi, cetakan; **editor** N redaktur, penyunting, editor; **editorial** N tajuk rencana

educate V mendidik; **education** N pendidikan

eel N [iel] belut

effect N pengaruh, efek; akibat, hasil; **effective** ADJ berhasil, efektif

efficient ADJ berdaya guna, tepat guna, efisien

effort N usaha, upaya

egg N telur; **eggplant** N terong

Egypt N [Ijipt] Mesir

eight ADJ, N [éit] delapan; **eighteen** ADJ, N delapan belas; **eighteenth** ADJ kedelapan belas; **eighth** ADJ kedelapan; **eighty** ADJ, N delapan puluh

either ADJ [ither, aither] salah satu; ~ ... or ... ... atau...

elaborate ADJ rumit, panjang lebar, teliti

elastic N karet; ADJ karet, kenyal, elastis

elbow N siku; V menyikut

elder N yang lebih tua; sesepuh; ADJ kakak; ~ *brother* kakak (laki-laki); **elderly** ADJ sepuh, sudah tua; **eldest** ADJ anak paling tua, sulung

elect V memilih; **election** N pemilihan

electric ADJ listrik; **electrician** N tukang listrik; **electricity** N listrik

electronic ADJ elektronik; **electronics** N, PL barang elektronik, elektronika

element N unsur, bagian, bahan, elemen; **elementary** ADJ dasar

elephant N [élefant] gajah

elevator N lift

eleven ADJ, N sebelas; **eleventh** ADJ kesebelas

elf N elves peri

eligible ADJ memenuhi syarat, dapat dipilih

eliminate V menyisihkan, menyingkirkan

elite ADJ elit

else ADV lain; **elsewhere** ADV di lain tempat

email N surat éléktronik, surel, imél; ~ *address* alamat imél

embarrass V memalukan,

mempermalukan
embassy N kedutaan
embrace V memeluk
embroidery N sulaman,
bordiran
emerald N zamrud; ADJ hijau
emerge V [emérj] timbul,
muncul
emergency N [emérjénsi]
keadaaan darurat
emigrant N emigran; **emigrate**
V pindah, beremigrasi;
emigration N emigrasi
emission N pancaran, buangan, emisi
emotion N perasaan, emosi;
emotional ADJ emosi
emperor N kaisar ← **empire**
emphasis N [émfasis] tekanan; **emphasize** V menekankan, menitikberatkan
empire N kekaisaran, kerajaan
employee N pegawai,
buruh, pekerja, karyawan,
karyawati; **employer** N
majikan; **employment** N
pekerjaan
empty ADJ kosong, hampa; V
mengosongkan
enable V memungkinkan
enchant V memesonakan,

memikat, menyihir
enclose V memagari;
melampirkan, menyertakan
encounter N pertemuan; V
bertemu, berjumpa
encourage V [énkarej] mendorong, mendukung, mem-
beri semangat; **encourage-
ment** N dorongan, desakan
end N akhir, ujung; V berakhir;
menyudahi; mengakhiri;
endless ADJ tanpa ujung,
tiada hentinya, tidak ada
akhirnya, tak terhingga,
tidak berkeputusan ← **end**
endurance N daya tahan;
endure V bertahan; menahan,
menderita, menempuh
enemy N musuh, seteru
energetic ADJ [énerjétik]
energik, bersemangat;
energy N tenaga, usaha
engage V memasang;
engagement N janji; pertunangan
engine N [énjin] mesin; **engineer** N insinyur; masinis; V
merekayasa; **engineering** N
ilmu teknik
England N [Ingland] Inggris;
English N bahasa Inggris

enhance v meningkatkan
enjoy v menikmati; **enjoyable** ADJ menyenangkan; **enjoyment** N kenikmatan, kesenangan
enlarge v membesarkan, memperbesar, memperluas
enormous ADJ sangat besar
enough ADJ [enaf] cukup, sudah
enrich v memperkaya
enroll v mendaftarkan; **enrolled** ADJ terdaftar
ensure v memastikan, menjamin
enter v masuk; memasuki, memasukkan
entertain v menghibur; **entertainment** N hiburan
enthusiasm N semangat, gairah, antusiasme, gelora; kegemaran, hobi; **enthusiastic** ADJ antusias, bersemangat
entire ADJ seluruh, seantero; **entirely** ADV benar-benar
entitled ADJ berhak
entrance N pintu masuk ← **enter**
entrepreneur N [ontreprenur] pengusaha, wiraswasta

entry N jalan masuk, pintu masuk ← **enter**
envelope N amplop
envious ADJ iri
environment N lingkungan; ~*ly friendly* ramah lingkungan
epidemic N wabah
epilepsy N penyakit ayan, epilepsi, sawan
equal N [ikuel] bandingan; v menyamai, menyamakan; ADJ sama, setara; **equality** N kesamaan
equator N katulistiwa
equestrian ADJ berkaitan dengan penunggangan kuda
equipment N perlengkapan
equivalent N yang sama atau setara
eraser N penghapus
erect v mendirikan, membangun; ADJ tegak, tegang
erotic ADJ erotis, merangsang
errand N urusan, pesan
erratic ADJ tidak menentu, tidak teratur
error N salah, kesalahan
erupt v meletus; **eruption** N letusan, erupsi
escalator N tangga berjalan, eskalator

escape N pelarian; v melarikan diri, kabur, menghindari

escort N pendamping, rombongan

especially ADV khususnya, terutama ← **special**

essay N karangan

essential ADJ mutlak

establish v mendirikan, mengadakan; menentukan, menetapkan; **establishment** N pendirian, penentuan, penetapan; pembangunan

estate N tanah milik; kebun, perkebunan

estimate N taksiran, anggaran, perkiraan; pendapat; v menaksir, memperkirakan

estuary N muara, kuala

eternal ADJ abadi, kekal

ethical ADJ etis; **ethics** N, PL etika

ethnic ADJ etnis, kesukuan; tradisional; ~ *group* suku (bangsa), kelompok etnis

etiquette N tata cara, sopan santun, etiket

Europe N [Yurop] Eropa

evacuate v mengungsi; mengungsikan; **evacuation** N pengungsian, evakuasi

evaluate v menilai; **evaluation** N evaluasi, penilaian

evaporate v menguap; **evaporation** N penguapan

eve N [iv] malam (sebelumnya); *New Year's* ~ Malam Tahun Baru

even ADJ rata; genap; pun; PREP bahkan; ~ *if* kalaupun; ~ *though* meskipun

evening N sore, petang; malam; *good* ~ selamat malam; *this* ~ nanti malam

event N peristiwa, kejadian, acara; **eventually** ADV akhirnya

ever ADJ [évir] pernah; ~ *since* (mulai) sejak; *have you* ~? pernahkah?; **everlasting** ADJ kekal, abadi

every ADJ setiap, tiap; **everybody, everyone** ADJ semua orang, setiap orang; **everyday** ADJ sehari-hari; **everything** N semua; **everywhere** ADJ di mana-mana

evidence N bukti; **evident** ADJ jelas, nyata, terang

evil N [ivel] kejahatan; ADJ jahat

evolution N evolusi

e-wallet N dompet elektronik,

263

e-dompet

exact ADJ tepat, persis; betul; **exactly** ADV persis

exaggerate v [egzajerét] membesar-besarkan; **exaggeration** N pernyataan yang berlebihan

exam, examination N ujian; **examine** v menguji, memeriksa

example N contoh, teladan; *for ~* (seperti) misalnya, seumpamanya

excellent ADJ bagus sekali, hebat

except PREP kecuali; v mengecualikan; **exception** N kekecualian, pengecualian; **exceptional** ADJ luar biasa, istimewa

excess N kelebihan

exchange N pertukaran, penukaran; kurs; v menukar

excite v merangsang, membangkitkan

exclaim v berseru

exclude v mengecualikan; **excluding** v tidak termasuk; **exclusive** ADJ eksklusif, elit

excursion N kunjungan

excuse N [ékskyus] alasan,

dalih; v [ékskyuz] memaafkan; *~ me* permisi

execute v melakukan, melaksanakan; menjalankan keputusan; melakukan hukuman mati; **execution** N pelaksanaan (hukuman mati); **executive** N pemimpin (harian), eksekutif; ADJ eksekutif

exercise N olahraga; latihan, pelajaran; v berlatih; melakukan

exhaustion N kecapekan yang luar biasa

exhibition N pameran

exile N buangan; pembuangan

exist v ada eksis; **existence** N keberadaan

exit N pintu atau jalan keluar; kepergian

exotic ADJ eksotik, dari negeri asing

expand v memperluas, mengembangkan; memuai; **expansion** N perluasan, pengembangan

expat, expatriate N orang asing, orang yang tinggal di luar negeri, ekspatriat

expect v berharap; mengharapkan, menantikan; **expect-**

ation N harapan

expense N belanja, biaya, ongkos; **expensive** ADJ mahal

experience N pengalaman; V mengalami

experiment N percobaan, uji coba; V mengadakan percobaan, menguji coba

expert N ahli, pakar; ADJ ahli

expire V kedaluwarsa, jatuh tempo; mati

explain V menjelaskan, menerangkan, menyatakan; **explanation** N penjelasan

explode V meletus, meledak

exploit V memanfaatkan, mengeksploitasi

explore V menjelajah; mengadakan penelitian; **explorer** N penjelajah

explosion N letusan, ledakan; **explosive** ADJ dapat meledak ← **explode**

export N, ADJ ekspor; V mengekspor; **exporter** N pengekspor, eksportir

expose V menyingkapkan, mempertunjukkan, memamerkan, membuka

express N yang cepat, kilat, ekspres; ADJ cepat,

kilat; V mengucapkan, mengungkapkan, menyatakan, mengutarakan; **expression** N ucapan, peribahasa; raut muka; **expressive** ADJ ekspresif, menyatakan perasaan

extend V merentangkan, membentangkan; memperluas; memperpanjang; **extension** N perpanjangan; **extensive** ADJ luas, panjang lebar

exterior N luar, luarnya

extinct ADJ punah; **extinction** N pemadaman; kepunahan

extra ADJ ekstra

extract V mencabut (gigi); mengambil

extraordinary ADJ [ékstro-dinari] luar biasa, istimewa

extravagant ADJ boros, berfoya-foya

extreme ADJ terlampau, ekstrem

eye N [ai] mata; **eyebrow** N alis; **eyelash** N bulu mata; **eyelid** N kelopak mata; **eyesight** N penglihatan; **eyewitness** N saksi mata

F

fable N dongeng, cerita rakyat

fabric N kain, bahan

fabulous ADJ hebat, menakjubkan

face N muka, paras, wajah; v menghadapi; **facial** N perawatan wajah

Facebook N fesbuk

facility N sarana, fasilitas; kemudahan

facsimile N salinan, kopi → **fax**

fact N kenyataan, fakta; *in* ~ sebenarnya

factory N pabrik

fade v luntur, pudar; mengecil (suara)

fail v gagal; tidak jadi; jatuh; tidak lulus; **failure** N kegagalan, gagalnya

faint N pingsan; v (jatuh) pingsan; ADJ lemah, kecil

fair N pameran, pekan raya, pasar malam; ADJ adil, berimbang

fairy N peri; ~ *tale* dongeng

faith N iman, kepercayaan; **faithful** ADJ beriman, setia

fake N tipuan; ADJ palsu

fall N kejatuhan, keruntuhan, keguguran; musim gugur, musim rontok; v **fell, fallen** jatuh, runtuh, gugur

fallen v, PF → **fall**

false ADJ palsu

fame N ketenaran

familiar ADJ dikenal; akrab; **family** N keluarga; rumah tangga

famous ADJ terkenal, ternama ← **fame**

fan N kipas; penggemar, fans

fanatic ADJ fanatic

fancy ADJ rumit, megah

fantastic ADJ ajaib, fantastis, tidak masuk akal; **fantasy** N fantasi, khayalan

far ADJ jauh

fare N ongkos perjalanan

farewell EJAC selamat tinggal, selamat jalan

farm N pertanian, peternakan; **farmer** N petani

farther, further ADJ, ADV lebih jauh

fascinate v memesonakan, menarik hati

fashion N mode; cara; v membentuk; **fashionable** ADJ

bergaya, gaya

fast N puasa; v berpuasa

fast ADJ cepat, laju; kokoh

fat N lemak; ADJ gemuk, tambun

fatal ADJ mematikan

fate N nasib

father N ayah, bapak; **father-in-law** N mertua (lelaki)

fatigue N [fatig] kelelahan, kecapekan; kerusakan

faucet N keran

fault N kesalahan, salah; cacat; **faulty** ADJ cacat, rusak, kurang sempurna

favor N pertolongan, karunia, anugerah; ampun; v lebih suka

favorite N kesukaan, anak emas; ADJ kesukaan, yang paling disukai, favorit

fax N ~ (machine) mesin faks; v (me)ngefaks, mengirim lewat faks ← **facsimile**

fear N ketakutan, rasa takut; v takut akan; **fearless** ADJ tidak takut, berani

feast N pesta, perjamuan, perayaan

feather N bulu

feature v mempertunjukkan, memperlihatkan

February N bulan Februari

fed v, PF → **feed**

federal ADJ federal, berserikat

fee N upah, gaji, biaya

feed N pakan, makanan hewan; ~ on makan (dari); v fed fed memberi makan; **feedback** N tanggapan

feel N rasa; v felt felt berasa, merasa; meraba; **feeling** N perasaan

feet N, PL → **foot**

fell v, PF → **fall**

fellow N lelaki; ADJ sesama

felt v, PF → **feel**

female N, ADJ perempuan, wanita; betina (binatang)

feminine ADJ feminin; yang berkaitan dengan kewanitaan

fence N pagar

ferocious ADJ ganas, buas

ferry N feri; v membawa penumpang bolak-balik, menyeberangkan

fertile ADJ subur; **fertilizer** N pupuk; **fertility** N kesuburan

festival N pesta, perayaan, hari raya, festival

fetch v menjemput (orang), mengambilkan

267

fever N demam; **feverish** ADJ demam, panas

few ADJ (hanya) sedikit; *a* ~ beberapa

fiancé N [fiansé] tunangan (laki-laki); **fiancée** N tunangan (perempuan)

fiber N [faiber] serabut, serat

field N bidang, daerah; padang, medan, ladang

fierce ADJ buas, galak, ganas

fifteen ADJ, N lima belas; **fifteenth** ADJ kelima belas ← **five**

fifth ADJ kelima ← **five**

fifty ADJ, N lima puluh

fight N [fait] pertengkaran; perkelahian; pertempuran, perjuangan; v **fought fought** bertengkar; berkelahi; bertempur, berperang, berjuang

figure N rupa, bentuk; bagan, gambar; angka; harga

file N berkas, arsip, dokumentasi; v menyimpan; mengikir

fill N jatah; v mengisi, menempati, memenuhi

film N film

filter N saringan, filter; v menyaring, menyeleksi

filthy ADJ kotor sekali

fin N sirip

final N (pertandingan) final; ADJ final, penghabisan, terakhir; **finally** ADV akhirnya

finance N keuangan; v membiayai, mendanai; **financial** ADJ keuangan

find N [faind] (hasil) temuan; v **found found** menemukan; menyimpulkan

fine N denda, tilang

fine ADJ bagus, baik; halus

finger N jari; **fingerprint** N sidik jari

finish N (garis) akhir; penghabisan, penyelesaian; v berhenti; mengakhiri, menghentikan; menyelesaikan; menghabiskan

Finland N Finlandia

fire N api; kebakaran; v melepaskan tembakan, menembak; **fireworks** N, PL kembang api, petasan, mercon

firm ADJ tetap, pasti, tegas

first ADJ pertama; ~ *name* nama depan; *at* ~ pada awalnya, semula; **firstly** ADV pertama-tama

fish N ikan; v memancing;

268

fisherman N nelayan; **fisheries** N perikanan; **fishing** N memancing; ~ *rod* joran

fist N tinju, kepalan tangan

fit ADJ pas, tepat, layak, patut; fit, sehat; v menyesuaikan; **fitness** N kebugaran, kesehatan

five ADJ, N lima

fix N masalah; v memperbaiki; menetapkan, memasang; **fixed** ADJ tetap

flag N bendera

flame N (kobaran) api

flannel N kain panas, flanel; handuk kecil untuk menyabuni

flap N tutup, penutup; v mengepak

flash N kilau; blits; v berkilat-kilat; **flashlight** N (lampu) senter

flask N botol minuman

flat N apartemen; ADJ rata, datar; **flatten** v meratakan

flavor N rasa; v membumbui

flea N kutu (binatang); ~ *market* pasar loak

fled v, PF → **flee**

flee v fled fled melarikan diri, kabur, minggat

fleet N armada (angkatan laut)

flesh N daging

flight N [flait] penerbangan; terbangnya

fling v **flung flung** melemparkan

flip N salto; v membalik, memutar-balikkan

flirt v bermain mata

float v mengapung, terapung

flood N banjir, air bah; v banjir; membanjiri; **flooded** ADJ banjir

floor N lantai, tingkat

flop v gagal; jatuh, tidak berdiri; **floppy** ADJ tidak tegak, lembut

florist N (pemilik) toko bunga

flour N tepung (terigu)

flow N aliran; v mengalir

flower N bunga, kembang

flown v, PF → **fly**

flu N flu, selesma ← **influenza**

fluent ADJ lancar, fasih

fluid N cairan

flung v, PF → **fling**

flush v memerah (muka); ~ *the toilet* menyiram WC

flute N suling

fly N lalat

fly v flew flown [flon] terbang; berkibar-kibar; mengibarkan

flyer, flier N selebaran, brosur

foam N buih, busa

focus N titik perhatian, pusat perhatian, fokus; V memfokuskan, memusatkan perhatian; **focused** ADJ terarah

fog N kabut

foil N kertas perak

fold N lipatan; V melipat

folk N orang; ~ *tale* cerita rakyat

follow V mengikuti, menuruti; **following** yang berikut

fond ADJ suka, gemar

font N jenis huruf (cetakan)

food N makanan, pangan, pakan (hewan)

fool N orang bodoh; **foolish** ADJ bodoh

foot N feet kaki; **football** N sepak bola; **footpath** N jalan setapak, trotoar; **footprint** N tapak kaki; **footwear** N sepatu

for PREP bagi, untuk; selama; CONJ karena

forbid V forbade forbidden melarang; **forbidden** ADJ terlarang, dilarang

force N kekuatan, tenaga, daya; V memaksa

forecast N ramalan

forehead N dahi, kening

foreign ADJ [foren] asing, luar negeri; **foreigner** N orang asing

forest N hutan; **forestry** N perhutanan

forever, forevermore ADV untuk selamanya

forgave V, PF → **forgive**

forget V forgot forgotten lupa, melupakan, terlupa; **forgetful** ADJ pelupa

forgive V forgave forgiven memaafkan, mengampuni

forgot, forgotten V, PF → **forget**

fork N garpu; belokan, pertigaan

form N bentuk, rupa; formulir, blangko; V merupakan, membentuk

formal ADJ formal, resmi

former ADJ dahulu, bekas, mantan (orang), lama

formula N rumus, formula

fort N benteng ← **fortress**

fortnight N dua minggu

fortunate ADJ beruntung; **fortunately** ADV secara beruntung; **fortune** N rezeki; harta karun

forty ADJ, N empat puluh ←
four

forward ADJ, ADV ke depan,
maju; v mengirimkan

fossil N fosil

foul ADJ jorok, kotor, najis,
jijik; v melanggar peraturan
(olahraga); mengotori

found v mendirikan; v, PF →
find; **foundation** N yayasan;
fondasi, alas; bedak dasar

fountain N air mancur,
pancuran air

four ADJ, N empat; **fourteen**
ADJ, N empat belas

fox N rubah; v menipu

fraction N pecahan

fracture N keretakan, patah

fragile ADJ mudah pecah atau
patah

fragrance N fragrant ADJ
[frégrant] harum, wangi

frame N rangka, kerangka;
bingkai, lis (gambar); kusen
(pintu); tubuh, badan; v
membingkai

France N Perancis

frangipani N bunga kamboja

fraud N penipuan, penipu

freak N orang dengan cacat
yang luar biasa; ADJ luar

biasa, kebetulan

freckle N bintik-bintik

free v membebaskan, melepaskan; ADJ bebas, merdeka;
cuma-cuma, gratis; **freedom**
N kemerdekaan, kebebasan

freeze v froze frozen membeku; **freezer** N lemari es

freight N [frét] muatan, kargo;
v mengirim

French N bahasa Perancis

frequent ADJ berulang kali,
sering; v sering mengunjungi

fresh ADJ segar; baru; sejuk

Friday N hari Jumat

fried ADJ goreng → fry

friend N [frénd] kawan,
sahabat, teman; **friendly**
ADJ ramah, bersahabat;
friendship N persahabatan

fright N [frait] rasa takut;
frighten v menakut-nakuti,
menakutkan

fringe N pinggir; poni

frog N kodok, katak

from PREP dari

front N bagian muka; hadapan;
ADJ muka; **frontier** N tapal
batas, perbatasan

frost N embun beku; **frosty** ADJ
dingin, tidak ramah

frown N [fraun] muka cemberut; v mengernyit dahi

froze, frozen V, PF → freeze

fruit N buah, buah-buahan

frustrate v menghambat; **frustration** N frustasi

fry v menggoreng; menjadi panas

fuel N bahan bakar

fulfill v memenuhi

full ADJ penuh; kenyang; lengkap

fun N keasyikan; ADJ asyik

function N fungsi; v berfungsi, berjalan, bekerja

fund N dana

funeral N (upacara) pemakaman

funnel N corong

funny ADJ lucu, jenaka; aneh

fur N bulu (binatang); **furry** ADJ berbulu

furious ADJ marah sekali, geram, naik pitam ← **fury**

furniture N mebel, perabot rumah

further ADJ lebih jauh, lebih lanjut; **furthermore** ADV lagipula

fury N kemarahan, berang

fuse N sumbu, sekering; v melebur, menyatu

fuss N repot; kekacauan; v cerewet; **fussy** ADJ teliti, cerewet

future N masa depan; ADJ yang akan datang, mendatang, bakal, calon (orang)

G

gadget N alat, perkakas

gain N untung, keuntungan, laba; v memperoleh, mendapat, mencapai

gale N angin besar, badai

gallery N serambi, ruang pameran, galeri

gamble v berjudi, bertaruh; **gambling** N judi, perjudian

game N permainan, pertandingan; ADJ berani

gang N kawanan, gerombolan, geng; **gangster** N preman, penjahat, perampok, garong

gap N lubang, celah, jurang pemisah

garage N [garaj] garasi; bengkel

garden N kebun, taman; **gardener** N tukang kebun;

gardening N berkebun

gargle V berkumur

garlic N bawang putih

gas N gas; bensin

gasoline N [gasolin] bensin ← **gas**

gasp N embusan napas; V menarik nafas dengan cepat

gate N pintu (masuk), gerbang

gather V berkumpul; mengumpulkan, memetik; **gathering** N perkumpulan

gauge N [géj] ukuran, kadar; V mengukur, menaksir

gay N orang homoseksual; ADJ senang hati, meriah

gaze V menatap, memandangi

gazelle N semacam rusa

GB ABBREV *gigabyte* gigabit

gear N peralatan, perkakas, perabot; persneling, gigi; gir

gecko N cicak

gee EJAC, SL wah, aduh

geese N, PL → **goose**

gem, gemstone N permata

gender N jenis kelamin; jender

gene N gen

general N jenderal; ADJ umum; *in ~* pada umumnya

generation N angkatan, generasi

generator N pembangkit listrik ← **generate**

generous ADJ murah hati, dermawan

genital N kemaluan

genius N [jinius] kecerdasan; jenius, orang berotak cemerlang

genre N [jonre] gaya, aliran

gentle ADJ (lemah) lembut, halus, jinak; **gentleman** N **gentlemen** tuan; orang pria; orang sopan; **gently** ADV perlahan-lahan, lemah lembut

genuine ADJ [jényuin] asli, sejati, tulen

geography N [jiografi] ilmu bumi, geografi

geologist N [jiolojist] geolog, ahli geologi; **geology** N geologi

geothermal ADJ [jiotérmal] berhubungan dengan panas bumi

germ N kuman

German N bahasa Jerman; **Germany** N Jerman

get V got gotten mendapat, menerima; mengerti; menjadi; *~ better* sembuh;

273

menjadi lebih baik; ~ *off*
turun; ~ *up* bangun; ~ *well
soon* semoga lekas sembuh
ghost N hantu
giant N, ADJ [jaiant] raksasa
gift [gift] kado, hadiah, pemberian; bakat
gigantic ADJ [jaigantik] besar
sekali, raksasa
giggle V cekikik; tertawa
terkikik-kikik
gin N [jin] jenewer, minuman
keras
ginger N [jinjer] jahe; ADJ
merah (rambut); kuning
(bulu kucing)
gipsy → **gypsy**
giraffe N [jiraf] jerapah
girl N [gerl] anak perempuan,
putri, gadis
give V [giv] **gave given**
memberi; ~ *birth* bersalin,
melahirkan; ~ *in* mengalah; ~
up menyerah, menyerahkan;
given ADJ tertentu
glacier N gletser
glad ADJ gembira, senang
glamorous ADJ memesona,
menarik, menawan, glamor
glass N kaca; gelas; **glasses**
N kacamata; **glasshouse** N

rumah kaca
glide V meluncur; **glider** N
pesawat peluncur, pesawat
layang; *hang-~* gantole
glitter N kegemilapan,
kemegahan; V gemilap
global ADJ seluruh dunia; ~
warming pemanasan bumi;
globalization N globalisasi;
globe N bola dunia; bola
lampu, bohlam
glorious ADJ megah, mulia,
agung; **glory** N kemuliaan;
kemenangan
gloss N kilau, kilap
glossary N daftar istilah
glossy ADJ licin, mengkilap
← **gloss**
glove N [glav] sarung tangan
glow N sinar, cahaya; V bersinar, berseri; berseri
glue N [glu] lem, perekat; V
mengelem
gnome N [nom] orang kerdil,
katai
go V **went gone** [gon] pergi,
berjalan; hilang; ~ *on*
meneruskan; ~ *out* keluar; ~
under bangkrut; *to have a
~* berusaha
goal N gawang, gol; tujuan;

v *(to score a)* ~ mencetak gol; **goalkeeper** N penjaga gawang, kiper

goat N kambing

god N dewa; **God** ISL, CHR Allah, Tuhan; CHR Bapa; **goddess** N, F dewi

going ~ *to* mau, akan; naik ← **go**

gold N emas; **golden** ADJ terbuat dari emas; **goldfish** N ikan emas

golf N golf; **golfer** N pegolf, pemain gulf

gone V, PF ← **go**

good ADJ baik, bagus; ~ *evening* selamat malam; ~ *night* selamat tidur; **goodbye** EJAC selamat tinggal, selamat jalan; **goodness** ~ *me* ampun

goods N, PL barang-barang

goose N **geese** [gis] angsa

gorge N jurang, ngarai

gorgeous ADJ [gorjes] sangat menawan atau menarik, indah

gorilla N gorila

gosh EJAC wah!

gossip N gosip, isu, gunjingan, buah bibir, kabar burung

got, gotten V, PF → **get**

government N [gaverment]
pemerintah, pemerintahan; **governor** N gubernur ← **govern**

gown N gaun; jubah

grab V merampas, menjambret, menyerobot, menangkap

grace N keanggunan; rahmat, anugerah, karunia; **graceful** ADJ anggun

grade N tingkat, pangkat, derajat; nilai (rapot); kelas; **gradual** ADJ lama-kelamaan, berangsurangsur

graduate N [gradyuet] lulusan, tamatan; sarjana; V [gradyuét] lulus, tamat; wisuda; **graduation** N tamat sekolah, acara lulus-lulusan; wisuda

grain N butir; sereal; biji-bijian

gram N gram

grand N besar, agung; bagus, mewah

grandchild N cucu; **granddaughter** N cucu (perempuan); **grandfather** N kakek; **grandma** N, SL nenek; nek; **grandmother** N nenek; **grandpa** N, SL kakek; kek; **grandson** N cucu (lelaki); **granny** N nenek, perempuan

275

tua ← **grandmother**
grant N (dana) pemberian, sumbangan, subsidi, beasiswa
grape N buah anggur; ADJ (rasa) anggur; **grapefruit** N semacam jeruk kuning yang besar
graphic ADJ grafik, bergambar, jelas
grasp V memegang, menggenggam, menangkap, mengerti
grass N rumput; **grasshopper** N belalang
grate V memarut; mengganggu; **grate, grating** N riol, kisi; ADJ kasar, mengganggu
grateful ADJ berterima kasih
grave ADJ berat, genting, gawat, serius
grave N kuburan, makam; **graveyard** N kuburan, tempat pemakaman
gravity N daya tarik bumi, gaya berat
gravy N [grévi] saus atau kuah daging
gray ADJ (warna) abu-abu, kelabu; suram
graze N goresan pada kulit; V mendapat goresan pada kulit

grease N [gris] gemuk, minyak; V [griz] memberi gemuk, meminyaki; **greasy** ADJ berlemak, berminyak
great ADJ [grét] besar, agung, mulia, raya
great-grandchild N cicit; **great-grandfather** N kakek buyut
Greece N Yunani
greedy ADJ rakus, tamak, loba
Greek N bahasa Yunani; orang Yunani ← **Greece**
green ADJ hijau; mentah; baru, muda; ramah lingkungan; **greenhouse** N rumah kaca; **greens** N, PL sayuran, sayur-mayur; partai hijau, partai peduli lingkungan
greet V memberi salam, menegur, menyambut; **greeting** N salam, ucapan selamat
grenade N granat
grew V, PF → **grow**
grey → **gray**
grid N jaringan
grief N kesedihan, duka cita
grill N pemanggangan, barbekiu; V memanggang
grin N senyum, seringai

grind v **ground ground** menggerinda, menggiling, mengasah; **grinder** N gerinda

grip N pegangan, genggaman; v memegang, menggenggam

grit N kerikil, pasir; kenekatan

groan N keluh, erang; v berkeluh, mengeluh, mengerang

grocery N toko bahan makanan; **groceries** N, PL bahan makanan

groom N *(bride)~* mempelai pria, pengantin pria, calon suami

gross N gros, 12 lusin, 144; ADJ sangat gemuk

ground v, PF → **grind**

ground N [graund] tanah, bumi; v mendasarkan; **grounds** N, PL pekarangan, taman; alasan

group N kelompok, grup; v mengelompokkan

grow v [gro] **grew grown** tumbuh; bertambah; menjadi; menanam

growl N [graul] geram; v menggeram

growth N pertumbuhan, pertambahan; benjolan ← **grow**

grudge N dendam

grumble N bersungut-sungut, menggerutu; keluhan

grumpy ADJ mengomel, marah-marah

grunt N dengkur; v mengeluarkan bunyi dengkur

guarantee N [garanti] jaminan; v menjamin, menanggung

guard N [gard] jaga, pengawal; kondektur; v menjaga, pengawal; **guardian** N wali, orang tua asuh; penjaga

guava N jambu

guess N [gés] tebakan, terkaan, sangkaan; v menebak, menerka

guest N [gést] tamu

guide N pemandu, pembimbing; v membimbing, memandu; **guidebook** N buku petunjuk, buku panduan; **guidelines** N, PL pedoman

guilt N [gilt] kesalahan, rasa bersalah; **guilty** ADJ bersalah

guitar N gitar

gulf N teluk besar; jurang

gum N getah

gum N gusi

gun N bedil, senapan, revolver, pistol; v menembak

gush N pancaran, semburan; v

277

memancar, mengalir dengan deras

gut N usus; **guts** N, PL nyali, keberanian

gutter N parit, selokan

guy N, SL [gai] orang, lelaki, cowok

gym N [jim] aula, tempat senam; pusat kebugaran; **gymnasium** N aula, tempat senam, gimnasium; **gymnast** N pesenam

gymnastics N senam

gynecologist N [gainekolojist] ginekolog

gypsy, gipsy N nomaden, orang jipsi

H

habit N kebiasaan

hack v memotong-motong, mencincang; memasuki jaringan komputer; **hacker** N orang yang memasuki jaringan komputer

had v, PF → **have**

hadn't (had not) ← **have**

hail, hailstone N hujan es

hair N rambut, bulu; **hairbrush**

N sikat rambut; **hairdresser** N penata rambut, potong rambut; **hairspray** N semprot rambut; **hairy** ADJ berbulu

half N [haf] **halves** ADJ setengah, separuh; ~ *past three* (jam) setengah empat; **halfway** ADJ setengah jalan

hall N [hol] aula, balai, ruang; lorong, koridor; **hallway** N lorong, koridor

halt N [holt] pemberhentian

ham N irisan daging babi

hamburger N burger

hammer N palu

hamper N bakul, keranjang (makanan)

hamster N marmot

hand N tangan; jarum (jam); jangan disentuh; **handbag** N tas tangan; **handbook** N buku panduan, pedoman

handicap N rintangan, cacat

handicraft N kerajinan tangan ← **hand**

handkerchief N sapu tangan

handle N pegangan; v menangani, memegang

handmade ADJ buatan tangan ← **hand**

handsome ADJ [handsam]

ganteng, tampan

handwriting N [handraiting] tulisan tangan ← **hand**

handy ADJ berguna, praktis; **handyman** N tukang ← **hand**

hang v bergantung; menggantung; ~*-gliding* gantolé

happen v terjadi; **happening** N kejadian, peristiwa

happiness N kebahagiaan; **happy** ADJ bahagia, berbahagia, senang

harbor N [harber] pelabuhan

hard ADJ keras; susah, sulit; dengan rajin

hardly ADV nyaris tidak, hampir tidak

hardware N alat-alat pertukangan; barang-barang dari logam dan besi; peranti keras ← **hard**

harm N bahaya; kerugian, kerusakan, kejahatan; v merusak, mengganggu; **harmful** ADJ membahayakan, merusak, merugikan; **harmless** ADJ tidak jahat

harmonica N harmonika

harness N tali pengaman, tali keselamatan; pakaian kuda

harsh ADJ kasar, keras hati; tidak ramah

harvest N (hasil) panen

hash N pagar (#)

hate N kebencian, rasa benci; v membenci; **hatred** N [hétred] kebencian, rasa benci

haul v menarik, menghela

haunt v menghantui

have v [hav] **had had** mempunyai, memiliki; ada; mendapat; menyuruh

hawk N burung elang

hawker N penjaja, pedagang kaki lima

hay N rumput kering, jerami; ~ *fever* alergi rumput

hazard N bahaya, risiko

he PRON, M [hi] dia, ia (subyek); **He** PRON Dia, Tuhan

head N [héd] kepala; pemimpin, direktur; v mengepalai; menyundul (bola); v mengepalai, memimpin; **headache** N sakit kepala, pusing; **heading** N judul (karangan); **headlights** N, PL lampu depan (mobil); **headline** N kepala berita; **headquarters** N markas besar

heal v menyembuhkan,

menyehatkan; **health** N
[hélth] kesehatan; **healthy**
ADJ sehat

heap N timbunan, tumpukan,
susunan

hear V **heard heard** [hérd]
mendengar; **hearing** N
(indera) pendengaran, sidang

heart N [hart] jantung; hati,
inti; **heartbeat** N denyut jantung; **heartbreak** N patah hati

heat N panas, kepanasan,
hangat; V memanaskan,
menghangatkan; **heater** N
alat pemanas

heaven N [héven] surga

heavy ADJ [hévi] berat,
berbobot

hedge N pagar hidup

hedgehog N landak

heel N tumit; hak

height N [hait] ketinggian;
tinggi badan; puncak

heir N [ér] **heiress** F ahli waris

helicopter N helikopter, heli

hell N neraka

hello, hallo EJAC halo; apa
kabar?

helmet N helm

help N pertolongan, bantuan;
V menolong, membantu;

helpful ADJ suka menolong;
berguna; **helpless** ADJ tidak
berdaya

hemorrhoid N [hémeroid]
wasir, ambeien

hen N, F ayam betina

hepatitis N [hépataitis]
hepatitis, radang hati

her PRON, F -nya (kepunyaan);
dia, ia (obyek)

herb N jamu, bumbu

herd N kawanan; V meng-
gembala

here ADV di sini

heritage N [héritej] warisan,
harta pusaka

hero N [hiro] pahlawan

heroin N [héroin] heroin,
putau

heroine N, F [héroin] pahlawan (wanita) ← **hero**

herring N ikan haring

hers PRON, F miliknya; **herself**
PRON dirinya, sendiri ← **her**

hesitant ADJ hesitate V ragu-
ragu, bimbang

hey EJAC he, oi

hiccup V cegukan, bersedu

hid, hidden V, PF → **hide**

hide V **hid hidden** bersembunyi, berlindung, me-

ngumpet; **menyembunyikan**

hiding N persembunyian; *in* ~
bersembunyi ← **hide**

high ADJ [hai] tinggi, mulia;
~ *chair* kursi bayi; ~ *school*
sekolah menengah (atas);
highlands N tanah tinggi,
pegunungan; **highway** N
jalan raya, jalan besar

hijack V membajak; **hijacker**
N membajak; **hijacking** N
pembajakan

hike N perjalanan kaki; V
berjalan kaki, mendaki
gunung

hill N bukit; **hillside** N lereng
bukit

him PRON, M dia, ia (obyek);
himself PRON dirinya, sendiri

Hindu N orang Hindu; ADJ
Hindu; **Hinduism** N agama
Hindu

hinge N [hinj] engsel; sendi

hint N tanda, isyarat, sindiran

hip N pangkal paha, pinggul

hire N sewa; V menyewa;
mempekerjakan

his PRON, M -nya (kepunyaan)

historic ADJ bersejarah;
history N sejarah, hikayat

hit N pukulan; V **hit hit** memu-

kul, kena, mengenai

hitchhike V menumpang
mobil orang yang lewat

hobby N hobi, kegemaran,
kesukaan

hockey N hoki; *ice* ~ hoki es

hoe N [ho] pacul, cangkul

hold N pegangan, genggaman;
palka; V **held held** memegang,
menggenggam; bermuatan

hole N lubang, liang

holiday N hari libur; *religious*
~ hari raya; V berlibur

Holland N, SL Belanda

hollow N rongga, ruang; ADJ
hampa, kosong

holy ADJ suci, kudus

home N rumah; panti (jompo);
ADJ di rumah, di kandang
sendiri; **hometown** N kampung (halaman); **homemade**
ADJ buatan sendiri; **homesick**
ADJ rindu pada rumah,
kampung halaman atau
negeri sendiri; **homework** N
pekerjaan rumah (PR)

homo SL orang homo; homoseksual

honest ADJ [onest] jujur;
honesty N kejujuran

honey N [hani] madu; sayang,

sayangku; **honeymoon** N bulan madu

honorable ADJ terhormat; **honorary** ADJ kehormatan; **honor** N hormat, kehormatan; v menghormati

hoof N **hooves** kuku (binatang)

hook N kait, kali; v mengait; **hooked** ADJ keranjingan

hooligan N penggemar sepak bola yang brutal

hop N lompat (pada satu kaki); v melompat-lompat, melonjak-lonjak

hope N harapan; v berharap; mengharapkan; **hopeful** ADJ penuh harapan; **hopeless** ADJ putus asa

horizon N [horaizon] cakrawala, kaki langit, ufuk, horison; **horizontal** ADJ [horizontel] melintang, horisontal

horn N tanduk; terompet, klakson

hornbill N burung enggang

horrible, horrific ADJ mengerikan, dahsyat; **horror** N kengerian, ketakutan, horor

horse N kuda; **horsepower** N daya kuda, PK (paarde-kracht); **horseshoe** N ladam, sepatu kuda

hose N selang

hospital N rumah sakit

hospitality N keramahtamahan

host N, M [hoost] tuan rumah

hostage N sandera, tawanan

hostel N asrama

hostess N, F [hoostés] nyonya rumah ← **host**

hot ADJ panas, hangat; pedas

hotel N hotel

hound N anjing pemburu

hour N [auer] jam; *half~, half an* ~ setengah jam; *quarter of an* ~ seperempat jam

house N rumah; dewan; **household** N rumah tangga; **housekeeper** N kepala pembantu; **housemaid** N, F pembantu, pramuwisma; **housewife** N, F ibu rumah tangga; **housework** N pekerjaan rumah; **housing** N perumahan

how ADV bagaimana; betapa; ~ *much?*, ~ *many?* Berapa banyak?; ~ *much is it?* Berapa harganya?; **however** ADV biarpun, akan tetapi, namun; bagaimanapun

howl N gonggong; teriak, tangis; V melolong; menangis (dengan keras)

hub N pusat (kota)

hug N pelukan; V berpelukan; memeluk

huge ADJ besar sekali

hum V bersenandung; mendengung

human N, ADJ manusia, orang; **humane** ADJ manusiawi, berperikemanusiaan

humble ADJ rendah hati; V merendahkan

humid ADJ lembab; **humidity** N kelembaban

humiliate V menghina, merendahkan; **humiliation** N penghinaan

humorous ADJ lucu, kocak, menggelikan; **humor** N kelucuan; sifat

hump N ponok (unta), bongkol

hunch N perasaan, firasat, dugaan

hunchback N, ADJ bungkuk

hundred N ratusan; ADJ seratus; ADJ keseratus

Hungary N Hongaria

hunger N [hangger] rasa lapar; **hungry** ADJ lapar

hunt N perburuan, buruan; V berburu; memburu; **hunter** N pemburu; **hunting** N pemburuan, perburuan

hurdle N gawang; rintangan; V melompati; mengatasi; **hurdles** N, PL lari gawang

hurrah, hurray EJAC hore

hurricane N angin topan

hurry N ketergopoh-gopohan; V bergegas; menggegaskan

hurt N sakit hati, luka; V melukai, menyakiti, mencederai, merusak

husband N suami

hush V diam

hut N pondok, gubuk

hydraulic ADJ [haidrolik] hidrolik, hidrolis

hygiene N [haijin] kebersihan; **hygienic** ADJ bersih; higienis

hypertension N hipertensi, darah tinggi

hypocrite N [hipokrit] orang munafik; **hypocritical** ADJ munafik

hysterical ADJ histeris

283

I

I PRON saya, aku

ice N es; **ice cream** N es krim; **iceberg** N gunung es; **icing** N lapisan gula di atas kue

icy ADJ [aisi] dingin sekali, sedingin es ← **ice**

idea N [aidia] ide, gagasan;

ideal ADJ [aidil] yang diinginkan atau diidamkan, ideal, yang terbaik

identical ADJ sama, serupa, identik

identification N pengenalan, indentifikasi; **identify** V mengenal, mengidentifikasi; **identity** N identitas, jati diri

idiom N ungkapan, idiom

idiot N orang dungu

idol N idola; berhala; **idolize** V mendewakan, memuji

if CONJ kalau, jika; apabila, bila

ignorant ADJ tidak tahu; **ignore** V tidak menghiraukan, tidak mengindahkan

iguana N iguana, sejenis biawak

ill N penyakit; ADJ sakit; jahat, salah; **illness** N penyakit

illegal ADJ melanggar hukum, tidak sah, ilegal

illegitimate ADJ lahir di luar nikah

illiterate ADJ buta huruf

illusion N ilusi, khayal

illustrate V menggambarkan, melukiskan; **illustration** N gambar, lukisan, ilustrasi

image N gambar; **imaginary** ADJ khayal; **imagination** N daya cipta, khayal, fantasi; **imagine** V membayang; membayangkan

imitate V meniru; **imitation** N tiruan, imitasi

immediate ADJ langsung; **immediately** ADV serta merta

immigrant N pendatang, imigran; **immigration** N imigrasi

immoral ADJ tuna susila, cabul

immortal ADJ kekal, abadi

immunization N imunisasi, pengebalan

impartial ADJ tidak memihak, adil, obyektif

impatient ADJ tidak sabar

imperial ADJ [impirial] kaisar; **imperialism** N imperialisme; **imperialist** N orang penjajah,

imperialis; ADJ imperialis,
penjajahan ← **empire**

impersonal ADJ bersikap
dingin; tidak mengenai
orang tertentu

implement N perkakas,
perabot, alat; v menerapkan,
melaksanakan; **implemen-
tation** N penerapan,
implementasi

implicate v melibatkan

import N barang impor,
pemasukan; v mengimpor,
mendatangkan

important ADJ penting

impossible ADJ mustahil, tidak
mungkin

impractical ADJ tidak praktis

impress v memberi kesan,
mengesankan; **impression** N
kesan; cetakan; **impressive**
ADJ mengesankan, hebat,
dahsyat

imprisonment N hukuman
penjara

improve v [impruv] memperbaiki; meningkatkan;
menjadi sembuh, membaik;
improvement N perbaikan,
peningkatan, kemajuan

impulse N kata hati, dorongan

hati; **impulsive** ADJ menurut
kata hati

in PREP di (dalam), dalam,
pada; ~ *Indonesian* dalam
Bahasa Indonesia

inability N ketidakmampuan

inaccurate ADJ tidak teliti,
tidak tepat

inadequate ADJ kurang, tidak
cukup

inappropriate ADJ tidak
pantas

inaugural ADJ [inogyural]
perdana

incense N dupa, kemenyan

inch N inci

incident N peristiwa, kejadian,
insiden

include v mengandung,
meliputi; **inclusive** ADJ
inklusif; sampai dengan

income N [incam] pendapatan,
penghasilan, gaji; **incoming**
ADJ yang masuk

incompatible ADJ tidak cocok

incompetent ADJ tidak
mampu

incomplete ADJ kurang
lengkap, tidak komplet

inconsiderate ADJ tidak
memperhatikan (perasaan

orang lain)

inconsistent ADJ tidak konsisten

inconvenient ADJ merepotkan, mengganggu

incorrect ADJ tidak benar, salah

increase N pertambahan, kenaikan; V tambah, bertambah; menambah, menaikkan, meningkatkan

incredible ADJ luar biasa, tidak dapat dipercaya, hebat

indecent ADJ tak senonoh, tidak sopan

indeed ADJ, ADV betul, sebetulnya; CONJ memang; bahkan

independence N kemerdekaan; kebebasan; **independent** ADJ mandiri, merdeka, bebas, tidak tergantung

index N daftar, indeks

India N India; **Indian** N orang India; orang Indian

indicate V menunjukkan; **indication** N tanda, petunjuk, alamat; **indicator** N penunjuk; indikator; lampu sein

Indies *the East* ~ Hindia Belanda

indigenous ADJ asli

indigestion N salah cerna

indignant ADJ marah, jengkel

indigo N nila; ADJ biru tua

indirect ADJ tidak langsung

individual N pribadi, orang, oknum; ADJ per seorangan

Indonesia N Indonesia; **Indonesian** N Bahasa Indonesia; orang Indonesia

indoor ADJ indoors ADV di dalam rumah atau gedung

industry N industri, perindustrian; kegiatan

inefficient ADJ tidak efisien, tidak jalan dengan baik

infant N, ADJ bayi, balita, anak kecil

infect V menulari, menjangkiti; **infection** N penyakit, infeksi, penularan; **infectious** ADJ menular

inferior ADJ [infirior] kurang bagus atau baik, bermutu rendah

infertile ADJ mandul, tidak subur

infinite ADJ [infinit] tak terhitung; **infinity** N jumlah tak berakhir

inflate V membesar

inflexible ADJ kaku

286

influence N [influens] pengaruh, efek; v memengaruhi

influenza N flu, selesma

inform v memberitahu, mengabarkan, menginformasikan

informal ADJ santai, tidak resmi

information N informasi, keterangan, penerangan ← **inform**

ingredient N [ingridient] bahan (mentah)

inhabit v mendiami, menghuni; **inhabitant** N penduduk, penghuni

inhale v menarik nafas, mengisap; **inhaler** N isapan, sedotan

inherit v mewarisi; **inheritance** N warisan

initial N huruf pertama, paraf; v teken, memaraf; ADJ pertama, perdana, permulaan; **initiation** N (upacara) pengenalan; **initiative** N prakarsa, inisiatif

inject v menyuntik, menyuntikkan; **injection** N suntik, suntikan; injeksi

injure v merugikan, melukai;

injury N luka; kerugian; hinaan

injustice N ketidakadilan

ink N tinta

inland N pedalaman

inn N penginapan

inner ADJ (di) dalam; batin

innocent ADJ tidak bersalah, tanpa dosa

innovation N ciptaan baru; **innovative** ADJ mampu menciptakan yang baru

input N masuknya; v memasukkan

inquiry, enquiry N pertanyaan; penyelidikan, pemeriksaan

insane ADJ gila, sakit jiwa

inscription N tulisan, suratan, prasasti

insect N serangga

insert N sisipan; v menyisipkan, menyelipkan, memasukkan

inside PREP, ADJ (di) dalam; **insider** N orang dalam

insight N [insait] wawasan, pemahaman

insist v mengotot, bersikeras, bersikukuh; mendesak

inspect v memeriksa;

inspection N pemeriksaan, inspeksi; **inspector** N pemeriksa

inspiration N ilham, inspirasi; **inspire** v mengilhami, memberi inspirasi

Instagram N instagram

install, instal v melantik; memasang; **installation** N pelantikan; pemasangan; **instalment, installment** N angsuran

instance *for* ~ misalnya, seumpamanya

instant N saat; **instantly** ADV saat itu juga, serta-merta

instead CONJ [instéd] alih-alih, melainkan, malah

institute N lembaga, institut

instruct v mengajar; memerintahkan, menginstruksikan; **instruction** N pengajaran; perintah, instruksi

instrument N alat, perkakas, pesawat

insult N cemoohan, hinaan; v menghina, mencemoohkan

insurance N asuransi, pertanggungan; **insure** v mengasuransikan

intake N masukan, asupan

integral ADJ perlu; pokok

intellect N akal budi, intelek; **intellectual** N cendekiawan; ADJ pandai

intelligence N kecerdasan; intelijen; **intelligent** ADJ cerdas, pandai

intend v berniat, bermaksud

intense ADJ hebat, mendalam, kuat, intens; **intensify** v meningkatkan; **intensive** ADJ intensif

intent, intention N maksud, niat, kehendak, tujuan; **intentional** ADJ sengaja ← **intend**

interaction N pergaulan, interaksi

interchange N simpang, belokan

interest N kepentingan; perhatian, minat; daya tarik; bunga (uang); **interested** ADJ tertarik, berminat; **interesting** ADJ menarik (perhatian)

interfere v [intérfir] campur tangan; mencampuri, mengganggu

interior N [intérior] pedalaman, dalamnya

288

intermediate ADJ sedang
internal ADJ dalam (negeri); **international** ADJ internasional, antar bangsa
Internet N internet, dunia maya; ~ *café* warung internet (warnét)
interpret V menafsirkan; menerjemahkan (secara lisan); **interpreter** N penerjemah, juru bahasa; **interpreting** N penerjemahan
interrogate V [intérogét] memeriksa, menginterogasi, menanyai; **interrogation** N pemeriksaan, interogasi
interrupt V menyela, menyeletuk, memotong pembicaraan
intersection N perempatan, simpang; persilangan
interval N antara, selang, jeda, waktu istirahat
intervention N halangan, campur tangan, intervensi
interview N wawancara, tanya jawab, interpiu; V mewawancarai
intestine N [intéstin] usus, isi perut
intimate ADJ [intimet] mesra,

intim, karib
intimidate V menakuti-nakuti, mengintimidasi
into PREP ke (dalam); menjadi; menuju
introduce V memperkenalkan; **introduction** N perkenalan; (kata) pengantar
intrude V mengganggu; **intruder** N orang yang memasuki tempat tanpa izin; maling
invade V menyerang, menyerbu
invaluable ADJ tak ternilai
invasion N serangan, serbuan ← **invade**
invent V menciptakan, menemukan; membuat-buat; **invention** N ciptaan
invest V menanamkan (modal), menginvestasikan
investigate V menyelidiki; **investigation** N penyelidikan; **investigator** N penyelidik
investment N penanaman modal, investasi ← **invest**
invisible ADJ tak terlihat, gaib
invitation N undangan, ajakan; **invite** V mengundang, mengajak; mempersilakan
involve V melibatkan
Iran N Iran

Iraq N Irak; **Iraqi** N orang Irak
Ireland N Irlandia
iron N besi; setrika; v menyetrika; **ironing** N setrikaan; kegiatan menyetrika
ironic ADJ ironis; **irony** N ironi
irregular ADJ tidak teratur, luar biasa
irrelevant ADJ tidak relevan
irresponsible ADJ tidak bertanggung jawab
irrigate v mengairi; **irrigation** N pengairan, irigasi
irritable ADJ cepat marah, marah-marah; **irritate** v mengganggu, membuat jengkel
Islam N agama Islam; **Islamic** ADJ berkaitan dengan agama Islam
island N [ailand] pulau
Israel N [Isrél] Israel
issue N [isyu] masalah, isu; terbitan
it PRON dia, ia (barang); -nya; itu
IT ABBREV *information technology* teknologi informasi, TI
italics N, PL [italiks] tulisan miring

Italy N Italia
itch N, v **itchy** ADJ gatal
item N [aitem] barang; pasal, ayat; nomor
its PRON -nya (barang)
itself PRON sendiri
ivory N [aivori] gading

J

jack N dongkrak, tuas, kuda-kuda
jacket N jaket; sampul buku
jade N batu giok
jaguar N semacam macan di Amerika
jail, gaol N penjara
jam N selai; v macet; menyumbat, menjepit
janitor N petugas pembersihan, penjaga
January N bulan Januari
Japan N Jepang
jar N kendi, stoples, botol
jasmine N [jasmin] bunga melati
Java N pulau Jawa; **Javanese** N bahasa Jawa
jaw N rahang
jealous ADJ [jélus] cemburu

jeep N mobil jip

jelly N agar-agar; **jellyfish** N ubur-ubur

jerk N sentakan, renggutan; V menyentak, merenggut

jersey N [jérsi] switer

Jesus N [Jisus] CHR Yesus; ISL Isa; ~ *Christ* Yesus Kristus

jet N semburan air; pancar gas; jet; V, SL terbang

jetty N jeti, dermaga

jewel N [jul] (batu) permata; **jeweler** N tukang emas; **jewelry** N perhiasan

Jewish ADJ Yahudi ← **Jew**

jigsaw N gergaji ukir; ~ *puzzle* teka-teki menyusun potongan kayu

job N pekerjaan, tugas; *part-time* ~ pekerjaan paruh waktu; **jobless** ADJ menganggur

jockey N joki

jog N, V lari pagi, lari sore

join V bergabung, ikut serta; menghubungkan, menggabungkan

joint N sendi, ruas; ADJ bersama

joke N senda gurau, lelucon, guyonan; **joker** N pelawak; joker (kartu)

jolly ADJ riang, gembira

Jordan N Yordania

journal N (buku) harian, majalah; **journalist** N wartawan, jurnalis

journey N [jurni] perjalanan

joy N kebahagiaan, kegembiraan

judge N hakim; V menghakimi, menilai; **judgment** N keputusan

judo N judo, yudo

jug N tempat untuk saus atau minuman; teko

juggle V bermain sunglap; bermain sulap; **juggling** N sunglapan

juice N air (buah), sari buah, jus; **juicy** ADJ berair banyak

jukebox N kotak musik, mesin pemutar lagu

July N bulan Juli

jumbo ADJ (berukuran) besar

jump N lompatan, loncatan; V melompat, meloncat; melompati

jumper N switer, baju hangat

junction N simpang (jalan), perempatan

June N bulan Juni

jungle N [janggel] hutan, rimba (raya)

291

junior N yunior; ADJ yunior, lebih muda, lebih rendah pangkatnya

junk N barang bekas, barang loak, sampah

jury N juri

just ADJ, ADV hanya, saja; tepat, persis; ~ *now* baru saja

just N adil; **justice** N keadilan; **justify** V membenarkan

K

kangaroo N kanguru, kangguru

kayak N dayung; kayak, kano; sampan

keen ADJ antusias; tajam

keep V kept kept menyimpan, memegang, menaruh, memelihara, menjaga; **keeper** N pemegang, penjaga, kurator

kennel N kandang anjing

kept V, PF → keep

kerosene N [kerosin] minyak tanah; ~ *lamp* lentera, lampu petromaks

kettle N teko; **kettledrum** N genderang kecil

key N [ki] (anak) kunci; tuts; nada; ADJ pokok; **keyboard** N kibor; papan tuts; **keyhole** N lubang kunci

kick N tendangan; V menendang, menyepak

kid N anak kambing; SL anak

kidnap V menculik; **kidnapper** N penculik

kidney N [kidni] ginjal

kill V membunuh; **killer** N pembunuh; **killing** N pembunuhan

kilogram, kilo N kilo, kilogram

kilometer, kilo N kilo, kilometer

kind N [kaind] macam, jenis, ragam; ADJ baik hati, simpatis; ~ *of* agak

kindness N [kaindness] kebaikan hati ← **kind**

king N raja; **kingdom** N kerajaan

kiosk N kios, loket, warung

kiss N ciuman, sun, kecupan; V mencium, (memberi) sun

kit N peralatan, perlengkapan

kitchen N dapur

kite N layang-layang

kitten N anak kucing; **kitty** N,

coll kucing (kecil)
kiwi N burung kiwi; **kiwifruit** N (buah) kiwi
knee N [ni] lutut, dengkul
kneel v [nil] **knelt knelt** berlutut
knew v, PF → **know**
knife N [naif] **knives** pisau; v menikam
knight N [nait] kesatria
knit v [nit] merajut; **knitting** N rajutan
knob N [nob] tombol, pegangan
knock N [nok] pukulan, ketok; v mengetuk; memukul; **knockout** N (pukulan) yang sangat hebat
knot N [not] simpul; buku, mata kayu; mil laut; v menyimpulkan
know v [no] **knew known** tahu, mengetahui; mengenal; mengerti; **knowledge** N [nolej] pengetahuan; **knowledgeable** ADJ banyak tahu; **known** ADJ dikenal
knuckle N [nakel] buku jari
koala N koala
Koran *the* ~ al-Quran
Korea N [Koria] Korea (Selatan)

L

label N merek; nama; v memberi nama, menulis nama pada barang
laboratory, lab N laboratorium
labor N pekerjaan (kasar); **laborer** N buruh, tukang, pekerja
lace N renda
lack N kekurangan; v kurang, tidak memiliki, tidak mempunyai
lacquer N [laker] lak, pernis; v memberi pernis
ladder N tangga, jenjang
lady N, F [lédi] nyonya, wanita; gelar bangsawan; **ladybird**, **ladybug** N kepik
lagoon N laguna
laid v, PF → **lay**
lain v, PF → **lie**
lake N danau, telaga
lamb N [lam] anak domba, anak biri-biri
laminate v melaminasi, melapis dengan lembaran plastik, laminating
lamp N lampu, pelita
land N tanah, bumi, darat; negeri, negara; v mendarat;

293

landing N pendaratan; tempat beristirahat di tangga; **landmark** N patokan, petunjuk; peristiwa penting; **landscape** N pemandangan, lanskap; **landslide** N tanah longsor

lane N gang, lorong; jalur; lajur

language N [languej] bahasa

lantern N lentera

Lao N bahasa Laos, orang Laos, ADJ berasal dari Laos

lap N haribaan, pangkuan

lapse N jatuh; kehilangan; selang; v kambuh, menjadi; habis

laptop N komputer laptop

large ADJ besar, luas; ~ *size* ukuran besar

laser N (sinar) laser

last v tahan, bertahan, berlangsung; awet; ADJ terakhir, penghabisan; ~ *night* tadi malam, semalam

late ADJ lambat, terlambat; mendiang; ISL almarhum; F almarhumah; **lately** ADV belum lama, belakangan ini, baru-baru ini

later ADJ, ADV nanti; kemudian

← **late**

latest ADJ, ADV terakhir, paling akhir

Latin N bahasa Latin, bahasa Romawi

latitude N lintang

latter N, ADJ yang kemudian, yang tersebut

laugh N, v [laf] tertawa, ketawa; **laughter** N ketawa, tawa

launch N peluncuran; kapal berkas; v meluncurkan

laundry N cucian, baju kotor; binatu

lava N lahar, lava

lavatory N [lavetori] kamar kecil, WC

lavender ADJ ungu muda; N semacam bunga harum berwarna ungu

law N hukum, undang-undang; peraturan

lawn N lapangan rumput

lawsuit N perkara, dakwaan

← **law**

lawyer N pengacara, advokat, praktisi hukum ← **law**

laxative N obat peluntur, pencahar

lay v **laid laid** meletakkan

layer N lapis, lapisan

layout N tata letak; rancangan, rencana ← **lay**

lazy ADJ malas

lead N [léd] timbal, timah hitam, plumbum

lead v [lid] **led led** memimpin; **leader** N pemimpin; **leadership** N kepemimpinan; **leading** ADJ penting, utama, terkemuka

leaf N **leaves** daun

leaflet N selebaran

leafy ADJ rimbun, rindang ← **leaf**

league N [lig] liga, persatuan, perserikatan

leak N, v bocor, merembes; **leaky** ADJ bocor, rembes

lean ADJ kurus; sedikit

lean v tidak lurus, condong, bersandar; **leaning** N kecenderungan

leap N lompatan; v melompat

leapt v, PF [lépt] → **leap**

learn v belajar; mendengar berita; **learner** N pelajar; **learning** N pembelajaran

lease N sewa; v mempersewakan

leash N pengikat binatang

least ADJ terkecil, paling sedikit; *at* ~ setidak-tidaknya, sekurang-kurangnya

leave N cuti; v **left left** berangkat, pergi, bertolak; membiarkan; meninggalkan

Lebanon N Libanon

lecture N kuliah, ceramah, pidato; v memberi kuliah; memberi teguran; **lecturer** N dosen, lektor

led v, PF → **lead**

leech N lintah

left N (sebelah) kiri

left ADJ, v, PF tertinggal → **leave**; **leftover** N, ADJ sisa

leg N kaki

legal ADJ sah, legal, menurut undang-undang

legend N legenda; kunci peta; **legendary** ADJ terkenal

leggings N, PL [légings] stoking tebal ← **leg**

legible ADJ [léjibel] dapat dibaca

legislation N perundang-undangan; **legislative** ADJ legislatif

legitimate ADJ sah

leisure N [lésyer] waktu luang, waktu senggang

lemon N jeruk nipis, limun;

lemonade N air jeruk nipis; Sprite

lend v **lent lent** meminjamkan; **lender** N pemberi pinjaman

length N panjang; jarak, lama; **lengthen** v memperpanjang; **lengthy** ADJ panjang lebar; panjang, lama

lens N lensa; *contact* ~ lensa kontak

leopard N [lépard] macan kumbang

lesbian lesbi

less ADJ kurang, lebih kecil; **lessen** v mengurangi, mengecilkan

lesson N pelajaran; les

let v **let let** membiarkan; menyewakan (rumah); ~ *us*, *let's* marilah

lethal ADJ [lithal] mematikan

letter N surat; huruf, aksara

lettuce N [létes] selada

leukaemia, leukemia N [lukimia] kanker darah

level ADJ [lével] datar, rata; N tingkat; permukaan

lever N pengungkit, tuas, tuil

liar N [laier] pembohong ← **lie**

liberal ADJ murah hati; liberal; **liberate** v membebaskan;

liberation N pembebasan; **liberty** N kemerdekaan, kebebasan

librarian N [laibrérian] pustakawan, kepala perpustakaan; **library** N perpustakaan

license, licence N [laisens] izin, ijazah

lick N jilatan; v menjilat

lie v bohong; v berbohong, membohong

lie v **lay lain** terletak, berada; berbaring

lieutenant N letnan

life N hidup, kehidupan; **lifeboat** N sekoci (penyelamat); **lifebuoy** N pelampung; **lifeguard** N penjaga pantai, penjaga kolam renang; **lifejacket** N baju pelampung; **lifelong** ADJ seumur hidup, sepanjang hidup; **lifesaver** N penjaga pantai; **lifestyle** N gaya hidup; **lifetime** N seumur hidup ← **live**

lift N lift, pengangkat barang; v mengangkat

light N [lait] cahaya, sinar; lampu; SL korek api; ADJ terang; ringan, enteng; v **lit**

lit menyalakan, memasang (lampu); **lighten** v meringankan, menerangkan; **lighter** N korek api, geretan; **lighthouse** N mercu suar; **lightning** N kilat, halilintar, geledek

like ADJ sama, serupa, sepadan, setara; CONJ seperti, sama dengan; v suka, menyukai, gemar; **likeable** ADJ ramah, menyenangkan; **likely** ADJ agaknya, kemungkinan

lily N [lili] teratai

lime N limau; kapur

limit N batas, limit; v membatasi; **limited** ADJ terbatas

limousine N [limosin], **limo** N, SL limosin, limo

limp v berjalan pincang; ADJ lemah

line N garis, gores; tali; baris, deret; v melapisi

linen N kain linan

liner N kapal penumpang yang besar

lingerie N [lonjeri] pakaian dalam wanita

linguistics N ilmu bahasa, ilmu linguistik

lining N lapisan, furing ← **line**

link N mata rantai, hubungan; **link** N tautan, pranala

lion N [laion] singa

lip N bibir; **lipstick** N lipstik

liquid ADJ cair; N cairan, zat cair

list N daftar; v mendaftar, menyebutkan

listen v [lisen] mendengarkan, menyimak; **listener** N pendengar; **listening** N (pelajaran) menyimak

lit v, PF → **light**

liter N liter

literally ADV secara harfiah; benar-benar; **literate** ADJ melek huruf; terpelajar; **literary** ADJ sastra; **literature** N kesusastraan

litre → **liter**

litter N sampah (di jalan); v membuang sampah sembarangan

little ADJ kecil; sedikit; ~ *finger* kelingking; N sedikit

live v [liv] hidup, tinggal, berdiam; v **live** ADJ [laiv] langsung; hidup

liver N [liver] hati, lever

livestock N hewan ternak

living N [living] mata

297

pencarian ← **live**

lizard N [lizerd] kadal, biawak, cicak

load N muatan, beban; v memuat, diisi

loaf N **loaves** roti; sejenis sepatu santai

loan N pinjaman; v meminjamkan, meminjami → **lend**

lobby N lobi (hotel); gerakan; v berusaha memengaruhi, memperjuangkan

lobster N udang karang, udang laut

local ADJ setempat, lokal; N orang setempat; **locate** v mencari; **location** N lokasi, tempat; penempatan

lock N kunci, gembok; pintu air; ~up sel tahanan; v mengunci; **locker** N loker

locket N liontin

locksmith N tukang kunci ← **lock**

locomotive N lokomotif, lok

lodge N pondok, pemondokan; v mondok, menginap; **lodging** N pemondokan; akomodasi

loft N loteng; **lofty** ADJ tinggi, mulia

log N catatan, buku harian; v mencatat; ~ *in* memasukkan nama atau kata kunci; ~ **off/ on** v masuk, keluar

log N batang kayu, kayu gelondongan; v menebang (pohon); **logging** N penebangan

logic N [lojik] logika, akal; **logical** ADJ logis, masuk akal

lone ADJ tunggal, sendiri; **loneliness** N (rasa) kesepian; **lonely** ADJ sepi, kesepian, sunyi, sendirian

long ADJ panjang; lama; *as* ~ *as* selama

long ~ *for* rindu akan, merindukan, mengidamkan; **longing** N hasrat, kerinduan

look N penampilan, gaya; v melihat; ~ *after* merawat, menjaga; ~ *for* mencari; ~ *on* menonton; ~ *out!* awas!; **lookout** N tempat meninjau; pengintai

loop N lingkaran, ikal, putaran; v menyimpulkan

loose ADJ longgar, kendur, terurai; lepas; **loosen** v melonggarkan, mengendurkan

298

looting N penjarahan

lord PRON tuan; **Lord** N, CHR Tuhan

lorry N truk

lose V [luz] hilang, kehilang-an; rugi, kalah; **loser** N yang kalah; **loss** N rugi, kerugian, kehilangan; **lost** ADJ hilang; tersesat; tewas

lotion N salep

lottery N lotere, undian ← lot

lotus N bunga seroja, bunga teratai

loud ADJ berisik, riuh, gempar, bising; **loudspeaker** N pengeras suara

louse N lice kutu; **lousy** ADJ, SL [lauzi] jelek

love N [lav] cinta, asmara, kasih (sayang); PRON kekasih, sayang; V mencintai, menya-yangi; **lovely** ADJ manis, cantik, asri; **lover** N kekasih; penggemar

low ADJ rendah, hina, murah; N titik rendah, nadir; **lower** ADJ lebih rendah; V menurunkan

loyal ADJ setia, setiakawan

lubricant N [lubrikant] pelumas

luck N untung; *good* ~ untung; semoga; **lucky** ADJ beruntung

luggage N bagasi, barang-barang

lukewarm ADJ [lukworm] suam-suam kuku

lullaby N [lalabai] (kidung) ninabobo

lumber N kayu; **lumberjack** N penebang kayu

lump N gumpal, bongkah; benjolan

lunar ADJ berkaitan dengan bulan

lunatic ADJ gila; N orang gila

lunch N, V makan siang

lungs N, PL paru-paru

luxurious ADJ [laksyurius] mewah, lux; **luxury** N kemewahan

lychee N buah leci

lyric N lirik, kata-kata yang dinyanyikan

M

m *meter* m (meter)

ma'am PRON Nyonya, Nona ← madam

macaroni N makaroni

299

machine N [masyin] mesin, alat

mad ADJ gila, tergila-gila; marah

madam PRON Nyonya

madness N kegilaan, penyakit gila ← **mad**

magazine N majalah

magic N [majik] ilmu sihir, ilmu sulap; **magical** ADJ berkaitan dengan sihir; ajaib; **magician** N penyihir, penyulap

magnet N magnet, maknit; **magnetic** ADJ magnetik

magnificent ADJ sangat bagus, mewah

magpie N burung murai

mahogany N pohon mahoni, kayu mahoni

maid N pembantu; gadis

mail N pos; surat email; V mengepos, mengirim lewat pos; **mailbox** N kotak surat

main ADJ utama; **mainly** ADV terutama

maintain V memelihara, mempertahankan; **main- tenance** N pemeliharaan

maize N jagung

majesty N keagungan; *Your* ~ Baginda, Sri Paduka

major ADJ utama, terbesar; N mayor; **majority** N kebanyakan, mayoritas

make N jenis, macam; V **made** **made** membuat, membikin, mengadakan; **make-up** N rias wajah; ~ *artist* perias; **maker** N pembuat, pencipta

Malay ADJ Melayu; N bahasa Melayu, bahasa Malaysia; orang Melayu; **Malaysia** N Malaysia; **Malaysian** N orang Malaysia

Maldives [Maldivs] *the* ~ (Kepulauan) Maladewa

male ADJ lelaki, pria; jantan

malfunction N kerusakan, kegagalan; V gagal

mama, mamma N, PRON ibu

man N **men** orang laki-laki, pria; suami, pasangan, pacar; V bertugas di

manage V mengelola, memimpin; mengurus, menangani; **management** N pimpinan, direksi; pengelolaan, pemerintahan, pengurus- an, manajemen; **manager** N manajer, pemimpin, pengurus

mango N mangga
mangosteen N manggis
mangrove N bakau
mania N [ménia] kegilaan,
demam
manicure N perawatan tangan,
manikur
manipulative ADJ suka
memanipulasi
mankind N [mankaind] umat
manusia ← **man**
manner N cara, jalan; macam
mansion N [mansyen] rumah
besar
mantelpiece N rak di atas
perapian
manual ADJ dengan tangan,
tidak otomatis; N pedoman,
buku panduan
manufacture N pembuatan;
v membuat; **manufacturer**
N pabrik
manure N pupuk (kotoran)
manuscript N naskah
many ADJ [méni] banyak
map N peta; v memetakan
marble N marmer, pualam;
kelereng
March N bulan Maret
march N perjalanan (militer);
mars; v jalan kaki

margarine N [marjarin]
mentega
marijuana N [marihuana]
ganja
marina N dermaga; **marine** ADJ
berhubungan dengan laut
mark N tanda, alamat; cap;
sasaran; bekas; nilai; v
menandai, mengecap; men-
catat, memperhatikan;
mengoreksi; **marker** N
penanda; spidol besar;
penilai
market N pasar, pasaran;
marketing N pemasaran
marmalade N selai jeruk
marriage N [marij] perkawinan, pernikahan; **married**
ADJ kawin, nikah; M beristri; F
bersuami ← **marry**
marry v menikah, kawin;
menikahi
marsh N rawa
marshmallow N penganan
manis yang putih dan empuk
marvelous ADJ ajaib, hebat,
mengagumkan
masculine ADJ [maskulin]
laki-laki, lelaki, jantan
mask N topeng; masker; v
menyamarkan

mass N massa; banyak sekali; misa

mass transit rail N MRT (Moda Raya Terpadu)

massage N pijatan; v memijat, mengurut

massive ADJ raksasa, besar sekali ← **mass**

mast N tiang (kapal)

master N tuan (rumah); ahli, guru; v menguasai; ~ *'s (degree)* S2, magister

mat N tikar; matras

match N korek api; tara, jodoh; pertandingan; v menyesuaikan; menyamai; menandingi; **matchmaker** N mak jomblang

mate N kawan, sahabat; pasangan; v kawin (binatang)

material N bahan, perkakas, alat; materi

maternal ADJ keibuan; dari pihak ibu

mathematics N, PL **math, maths** SL matematika

matron N [métron] kepala perawat, suster

matter N perkara, hal, perihal; bahan; v berarti

mattress N kasur

mature ADJ dewasa, tua, matang

maximal ADJ maksimal, sebanyak-banyaknya; **maximum** ADJ, N maksimum, sebanyak-banyaknya

May N bulan Mei

may v, AUX boleh, dapat; **maybe** ADV [mébi] mungkin, barangkali, boleh jadi

mayor N [mér] walikota

maze N labirin

me PRON, OBJ saya, aku

meadow N [médo] padang rumput

meal N makanan, santapan

mean ADJ jahat, membuat sakit hati

mean v **meant meant** [mént] berarti, bermaksud; memaksudkan, menghendaki; **meaning** N arti, maksud

meanwhile ADV sementara itu

measles N, PL [mizels] penyakit campak

measure N [mésyer] ukuran, takaran; besarnya; tindakan; v mengukur

meat N daging

mechanic N [mekanik] montir, ahli mesin; **mechanical** ADJ

302

teknik
medal N medali
media N, PL [midia] pers;
perantara, bahan ← **medium**
medical ADJ kedokteran,
medis; **medicine** N [médisin]
obat; jurusan kedokteran,
ilmu kedokteran
medieval ADJ [médiivel] dari
Abad Pertengahan
meditate V bermeditasi,
bersemadi
medium ADJ sedang; **media** N
cenayang, dukun, perantara;
bahan
meet N perlombaan atletik
atau renang; V **met met**
bertemu, berjumpa; mene-
mui; berkumpul; **meeting** N
rapat, pertemuan
melody N lagu
melon N semangka
melt V meleleh, mencair,
melebur; melelehkan,
meleburkan
member N anggota
memo N memorandum, surat
peringatan; **memorial** ADJ
peringatan; N tanda atau tugu
peringatan; **memorize** V
menghafalkan; **memory** N

ingatan, memori
mend V memperbaiki,
membetulkan; menambal
menstruation N datang bulan,
mens
mental ADJ jiwa
mention N [ménsyen] sebutan;
V menyebutkan
menu N daftar makanan, menu
merchant N pedagang,
saudagar
mercy N belas kasih, kemu-
rahan hati
merge V menyatu; menggabungkan
mermaid N putri duyung
merry ADJ ria
mess N kekacauan, keadaan
berantakan; V mengacaukan;
mengacaukan
message N pesan; **messenger**
N pesuruh, kurir
messy ADJ berantakan, tidak
rapi ← **mess**
metal N logam
meteor N [mitior] bintang
jatuh
meter N meter
method N metode, cara, jalan
metre → **meter**
Mexico N Meksiko

303

mice N, PL ← **mouse**
microphone N [maikrofon] mikrofon, corong radio
microscope N [maikroskop] mikroskop
midday N tengah hari, jam 12 siang
middle ADJ tengah, menengah; N pertengahan, titik tengah
midnight N [midnait] tengah malam, jam 12 malam
midwife N bidan
might V, AUX [mait] mungkin, boleh jadi
mighty ADJ berkuasa; besar
migraine N [maigrén] migren, sakit kepala sebelah
migrant N [maigrant] pendatang; **migrate** V pindah, bermigrasi
mild ADJ [maild] lembut, ringan, enteng
mile N mil
military ADJ, N militer, ketentaraan
milk N susu; V memerah susu
millimeter N mili, milimeter
million N juta; **millionaire** N jutawan, milyuner
mimic V mimicked mimicked meniru

minaret N [minarét] menara (mesjid)
mince N (daging) cincang; V mencincang, mengiris
mind N [maind] akal (budi), pikiran, jiwa; V ingat akan, memperhatikan, mengindahkan; merasa keberatan
mine PRON, POSS milikku, saya punya
mine N ranjau; **minefield** N daerah ranjau
mine N tambang; **miner** N buruh tambang; **mineral** N [mineral] barang tambang, barang galian
mini ADJ, SL kecil, mungil, mini; **miniature** ADJ kecil
minimum ADJ, N minimum, sedikit-sedikitnya, terendah
mining N [maining] pertambangan
minister N menteri; pendeta; **ministry** N kementerian, departemen
minor ADJ [mainor] kecil; **minority** N golongan kecil, minoritas
mint N percetakan mata uang
mint N sejenis kemangi;

304

permen penyegar mulut

minus v [mainus] kurang; tanpa

minute N [minet] menit

miracle N [mirakel] keajaiban, mukjizat

mirror N cermin; v mencerminkan

miscarriage N [miskarej] keguguran

mischievous ADJ nakal, jahil

miserable ADJ [mizerabel] sedih, murung

mislead v **misled misled** menipu, menyesatkan

misprint N salah cetak

miss N, PRON Nona (before a surname)

miss v meleset; rindu akan, merindukan

missionary N misionaris

mist N kabut, halimun

mistake N kesalahan; v **mistook mistaken** keliru, salah mengerti

mister PRON Tuan (before a surname); **mistress** N kekasih, gundik

misty ADJ berkabut ← **mist**

misunderstand v **misunderstood misunderstood**

salah mengerti, salah paham, salah tangkap

mitten N sarung tangan, kaus tangan

mix N campuran; v mencampur(kan); **mixture** N campuran, adonan

moan N erangan; keluhan; v mengerang, mengeluh

mobile ADJ dapat bergerak, dapat dipindahkan; ~ *phone* telepon genggam, ponsel

mock ADJ palsu, pura-pura, tiruan; v mengejek

model ADJ contoh; N contoh, macam, model; peragawati, peragawan; v memperagakan

modern ADJ modern, baru, kini

moist ADJ basah, lembab; **moisture** N embun, kelembaban; **moisturizer** N pelembab

moldy, mouldy ADJ berjamur, jamuran, apak

mole N sejenis tikus; tahi lalat

Moluccas *the* ~ Maluku

Mom, Mum PRON Bu, Mak

moment N saat; *in a* ~, *just a* ~ sebentar

mommy, mummy PRON Ibu, Mama, Mami ← **mom**

305

Monday N [Mandé] hari Senin

monetary ADJ [manetéri] keuangan, moneter; **money** N uang; **moneybox** N celengan

Mongolia N Mongolia

mongrel N [manggrel]; anjing kampung

monitor N pengawas; layar (komputer); V mengawasi

monkey N [mangki] monyet

monorail N monorel

monsoon N musim hujan, muson

monster ADJ raksasa; N makhluk besar yang mengerikan

month N [manth] bulan; **monthly** ADJ, ADV bulanan

monument N monumen, tanda peringatan, tugu peringatan

mood N suasana hati

moon N bulan, rembulan; **moonlight** N [munlait] sinar bulan

moral N [morel] kesusilaan, etika; moral, moril

more ADV lebih, lagi; **moreover** ADV lagipula

morning N pagi (hari); good

~ selamat pagi (diucapkan sampai jam 12 siang)

Morocco N Maroko

Moslem → **Muslim**

mosque N [mosk] mesjid

mosquito N [moskito] nyamuk; ~ *net* kelambu

most ADV paling, maha; **mostly** ADV kebanyakan

motel N hotel transit

moth N ngengat

mother N [mather] ibu; induk; PRON Ibu; ~*-in-law* (ibu) mertua; ~ *tongue* bahasa ibu

motion N gerak; mosi, usul

motivation N dorongan, dukungan, motivasi; **motive** N [motiv] alasan, dalil, motif

motor N motor, mesin; **motorboat** N perahu bermotor; **motorcycle** N **motorbike** SL sepeda motor; **motorist** N pengendara mobil; **motorway** N jalan bebas hambatan

mould → **mold**

mount N (nama) gunung; ~ *Bromo* Gunung Bromo; **mountain** N [maunten] gunung

mouse N **mice** tikus; ~ *(of computer)* N tetikus; **mouse-**

trap N perangkap tikus
mouth N mulut; muara;
mouthful N sesuap;
mouthwash N obat kumur
move N perpindahan, gerakan;
v bergerak; berpindah
(rumah); menggerakkan,
memindahkan; **movement** N
gerak, gerakan, pergerakan
movie N, SL [muvi] film
mower N mesin pemotong
rumput
Mt *Mount* Gg., (gunung)
much ADV, N banyak; *so* ~
sekian; *as* ~ *as* sebanyak
mud N lumpur
muddle N kekacauan, kekusutan; v mengacaukan
muddy ADJ berlumpur ← **mud**
mudguard N [madgard]
sepakbor ← **mud**
muffler N kenalpot; selendang
mug N cangkir besar; v menodong, merampok; **mugger** N
penodong
muggy ADJ lembab (cuaca)
multi- PREF lebih dari satu,
aneka; **multi-colored** ADJ
warna-warni, beraneka warna
multiple ADJ [maltipel] ber-
lipat ganda; **multiplication**

N perkalian; **multiply**
v berkembang biak;
mengalikan
mumble v bergumam,
berkomat-kamit
mummy N mumi → **mommy**
mumps N penyakit gondok
munch v mengunyah
municipality N [munisipaliti]
kota (praja), kotamadya
mural N lukisan pada tembok
atau dinding
murder N pembunuhan; v
membunuh; **murderer** N
pembunuh
murmur N bisikan; v berbisik
muscle N [masel] urat, otot;
kekuatan
museum N musium
mushroom N cendawan,
jamur
music N musik, lagu; **musical**
ADJ (berbakat) musik; **musi-**
cian N musikus, pemain
musik
Muslim, Moslem ADJ Islam,
Muslim; N orang Islam
must N keharusan; v, AUX
harus, wajib, terpaksa
mustache, moustache N
[mustasy] kumis, misai

307

mute ADJ bisu
mutilate V memotong
mutter V bergumam, berkomat-kamit
mutual ADJ [myutyual] saling, dari kedua pihak, timbal balik
my PRON, POSS saya, -ku
myself PRON saya sendiri; sendirian
mysterious ADJ gaib, misterius; **mystery** N kegaiban, misteri
myth N [mith] isapan jempol, dongeng, mitos

N

nail N paku; kuku; V memaku; **nailbrush** N sikat kuku
naked ADJ [néked] telanjang
name N nama; V menamai, menamakan, memberi nama; **named** ADJ bernama; **namely** CONJ yakni, yaitu
nanny N penjaga anak, pengasuh anak
nap N tidur siang
napkin N serbet; popok; **nappy** N popok; *disposable* ~

pampers, popok plastik
narrator N orang yang bercerita
narrow ADJ sempit
nasty ADJ buruk, jahat
nation N [nésyen] negara, bangsa; **national** N, ADJ [nasyonal] nasional, kebangsaan; **nationality** N kebangsaan, kewarganegaraan
native ADJ [nétif] asli; N orang asli, pribumi
natural ADJ [natyurel] alami, alamiah; **naturally** ADV tentu, memang; **nature** N alam (semesta); tabiat, kepribadian, sifat
naughty ADJ [noti] nakal, jahil
nausea N [nozia] (rasa) mual, mabuk
navel N pusar
navigate V [navigét] melayari, mengemudikan kapal; **navigator** N mualim, navigator; **navy** N [névi] angkatan laut
near ADJ dekat; **nearby** ADV [nirbai] dekat; **nearly** ADV hampir
neat ADJ apik, rapi, bersih; SL

308

hebat, bagus

necessary ADJ [néseséri] perlu; **necessity** N kebutuhan, keperluan

neck N leher; **necklace** N kalung; **necktie** N dasi

need N kebutuhan, keperluan; V membutuhkan, memerlukan

needle N jarum; **needlepoint**, **needlework** N semacam sulaman

negative ADJ negatif, buruk; N klise

neglect N keadaan telantar; V mengabaikan

negotiate V bermusyawarah, berunding; merundingkan; **negotiation** N negosiasi, perundingan

neigh V [néi] meringkik

neighbor N [nébor] tetangga; **neighborhood** N lingkungan (dekat rumah)

neither CONJ [nither, naither] kedua-duanya (tidak); ~ ... *nor* bukan ... maupun

nephew N, M [néfyu] keponakan (lelaki)

nerve N saraf; nyali, keberanian; **nervous** ADJ gelisah, gugup

nest N sarang; V bersarang

net ADJ bersih, netto; N jala, jaring

Netherlands *the* ~ (negeri) Belanda

network N jaringan; V menjalin hubungan

neutral ADJ [nutral] netral, tidak memihak

never ADV [néver] tidak pernah

nevertheless CONJ [néverthelés] walaupun demikian, namun

new ADJ baru; ~ *Year* tahun baru; ~ *Zealand* Selandia Baru; *Papua* ~ *Guinea* Papua Nugini; **newborn** ADJ baru saja lahir; **newcomer** N pendatang baru; **newly** ADV baru saja, belum lama; **news** N, s berita, warta, warta berita; kabar; **newsletter** N selebaran; **newspaper** N surat kabar, koran

next PREP berikut, sebelah, samping

nibble N [nibel] gigit; V menggigit, mengunggis

nice ADJ enak, sedap; manis, cantik, apik

nick N torehan; V, SL mengutil

nickname N nama kecil, nama panggilan

niece N, F [nis] keponakan (perempuan)

night N [nait] malam; *at ~* pada waktu malam, malam hari; *good ~* selamat tidur; *last ~* tadi malam, semalam; **nightie** SL daster; **nightfall** N senja, magrib; **nightingale** N bulbul; **nightlife** N kehidupan malam; **nightly** ADV tiap malam; **nightmare** N mimpi buruk

nine N, ADJ sembilan; **nineteen** N, ADJ sembilan belas; **ninety** ADJ, N sembilan puluh; **ninth** ADJ [nainth] kesembilan

nip N gigitan kecil; V mencubit, menggigit

nipple N [nipel] puting, pentil, dot

no tidak; bukan

noble ADJ bangsawan, ningrat

nobody N [nobodi] bukan siapa-siapa; PRON tidak seorang pun

nod N anggukan, tanda setuju

noise N bunyi, kegaduhan, keributan, suara bising; **noisy** ADJ gaduh, ribut, berisik, bising

nominate V mencalonkan; **nomination** N pencalonan, nominasi

non- PREF tidak, non-

none N [nan] seorang pun tidak, sesuatu pun tidak; tidak sama sekali

nonsense N omong kosong

noon *(at)* ~ jam duabelas siang

nor → **neither**

normal ADJ biasa, lazim, lumrah, umum; normal; **normally** ADV biasanya, pada umumnya

north ADJ, ADV utara; N (sebelah) utara; ~ *Korea* Korea Utara (Korut); **northeast** ADJ, N timur laut; **northern** ADJ utara; **northwest** ADJ, N barat laut

Norway N Norwegia; **Norwegian** ADJ [Norwijen] berasal dari Norwegia

nose N hidung; **nostril** N lubang hidung; **nosy** ADJ ingin tahu

not ADV tidak, tak; belum; bukan; ~ *yet* belum

note N catatan, peringatan; nada; not; nota; V mencatat, menulis; memperhatikan; **notebook** N buku catatan, buku tulis, notes; **noted** ADJ masyhur, tersohor, kenama-an; **notepaper** N kertas tulis

nothing N [nathing] tidak sesuatu pun

notice N [notis] perhatian; pemberitahuan, maklumat; V melihat; memerhatikan; **noticeable** ADJ [notisabel] nyata, tampak, kelihatan

notification N [notifikésyen] pemberitahuan surat panggilan; **notify** V memberitahu; memberitahukan

nought, naught N, ARCH [not] nol, kosong; tanpa hasil

noun N [naun] kata benda

nourishing ADJ bergizi

novel ADJ baru; N buku roman, novel

November N bulan November

now PREP [nau] sekarang, kini; *just ~* baru saja, tadi; *from ~ (on)* mulai sekarang; CONJ nah; **nowadays** PREP sekarang (ini)

nowhere ADV, PRON [nowér] tidak di mana-mana

nuclear ADJ nuklir

nude ADJ telanjang, bugil

nudge N [naj] sentuhan; V menyentuh, menyinggung

nuisance N [nusens] gang-guan; orang pengganggu

numb ADJ [nam] mati rasa, kesemutan

number N nomor; bilangan, angka; banyaknya; **numeral** N angka; *Roman ~s* angka Romawi

nun N biarawati, suster

nurse N juru rawat, perawat; V merawat; menyusui; **nursery** N kamar anak; toko tanam-an; **nursing** ADJ menyusui; *~ home* panti asuhan

nut N kacang; SL penggemar berat, penggila; **nutmeg** N pala

nutrient N [nutrient] gizi; **nutrition** N [nutrisyen] ilmu gizi; **nutritious** ADJ bergizi

O

oar N dayung

oatmeal N havermut

oath N sumpah; umpatan

oats N, PL sejenis gandum

obese ADJ [obis] gemuk sekali

obey V [obé] taat, patuh

object N benda, obyek; V berkeberatan; **objection** N keberatan; **objective** ADJ obyektif, tidak memihak; N tujuan

oboe N obo

obscene ADJ [obsin] cabul, jorok

observe V mengamati, meninjau; menghormati; **observer** N pengamat, peninjau

obsession N obsesi

obstacle N [obstakel] rintangan, hambatan

obtain V memperoleh, mendapatkan, menerima

obvious ADJ [obvius] jelas, terang, nyata

occasion N [okésyen] kesempatan; peristiwa, acara

occupant N penghuni; **occupation** N pekerjaan; pendudukan; **occupy** V [okupai] mengisi; menduduki

occur V terjadi; **occurrence** N kejadian, peristiwa

ocean N [osyan] samudera, lautan

o'clock jam, pukul; *it's six ~* sekarang jam enam

octagon N segi delapan

October N bulan Oktober

octopus N ikan gurita

odd ADJ aneh, ganjil

odor N bau

of PREP [ov] milik; dari, daripada

off PREP jauh; ADJ mati, tidak hidup; basi (makanan); tidak jadi; *day ~* hari libur

offend V menghina, membuat tersinggung; melanggar hukum; **offensive** ADJ menghina, tidak sopan; serangan

offer N tawaran, penawaran; V menawarkan, menawari; mempersembahkan; **offering** N persembahan, sesajen

office N [ofis] kantor, ruangan, tempat kerja; jabatan; **officer** N pegawai, petugas; perwira; **official** ADJ resmi; N pegawai, pejabat

often ADV sering

ogre N [oger] raksasa

oil N minyak; V meminyaki; *~ colors, ~ paint* cat minyak; *~ palm* kelapa sawit; **oilfield**

N ladang minyak; **oily** ADJ berminyak

ointment N salep, balsem

OK, okay N [oké] baik, oke, jadi; V menyetujui

old ADJ tua; sepuh, lanjut usia; **olden** ~ *days* masa lalu, tempo dulu, zaman baheula

olive N [oliv] (buah) zaitun

Olympic ADJ Olimpiade; ~ *Games* Pertandingan Olimpiade; **Olympics** *the* ~ Olimpiade

omelet, omelette N telur dadar

omen N tanda, pertanda, alamat

omit V melupakan, meng-hilangkan

on ADJ hidup; PREP di (atas), pada; ~ *the way* sedang dalam perjalanan; sedang berjalan, sedang berlangsung

once ADV [wans] sekali (waktu); dahulu kala; *all at* ~ serentak; tiba-tiba; *at* ~ pada saat itu juga, segera ← **one**

one N, ADJ [wan] satu, suatu; seorang; PRON orang; ~ *another* satu sama lain; ~*-way street* jalan satu arah; ~ *by* ~ satu per satu

ongoing ADJ terus-menerus ← **on**

onion N [anien] bawang

online shopping N belanja online, belanja daring

only ADJ tunggal; ~ *child* anak tunggal; *one and* ~ satu-satunya; ADV saja, hanya; *not* ~ ... *but also* tidak hanya ... tetapi juga

onyx N [oniks] batu akik

opal N opal, baiduri

opaque ADJ [opék] tidak tembus pandang, buram

open ADJ buka, terbuka; terang-terangan; V membuka; **opener** N pembuka; **opening** ADJ pembuka; N pembukaan; lubang, celah, lowongan

opera N opera

operate V [operét] membedah, mengoperasi; beroperasi; menjalankan (mesin), meng-operasikan; **operation** N pembedahan, operasi; cara menjalankan; **operator** N penjaga mesin, penjaga telefon

opinion N [opinion] pendapat; *in my* ~ menurut pendapat saya

313

opium N candu

opossum, possum N semacam tupai

opponent N lawan

opportunity N kesempatan, peluang

opposite N, ADJ [opozet] berlawanan, bertentangan, lawan (kata); **opposition** N perlawanan, oposisi

optical ADJ optik; **optician** N ahli kaca mata

optimist N **optimistic** ADJ optimis

option N [opsyen] opsi, pilihan; **optional** ADJ bebas (memilih)

optometrist N dokter mata; ahli kacamata

or CONJ atau; *either ... ~* salah satu

oral ADJ lisan, berkaitan dengan mulut

orange ADJ [orenj] oranye, jingga; N jeruk

orangutan N orang hutan

orchard N [orced] kebun buah

orchestra N [orkestra] orkes

orchid N [orkid] (bunga) anggrek

order N urutan; peraturan; perintah; pemesanan; v

memerintahkan, menyuruh, mengatur, memesan

ordinary ADJ [ordineri] biasa, lazim

organ N orgel, organ

organ N bagian badan; **organic** ADJ organik

organization N organisasi, persatuan; penyusunan, pengaturan; **organize** v menyusun, mengatur, mengurus

oriental ADJ timur, ketimuran

origin N asal, asal-usul; **original** ADJ orisinil, asli

ornament N hiasan

orphan N [orfan] anak yatim (piatu); **orphanage** N rumah yatim piatu

ostrich N burung unta

other PRON, ADJ [ather] lain, berlainan; *the ~ day* kemarin, belum lama ini; **otherwise** CONJ kalau tidak, bila tidak

otter N berang-berang

ouch EXCL [auc] aduh, sakit

ought AUX, V [out] seharusnya, semestinya, sebaiknya

ounce N [auns] ons

our PRON kita, kami; **ours** PRON milik kita, milik kami; **ourselves** PRON kita sendiri,

314

kami sendiri

out PREP (di) luar; ADJ di luar, tidak ada; tidak berlaku lagi; **outburst** N letusan, ledakan; **outdated** ADJ ketinggalan zaman, kuno; **outdoor** ADJ **outdoors** PREP (di) luar (rumah); **outer** ADJ bagian luar; **outfit** N busana; **outgoing** ADJ ramah; **outlet** N jalan keluar, saluran pembuangan; toko, cabang; **outline** N garis besar; **outlook** N wawasan; **output** N hasil, produksi; keluaran; **outside** N, PREP (di) luar, ke luar, bagian luar; **outsider** N orang luar; **outspoken** ADJ blak-blakan, terang-terangan; **outstanding** ADJ luar biasa

oval ADJ lonjong; N (lapangan) bulat panjang

oven N [aven] oven, kompor, tungku

over ADJ selesai, rampung; PREP di atas; melalui; tentang, mengenai; lebih daripada; **overact** V bertindak secara berlebihan; **overall** ADJ secara keseluruhan; **overcharge** V meminta bayaran terlalu

tinggi; **overcome** V **overcame** mengalahkan, mengatasi; **overdose** N overdosis, OD; V OD; **overdue** ADJ kedaluwarsa, terlambat; **overhead** ADJ di atas (kepala); **overhear** V **overheard** **overheard** menguping; terdengar; **overnight** ADJ, PREP semalaman; **overpass** N jembatan penyeberangan; **overpower** V menguasai; **overseas** ADV, ADJ (di) luar negeri; **overtake** V **overtook** **overtaken** menyalip; **overthrow** V **overthrew** **overthrown** menjatuhkan, meruntuhkan; **overweight** ADJ kelebihan berat (badan); **overwhelmed** ADJ kewalahan

owe V [o] berhutang

owl N [aul] burung hantu

own ADJ [oun] sendiri; V memiliki, mempunyai; **owner** N pemilik; **ownership** N kepemilikan, hak milik

ox N **oxen** sapi, lembu

oxygen N [oksijen] oksigen

oyster N tiram

ozone N, PL ozon

P

p *page*, **pp** (*pages*) halaman
Pa PRON, SL Pak, Yah
pace N langkah; kecepatan
Pacific ~ *Ocean* Lautan Teduh, Samudera Pasifik
pack N bungkusan; pak; V membungkus, mengepak, menyusun; **package** N bungkus; bingkisan, paket; **packet** N paket, pak, bungkus
pact N pakta, perjanjian
pad N bantalan
paddle N [padel] kayuh; V mengayuh
paddy N ~ (*field*) sawah
padlock N gembok; V mengunci, menggembok
page N halaman, lembar
pagoda N kuil
paid V, PF → **pay**
pain N rasa sakit, rasa nyeri; *in* ~ kesakitan; **painful** ADJ sakit, pedih
paint N cat; V mengecat; **painter** N tukang cat; pelukis; **painting** N lukisan; seni lukis
pair N pasang, rangkap; pasa-ngan
pajamas → **pyjamas**
Pakistan N Pakistan; **Pakistani** N orang Pakistan
palace N [pales] istana, puri
palate N [palet] langit-langit
pale ADJ pucat, lemah
Palestine N [Palestain] Palestina; **Palestinian** N orang Palestina
palm N [pam] palem; telapak tangan
pamphlet N brosur, selebaran, pamflet
pan N panci, wajan, kuali; **pancake** N panekuk
panel N panel; sehelai papan
panic N panik, ketakutan; V panik
panther N macan kumbang
pantry N [pantri] gudang (dapur), lemari untuk menyimpan makanan kering
pants N, PL celana
panty ~ *liner* pembalut (tipis); **panties** N, PL celana dalam wanita
papa PRON pak, ayah
papaya N pepaya
paper N kertas; koran, surat kabar; makalah; **paperboy** N

tukang koran, loper koran; **paperwork** N pekerjaan tulis-menulis

Papua N Irian (Jaya); ~ *New Guinea (PNG)* Papua Nugini

parachute N payung, parasut; v terjun payung

parade N [paréid] pawai, ara-karakan; jalan

paradise N surga

paragraph N paragraf, alinea

parakeet N burung bayan, burung parkit

parallel ADJ sejajar, paralel

paralyzed ADJ lumpuh

parasite N [parasait] parasit, benalu

parcel N bingkisan, paket; parsel

pardon N ampun, maaf; grasi; v mengampuni, memaafkan

parent N [pérent] orang tua, ibu bapak, ayah bunda

park N taman; v parkir; memarkirkan mobil

parliament N Dewan Perwakilan Rakyat (DPR), parlemen

parrot N burung nuri

parsley N [parsli] peterseli

part N bagian, potong; peran-an; belahan; v membagi, memisahkan; ~ *with* melepaskan

participant N peserta; **participate** v ikut serta, mengambil bagian

particular ADJ istimewa, spe-sial, khusus

parting N perpisahan; belahan (rambut) ← **part**

partly ADV sebagian ← **part**

partner N pasangan, mitra

party N pesta, perayaan; partai, kelompok, pihak; rombongan; v berpesta

pass N surat izin masuk, pas jalan; jalan kecil; v lulus ujian; lewat; melalui; melewati; mengesahkan; ~ *away* meninggal dunia, berpulang; **passage** N [pasej] jalan lintas, jalan tembus, lorong, terusan; bagian dari tulisan; pelayaran; **passenger** N [pasenjer] penumpang

passion N [pasyen] hawa nafsu, gairah; **passionate** ADJ [pasyenet] bernafsu, bergairah, bersemangat

passive ADJ pasif, terdiam

passport N paspor

317

password N kata sandi

past ADJ lalu, lewat, lampau, silam; N masa lalu

paste N [pést] adonan, pasta; V tempel

pastel N warna pastel; kapur berwarna

pastor N pastor, pendeta

pastry N [péstri] kue

pat N tepukan; V menepuk, mengelus

patch N tambal, tempelan

paternal ADJ [patérnal] dari pihak bapak

path N jalan (tapak), lorong

patience N [pésyens] kesabaran; soliter; **patient** ADJ sabar; N pasien

patriotic ADJ cinta tanah air

patrol N patroli, ronda; V berpatroli, meronda

pattern N pola, corak; patron, contoh

patty N perkedel

pause N [pouz] jeda, waktu istirahat; V berhenti sebentar; menghentikan sementara

pavement N trotoar

pavilion N [pavilion] anjungan; tenda besar; bangunan dekat taman atau lapangan

paw N kaki binatang

pay N pembayaran; gaji, upah; V **paid paid** membayar; **payment** N pembayaran; **payphone** N telepon umum

pea N kacang polong

peace N perdamaian; **peaceful** ADJ damai, tenteram, tenang

peach N buah persik

peacock N, M burung merak

peak N, ADJ puncak; V memuncak

peanut N kacang tanah

pear N [pér] buah pir

pearl N mutiara

peculiar ADJ [pekyulier] aneh, ganjil

pedal N [pédel] injakan kaki, pedal; V mengayuh (sepeda)

pedestrian N [pedéstrien] pejalan kaki

pedicab N [pedikab] becak

pedicure N pedikur, perawatan kaki

pee V, SL kencing, pipis

peek V mengintip, menengok sejenak

peel N kulit (buah); V mengelupas; menguliti, mengupas; **peeler** N alat pengupas

peep V mengintip, mengintai; menengok

318

peer v melihat dengan susah

peg N pasak; sangkutan; patokan; v mematok, memasak

pelican N [pélikan] burung pelikan

pen N pena, kalam; bolpoin, pulpen

penalize v menghukum; **penalty** N denda, hukuman, penalti

pencil N pensil

penguin N pinguin

peninsula N [peninsula] semenanjung

penknife N [pén naif] pisau lipat ← **pen**

pension N [pénsyen] pensiun

penthouse N [pént haus] apartemen (mewah)

people N, PL [pipel] orang, bangsa, rakyat, kaum

pepper N merica, lada; **peppermint** ADJ mint, mentol; N permen

per PREP setiap, tiap, per

percent N persen; **percentage** N persentase

perfect ADJ [pérfekt] sempurna

perform v melakukan, menye-

lenggarakan, memainkan (peran); **performance** N pertunjukan; **performer** N pemain, pemeran

perfume N wewangian, minyak wangi, parfum; wangi

perhaps ADV mungkin, barangkali

period N [piried] zaman, masa, kala, waktu; titik; datang bulan, haid

permanent ADJ tetap, permanen

permission N izin; **permit** N surat izin; v mengizinkan, memperboleh

persist v tetap (melakukan), bertekun, bertahan

person N **people** [pipel] orang, pribadi; **personal** ADJ pribadi; perorangan; **personality** N kepribadian; tokoh; **personnel** N [pérsonél] personalia, para karyawan

persuade v [pérsuéd] meyakinkan

pessimistic ADJ pesimis, bersangka buruk

pest N hama; gangguan

pesticide N [péstisaid] pestisida, obat pembasmi

serangga
pestle N alu
pet ADJ kesayangan; N hewan peliharaan; v mengelus
petal N [pétel] daun bunga
petition N [petisyen] permohonan, petisi; v memohon
petrol N bensin
petticoat N rok dalam
phantom N [fantom] hantu, momok
pharmacy N apotik
Philippines [filipins] *the ~* Filipina
philosophy N (ilmu) filsafat
phone N, SL telepon; v menelepon ← **telephone**
photo N, SL foto; **photocopy** N fotokopi; v memfotokopi; **photograph** N foto, potret, gambar; v memotret; **photographer** N tukang foto, tukang potret, fotografer; **photography** N potretmemotret, fotografi
phrase N [fréz] frasa, kelampok kata
physical ADJ (secara) fisik; jasmani
physics N, PL ilmu fisika
physiotherapy N fisioterapi

piano N piano
pick v memilih; mencungkil; memetik; *~ up* mengambil; menjemput
pickpocket N copet, pencopet
pickup N pikap
picnic N piknik
picture N gambar, lukisan
piece N [pis] potong, keping, bagian
pier N [pir] jeti, dermaga, pelabuhan
pierce v [pirs] menembus, menindik, menusuk
pig N babi
pigeon N [pijen] burung merpati, burung dara
pile N timbunan; v menimbun
pilgrim N haji; peziarah
pill N pil, obat
pillar N [piler] tiang, soko guru
pillow N [pilo] bantal
pilot ADJ percontohan; N pilot, penerbang, pandu; contoh
pimple N [pimpel] jerawat
pin N peniti; v menyematkan
pinch v mencubit
pine N *~ (tree)* pohon pinus
pineapple N nanas
pingpong N tenis meja, pingpong

pink ADJ merah muda, merah jambu, pink

pioneer N [payonir] perintis, pelopor

pipe N pipa; V menyalurkan; **pipeline** N saluran pipa

pirate N [pairat] bajak laut, pembajak; **pirated** ADJ bajakan

pit N lubang, terowongan dalam tambang

pitch N pola titinada; V melemparkan; **pitcher** N kendi, tempat air

pitiful ADJ [pitiful] memelas, menyedihkan; **pity** N belas kasihan; V mengasihani; *what a ~* sayang (sekali)

place N tempat; kedudukan

plague N [plég] penyakit sampar, wabah

plain ADJ polos; sederhana, bersahaja; nyata; N medan, dataran; **plainly** ADV terus terang

plan N rencana, rancangan, bagan, denah; V merancang, merencanakan; **planning** N perencanaan

plane N, SL pesawat terbang ← **aeroplane**

planet N planet; *~ Earth* Bumi

plank N papan

planner N perencana ← **plan**

plant N tetumbuhan, tanaman; pabrik; V menanam, menanamkan; **plantation** N perkebunan

plaster N kapur, gips, plester

plastic ADJ, N plastik; *~ bag* keresek, kantong plastik

plate N piring; pelat

platform N peron; panggung

platinum N [platinum] platina, emas putih

play N pertunjukan, sandiwara; permainan; V main, bermain; memainkan; **playboy** N lelaki yang suka mempermainkan perempuan; seorang Arjuna; **player** N pemain; **playground** N tempat bermain, tempat ayunan; **playpen** N boks (bayi)

plaza N alun-alun

pleasant ADJ [plézant] menyenangkan, enak, nyaman, nikmat; sopan; **please** tolong; silahkan; coba; *~ help me* tolong bantu saya; *~ sit down* silahkan duduk; *~ try* cobalah; V menyenangkan; **pleasure** N [plézyur]

kesukaan, kenikmatan

plenty ADJ banyak, cukup

plot v merencanakan; berkomplot, bersekongkol

plow, plough N [plau] bajak; v membajak

plug N sumbat, steker, stopkontak; v menyumbat

plumber N [plamer] tukang ledeng

plump ADJ tambun, subur

plural ADJ jamak

plus [plas] plus, ditambah

pneumonia N [nyumonia] radang paru-paru

pocket N saku, kantong, kocek; **pocketknife** N [poketnaif] pisau lipat

poem N [poem] syair, pantun; **poet** N penyair; **poetry** N puisi

point N titik, noktah; tanjung; v menunjuk, menunjukkan; **pointed** ADJ runcing, tajam; **pointless** ADJ tiada gunanya

poison N racun; bisa; v meracuni; **poisonous** ADJ beracun, berbisa

poke v menyodok, menusuk

Poland N Polandia

polar ADJ berhubungan dengan kutub; ~ *bear* beruang kutub; **pole** N kutub

pole N tiang

police N [polis] polisi; ~ *station* kantor polisi, pos polisi; **policeman** N, M polisi; **policewoman** N, F polisi wanita (polwan)

policy N kebijaksanaan

polio N penyakit lumpuh layuh, penyakit polio

polish N pelitur, semir; v menggosok, menyemir

polite ADJ sopan (santun)

political ADJ politik; **politician** N [politisyen] politikus, politisi

pollute v mencemarkan; **pollution** N pencemaran, kecemaran, polusi

polygamy N poligami

pond N kolam

pony N kuda kerdil, kuda poni

poo, pooh N, SL tahi; v berak

pool N kolam (renang); bilyar

poor ADJ miskin, papa; hina, malang

pop v meletup; ~ *up* muncul

Pope *the* ~ Sri Paus

popular ADJ populer, laku;

322

population N (jumlah) penduduk, populasi

pork N daging babi

pornography N pornografi

porpoise N [porpus] lumba-lumba

porridge N [porij] bubur

port ADJ kiri (di kapal); N pelabuhan; lubang, colokan

portable ADJ dapat dibawa ke mana-mana, jinjing

porter N kuli

portion N porsi, bagian

portrait N potret, lukisan, gambar

pose N [poz] gaya, lagak; V bergaya

position N [posisyen] letak, kedudukan, pangkat, jabatan; keadaan

positive ADJ, N positif, pasti, tentu

possess V memiliki, mempunyai

possibility N kemungkinan; **possible** ADJ [posibel] mungkin; **possibly** ADV barangkali, mungkin

post ADJ sesudah, pasca

post N pos; jabatan; tiang; layanan pos; ~ *office* kantor pos; V mengeposkan; menempelkan; **postcard** N kartu pos; **poster** N plakat, gambar

postman N tukang pos

postpone V menunda, mengundurkan

pot N pot, periuk, tempat bunga, tempat tanaman

potato N [potéto] kentang; ~ *chips* kentang goreng

potential ADJ mungkin, berpeluang, calon

pothole N [pot hol] lubang di jalan

pottery N tembikar, pecah belah, keramik

poultry N [poltri] unggas

pour V mengalir; menuangkan, mencurahkan; menyiram

poverty N [poverti] kemiskinan

powder N [pauder] bubuk, serbuk, puyer; bedak; V membedaki

power N kekuasaan, kekuatan, daya, tenaga; **powerful** ADJ berkuasa, kuat

practical N praktis, berguna; **practically** ADV hampir-hampir, benar-benar; **practice** N praktek, kebiasaan, adat;

323

latihan; mempraktekkan, melatih

praise N [préiz] pujian; v memuji

pram N kereta bayi, kereta anak-anak

prank N gurauan, permainan

pre- PREF [pri] pra-, sebelum

preacher N pemuka agama; ISL khatib, dai

precious ADJ [présyus] berharga, mahal; mulia

precise ADJ tepat, saksama

predict v meramalkan; **prediction** N ramalan

prefer v lebih suka, memilih; **preference** N kecenderungan, pilihan

prefix N awalan

pregnancy N (masa) kehamilan; **pregnant** ADJ hamil, mengandung

prehistoric ADJ prasejarah

prejudice N [préjudis] prasangka

premature ADJ prematur, sebelum waktunya, pradini

premier ADJ utama, terbaik

premiere N [prémiér] pemutaran perdana, pertunjukan perdana

prepaid ADJ prabayar

preparation N [préparé-syen] persiapan; **prepare** v menyiapkan, mempersiapkan

preposition N [préposisyen] kata depan

prescription N resep

presence N [prézens] hadirat, hadapan; kehadiran; **present** ADJ [prézent] sekarang, kini; hadir; N hadiah, kado, pemberian; v [prezént] menyajikan, mempersembahkan; **presentation** N penyajian, presentasi; **presently** ADV segera

preservation N [préservésyen] perlindungan; preservasi; **preserve** N [présérv] cagar; selai; v mengawetkan, melindungi, memelihara

president N presiden; ketua

press N percetakan; pers; alat penekan; v menekan, menindih, mendesak; **pressure** N [présyur] tekanan

presume v menganggap; mengira

pretend v berpura-pura, berdalih

pretty ADJ [priti] manis,

cantik, molek; **ADV** cukup

prevent **V** [prevént] mencegah, menghalangi, menangkis; **prevention** **N** pencegahan

previous **ADJ** yang dahulu, yang sebelumnya

price **N** harga; **priceless** **ADJ** tidak ternilai

prick **N** tusukan; **V** menusuk; **prickly** **ADJ** tajam, berduri, menusuk

pride **N** kesombongan, kebanggaan, harga diri

priest **N**, **CATH** [prist] pastor; **HIND** pedanda

primary **ADJ** pertama, terpenting, dasar; **prime** **ADJ** perdana, utama; ~ *minister (PM)* Perdana Menteri (PM)

primitive **ADJ** sederhana, primitif

prince **N**, **M** pangeran; **princess** **N**, **F** putri, permaisuri

principal **ADJ** utama; **N** kepala sekolah; uang pokok

principle **N** [prinsipel] asas, prinsip

print **N** tapak (kaki); gambar, reproduksi; tulisan, ketikan; **V** mencetak; **printer** **N** printer,

pencetak; **printout** **N** hasil cetak

prior **ADJ** [praior] terlebih dahulu; **priority** **N** prioritas

prison **N** [prizon] penjara; **prisoner** **N** orang yang dipenjara, terpidana

private **ADJ** [praivet] pribadi; swasta; milik sendiri

privilege **N** [privilej] hak istimewa

prize **N** hadiah

probably **ADV** kemungkinan besar, mungkin

problem **N** masalah, soal

procedure **N** prosedur, tata cara; **process** **N** cara, proses; **V** memproses, mengolah; **procession** **N** arak-arakan, prosesi

proclamation **N** proklamasi, pengumuman

produce **N** hasil; **V** menghasilkan; **producer** **N** produsen; **product** **N** hasil, produk; **production** **N** produksi, pertunjukan

profession **N** profesi, pekerjaan; pernyataan; **professional** **ADJ** profesional

professor **N** guru besar

325

profile N profil

profit N untung, keuntungan, laba; V beruntung, memperoleh keuntungan; **profitable** ADJ menguntungkan

program, programme N acara, program; V memprogram

progress N kemajuan; V maju

project N proyek; V memproyeksikan; **projector** N proyektor

promise N [promis] janji; V berjanji; menjanjikan

promote V memajukan, menaikkan pangkat, mempromosikan; **promotion** N kenaikan pangkat; promosi

pronunciation N lafal

proof N bukti

propeller N baling-baling

proper ADJ benar, betul, patut, layak; **properly** ADV benar-benar, dengan betul

property N kepunyaan, (harta) milik; sifat

proposal N usul; lamaran; **propose** V mengusulkan; meminang

protect V melindungi; **pro-**

tection N perlindungan; **protective** ADJ [protéktif] bersifat melindungi; pencegah

protest N protes, pembangkangan, unjuk rasa; V memprotes, melawan, membangkang, berunjuk rasa

proud ADJ bangga; angkuh, sombong

prove V [pruv] membuktikan

proverb N peribahasa

provide V menyediakan, membekali, melengkapi; **provided, providing** ~ *(that)* asal, asalkan

province N propinsi; **provincial** ADJ berhubungan dengan provinsi; picik, kampungan

prune N buah prem kering

pseudonym N [siudonim] nama samaran

psychiatrist N [saikayetrist] psikiater, ahli jiwa

psychic ADJ, N [saikik] mempunyai indera keenam, cenayang

psychologist N psikolog, ahli ilmu jiwa; **psychology** N ilmu jiwa, psikologi

PTO ABBREV *please turn over* di

326

halaman berikut

public N orang banyak, umum; **publication** N terbitan, keluaran; pengumuman

publish V menerbitkan, mengeluarkan, mengumumkan; **publisher** N penerbit

pudding N puding, pencuci mulut, podeng

puddle N [padel] genangan

pull N tarikan, daya tarik; [pul] menarik; **pullover** N switer, baju hangat

pulse N nadi

pump N pompa; V memompa

pumpkin N labu

punch V menghantam, meninju, menonjok

punctual ADJ tepat waktu

punctuation N [pangktyu-ésyen] pemberian tanda-tanda baca

punish V [panisy] menghukum; **punishment** N hukuman

pupil N murid; anak mata

puppet N boneka; wayang

puppy N [papi] anak anjing

purchase V membeli

pure ADJ murni, bersih

purple N, ADJ ungu, lembayung

purpose N maksud, niat, tujuan; *on ~* dengan sengaja

purr N dengkur (kucing); V mendengkur

purse N dompet

push N [pusy] dorongan; V mendorong; **pusher** N kereta anak

puss, pussycat N, SL [pus, pusikat] kucing

put V **put put** [put] meletakkan, menaruh, menyimpan; menempatkan

puzzle N [pazel] mainan, teka-teki

pyjamas, pajamas N, PL piyama, baju tidur

python N [paithon] ular sanca, piton

Q

quake N gempa; V gemetar

qualification N kualifikasi, ijazah; **qualified** ADJ berkualifikasi, berhak, berijazah

quality N mutu, kualitas; sifat

quantity N [kuontiti] banyaknya, kuantitas

quarantine N [kuorantin] karantina

quarrel N [kuorel] pertengkaran, percekcokan

quarter N [kuorter] perempat; kampung, daerah, lingkungan

quay N [ki] dermaga

queen N ratu

queer ADJ aneh

query N [kuiri] pertanyaan; V menanyakan, meragukan

quest N pencarian

question N pertanyaan; masalah, soal; V bertanya, memeriksa; **questionnaire** N [kuéstioner] angket

queue N [kyu] antre, antrean; V antri, berantri

quick ADJ cepat

quiet ADJ [kuayet] teduh, tenang

quilt N selimut tebal

quit V quit quit putus asa, berhenti, meninggalkan

quite ADV cukup sama, rada, lumayan

quiz N kuis, ulangan singkat, tanya jawab; V menanyai

quotation N kutipan; penawaran; **quote** V mengutip, menyebut, mencatat

R

rabbit N kelinci

race N lomba, balap, pacuan; V berlomba, membalap; **racehorse** N kuda pacu, kuda balap; **racetrack** N sirkuit; pacuan kuda

race N (suku) bangsa, ras; **racism** N [résizem] rasisme, pembedaan rasial; **racist** ADJ rasis

rack N rak

racket, racquet N raket

radio N [rédio] radio

radish N [radisy] lobak

raffle N [rafel] undian

raft N rakit

rag N lap, kain jelek

rage N kemarahan, geram

raid N razia, serangan, penggerebekan; V merazia, menyerang, menyerbu

rail N rel; **railing** N susuran; **railroad, railway** N jalan kereta api

rain N, V hujan; **rainbow** N pelangi, bianglala; **raincoat** N jas hujan; **rainy** ADJ banyak hujan

raise v mengangkat, menaikkan, meninggikan; membesarkan (anak-anak); menimbulkan

raisin N kismis

rally N reli; pertemuan

ramp N jalur mendaki, jalur yang melandai

ranch N peternakan, pertanian

range N [rénj] jajaran, barisan; kisaran, jangkauan; lapangan, tempat; **ranger** N penjaga hutan

rank N pangkat, derajat; v menduduki; mengatur, menyusun; menggolongkan; **ranking** N urutan

ransom N (uang) tebusan, penebusan

rap N musik rap; ketukan; v mengetuk

rape N perkosaan, pemerkosaan; v memerkosa

rapid ADJ [rapid] cepat, lekas; **rapids** N, PL jeram

rare ADJ mentah; jarang; **rarely** ADV jarang

raspberry N frambozen

rat N tikus (besar)

rate N tarif, perbandingan, angka; kecepatan

rather ADV agak, rada, cukup; melainkan; ~ *than* daripada

rating N penilaian

ration N rangsum, jatah

rattan N rotan

raven N burung gagak

raw ADJ mentah; kasar

ray N sinar

razor N pisau cukur

reach v sampai, tiba, mencapai; menghubungi

react v [riakt] bereaksi; menanggapi; **reaction** N tanggapan, reaksi

read v read read [réd] membaca; **reader** N pembaca; buku bacaan; **reading** N membaca; bacaan ← read

ready ADJ [rédi] siap, sedia; selesai, sudah

real ADJ nyata, betul, sejati; ADV sangat, benar-benar; **reality** N kenyataan, realitas; **realize** v sadar; mewujudkan, melaksanakan

rear ADJ, N (bagian) belakang; pantat

reason N sebab, alasan; akal (budi); **reasonable** ADJ masuk akal

rebel N [rébel] pemberontak; **rebellion** N pemberontakan

recall V ingat; memanggil kembali, menarik kembali

receipt N [risit] kuitansi, tanda terima, struk; penerimaan;

receive V menerima, mendapat, memperoleh; menyambut

recent ADJ baru; **recently** ADV baru-baru ini

reception N resepsi ← receive

recharge V mengecas, mengisi ulang

recipe N [résipi] resep

recognize V mengenal, mengenali; mengakui, menghargai

recommend V menganjurkan; memuji; **recommendation** N rekomendasi, saran

record N [rékord] catatan; daftar; rekor; piringan hitam; dokumen; V [rékord] mencatat, mendaftar, merekam

recover V [rikaver] sembuh, pulih; menemukan kembali, menyelamatkan

recreation N [rékriésyen] hiburan, rekreasi

recruit N rekrut; V merekrut

rectangle N [rektanggel] empat persegi panjang

recycle V [risaikel] didaur ulang; **recycling** N daur ulang

red ADJ merah

reduce V mengurangi, memperkecil

reef N (batu) karang

refer V mengacu; menunjukkan; mengenai; **referee** N wasit; **reference** N surat keterangan, referensi

refill N isi ulang; pengisian kembali

refine V menghaluskan, menyaring; **refinery** N kilang

reflect V membayang; mencerminkan, memantulkan; merenung, merenungkan; **reflection** N bayangan; renungan

reforestation N reboisasi

reform N perubahan, reformasi; V berubah; mengubah; menyusun kembali

refresh V menyegarkan

refrigerator N lemari es, kulkas

refugee N pengungsi

refund N pembayaran kembali; V mengembalikan uang

refusal N penolakan; **refuse** V

[refyuz] menolak
regard N hormat; v menganggap
regency N kabupaten; daerah; **regent** N bupati
region N daerah, wilayah; **regional** ADJ daerah
register N [réjister] daftar; v daftar; mendaftarkan; mencatat; **registration** N pendaftaran, pencatatan; **registry** N (kantor) pendaftaran
regret N rasa sesal; v menyesal
regular ADJ biasa; teratur; tetap
rehearsal N [rihérsal] latihan
reign N [réin] pemerintahan, masa bertakhta
reindeer N [reindir] **reindeer** rusa kutub
reject v [rejékt] menolak; **rejection** N penolakan
relate v menceritakan; mengaitkan, menghubungkan; **relation** N saudara, keluarga; hubungan; **relationship** N hubungan; **relative** ADJ relatif; N saudara, keluarga
relax v bersantai-santai; mengendurkan; **relaxation** N relaksasi; **relaxing** ADJ santai

release N pembebasan; rilis, keluaran; v melepaskan, membebaskan, memerdekakan
relevant ADJ bersangkut paut, relevan
reliable ADJ andal, terpercaya ← **rely**
relief N [rilif] bantuan, pertolongan, sumbangan; rasa lega; **relieve** v membantu, menolong
religion N [rilijen] agama
reluctant ADJ enggan
rely v [relai] mengandalkan
remain v tinggal, tetap; ~s sisa; **remainder** N sisa
remark N komentar; catatan; v berkomentar, mengomentari; berkata; **remarkable** ADJ pantas diperhatikan, luar biasa
remember v ingat
remind v [remaind] mengingatkan; **reminder** N surat peringatan
remote ADJ, N terpencil; ~ *control* remot
removal N [remuvel] pemindahan; **remove** v memindahkan; menjauhkan
renew v memperbarui,

331

memperpanjang

renovate v merenovasi, memperbaiki

rent N (uang) sewa; v menyewa; ~ *out* menyewakan

repair N perbaikan, reparasi; v memperbaiki

repay v repaid repaid membayar kembali, mengganti

repeat N tayangan ulang; v mengulangi

replace v mengganti, menggantikan

reply N [replai] jawaban, sahutan, balasan; v menjawab, menyahut, membalas

report N laporan, pemberitaan; v melapor, melaporkan, memberitakan; **reporter** N wartawan

represent v mewakili; menggambarkan, melambangkan; **representative** N wakil, utusan

reprint N cetak ulang; v mencetak ulang

reproduce v mempunyai keturunan, berkembang biak; meniru; **reproduction** N reproduksi

reptile N binatang melata

republic N republik; **republican** ADJ berkaitan dengan republik, republikan

reputation N nama baik, reputasi

request N permohonan, permintaan; v memohon, minta

require v memerlukan

rescue N penyelamatan; v menolong, menyelamatkan

research N penelitian, riset; v meneliti, meriset

resemble v menyerupai, mirip

reservation N reservasi, pesanan, buking; **reserve** N cadangan, persediaan; v memesan, menyediakan

reshuffle N perombakan; v merombak

residence N kediaman; **resident** N penduduk, penghuni; ARCH residen

resign v [rizain] mundur, mengundurkan diri, berhenti bekerja

resist v [rezist] melawan, menahan; **resistance** N perlawanan, pertahanan

resort N tempat beristirahat, resor

resource N sumber daya
respect V hormat; hal; **respectable** ADJ baik-baik, terhormat; **respectful** ADJ (penuh) hormat
respective ADJ masing-masing
respond V membalas, menjawab, menanggapi; **response** N tanggapan, jawaban, respons
responsibility N [responsibiliti] tanggung jawab; **responsible** ADJ bertanggung jawab
rest N (waktu) istirahat; sisa; V berhenti, beristirahat, mengaso; tinggal; **restroom** N toilet, WC
restaurant N restoran, rumah makan
restrict V membatasi; **restriction** N pembatasan
result N akibat, hasil
resumé, resume N [rézumé] riwayat hidup
resume V mulai lagi, meneruskan
resurrect V menghidupkan kembali
retail ADJ [ritél] eceran, ritel; N perdagangan eceran; **retailer**

N pengecer, pedagang eceran
retain V menyimpan, menahan, tetap
retarded ADJ tunagrahita, terkebelakang
retire V pensiun; **retirement** N masa pensiun
retreat N [retrit] retret; V mundur, menarik diri
retrieve V [retriv] mengambil, mendapat kembali
return N kembali, pemulangan, perjalanan pulang; V pulang, kembali; mengembalikan, membalas
reveal V [revil] membuka, menyingkapkan; menyatakan
revenge N (rasa) dendam, pembalasan
reverse ADJ terbalik; N sisi balik; V mundur, memundurkan kendaraan; membalikkan
review N [revyu] tinjauan; resensi; majalah; V meninjau kembali; menilai; **reviewer** N penulis resensi
revolution N revolusi; peredaran
reward N [reword] hadiah, imbalan, ganjaran; V meng-

ganjar; menghadiahi; **rewarding** ADJ menguntungkan, berguna

rheumatism N [rumatizem] encok, rematik, sengal

rhinoceros N [rainoseres] **rhino** SL badak

rhyme N [raim] sajak; v bersajak; **rhythm** N [rithem] irama, ritme

rib N tulang rusuk, iga

ribbon N pita

rice N padi; beras; nasi

rich ADJ kaya, subur

rickshaw N becak

rid v membersihkan, membebaskan

riddle N teka-teki

ride N perjalanan; v **rode ridden** mengendarai, naik; **rider** N penunggang; pengendara

ridiculous ADJ menggelikan

rifle N [raifel] senapan, bedil

right ADJ [rait] (sebelah) kanan; betul, benar; patut, layak

ring N cincin; lingkaran; jaringan; gelanggang; dering; **rang rung** berdering; COLL telepon, menelepon

rink *ice (skating)* ~ gelanggang es

rinse N bilasan; v membilas

riot N [raiot] kerusuhan; kegaduhan

rip N robekan, sobekan; v menyobek, merobek

ripe ADJ masak, matang

rise N kenaikan; v **rose risen** [rizen] bangkit, terbit, berdiri

risk N risiko; v mengambil risiko

ritual N upacara (agama)

rival N saingan, lawan; v menyaingi

river N [river] sungai, kali

road N jalan (raya); **roadwork** N perbaikan jalan

roast ADJ panggang; N daging panggang; v memanggang, membakar

rob v merampok, merampas; **robber** N perampok; **robbery** N perampokan

rock N batu, cadas; v mengayunkan; menggoncang

rocket N roket; v meroket

role N peran, peranan

roll N gulung, gulungan; roti bulat; daftar; v berguling, berputar; menggulung, menggulungkan, mengge-

334

lindingkan; **roller** ~ *blades*, ~ *skates* sepatu roda

Roman N Romawi

romance N cerita cinta

roof N atap

room N ruang, ruangan; kamar; v kos

rooster N ayam jago

root N akar

rope N tali

rose N bunga mawar, bunga ros; v, PF → **rise**

rot v membusuk

rotate v berputar, berkisar

rotten ADJ busuk ← **rot**

rough ADJ [raf] kasar; mentah; **roughly** ADV kurang lebih, kira-kira; secara kasar

round ADJ bulat, bundar; di sekitar; N giliran, putaran, ronde; v mengelilingi; **roundabout** N bundaran; komidi putar

route N [rut] trayek, jalur, rute

router N penghala

row N [ro] baris, jajar, deretan

row v [ro] berkayuh; mendayung, mengayuh

rub v menggosok, menggosok-gosok; ~ *out* menghapus;

rubber N karet; penghapus

rubbish N sampah; omong kosong

ruby N batu mirah

rucksack N ransel

rude ADJ kasar, tidak sopan

ruin N reruntuhan, puing-puing; v meruntuhkan, merobohkan, merusak

rule N aturan, peraturan; pemerintahan; v memerintah; **ruler** N kepala pemerintah; penggaris

rum N room

rumor N kabar angin, kabar burung, desas-desus

run N perjalanan, latihan berlari, perlombaan; v **ran** run lari; berlangsung; mengalir; memimpin; menjalankan; **runaway** N pelarian

runner N pelari; pesuruh, pengantar ← **run**

runway N landasan pacu

rural ADJ pedesaan, pedalaman

rush N ketergesa-gesaan; ~ *hour* jam padat; v terburu-buru; menyerbu

Russia N Rusia; **Russian** N bahasa Rusia; orang Rusia

rust N karat; v berkarat; **rusty**

335

ADJ berkarat, karatan
ruthless ADJ [ruthles] keji, kejam, tanpa belas kasihan

S

sabotage N [sabotaj] sabotase; v menyabotase

sachet N [sasyé] sase, saset, kemasan (kecil) (berisi saus, sampo dll)

sack N karung, goni

sacred ADJ [sékred] suci, kudus

sacrifice N [sakrifais] korban, pengorbanan; ISL kurban, qurban; v berkurban; mengorbankan

sad ADJ susah, sedih

saddle N pelana, sadel, tempat duduk

safe ADJ selamat; aman, dapat dipercaya; **safety** N keselamatan; keamanan

sail N layar; v berlayar; **sailing** N berlayar; **sailor** N pelaut, anak buah kapal (ABK)

salad N selada

salary N [salari] gaji

sale N obral; *for* ~ dijual; **sales** N penjualan; **salesperson** N

agen; pelayan toko

salmon N [samen] ikan salmon

salt N garam; **salty** ADJ asin

salute N pemberian hormat; v v memberi hormat

same ADJ sama; serupa

sample N [sampel] contoh; v coba

sand N pasir

sandal N [sandel] sepatu sandal

sandpaper N kertas gosok, ampelas ← **sand**

sandwich N [sandwij] roti lapis

sapphire N [safair] batu nilam, batu safir

sarong N sarung

satellite N [satelait] satelit; bulan; ~ *dish* parabola

satisfaction N kepuasan; **satisfactory** ADJ memuaskan, cukup; **satisfy** v [satisfai] memuaskan; memenuhi

Saturday ADJ, N [saterdé] hari Sabtu

sauce N kuah, saus

saucer N piring cawan

Saudi Arabia N Arab Saudi

savage ADJ [savej] buas, liar, ganas

save N penyelamatan, tangkap-an; PREP kecuali; v menyelamatkan; **savings** N, PL (uang) tabungan, simpanan

saw N gergaji; v, PF → **see**; **sawdust** N serbuk kayu

sax, saxophone N saksofon

say v said said [séd] kata, berkata; mengatakan; **saying** N pepatah, peribahasa

scale N skala, ukuran; sisik, kulit; **scales** N, PL timbangan, neraca

scan N peninjauan; v meninjau; pindai, memindai

scandal N skandal, keonaran

scanner N pemindai, scanner ← **scan**

scar N bekas (luka); v membekas, menggoresi

scare N [skér] peristiwa yang menakutkan; v menakut-nakuti, menakutkan; **scared** ADJ takut

scarf N syal

scary ADJ [skéri] menakutkan ← **scare**

scavenger N pemulung

scene N [sin] pemandangan; adegan; **scenery** N pemandangan alam

scent N [sént] (minyak) wangi, harum, bau

schedule N [skédyul] jadwal, program, daftar acara; v merencanakan, mengatur

scheme N [skim] rencana; bagan, skema, rancangan; v merekayasa

scholar N [skolar] pelajar; orang terpelajar; **scholarship** N beasiswa; **school** N sekolah

science N ilmu (pengetahuan alam, IPA); sains; **scientist** N ilmuwan

scooter N otopet, skuter

scorch v membakar (tidak sengaja)

score N skor, angka, nilai; v mencetak gol, angka atau poin; memperoleh nilai; **scoreboard** N papan angka

scorpion N kalajengking

Scotland N Skotlandia

scout N pandu, pramuka; pengintai

scramble N perebutan; v berebut; mengocok

scrap ADJ bekas; ~ *metal* besi tua; ~ *paper* kertas bekas; N sisa, carik

scrape v bergeseran; menggores, menggesekkan

scratch N goresan; v menggores, menggaruk, mencoret

scrawl N tulisan cakar ayam

scream N jeritan; v berteriak, menjerit

screen N tabir; layar putih; **screening** N pemutaran film

screw N sekrup; v menyekrup; **screwdriver** N obeng

scribble v mencoret-coret

script N tulisan; naskah

scroll v menggulung, naik

scrub N semak, belukar

scrub v menggosok

scuba ~ *diving* selam dengan tangki udara

sculptor N perupa, pematung, pemahat patung

sea N laut; ~ *level* permukaan laut; ~ *urchin* bulu babi; **seafood** N makanan laut; **seagull** N burung camar; **seahorse** N kuda laut

seal N anjing laut

seal N meterai, cap; v menutup

sealion N [silayon] singa laut ← **sea**

search N [sérc] pencarian, penggeledahan; v mencari, memeriksa, menggeledah

search engine N mesin pencari

seashell N kerang (laut) ← **sea**

seashore N pantai laut ← **sea**

seasick ADJ mabuk laut ← **sea**

seaside N tepi laut ← **sea**

season N [sizen] musim; *the dry* ~ musim kemarau

seasoning N bumbu

seat N tempat duduk, bangku, kursi

seaweed N ganggang laut, rumput laut

second N [sékond] detik

second ADJ [sékond] kedua; ~-*hand* bekas; **secondary** ADJ sekunder

secretary N sekretaris, panitera

section N seksi, bagian, belahan; **sector** N sektor, bidang

security N keamanan

see v **saw** **seen** melihat; berkunjung

seed N biji, benih

seek v **sought** **sought** [sot] mencari

seem v nampak; ternyata, kelihatannya; rupanya, rasanya

seize v [siz] menangkap; menyita

seldom ADV jarang

select v [selékt] memilih, menyaring; **selection** N pilihan, pemilihan, seleksi

self PRON sendiri, pribadi; **selfish** ADJ egois, suka mementingkan diri sendiri

selfie N swafoto, selfi

sell v sold sold menjual, berjualan; **seller** N penjual

semi- PREF tengah, separuh; ~*colon* titik koma

send v sent sent mengirim, mengirimkan, mengirimi

senior ADJ [sinior] lebih tua, tertua, senior; N orang yang lebih tua; ~ *high school* sekolah menengah atas (SMA)

sensation N kegemparan, sensasi

sense N indera; perasaan; arti, pengertian; **sensible** ADJ waras, berpikiran sehat, berakal sehat; **sensitive** ADJ peka, sensitif

sentimental ADJ sentimentil

separate ADJ [séperet] terpisah; v [séperét] berpisah; pisah ranjang; memisahkan

September N bulan September

sequel N [sikuel] lanjutan, sambungan

sergeant N [sarjent] sersan

serial N [siriel] seri; film seri; cerita bersambung (cerber); **series** N seri, rangkaian

serious ADJ sungguh-sungguh, serius

servant N pembantu, pelayan, pramuwisma, babu; **serve** v melayani, mengabdi; menghidangkan; **service** N pelayanan; pemeliharaan; kebaktian; masa bakti; jasa; v memperbaiki (mobil)

serviette N [sérviét] serbet

sesame N [sésami] wijen

set ADJ sudah ditentukan; siap; N sepasang, seperangkat, perlengkapan; pesawat (radio/televisi); kelompok; v set set menaruh, memasang, menyetel; menetapkan; terbenam (matahari)

settle v [sétel] berdiam; menempati; menyelesaikan; menenangkan; mengatur, mengurus; **settlement** N perkampungan; penyelesai-

339

an; **settler** N pendatang, pemukim awal

seven ADJ, N [séven] tujuh; **seventeen** ADJ, N tujuh belas; **seventh** ADJ ketujuh; **seventy** ADJ, N tujuh puluh

several ADJ [séveral] beberapa

sew V [so] sewed sewn menjahit

sewn V, PF [son] → **sew**

sex N jenis kelamin; (hubungan) seks, persetubuhan, sanggama; **sexy** ADJ seksi

shade N naungan, tempat teduh; krei; warna

shadow N [syado] bayangan; V membayangi; membuntuti

shake N minuman bercampur (coklat, dsb) ← **milkshake**; goncangan, gelengan (kepala); jabat tangan; V **shook shaken** mengguncang, mengocok

shall V, AUX akan

shallow ADJ dangkal

shame N malu

shampoo N [syampu] sampo; V berkeramas

shan't V takkan, tidak akan ← **shall**

shape N bentuk; V membentuk

share N bagian, andil, saham; V berbagi; membagi; **shareholder** N pemegang saham

shark N ikan hiu

sharp ADJ tajam, runcing; cerdik; **sharpen** V meruncingkan, mengasah, meraut; **sharpener** N raut pensil

shave V bercukur; mencukur; mengiris; **shaver** N alat cukur (listrik)

shawl N syal, selendang

she PRON, F [syi] dia

shed N gudang

sheep N sheep domba, biri-biri; **sheepdog** N anjing gembala

sheet N helai, lembar; seprai

shelf N papan, rak

shell N kulit, kerang; V mengupas; **shellfish** N kerang-kerangan

shelter N tempat berlindung, tempat teduh; V berlindung, bernaung; melindungi

shepherd N [shéperd] gembala

shield N [syild] perisai, tameng; V melindungi

shift N perubahan, pergeseran; jam kerja; V berpindah

tempat, beralih; mengubah, menggeser

shine N cahaya, sinar; v **shone shone** [syon] bercahaya, bersinar; memancarkan

shiny ADJ berkilap, mengkilap ← **shine**

ship N kapal, perahu; **shipping** N perkapalan, pengiriman dengan kapal; **shipwreck** N [syiprék] peristiwa kapal karam; **shipyard** N galangan kapal

shirt N baju, kemeja

shiver v menggigil, gemetar

shock N guncangan; kejut-an; *electric* ~ kena setrum; **shocking** ADJ mengejutkan

shoe N [syu] sepatu; **shoelace** N tali sepatu

shoot v **shot shot** menembak; merekam; **shooting** N penembakan; menembak (olahraga); syuting, peng-ambilan gambar

shop N toko; v berbelanja; **shopkeeper** N pemilik toko; **shoplift** v mengutil atau mencuri dari toko; **shopper** N orang yang berbelanja, pembeli; **shopping** N hasil

belanja, belanjaan; ~ *center*, ~ *mall* (pusat) pertokoan, mal

shore N pantai, tepi

short ADJ pendek, ringkas, singkat; kurang; kekurangan; N film pendek; **shortage** N [shortej] kekurangan; **shortly** ADV tidak lama lagi; **shorts** N, PL celana pendek, kolor

shot N tembakan; suntikan; v, PF → **shoot**

should v, AUX [syud] seharus-nya, sebaiknya, semestinya

shoulder N [syolder] bahu, pundak; *hard* ~ bahu jalan

shout N [syaut] teriakan; v berteriak

shove N [shav] dorongan; v mendorong dengan kasar

shovel N [shavel] sekop; v menyekop

show N [sho] pertunjukan, tontonan; acara di televisi; pameran; v memperlihat-kan, mempertunjukkan; menunjukkan, menampak-kan; membuktikan; **show-down** N [shodaun] bentrokan

shower N [syauer] pancuran (mandi); hujan sebentar; v

341

mandi (di pancuran); meng-hujani, menaburi

shred N carik, sobekan; V mencarik, memarut

shriek N [syrik] jeritan, peki-kan; V menjerit

shrimp N udang

shrine N kuil, tempat keramat

shrink V **shrank shrunk** susut; menyusutkan

shrunk V, PF → **shrink**; **shrunken** ADJ berkerut, menyusut

shuffle V mengocok; menyeret kaki

shut V **shut shut** tutup; menu-tup; **shutter** N daun penutup jendela

shuttle ADJ [syatel] ulang-alik; N kendaraan ulang-alik

shy ADJ [syai] malu, pemalu

sick ADJ sakit

sickly ADJ sering sakit, sakit-sakitan ← **sick**

side N sisi, segi; samping; **sidewalk** N trotoar; **sideways** ADV miring, ke samping

sieve N [siv] ayakan, saringan

sift V mengayak; menyaring

sigh N [sai] keluh, nafas panjang; V menarik nafas panjang; mendesah

sight N [sait] pemandangan; penglihatan; **sightseeing** N wisata, tamasya

sign N [sain] tanda, pertanda, isyarat; rambu; plang; V menandatangani; teken, mem-beri paraf; **signal** N [signal] tanda, isyarat; V memberi tanda; mengisyaratkan; **signature** N [signatyur] tanda tangan

significant ADJ berarti, penting

signpost N [sainpost] rambu

silence N keheningan; V mendiamkan; **silent** ADJ diam

silk ADJ, N sutera

silly ADJ bodoh, tolol; lucu

silver ADJ, N perak

similar ADJ [similer] serupa, mirip

simple ADJ [simpel] sederhana, bersahaja; **simply** ADV dengan sederhana; hanya; benar-benar, sungguh-sungguh

sin N dosa; V berdosa

since CONJ sejak, sedari; sebab, karena

sincere ADJ [sinsir] tulus (hati), ikhlas; bersungguh-sungguh

sing v **sang sung** bernyanyi, menyanyi; menyanyikan; **singer** N penyanyi

Singapore N Singapura

singer N penyanyi

single ADJ [singgel] tunggal, sendiri; lajang, M bujangan; lagu

singlet N singlet

sink N tempat cuci (piring); v **sank sunk** tenggelam, mengendap; menenggelamkan

sip N isapan; v mengisap, meminum sedikit

sir PRON tuan

siren N sirene

sister N saudara perempuan, adik atau kakak perempuan; kepala perawat, suster

sit v **sat sat** duduk

site N lokasi, situs

situated ADJ [situyuéted] terletak; **situation** N keadaan, situasi

six ADJ, N enam; **sixteen** ADJ, N enam belas; **sixth** ADJ keenam; **sixty** ADJ, N enam puluh

size N ukuran, nomor; besarnya

skate N sepatu luncur, sepatu es; *ice-~* sepatu es; v bermain sepatu luncur atau sepatu roda; **skating** N bermain sepatu luncur

skeleton N [skéleton] kerangka

sketch N sketsa; gambar

ski N (sepatu) ski; v main ski; **skiing** N main ski

skill N keterampilan, keahlian; **skillful, skilful** ADJ terampil

skin N kulit

skinny ADJ [skini] kurus, ceking

skip v melompat-lompat; melewati; meloncati

skirt N rok

skull N tengkorak, batok kepala

sky N langit, angkasa, udara; **skydiving** N terjun payung; **skyscraper** N pencakar langit

slang N bahasa percakapan, bahasa gaul

slap N tampar, tamparan; v menampar

slaughter N [sloter] pembantaian; penyembelihan; v membantai; memotong; menyembelih

slave N budak; **slavery** N

343

perbudakan

sled, sledge N kereta luncur

sleep V slept slept tidur; **sleepy** ADJ mengantuk

sleeve N lengan baju; sisipan kertas di CD; **sleeveless** ADJ tanpa lengan

slender ADJ ramping, langsing

slice N irisan, sayatan; V mengiris, menyayat

slide N perosotan; V slid slid meluncur; tergelincir

slightly ADV sedikit

slim ADJ ramping, langsing, lampai

slip N kesalahan; longsor; rok dalam; V tergelincir; terlupa

slipper N selop; sandal

slippery ADJ licin ← slip

slogan N semboyan, slogan

slope N lereng; V melandai

sloppy ADJ tidak rapi; cengeng

slow ADJ perlahan-lahan, pelan-pelan; lambat, lamban; **slowly** ADV pelan-pelan

slug N semacam siput

slum N daerah kumuh

slump N kemerosotan; V merosot; terjatuh

smack N tampar, tamparan, tempeleng; SL heroin; V

menampar, menempeleng

small ADJ kecil

smart ADJ cerdas, pintar; cantik, tampan; cepat; V pedih, sakit

smart TV N televisi pintar

smartphone N pesawat selular pintar, ponsel pintar

smash N tabrakan, kecelakaan (mobil); V memecahkan, menghancurkan

smell N bau; V bau; **smelly** ADJ berbau (tidak sedap)

smile N senyum, senyuman; V tersenyum

smith N pandai besi

smog N asbut (asap kabut)

smoke N asap; SL rokok; V berasap; merokok; **smoking** *no* ~ dilarang merokok; **smoky** ADJ berasap

smooth ADJ licin; lancar

SMS N pesan (singkat)

smuggle V [smagel] menyelundupkan

snack N makanan kecil, camilan

snail N keong, siput

snake N ular

snapshot N potret, foto

snatch V menjambret,

merampas

sneak N orang yang melaporkan kawan; v menyelinap;
sneakers N sepatu kets, sepatu olahraga; **sneaky** ADJ tidak terus terang

sneer N mimik wajah yang menyeringai; v menyeringai

sneeze N, v bersin

sniff N hirupan; v mencium, mencium-cium

sniffle N [snifel] pilek; v tersedu-sedu

sniper N penembak jitu

snob N, SL orang sombong

snooze N, SL tidur sebentar

snore v mendengkur; SL mengorok

snow N salju; v hujan salju; **snowball** N bola salju; **snowman** N boneka salju; **snowy** ADJ bersalju

snug ADJ hangat, nyaman; pas

so ADV begitu; sangat; demikian; CONJ jadi, maka, oleh sebab itu

soak v merendam

soap N sabun

sob N sedu; v tersedu-sedu

soccer N sepak bola

social ADJ [sosyal] sosial,

kemasyarakatan; ramah;
socialism N [sosyalizem] sosialisme; **society** N [sosayeti] masyarakat; perkumpulan, perhimpunan;
sociology N sosiologi, ilmu masyarakat

social media N média sosial (medsos), jejaring sosial

sock N kaus kaki

socket N lubang, stopkontak

soda ~ *water* air soda

sofa N dipan, sofa, kursi empuk

soft ADJ lunak, lembek, lembut; ~ *toy* boneka; **softball** N sofbal

soil N tanah; v mengotori

solar ADJ [soler] berhubungan dengan matahari

soldier N [soljer] tentara, laskar, serdadu

sole N telapak kaki, alas sepatu

solicitor N [solisiter] pengacara, ahli hukum

solid ADJ padat; kuat, kokoh

solo ADJ, ADV sendiri, solo

solution N cara pemecahan, cara penyelesaian, solusi; **solve** v memecahkan;

menyelesaikan

some ADJ [sam] beberapa; kurang lebih; salah satu; sedikit; **somebody** PRON seseorang, ada orang; **somehow** ADV bagaimanapun juga; **someone** PRON [samwan] seseorang, ada orang; **something** PRON [samthing] sesuatu; **sometimes** ADV [samtaimz] kadang-kadang; **somewhere** ADV [samwér] entah di mana

son N [san] anak (lelaki), putera; ~-*in-law* menantu

song N nyanyian, lagu

soon ADV segera, lekas

sophisticated ADJ [sofistikéted] canggih, pintar, berpengalaman

sore ADJ sakit, pedih

sorry ADJ menyesal; maaf

sort N macam, jenis; v menyortir, memilih, memilah-milah

soul N sukma, nyawa, jiwa, semangat

sound ADJ sehat, kuat; N bunyi, suara

soup N [sup] sop, sup

source N [sors] sumber, mata air; narasumber

south ADJ, N [sauth] selatan; **southeast** ADJ, N [sauth ist] tenggara

souvenir N [suvenir] oleh-oleh, kenang-kenangan, cenderamata

sow v [so] menaburkan

soy ~ *milk* susu kedelai; **soya** ~ *bean* kacang kedelai

space N ruang, tempat; spasi, jarak; angkasa

spaghetti N spageti

Spain N Spanyol

spare ADJ cadangan

spark N (percikan) api; **sparkle** N kilau; v berkilau-kilauan, bergemerlapan

sparrow N [sparo] burung gereja

speak v **spoke spoken** berbicara, berkata; **speaker** N pembicara; Ketua Dewan

spear N tombak, lembing

special ADJ [spésyal] istimewa, khusus, spesial; **specialist** N spesialis, ahli

specific ADJ khusus, tertentu, spesifik

spectacular ADJ hebat, spektakuler; **spectator** N

penonton

speech N pidato; cara bicara
← **speak**

speed N laju, kecepatan;
speedboat N perahu motor
cepat; **speedy** ADJ lekas, cepat

spend V spent spent membe-
lanjakan, memakai

sperm N sperma, air mani

spice N bumbu, rempah-
rempah; **spicy** ADJ pedas

spider N laba-laba

spill V tumpah; menumpahkan

spin V spun spun berputar-
putar; memintal

spinach N [spinec] bayam

spine N tulang punggung

spiral ADJ [spairal] spiral; V
bergerak naik/turun

spirit N [spirit] semangat; roh,
hantu; **spiritual** ADJ batin,
rohani; keagamaan

splash N bunyi ceburan atau
cemplungan; V bepercikan;
memercikkan

splendid ADJ bagus sekali

split ADJ retak, sobek; N belahan, retakan; V split split
retak, membelah; membagi

spoil V memanjakan; merusak;
spoilt ADJ manja

spokesperson N juru bicara

sponge N [spanj] spons, bunga
karang

sponsor N sponsor

spoon N sendok

sport N olahraga; **sporting** ADJ
sportif; **sportsperson** N olahragawan

spot N titik, noda; SL jerawat;
V melihat; **spotlight** N lampu
sorot; **spotty** ADJ berjerawat,
jerawatan

spout N bibir, corot

sprain N, V salah urat, keseleo

spray N percikan, semprotan;
V menyemprot, memercik

spread N [spréd] penyebaran;
sajian; mentega, selai; V
spread spread mengolesi;
menyiarkan, menyebarkan,
membentangkan

spring N musim semi, musim
bunga; sumber (air); per,
pegas; V sprang sprung
melompat, meloncat

sprinkler N alat penyiram

spy N mata-mata, spion; V
memata-matai

square ADJ [skuér] persegi;
N persegi empat; alun-alun,
medan

347

squash N [skuosy] semacam labu; v memasukkan dengan paksa

squat v [skuot] jongkok, berjongkok

squeak N [skuik] ciutan; cicit; v menciut-ciut; mencicit

squeeze v memeras; memeluk

squirrel N bajing

stab v menikam

stable ADJ [stébel] mantap, stabil; kandang kuda, istal

stadium N stadion, gelang-gang, arena

staff N staf, para karyawan, para pegawai; para guru atau pengajar

stage N panggung, pentas; tahap

stain N noda

stair N anak tangga; **stairs** PL tangga; **staircase, stairway** N tangga

stale ADJ keras (roti); basi, pengap, apak

stall N [stol] warung, kedai, kios; kandang

stamina N daya tahan

stamp N perangko; meterai, segel, tera, cap; v mem-bubuhi prangko, memberi meterai, mengecap

stand N tribune; pendirian, sikap; kios; v **stood stood** berdiri; tahan

standard ADJ baku, standar, tolok; N patokan, ukuran, norma, standar

staple v [stépel] menjepret (kertas); **stapler** N jepretan

star N bintang

stare v memelototkan mata; memandang, menatap

starfish N bintang laut ← **star**

start v mulai, berangkat; me-mulai; menghidupkan mesin

starve v (mati) kelapar

state ADJ kenegaraan; N negara (bagian); keadaan, suasana; v menyatakan, menyebutkan, memaparkan; **statement** N pernyataan, pengumuman

station N stasiun, pos; pangkalan

stationery N alat tulis

statistics N, PL statistik, angka

statue N [statyu] patung

status N keadaan, kedudukan, status; pangkat, derajat

stay N (masa) tinggal; v tinggal, menginap; bertahan

steady ADJ [stédi] tetap, terus-

348

menerus, teguh, mantap
steak N [sték] stek, bistek
steal V stole stolen mencuri
steam N uap; V beruap;
mengukus
steel N baja
steep ADJ curam, terjal; SL
mahal
steer V mengemudikan
stem N batang
step N langkah, jejak; anak
tangga; tahap; V melangkah;
stepfather N bapak tiri, ayah
tiri; **stepmother** N ibu tiri
sterile ADJ [stérail] steril,
sucihama; mandul; **sterilize**
V menyucihamakan,
mensterilkan
stick N tongkat, batang;
V stuck stuck bertekun,
bertahan; melekatkan;
sticker N stiker, tempelan
stiff ADJ keras, kaku; pegal
still ADJ tenang, teduh, sepi;
ADV masih; CONJ bahkan,
tetapi
sting N sengat; V stung stung
menyengat
stir N [ster] keributan, kekacauan; V bergerak; menga-
duk; mengacaukan

stitch N jahitan; V menjahit
stock N persediaan; hewan
ternak
stocking N stoking
stomach N [stamek] perut,
lambung
stone N batu; biji (buah)
stool N bangku, dingklik
stop V berhenti, menahan
store N toko; persediaan,
perbekalan, gudang; V
menyimpan
stork N (burung) bangau
storm N angin badai; **stormy**
ADJ (berangin) ribut
story, storey N lantai, tingkat
story N cerita, riwayat, kisah,
dongeng
stove N kompor
straight ADJ [strét] lurus,
terus; ADV langsung; jujur,
terus terang; **straighten** V
meluruskan
strain N ketegangan; V bersu-
sah payah; mengejan;
menyaring; memaksakan;
strainer N saringan
strait N selat
strange ADJ [strénj] aneh,
ganjil, asing; **stranger** N
orang asing, orang luar

strangle v [stranggel] mencekik

strap N tali; cambuk

straw N sedotan; jerami, merang

strawberry N stroberi, arbei

stream N sungai, kali; aliran; v mengalir

street N jalan; **streetcar** N trem

strength N kekuatan, tenaga, kekuasaan; **strengthen** v memperkuat, memperkokoh ← **strong**

stress N tekanan; ketegangan, stres; v menekan, mementingkan, menitikberatkan

stretch v menegangkan; merentangkan

stretcher N usungan

strict ADJ keras; streng (guru)

strike N pukulan; pemogokan, mogok kerja; serangan; v **struck struck** memukul; menyerang; mogok

string N tali; senar (raket, alat musik); untaian

strip N garis, jalur; v menghilangkan, membersihkan

stripe N garis, belang

stroke N pukulan; gaya

(renang); serangan otak

strong ADJ kuat, kokoh; keras (minuman)

struggle N [stragel] perjuangan; v berjuang

stubborn ADJ keras kepala

stuck N terjebak, terjepit; v, PF → **stick**

student N pelajar, murid, mahasiswa

studio N studio; sanggar

study N [stadi] pelajaran, studi; penelitian, riset; ruang belajar; v belajar, mempelajari, mengkaji

stuff N bahan; barang-barang; v mengisi

stunt N perbuatan yang luar biasa; pertunjukan, akrobatik

stupid ADJ bodoh, dungu

sturdy ADJ kokoh

style N [stail] gaya, cara; **stylish** ADJ bergaya

sub- PREF (di) bawah

subject N soal, topik, subyek; mata pelajaran

submarine N [sabmarin] kapal selam

submit v menyerahkan, menyampaikan

subscribe v berlangganan;

menganut

subsequent ADJ berikut

subsidize V mensubsidi, memberi subsidi; **subsidy** N tunjangan, subsidi

substitute ADJ, N ganti, pengganti; wakil; V mengganti

subtitles N, PL teks

subtract V mengurangi

suburb N [sabérb] daerah perumahan, daerah perkotaan

subway N kereta api bawah tanah; terowongan penyeberangan

succeed V [saksid] berhasil, menjadi sukses; mengganti; **success** N keberhasilan, sukses; **successful** ADJ berhasil, sukses

such ADJ seperti itu, sedemikian; sungguh; ADV demikian, begini, begitu; PRON demikian, begitu

suck V mengisap, mengemut

sudden ADJ tiba-tiba, mendadak; **suddenly** ADV tiba-tiba, secara mendadak

suffer V menderita

sufficient ADJ [safisyent]

cukup

sugar N [syuger] gula

suggest V [sejést] menyarankan, mengusulkan, menganjurkan; **suggestion** N saran, usul, anjuran

suicide N [suisaid] bunuh diri

suit N [sut] setelan (pakaian); rupa (kartu); V cocok; berpadanan; **suitable** ADJ patut, layak, cocok; **suitcase** N koper

Sumatra N (pulau) Sumatera

summary N ringkasan, ikhtisar

summer N musim panas

sun N matahari; **sunburn** N, V terbakar sinar matahari; **sunny** ADJ cerah; riang

sundae N [sandé] es krim dengan sirop

Sundanese N bahasa Sunda; orang Sunda

Sunday N hari Minggu ← **sun**

sundown N matahari terbenam, matahari tenggelam, magrib ← **sun**

sunglasses N, PL kacamata hitam ← **sun**

sunk ADJ tenggelam; V, PF → **sink**

351

sunlight N [sanlait] cahaya matahari ← **sun**

sunrise N matahari terbit ← **sun**

sunset N matahari terbenam, matahari tenggelam, magrib ← **sun**

sunshine N sinar matahari, cahaya matahari ← **sun**

super ADJ luar biasa, hebat

superior ADJ [supirior] ulung, unggul, tinggi; sombong; N atasan

supermarket N (toko) swalayan

superstitious ADJ [superstisyes] sering percaya takhayul

supervise V mengawasi; **supervisor** N [supervaizer] pengawas

supper N makan malam

supply N pasokan, persediaan, suplai; V memasok, menyediakan

support N dukungan, bantuan; V mendukung, membantu; **supporter** N pendukung

suppose V mengandaikan, menganggap, mengira

supreme ADJ unggul, teratas

sure ADJ [syur] tentu, pasti; yakin

surf N buih ombak; V berselancar

surface N [sérfes] muka, permukaan

surgeon N [serjen] ahli bedah; **surgery** N pembedahan, operasi; tempat praktek dokter

surname N nama keluarga, nama marga

surprise N kejutan; V membuat kejutan, mengejutkan

surround V mengelilingi, mengepung

survey N angket; penelitian; peninjauan

survival N kelangsungan hidup; **survive** V bertahan (hidup), tetap hidup, selamat

suspect N [saspekt] tersangka; V [saspékt] menyangka; **suspicious** ADJ curiga, mencurigakan

swallow V [swolo] menelan

swamp [swomp] paya, rawa

swap, swop N pertukaran; V bertukar; menukar

swear V [suér] swore sworn bersumpah; mengumpat

sweat N [swét] keringat, peluh; v berkeringat

Sweden N Swedia

sweep v swept swept menyapu

sweet ADJ manis; N permen

swim v swam swum berenang, mandi; **swimming** N renang; **swimsuit, swimwear** N baju renang

swing N swung swung ayunan; pergeseran; v bergoyang, berayun

swipe v menggesek; memukul; mencuri

switch N sakelar, penghubung; pertukaran

Switzerland N (negeri) Swis

swollen ADJ bengkak, kembung ← **swell**

sword N [sord] pedang

symbol N lambang, simbol

symptom N gejala

syringe N [sirinj] alat suntik, suntikan

syrup N sirop

system N sistem, susunan, jaringan

T

T ~-shirt kaus (oblong)

tab N label

table N [tébel] meja; daftar; **tablecloth** N taplak meja; **tablespoon** N sendok besar

tablet N pil, tablet; *(computer)* tablet

tag N label, merek, nama, kartu

tail N ekor, buntut; bagian belakang

tailor N tukang jahit, modist

Taiwan N Taiwan

take v took taken mengambil, membawa (pergi); menganggap; menangkap, menerima; makan (waktu), memerlukan; **takeaway** ADJ, N dibungkus, bawa pulang

talcum ~ *powder* bedak

tale N cerita, dongeng

talent N [talent] bakat; **talented** ADJ berbakat

talk N [tok] percakapan, pembicaraan, ceramah; v berbicara, berunding, bertutur; **talkshow** N acara

diskusi

tall ADJ [tol] tinggi, jangkung

tambourine N [tamburin] rebana

tame ADJ jinak; v menjinakkan

Tamil ADJ berasal dari kebudayaan Tamil atau Keling; N bahasa Tamil

tan ADJ coklat muda; N kulit berwarna coklat

tangerine N [tanjerin] jeruk garut, jeruk keprok

tangle N [tanggel] kekusutan, kekacauan

tank N tangki; panser; **tanker** N kapal tangki

tap N keran; ketukan; v mengetuk; menyadap

tape N pita; plester; kaset; v membalut; merekam

target N sasaran, tujuan, target; v mengincar

tariff N tarif, ongkos

taro N talas

tart N kue kecil yang bulat

task N tugas, pekerjaan

taste N [tést] (cita) rasa; nuansa; selera; v mengecap, merasai; **tasty** ADJ enak, sedap

tattoo N tato, rajah

tax N pajak, bea; v mengenakan pajak atau bea; **taxation** N pajak, perpajakan

taxi, taxicab N taksi

taxpayer N pembayar pajak ← **tax**

tea N [ti] teh

teach v taught taught [tot] mengajar; **teacher** N guru, pengajar

teacup N cangkir teh, cawan teh ← **tea**

teak N (kayu) jati

team N regu, tim; **teamwork** N kerjasama sekelompok

tear N [tér] sobekan, robekan; v tore torn menyobek, merobek, mengoyak

tear N [tir] air mata

tease v mengganggu, meledek, mengusik

teaspoon N sendok teh ← **tea**

technical ADJ [téknikel] teknis; **technician** N teknisi

technology N teknologi

teenage ADJ remaja, umur belasan tahun; **teenager** N (anak) remaja

telephone N (pesawat) telepon, telefon; v menelepon

telescope N teropong (bintang), teleskop

354

television (TV) N televisi (teve, tivi)

tell V **told told** bercerita; menceritakan, memberitahukan; menyuruh, memerintahkan

temper N sifat, watak

temperature N suhu

temple N candi, kuil; HIND pura, kuil

temporary ADJ untuk sementara

ten ADJ, N sepuluh

tend V cenderung; merawat, memelihara

tennis N tenis

tense N masa; *past* ~ bentuk lampau

tense ADJ tegang; **tension** N ketegangan, tegangan

tent N kemah, tenda

tenth ADJ kesepuluh ← **ten**

term N istilah; jangka waktu; **semester** triwulan, caturwulan (cawu); **terms** N, PL syarat-syarat; hubungan

terminal N terminal, pangkalan

termite N rayap, anai-anai

terrace N teras

terrible ADJ [téribel] mengerikan, menakutkan, buruk sekali

terrific ADJ [terifik] hebat

territory N daerah, wilayah

terror N rasa takut, teror; **terrorism** N [térorizem] terorisme; **terrorist** N teroris; **terrorize** V meneror

tertiary ADJ [térsyeri] ketiga; ~ *education* pendidikan di perguruan tinggi

test N ujian, pemeriksaan, tes; percobaan, uji coba; V memeriksa, menguji; mengujicoba

text N naskah, teks; V mengirim pesan singkat; **textbook** N buku pelajaran

textiles N, PL tekstil, barang tenunan

Thailand N Thailand

than CONJ daripada, dari; *bigger* ~ lebih besar daripada

thank V mengucapkan terima kasih; ~ *God* ISL alhamdulillah; CHR puji Tuhan; **thanks** COLL terima kasih, makasih; ~ *very much* terima kasih banyak

that CONJ bahwa; yang; supaya; ~ *way* begitu; ke arah sana; **those** PRON itu

355

the ART itu, -nya

theater N (gedung) teater

theft N pencurian ← **thief**

their PRON, POSS, PL [thér]
theirs mereka (punya), milik mereka; **them** PRON, OBJ, PL mereka; **themselves** PRON, PL mereka sendiri

then ADV pada waktu itu; CONJ sesudah itu, kemudian, lalu; maka; N waktu itu

there ADV [thér] (di) situ; (di) sana; EJAC nah; N sana; itu; ~ *is*, ~ *are* ada; **therefore** CONJ maka, oleh sebab itu

thermometer N termometer

these PRON, PL ini ← **this**

they PRON, PL [thé] mereka

thick ADJ gemuk; tebal; kental

thief N [thif] **thieves** pencuri, maling

thigh N [thai] paha

thin ADJ kurus; tipis; encer

thing N barang, benda, alat

think V thought thought [thot] pikir, berpikir; berpendapat

third ADJ, N ketiga; pertiga

thirsty ADJ haus

thirteen ADJ, N tiga belas

thirty ADJ, N tiga puluh

this PRON these ini; ~ *evening*

nanti malam; malam ini; ~ *morning* tadi pagi; pagi ini

thorn N duri

those PRON, PL itu ← **this**

though ADV [tho] bagaimanapun; CONJ sungguhpun, meskipun, biarpun; *even* ~ walaupun

thought N [thot] pikiran, ide; V, PF → **think**

thousand ADJ, N ribu; *one* ~, *a* ~ seribu

thread N [thréd] benang; urutan

threat N [thrét] ancaman; **threaten** V mengancam

three ADJ, N tiga

thriller N film atau buku yang menyeramkan; **thrilling** ADJ menggetarkan

throat N tenggorokan, kerongkongan

through ADJ [thru] selesai; ADV terus; PREP melalui, melewati, oleh, karena, terus

throw V threw thrown N lemparan; V membuang, melemparkan

thumb N [tham] jempol, ibu jari; V membaca sepintas lalu (buku)

thunder N gemuruh, geluduk; **thunderbolt, thunderclap** N petir; **thunderstorm** N petir; **thunderstorm** N gemuruh dan petir

Thursday ADJ, N (hari) Kamis

thus CONJ, ARCH maka

tick V tanda ✓; detik; kutu (binatang); V berdetik

ticket N karcis, tiket

tickle V [tikel] menggelitik

tide high ~, ~'s in air pasang; low ~, ~'s out air surut

tidy ADJ apik, rapi; N tempat menyimpan barang

tie N tali, ikat; dasi; pertalian; seri

tiger N harimau, macan

tight ADJ [tait] erat, tegang, ketat; COLL sukar, sulit

tile N ubin, tegel, keramik; genteng

till CONJ, COLL sampai, sehingga

timber N kayu (bahan bangunan)

time N waktu, masa; kali; in ~ sebelum waktunya; on ~ tepat waktu; all the ~ selalu, senantiasa; sejak semula; V mencatat waktu; **times** kali; **timer** N jam (pasir), pencatat waktu; **timetable** N jadwal

tin N timah; kaleng; **tinfoil** N kertas perak

tiny ADJ [taini] kecil sekali, mungil

tip N ujung; uang rokok, tip; saran, tips; tempat pembuangan akhir (TPA); V memberi tip; menumpahkan

tiptoe V jalan berjinjit

tire, tyre N ban

tired ADJ lelah, capek, letih

tissue N tisu; jaringan

title N [taitel] gelar; judul

T-junction N pertigaan, simpang tiga

to PREP [tu] ke, kepada; untuk; lawan; five (minutes) ~ three jam tiga kurang lima (menit)

toad N katak, kodok; **toadstool** N cendawan, jamur payung

toast N sulangan; V bersulang

toast N roti panggang; **toaster** N alat pemanggang roti

tobacco N tembakau

today ADV, N [tudé] hari ini; (masa) kini

toddler N (anak) batita (bawah tiga tahun)

toe N [to] jari kaki; ujung (kaus kaki)

together ADV [tugéther]

bersama, bersama-sama

toilet N kamar kecil, WC; kloset; **toiletries** N, PL perlengkapan mandi, alat-alat kecantikan

token N tanda (penghargaan), tanda masuk

toll N tol, bea; jumlah korban; ~ *road* jalan tol

tomato N **tomatoes** tomat

tomorrow ADV, N [tumoro] besok, esok (hari); masa depan; *the day after* ~ lusa

tone N bunyi, nada; warna, rona

tongs N, PL jepitan

tongue N [tang] lidah; bahasa

tonight ADV, N [tunait] malam ini, nanti malam

tonsils N, PL amandel

too ADV terlalu, terlampau; sekali; juga

tool N alat, perkakas; **tools** N, PL peralatan; **toolbox** N tempat peralatan

tooth N **teeth** gigi; **toothbrush** N sikat gigi; **toothpaste** N pasta gigi; **toothpick** N tusuk gigi

top ADJ atas; teratas, terbaik, tertinggi; N puncak, (bagian) atas, ujung; tutup; gasing

topic N topik, isu

torch N obor, suluh; senter

tortoise N [tortes] kura-kura

torture N siksaan; v menyiksa

toss N lemparan; v melempar-kan, melontarkan, melambungkan; mengundi

total ADJ sama sekali, seluruh; N jumlah, total

touch N [tac] sentuhan, nuansa; v menyentuh, menyinggung, mengenai; **touching** ADJ bersentuhan; mengharukan

tough ADJ [taf] kasar; liat, alot, awet; ~ *luck* sayang sekali

tour N tamasya, tur, perjalan-an, pelayaran; **tourism** N wisata, pariwisata, turisme; **tourist** N wisatawan, turis

tournament N kejuaraan, pertandingan, turnamen

tow v [to] menarik, menderek

toward [tuwod] **towards** PREP ke (arah); kepada, akan, untuk, terhadap; menjelang; menuju

towel N [taul] handuk

tower N [tauer] menara

town N kota; **township** N kota

toy N mainan

trace N bekas, jejak; v meru-nut, mengikuti jejak, memetakan

track N jejak, tapak jalan

tractor N traktor

trade N niaga, perniagaan, perdagangan; v berdagang, berbisnis; bertukar; tukar-menukar; **trader** N pedagang; **tradesman** N tukang

tradition N [tradisyen] adat (istiadat), tradisi; **traditional** ADJ menurut adat, tradisional

traffic N lalu lintas; peredaran, perdagangan

tragedy N [trajedi] cerita sedih; kecelakaan

trail N tapak jalan, bekas, jejak

train N kereta api

train v melatih; **trainee** ADJ calon; N orang yang ikut latihan, orang yang magang; **trainer** N pelatih; **training** N latihan, pelatihan, pendidikan

tram N trem

transfer N pemindahan, mutasi; v memindahkan

translate v menerjemahkan; **translation** N terjemahan, penerjemahan; **translator** N penerjemah

transmigration N transmigrasi

transparent ADJ bening, tembus cahaya

transport N angkutan, pengangkutan, transportasi; v mengangkut, membawa; **transportation** N transportasi

trap N perangkap, jerat, jebakan; v memerangkap, menjerat, menjebak; **trapdoor** N pintu di lantai atau plafon

trash N sampah

trauma N [troma] pengalaman buruk, trauma

travel v jalan, berjalan; bepergian; **traveler** N orang yang sedang dalam perjalanan, musafir

tray N dulang; baki

tread v [tréd] **trod trodden** menginjak, memijak

treasure N [trésyur] barang berharga tinggi

treasurer N [trésyurer] bendahara; Menteri Keuangan

treat N [trit] sesuatu yang menyenangkan; v mengobati; memperlakukan; **treatment** N pengobatan, perawatan;

359

perlakuan

tree N pohon

tremendous ADJ [treméndus] hebat, dahsyat

tremor N gemetaran; gempa bumi

trend N mode, gaya, tren; kecenderungan; **trendy** ADJ gaya, bergaya, modis

triangle N [trayanggel] segi tiga; keincing

tribe N suku (bangsa)

trick N tipu daya; permainan; v menipu; **tricky** ADJ sulit, rumit

tricycle N [traisikel] sepeda roda tiga

trim ADJ langsing, rapi; v menggunting; menghiasi

trip N perjalanan; v tersandung; menjebloskan

triple ADJ [tripel] lipat tiga; N rangkap tiga

tripod N [traipod] (tumpuan) kaki tiga, tripod

triumph N [trayemf] kemenangan, keberhasilan; v menang, berhasil

trolley N kereta dorong, troli

troop N pasukan; v jalan ramai-ramai; **trooper** N polisi

trophy N [trofi] piala

tropical ADJ tropis

trouble N [trabel] kesusahan, kesulitan; gangguan; kerusakan; repot

trousers N, PL [trauzerz] celana panjang

truck N truk

true ADJ [tru] benar, betul, sungguh; setia; **truly** ADV sesungguhnya, sungguh-sungguh

trumpet N trompet

trust N kepercayaan; v memercayakan, mempercayai

truth N [truth] kebenaran; **truthful** ADJ jujur

try N usaha, percobaan; v mencoba, berusaha; **tryout** N seleksi, percobaan

T-shirt N kaus (oblong) ← **T**

tub N bak mandi

tube N tabung; pipa, pembuluh

tuberculosis N radang paru-paru, tebese, TBC

Tuesday ADJ, N [Tyusdé] (hari) Selasa

tug N sentakan, tarikan; v menarik, menyentak; **tugboat** N kapal penarik

tuition N [tuwisyen] pengajaran; uang belajar

tulip N bunga tulip, tulpen

tumor N benjolan, tumbuhan, tumor

tuna N ikan tongkol

tune N bunyi, lagu; melodi; V menyetel; menala

tunnel N terowongan; V menggali terowongan atau lubang

Turkey N Turki

turkey N kalkun

turn N putaran; giliran; belok; V berputar, membelok, menoleh; memutar, membalikkan

turnip N lobak cina

turnoff N pintu keluar (jalan tol) ← **turn**

turquoise ADJ [térkoiz] biru toska; N (batu) pirus

turtle N kura-kura, penyu

tutor N guru pribadi; wali kelas; V memberi les privat kepada; **tutorial** N kelas diskusi

TV ABBREV *television* teve, tivi, TV (televisi)

tweet N twit; V ngetwit

tweezers N, PL pinset, penyepit

twelfth ADJ kedua belas;

twelve ADJ, N dua belas

twenty ADJ, N dua puluh

twice ADV dua kali

twilight ADJ, N [twailait] senjakala

twin N kembar

twist N tikungan; pelintir; putaran; V memutar, memintal, menganyam

two ADJ, N [tu] dua

tycoon N [taikun] hartawan, taipan

type N macam, jenis, bentuk, tipe; golongan; huruf cetak; V mengetik

typhoid N [taifoid] ~ *(fever)* tifus, tipus

typhoon N [taifun] (angin) topan

U

UFO ABBREV *unidentified flying object* piring terbang

ugly ADJ buruk (rupa), jelek

UK ABBREV *United Kingdom* Kerajaan Inggris

Ukraine N [Yukrén] Ukraina

ulcer N bisul, borok

um INTERJ anu, er

umbrella N payung
umpire N wasit
UN ABBREV *United Nations* PBB (Persatuan Bangsa-Bangsa)
unable ADJ [anébel] tidak mampu, tidak dapat, tidak bisa ← **able**
unauthorized ADJ [anothoraizd] tanpa wewenang, tidak sah ← **authorize**
unbearable ADJ [anbérabel] tak tertahankan ← **bear**
unbelievable ADJ [anbelivabel] tidak dapat dipercaya, bukan main ← **believe**
unbolt V membuka (kunci selot) ← **bolt**
unborn ADJ belum lahir; ~ *baby*, ~ *child* janin ← **born**
unbreakable ADJ [anbrékabel] tahan banting, anti pecah ← **break**
uncle N [angkel] paman, om
unclear ADJ kurang jelas ← **clear**
uncomfortable ADJ [ankamftabel] tidak enak, kurang nyaman ← **comfortable**
unconscious ADJ [ankonsyus] pingsan, tidak sadar ← **conscious**

uncover ADJ [ankaver] membuka ← **cover**
under CONJ menurut; PREP (di) bawah; **underage** ADJ di bawah umur; **underclothes** N, PL pakaian dalam; **undergo** V **underwent undergone** menempuh, mengalami; **undergraduate** ADJ, N sarjana muda; **underground** ADJ (di) bawah tanah; **underline** V menggarisbawahi; **underneath** ADV, PREP (di) bawah; **underpass** N terowongan (di bawah jalan); **underscore** N tanda
understand V **understood understood** mengerti, paham; memahami; **understanding** ADJ pengertian; N pengertian, pemahaman
undertake V **undertook undertaken** menjalankan, melakukan
underwater ADJ [anderwoter] (di) dalam air ← **under**
underwear N pakaian dalam ← **under**
undo V [andu] **undid undone** membuka ← **do**
undress V membuka pakaian,

362

melepas pakaian ← **dress**
unemployed ADJ, N [anem-
ploid] pengangguran ←
employ
uneven ADJ [aniven] tidak
rata, bergelombang; tidak
konsisten, tidak seimbang
← **even**
unexpected ADJ [anékspékted]
tidak terduga; **unexpectedly**
ADV tiba-tiba ← **expect**
unfair ADJ tidak adil, tidak
jujur
unfaithful ADJ tidak setia,
durhaka; menyeleweng ←
faithful
unforgettable ADJ [anfor-
gétabel] tak terlupakan ←
forget
unfortunate ADJ [anfortyunet]
malang, sial; **unfortunately**
ADV sayang ← **fortunate**
unhappy ADJ tidak bahagia;
sedih; malang ← **happy**
uniform ADJ, N [yuniform]
(pakaian) seragam
union N [yunien] persatuan,
serikat, uni
unique ADJ tunggal, unik,
tiada duanya
unit N [yunit] unit, satuan

unite V [yunait] bersatu,
menyatu; menyatukan,
mempersatukan; **united** ADJ
bersatu, serikat
universal ADJ [yunivérsel]
umum, universal; **universe** N
alam semesta
university N [yunivérsiti]
universitas
unkind ADJ [ankaind] kejam,
bengis ← **kind**
unknown ADJ tidak ketahuan,
tidak dikenal ← **knowing**
unless CONJ (kecuali) kalau
unlike ADJ tidak seperti, tidak
sama ← **like**
unlikely ADJ kemungkinan
kecil; tidak dapat dipercaya
← **likely**
unlucky ADJ celaka, sial,
malang ← **lucky**
unmarried ADJ [anmarid]
belum kawin, tidak kawin,
lajang ← **married**
unpaid ADJ tidak dibayar,
belum dibayar ← **pay, paid**
unrealistic ADJ tidak realistis
← **real**
unreasonable ADJ [anriz-
nabel] tidak masuk akal ←
reasonable

363

unreliable ADJ [anrelayabel]
tidak dapat dipercayai, tidak
dapat diandalkan ← **reliable**

unsafe ADJ tidak aman,
berbahaya ← **safe**

unstable ADJ [anstébel]
goyah, tidak stabil; mudah
tergoncang ← **stable**

unsuccessful ADJ [ansaksés-
ful] tidak berhasil, tidak
lulus, gagal ← **successful**

unsuitable ADJ [ansutabel]
tidak cocok ← **suitable**

unsure ADJ [ansyur] tidak
yakin, tidak pasti ← **sure**

untidy ADJ [antaidi] tidak rapi,
tidak teratur, jorok ← **tidy**

untie V [antai] membuka (tali),
menguraikan ← **tie**

until CONJ sampai; PREP hingga,
sampai (dengan)

unusual ADJ [anyusyuel] tidak
biasa, tidak lazim ← **usual**

unwell ADJ tidak enak badan
← **well**

unwrap V [anrap] membuka
(bungkus)

unzip V membuka ritsleting
← **zip**

up ADJ habis; bangun; naik;
what's ~? apa kabar? ada

apa?; ADV ke atas; naik; PREP
(di) atas; ke atas; **upcoming**
ADJ [apkaming] yang mendatang; **update** N laporan
terbaru; V memperbarui;
upfront ADJ [apfrant] terus
terang, jujur; **upgrade** N
penataran; V menaikkan kelas

upon PREP [apon] (di) atas
→ **on**

upper ADJ (tingkat) atas; tinggi
← **up**

uprising N pemberontakan

upset ADJ tersinggung;
tidak tenang; terganggu;
V membuat tersinggung,
mengganggu, merusak

upside ~ *down* terbalik ← **up**

upstairs ADJ di (lantai) atas;
ADV ke (lantai) atas; N lantai
atas ← **up**

urban ADJ [érben] perkotaan

urgent ADJ mendesak, penting,
genting

urinate V [yurinét] kencing,
buang air kecil; **urine** N air
kencing, air seni

US ABBREV *United States* AS
(Amerika Serikat)

us PRON, OBJ kita (termasuk

364

lawan bicara); kami

use N [yus] pemakaian, penggunaan; V [yuz] memakai, menggunakan; *~ up* menghabiskan; used ADJ bekas (pakai); *~ to* terbiasa; dulu; **useful** ADJ [yusfel] berguna, bermanfaat; **useless** ADJ tidak berguna, sia-sia; tidak dapat dipakai; **user** N [yuzer] pemakai

usual ADJ [yusyual] biasa, lazim, lumrah; *as ~* seperti biasa; **usually** ADV biasanya ← **use**

utensil N [yuténsil] alat (masak)

V

vacancy N lowongan; ada kamar; **vacant** ADJ kosong

vacation N [vakésyen] liburan

vacuum N [vakyum] menyedot debu

vague ADJ [vég] tidak jelas, samar-samar

valet N, M [valé] pelayan pria

valid ADJ [valid] berlaku, sah

valley N [vali] lembah

valuable ADJ [valyuabel] berharga; mahal; **valuables** N, PL barang-barang berharga; **value** N nilai; PL norma, nilai; V menghargai, menilai

valve N [valv] klep, katup, pentil

van N mobil bagasi; gerbong

vanilla N panili, vanili

vanish V [vanisy] hilang, menghilang, lenyap

variable ADJ [vériabel] berubah-ubah, tidak tetap ← **vary**

variety N [varayeti] macam; keanekaragaman; **various** ADJ [vérius] berjenis-jenis, bermacam-macam ← **vary**

varnish N pernis

vary V [véri] berubah-ubah, berbeda-beda; mengubah

vase N vas, jambangan

vast ADJ luas, besar sekali

vat N tong

vault N kuda-kuda loncat; V meloncat (dengan galah)

veal N daging anak sapi

vegan N orang yang tidak makan atau memakai produk dari hewan

vegetable ADJ [véjtebel]

nabati; N sayur, PL sayur-sayuran, sayur-mayur; **vegetarian** N [véjétérien] orang yang hanya makan sayur, orang vegetarian

vehicle N [viekel] kendaraan, wahana

veil N [vél] kerudung, kudungan; jilbab; tudung

vendor N penjaja, penjual

vent N lubang angin; **ventilation** N ventilasi, peredaran udara, sirkulasi udara

venue N [vényu] tempat acara berlangsung

veranda(h) N beranda

verb N kata kerja

verse N [vérs] ayat; sajak, syair; pantun; bagian (dari sajak)

version N [vérsyen] versi

versus (vs) CONJ lawan, melawan

vertical ADJ tegak lurus, vertikal

very ADV [véri] amat, sangat, sekali; benar, betul

vest N rompi; singlet

vet N, COLL dokter hewan (drh)
← **veterinarian**

veteran ADJ [vétran] kawakan; N veteran

veterinarian, vet N [véterin-érian] dokter hewan

via PREP [vaya] lewat, via; melalui

vibrate V bergetar; **vibration** N getaran, vibrasi

vice N sifat buruk atau jahat

vice- PREF wakil, muda

vicious ADJ [visyes] kejam, jahat

victim N korban

video [vidio] alat perekam kaset video; **videotape** N kaset video; V merekam pada kaset video

Vietnam N Vietnam

view N [vyu] pemandangan; pandangan, pendapat; V melihat, meninjau; **viewer** N pemirsa

villa N vila

village N [vilej] desa, kampung, dusun; **villager** N orang desa

vine N tanaman anggur; tanaman merambat

vinegar N [vineger] cuka

vineyard N [vinyerd] kebun anggur

violence N [vayolens] kekerasan; **violent** ADJ kasar; suka

366

memukul; keras, hebat

violet ADJ [vayolet] ungu muda

violin N [vayolin] biola

virgin N [vérjin] perawan, gadis

virtual ADJ [vértyuel] nyaris; maya; ~ *reality* realitas maya

virus N [vairus] virus

visa N [viza] visa

visit N [vizit] kunjungan; v berkunjung; mengunjungi; **visitor** N tamu, pengunjung

visual ADJ [visyuel] berkaitan dengan mata atau penglihatan; ~ *arts* seni rupa

vital ADJ penting sekali

vitamin N vitamin

vivid ADJ [vivid] hidup, jelas, terang

vocabulary N **vocab** COLL [vokabuleri] kosa kata

vocal ADJ bersuara; berkaitan dengan suara; N pembawaan lagu; **vocalist** N penyanyi, vokalis

voice N [vois] suara; v menyuarakan, mengatakan

volcano N [volkéno] gunung api, gunung berapi

volleyball N bola voli

volume N [volyum] isi,

muatan, volume; jilid

volunteer ADJ sukarelawan

vomit N muntah; v muntah

vote N (pemungutan) suara; hak memilih; v memberikan suara; memutuskan; memilih; **voter** N pemilih; **voting** N pemungutan suara

voucher N [vaucer] vocer, bon

vow N janji; v bersumpah

voyage N [voyej] pelayaran, perjalanan lewat laut

W

wade v berjalan dalam air; mengarungi

wafer N biskuit tipis

waffle N [wofel] wafel

wag v mengibas, mengibas-sibas; mengibaskan

wage N upah

wagon N [wagon] gerbong, kereta

wail N ratapan; v meratap

waist N pinggang; **waistcoat** N rompi

wait N masa menunggu; penantian; v menunggu, menanti; **waiter** N, M pelayan;

367

waitress N, F pelayan

wake N selamatan sesudah upacara pemakaman; v **woke woken** membangunkan; **waken** v bangun; membangkitkan

walk N [wok] jalan-jalan, jarak yang dijalani; v jalan (kaki), berjalan (kaki); **walking** ADJ berjalan; **walkout** N aksi mogok

wall [wol] N tembok, dinding

wallet N [wolet] dompet

wallpaper N [wolpéper] kertas dinding

walnut N [wolnat] sejenis kenari

walrus N [wolras] singa laut

wander N jalan-jalan; v mengembara, berkelana, berputar-putar

want N [wont] keinginan; v ingin; menginginkan, menghendaki; membutuhkan, memerlukan; **wanted** ADJ dicari

war N [wor] perang

ward N [word] bangsal, ruang; wilayah

wardrobe N [wordrob] lemari baju, lemari pakaian

warehouse N [wérhaus] gudang

warm ADJ [worm] hangat, panas; v memanaskan, menghangatkan; **warmth** N panas, kehangatan

warn v [worn] memperingatkan; **warning** N peringatan

warranty N [woranti] jaminan, garansi

warrior N [worier] pejuang, prajurit, kesatria

wart N [wort] kutil

was v, PF [woz] → **be**

wash N [wosy] cucian; mandi; v mencuci, membasuh; memandikan (orang); **washbasin** N tempat cuci muka, wastafel; **washcloth** N lap; **washing** N cucian; **washroom** N kamar kecil, WC

wasp N [wosp] tawon

waste N [wést] sampah; pemborosan; v memboroskan, membuang; **wasteful** ADJ boros

watch N [woc] jam tangan; jaga

watch v [woc] menonton; menjaga; **watchdog** N (anjing) penjaga

368

water N [woter] air; v berliur; menyirami, mengairi; **watercolors** N, PL cat air; **waterfall** N air terjun; **watermelon** N semangka; **waterproof** ADJ kedap air; **waterski** N [woterski] ski air

wave N ombak, gelombang; v berkibar; melambaikan; **wavy** ADJ bergelombang, berombak

wax N lilin; malam (untuk batik)

way N jalan; arah; cara

we PRON, PL kami; kita

weak ADJ [wik] lemah

wealth ADJ [wélth] kekayaan; **wealthy** ADJ kaya

weapon N [wépen] senjata

wear N [wér] pakaian; perlengkapan; v **wore worn** memakai

weather N [wéther] cuaca

weave v [wiv] **wove woven** bertenun; menenun; **weaver** N penenun, tukang tenun

web N jaringan; rumah laba-laba

wedding N (acara) perkawinan, pernikahan

Wednesday ADJ, N [Wénsdé] (hari) Rabu

week N minggu; **weekday** N hari kerja; **weekend** N akhir minggu, akhir pekan

weep v **wept wept** menangis

weigh v [wé] menimbang; **weight** N berat, bobot; **weightlifting** N angkat besi

weird ADJ [wird] aneh, ganjil

welcome N [wélkem] sambutan; v (mengucapkan) selamat datang

well ADV baik; sehat; *as ~* (begitu) juga, demikian juga

well N (sumber) mata air, sumur

Welsh ADJ berasal dari Wales

west ADJ, N barat; **western** ADJ barat; **westerner** N orang Barat

wet ADJ basah, berair; v **wet wet** membasahi

whale N [wél] ikan paus

wharf N [worf] **wharves** dermaga

what ADJ [wot] apa; alangkah; INTERROG [wot] apa; *~ 's your name?* siapa namanya?; **whatever** ADJ apa saja, apa pun

wheat N [wit] gandum

wheel N [wil] roda; **wheel-**

369

barrow N [wilbaro] kereta dorong, gerobak; **wheelchair** N kursi roda

when CONJ [wén] ketika; bila, kalau; INTERROG kapan; **whenever** ADV, CONJ [wénéver] kapan saja

where ADV, CONJ, PRON [wér] di mana; INTERROG di mana

whereas CONJ [wéraz] sedangkan, padahal

wherever ADV, CONJ [wéréver] di mana saja, di mana pun

whether CONJ [wéther] apakah

which CONJ, PRON [wic] mana; **whichever** PRON [wicéver] mana saja

while, whilst CONJ [wail] selama; saat, ketika; sedangkan; N waktu

whip N [wip] cambuk, cemeti; V mencambuk, mencemeti

whisper V [wisper] berbisik; membisikkan

whistle N [wisel] peluit; V bersiul

white ADJ [wait] (berkulit) putih

who CONJ [hu] yang; INTERROG, PRON siapa; **whoever** PRON [huéver] barang siapa

whole ADJ [hol] seantero, seluruh, semua; lengkap, utuh; N semua, keseluruhan;

wholemeal ADJ tepung terigu yang masih mengandung biji-biji; gandum

whom PRON, OBJ [hum] siapa

whose CONJ yang; PRON, POSS [huz] milik siapa

why CONJ, INTERROG [wai] mengapa; EJAC nah

wicked ADJ [wiked] jahat

wide ADJ [waid] lebar, longgar, luas; ADV jauh, lebar

widespread ADJ [waidspréd] tersebar luas

widow N, F [wido] janda (mati)

width N lebar(nya) ← **wide**

wife N **wives** isteri

Wifi N wifi

wig N rambut palsu, wig

wild ADJ [waild] liar, ganas, buas; gila; **wildlife** N [waildlaif] margasatwa, fauna

will N kehendak, kemauan; wasiat; V **would** [wud] akan, mau, hendak; **willing** ADJ rela, bersedia, sudi

win V **won won** [wan] menang; memenangkan; memperoleh,

mendapat
wind N (mata) angin
wind N [waind] belok, belokan, belitan; v **wound wound** memutar, menggulung; membelit, membalutkan
windmill N kincir angin ← **wind**
window N [windo] jendela
windscreen, windshield N [windsyild] kaca depan mobil ← **wind**
windy ADJ banyak angin, berangin ← **wind**
wine N (minuman) anggur
wing N sayap; sisi (panggung)
wink N kedip, kedipan; v kedip, berkedip; mengedipkan mata
winner N pemenang; **winnings** N hasil kemenangan ← **win**
winter ADJ, N musim dingin; *in* ~ pada musim dingin
wipe v menyapu, menyeka, menghapus
wire N [wair] kawat
wisdom N kearifan, kebijaksanaan; **wise** ADJ arif, bijaksana
wish N keinginan; v ingin, menginginkan; mengharap-

kan
witch N, F penyihir, tukang sihir
with PREP dengan, bersama, serta; pakai; **withdraw** v **withdrew withdrawn** mundur, mengundurkan diri; menarik, mencabut; **withdrawal** N pengunduran; penarikan (uang); **withdrawn** ADJ pendiam, suka menyendiri
within ADV, PREP (di) dalam ← **with**
without PREP tanpa, dengan tidak ← **with**
witness N saksi; v menyaksikan
wives N, PL → **wife**
wizard N, M [wizerd] penyihir, tukang sihir
wobbly ADJ goyang
woke, woken v, PF → **wake**
wolf N [wulf] serigala
woman N [wumen] **women** [wimen] perempuan, wanita
wonder N [wander] keajaiban; v berpikir, berpikir-pikir; **wonderful** ADJ ajaib, mengherankan
won't v, AUX takkan → **will**

371

wood N kayu; hutan; **wooden** ADJ terbuat dari kayu; **woods** N, PL hutan; **woodwork** N prakarya, pelajaran memotong dan mengolah kayu

wool N wol, bulu domba; **woolen** ADJ terbuat dari wol

word N [wérd] kata

wore V, PF → **wear**

work N [wérk] pekerjaan, karya, kerja; kantor, tempat kerja; *at ~* sedang bekerja; di kantor; *hard ~* kerja keras; V bekerja, berjalan, jalan; **workbook** N buku tulis; **worker** N pekerja, buruh; **workforce** N tenaga kerja; **working** ADJ *~ class* kaum buruh, rakyat jelata; **workman** N pekerja, tukang; **workout** N latihan; **works** N, PL pabrik; mesin; **worksheet** N kertas tugas belajar; **workshop** N bengkel

world N [wérld] dunia, alam; planet; **worldwide** ADJ yang meliputi seluruh dunia

worm N [wérm] cacing, ulat

worn V, PF → **wear**

worry N [wari] kekhawatiran,

beban pikiran, urusan, kesusahan; V khawatir, merasa cemas; *~ about* mencemaskan; *don't ~* jangan khawatir; *no worries* tidak masalah

worse ADJ, ADV [wérs] lebih buruk, lebih jelek ← **bad**

worship V memuja, menyembah

worst ADJ, ADV [wérst] paling buruk, paling jelek, terburuk ← **bad**

worth ADJ bernilai, bermanfaat, berharga; N [wérth] nilai, harga, guna; **worthwhile** ADJ berguna, bermanfaat

would V, AUX, PF [wud] akan → **will**; **wouldn't** V AUX, NEG [wudent] tidak akan, takkan

wound N [wund] luka; V melukai

wow EJAC [wau] wah

wrap N [rap] semacam roti isi yang digulung; V membungkus; **wrapper** N bungkus, pembungkus

wreck V merusak, menghancurkan

wrench N [rénc] *(monkey) ~* kunci Inggris; renggutan; V

merenggut
wrestle N [résel] pergumulan, pergulatan; **v** bergumul, bergulat; **wrestler** N [résler] pegulat; **wrestling** N [résling] gulat
wrinkle N [ringkel] (garis) keriput, kerut
wrist N [rist] pergelangan tangan; **wristwatch** N jam tangan
write v [rait] **wrote written** menulis, mengarang; **writer** N penulis, pengarang; **writing** N tulisan, karangan; **written** ADJ tertulis
wrong ADJ [rong] salah, keliru; N kesalahan

X

X-ray N [éksré] rontgen, sinar X; v merontgen, menyinar
xylophone N [zailofon] xilofon

Y

yacht N [yot] kapal layar, kapal pesiar
yard N pekarangan, halaman; ukuran panjang sebesar 0.9144 m
yarn N benang (rajutan)
yawn v menguap
yeah SL [yéa] ya, iya ← **yes**
year N [yir] tahun
yell N pekik, pekikan; v memekik
yellow ADJ [yélo] kuning; SL takut
yes ya
yesterday ADV, N kemarin; *the day before* ~ kemarin dulu
yet ADV masih (belum); *as* ~ sampai sekarang, sehingga kini; CONJ namun
yolk N [yok] kuning telur
you PRON [yu] kamu, engkau; FORM anda; PL kalian; ~ *all* kalian, Anda sekalian; **you'll** anda akan ← **you will**
young ADJ [yang] muda; N anak (binatang)
your PRON -mu, kamu punya,

milik anda, kepunyaan
anda; **you're** kamu adalah
← **you are**; **yours** PRON,
POSS milikmu, milik anda;
yourself PRON **yourselves**
engkau sendiri, kamu sen-
diri, anda sendiri ← **you**
youth N [yuth] masa muda;
kaum muda; ~ *hostel* losmen
you've [yuv] kamu sudah ←
you have

yum EJAC sedap, enak; **yummy**
ADJ enak, sedap; EJAC enak,
nyam-nyam

Z

zebra N kuda zebra, kuda
belang
zero ADJ, N [ziro] nol, kosong
zigzag ADJ, V berkelok-kelok,
berliku-liku
zinc N seng
zipper, zip N ritsleting,
kancing tarik
zone N zona, daerah
zoo N kebun binatang
zoom ~ *in* memfokuskan lebih
dekat pada

ABOUT TUTTLE
"Books to Span the East and West"

Our core mission at Tuttle Publishing is to create books which bring people together one page at a time. Tuttle was founded in 1832 in the small New England town of Rutland, Vermont (USA). Our fundamental values remain as strong today as they were then—to publish best-in-class books informing the English-speaking world about the countries and peoples of Asia. The world has become a smaller place today and Asia's economic, cultural and political influence has expanded, yet the need for meaningful dialogue and information about this diverse region has never been greater. Since 1948, Tuttle has been a leader in publishing books on the cultures, arts, cuisines, languages and literatures of Asia. Our authors and photographers have won numerous awards and Tuttle has published thousands of books on subjects ranging from martial arts to paper crafts. We welcome you to explore the wealth of information available on Asia at **www.tuttlepublishing.com**.